THE BOYS OF SUMMER

Also by Roger Kahn

The Era, When the Yankees,
the Giants and the Dodgers
Ruled the World, 1993
Games We Used to Play, 1992
Joe & Marilyn, 1986
Good Enough to Dream, 1985
The Seventh Game, 1982
But Not to Keep, 1978
A Season in the Sun, 1977
How the Weather Was, 1973
The Boys of Summer, 1972
The Battle for Morningside Heights, 1970
The Passionate People, 1968

Dear Sports Fan,

The Boys of Summer has been described as 'the most celebrated baseball book of the last 50 years', and was voted by *Sports Illustrated* magazine as one of the greatest sports books of all time. Its genius is not only to tell the story of the celebrated Brooklyn Dodgers of the 1950s, or the story of race and sport, victory and obsession. The magic of *The Boys of Summer* is that it tells the story of the making of modern America, one that each of us can understand even if we've never even watched a game of baseball.

The Boys of Summer is one of six books that begin our Aurum classics sports list. Publishing sports writing that does justice to the story being told has always been our priority at Aurum. This new series, which covers sports ranging from cricket to boxing, rugby to baseball, gives us the opportunity to celebrate both our own books that, over the years, have come to obtain classic status, and also bring back into print neglected books that deserve to be acclaimed as such. I hope that you will enjoy them all whether you are coming to the subject, the sport, or the writer for the first time.

At Aurum Press we take great care in shaping our sports list to be as diverse and inspiring as possible and we would love to hear what you think of the classics. Let us know on twitter at #aurumsportsclassics. Every month new tweets will be entered into a draw to win a set of all the titles. You can also email me at aurumclassics@aurumpress.co.uk to find out more about our forthcoming titles.

I would also be delighted to hear your suggestions for other forgotten classics, which you think merit re-publishing for a new generation.

Yours sincerely,
Robin Harvie

July 2013

The Boys of Summer

ROGER KAHN

First published in Great Britain
2013 by Aurum Press Ltd
74–77 White Lion Street
London N1 9PF
www.aurumpress.co.uk

Portions of this book have appeared in slightly different form in *Sport* magazine. Grateful acknowledgement is made for permission to reprint excerpts from the following:

Lines on pages xix, from 'Carpe Diem', and on page 81, from 'I Could Give All to Time', are from *The Poetry of Robert Frost* edited by Holt, Rinehart and Winston, Inc. Copyright © 1970 by Lesley Frost Ballantine. Reprinted by permission of Holt, Rinehart and Winston, Inc. and Jonathan Cape Ltd.

Lines on page 6, from 'Border Line', are from *Selected Poems* by Langston Hughes. Copyright 1947 by Langston Hughes. Reprinted by permission of Alfred A. Knopf, Inc.

Lines on page 205, from '…Did I ever dream…' by Saigyō, are from *Anthology of Japanese Literature: From the Earliest Era to the Mid-Nineteenth Century*, compiled and edited by Donald Keene. Copyright © 1955 by Grove Press, Inc. Reprinted by permission of Grove Press, Inc.

Lines on page 207, from 'The Return', are from *Personae* by Ezra Pound. Copyright 1926 by Ezra Pound. Reprinted by permission of New Direction Publishing Corporation and Faber & Faber Ltd.

Lines on page 152, from 'The Cremation of Sam McGee', are from *The Collected Poems of Robert Service*. Reprinted by permission of Dodd, Mead & Company, McGraw-Hill Ryerson Ltd and Ernest Benn Ltd.

Lines on page ix, from 'I See the Boys of Summer', are from *Collected Poems* by Dylan Thomas. Copyright 1939 by New Directions Publishing Corporation. Reprinted by permission of New Directions Publishing Corporation and J. M. Dent & Sons Ltd and the Trustees for the Copyrights of the late Dylan Thomas.

Every effort has been made to trace the copyright holders of material quoted in this book. If application is made in writing to the publisher, any omissions will be included in future editions.

A catalogue record for this book is available from the British Library.

ISBN 978 1 78131 178 3

1 3 5 7 9 10 8 6 4 2
2013 20150 2017 2016 2014

Printed and bound in Great Britain by
CPI Group (UK) Ltd, Croydon, CR0 4YY

In Memoriam
G.J.K., 1901–1953

CONTENTS

Groups of photographs will be found following pages 138 and 266.

I see the boys of summer in their ruin
Lay the gold tithings barren,
Setting no store by harvest, freeze the soils.

DYLAN THOMAS

LINES ON THE
TRANSPONTINE MADNESS

At a point in life when one is through with boyhood, but has
not yet discovered how to be a man, it was my fortune to travel
with the most marvelously appealing of teams. During the early
1950s the Jackie Robinson Brooklyn Dodgers were outspoken,
opinionated, bigoted, tolerant, black, white, open, passionate:
in short, a fascinating mix of vigorous men. They were not,
however, the most successful team in baseball.

During four consecutive years they entered autumn full of
hope and found catastrophe. Twice they lost pennants in the
concluding inning of the concluding game of a season. Twice
they won pennants and lost the World Series to the New York
Yankees. These narrow setbacks did not proceed, as some suggested, from failings of courage or of character. The Dodgers
were simply unfortunate—it is dreamstuff that luck plays everyone the same—and, not to become obsessively technical, they
lacked the kind of pitching that makes victory sure. In the next
decade, a weaker Dodger team, rallying around Sandy Koufax,
won the World Series twice.

But I mean to be less concerned with curve balls than with
the lure of the team. Ebbets Field was a narrow cockpit, built

of brick and iron and concrete, alongside a steep cobblestone slope of Bedford Avenue. Two tiers of grandstand pressed the playing area from three sides, and in thousands of seats fans could hear a ball player's chatter, notice details of a ball player's gait and, at a time when television had not yet assaulted illusion with the Zoomar lens, you could see, you could actually see, the actual expression on the actual face of an actual major leaguer as he played. *You could know what he was like!*

"I start in toward the bench, holding the ball now with the five fingers of my bare left hand, and when I get to the infield —having come down hard with one foot on the bag at second base—I shoot it, with just a flick of the wrist, gently at the opposing team's shortstop as he comes trotting out onto the field, and without breaking stride, go loping in all the way, shoulders shifting, head hanging, a touch pigeon-toed, my knees coming slowly up and down in an altogether brilliant imitation of The Duke." Philip Roth as Alexander Portnoy as Duke Snider. In the intimacy of Ebbets Field it was a short trip from the grandstand to the fantasy that you were in the game.

My years with the Dodgers were 1952 and 1953, two seasons in which they lost the World Series to the Yankees. You may glory in a team triumphant, but you fall in love with a team in defeat. Losing after great striving is the story of man, who was born to sorrow, whose sweetest songs tell of saddest thought, and who, if he is a hero, does nothing in life as becomingly as leaving it. A whole country was stirred by the high deeds and thwarted longings of The Duke, Preacher, Pee Wee, Skoonj and the rest. The team was awesomely good and yet defeated. Their skills lifted everyman's spirit and their defeat joined them with everyman's existence, a national team, with a country in thrall, irresistible and unable to beat the Yankees.

"Baseball writers develop a great attachment for the Brooklyn club if long exposed," Stanley Woodward, an extraordinary sports editor, complained in 1949.

This was so in the days of Uncle Wilbert Robinson [1920] and it is so now. We found it advisable [on the New York *Herald Tribune*] to shift Brooklyn writers frequently. If we hadn't, we would have had on our hands a member of the Brooklyn baseball club, rather than a newspaper reporter. The transpontine madness seems to affect all baseball writers, no matter how sensible they outwardly seem. You must watch a Brooklyn writer for symptoms and, before they become virulent, shift him to the Yankees or to tennis or golf.

By the time Woodward was writing, the concept of the Dodgers as appealing incompetents—"Dem Bums" in a persistent poor joke—was dying. Research suggests that when they were incompetent, the Dodgers appealed as a conversation piece, but not as an entertainment. I remember a succession of mots about a shortstop named Lonny Frey, *fl. c.* 1935, who made more than fifty errors in one season. People said, "There's an infielder with only one weakness. Batted balls." Everyone laughed, but few chose to pay to see Frey fumble. Attendance was so poor that by the late 1930s the Dodgers, "a chronic second division team," to quote the sportswriters, had passed from family ownership to the Brooklyn Trust Company. It took a succession of winning teams, with dependable shortstops named Durocher and Reese, to rescue the franchise from receivership.

Accents echo in the phrase "Brooklyn Dodgers." The words strike each other pleasantly, if not poetically, suggesting a good-humored bumping about. You get an altogether different sense from other nicknames. The Brooklyn Astros would skate in the Roller Derby. The Brooklyn Tigers would play football in a stony sandlot. The Brooklyn Braves would be an all-black schoolyard basketball team in 1945. The Brooklyn Yankees will not penetrate the consciousness. It is an antiphrase, like the Roman Greeks.

As far as anyone knows, the nickname proceeded from benign absurdity. Brooklyn, being flat, extensive and populous, was an early stronghold of the trolley car. Enter absurdity. To survive in Brooklyn one had to be a dodger of trolleys. After several unfortunate experiments in nomenclature, the Brooklyn National League Baseball Team became the Dodgers during the 1920s, and the nickname endured after polluting buses had come and the last Brooklyn trolley had been shipped from Vanderbilt Avenue to Karachi.

Brooklyn is not an inherently funny word, although the old Brooklyn accent, in which one pronounced "oil" as "earl" and "earl" as "oil," was amusing. The native ground might be enunciated "Bvooklyn" and "thirty" was a phonetist's Armageddon. It could be "tirdy," "toidy," "dirty," "doity," "tirty," "toity," "dirdy" or "doidy." But dialect, all dialect, Brooklyn, Boston, German, Jewish, British, Russian, Italian dialect, is the stuff of easy rough humor. Have you ever heard a Georgia belle insert four question marks into a declarative paragraph? "Ah went to Rollins? That's in Florida? South of heah? An' real pretty?" When a Georgia girl says *no*, she asks a question.

The lingering sense of Brooklyn as a land of boundless mirth with baseball obbligato was the creation of certain screen writers and comedians. Working for a living, they synthesized *that* Brooklyn. In one old patriotic movie, Bing Crosby defends the American flag against a cynic by asking others "to say what Old Glory stands for." A Southerner talks of red clay and pine trees. A Westerner describes sunset in the Rocky Mountains. But it is a Brooklynite who carries the back lot at Paramount Pictures. His speech begins with the apothegm, "Hey, Mac. Ever see steam comin' out a sewer in Flatbush?" As if that were not enough, can anyone forget William Bendix dying happy in a mangrove swamp? Just before a Japanese machine gunner cut him in two, Bendix had heard by shortwave that the Dodgers scored four in the ninth. *Requiescat in pace*. Winning pitcher: Gregg (7 and 5).

The Brooklyn of reality, where one Harold Dana Gregg

pitched inconsistently for five seasons, suffered a wartime dis-affection from baseball. Selective Service hit the Dodgers par-ticularly hard and the 1944 team finished seventh. At about the time screenwriters were conceiving other, yet more heroic deaths for Baseball Bill Bendix, genuine Dodger fans sang paro-dies of the soldier's song, "Bless 'Em All." In Brooklyn, the words went, "Lose 'em all." That was the darkness before the sunburst of peace and the great Jackie Robinson team.

After World War II, Brooklyn, like most urban settlements, began a struggle to adjust which presently turned and became a struggle to survive. Brooklyn had been a heterogeneous, dominantly middle-class community, with remarkable schools, good libraries and not only major league baseball, but extensive concert series, second-run movie houses, expensive neighbor-hoods and a lovely rolling stretch of acreage called Prospect Park. For all the outsiders' jokes, middle-brow Brooklyn was reasonably sure of its cosmic place, and safe.

Then, with postwar prosperity came new highways and the conqueror automobile. Families whose wanderings had not ex-tended beyond the route of the New Lots Avenue subway at last were able to liberate themselves. For $300 down one could buy a Ford, a Studebaker or a Kaiser, after which one could drive anywhere. California. Canada. *Anywhere.* Whole families left their blocks for outings. California was a little far and Canada was said to be cold, but there was Jones Beach on the south shore to the east and Kiamesha Lake in the Catskill Mountains to the northwest. Soon families began to leave their blocks for good. They had been overwhelmed by the appeal of a split-level house (nothing down to qualified Vets) on a treeless sixty-by-ninety foot corner of an old Long Island potato farm. What did it matter about no trees? A tree could always come later, like a television.

Exodus worked on the ethnic patterns and economic struc-ture and so at the very nature of Brooklyn. As old families, mostly white, moved out, new groups, many black and Puerto Rican, moved in. The flux terrified people on both sides. Could Brooklyn continue as a suitable place for the middle class to live? That was what the Irish, Italian and Jewish families asked themselves. Are we doomed? wondered blacks, up from Carolina dirt farms and shacks in the West Indies. Was black life always to be poverty, degradation, rotgut? The answers, like the American urb itself, are still in doubt.

Against this uncertain backdrop, the dominant truth of the Jackie Robinson Dodgers was integration. They were the first integrated major league baseball team and so the most consciously integrated team and, perhaps, the most intensely integrated team. All of them, black and white, became targets for the intolerance in which baseball has been rich.

As many ball players, officials, umpires and journalists envisioned it, the entity of baseball rose in alabaster, a temple of white supremacy. To them, the Robinson presence was a defilement and the whites who consented to play at his side were whores. Opposing pitchers forever threw fast balls at Dodger heads. Opposing bench jockeys forever shouted "black bastard," "nigger lover" and "monkey-fucker." Hate was always threatening the team. But the Dodgers, the dozen or so athletes who were at the core of the team, and are at the core of this book, stood together in purpose and for the most part in camaraderie. They respected one another as competitors and they knew that they were set apart. No one prattled about team spirit. No one made speeches on the Rights of Man. No one sang "Let My People Go." But without pretense or visible fear these men marched unevenly against the sin of bigotry.

That spirit leaped from the field into the surrounding two-tiered grandstand. A man felt it; it became part of him, quite painlessly. You rooted for the team, didn't you? You'd rooted for the team all your life. All right. They got this black guy now, and he can run and he can bunt, but can he hit?

Below, Robinson lines a double into the left-field corner. He steals third. He scores on a short passed ball, sliding clear around the catcher, Del Rice.

The stands erupt. The Dodgers win. We beat the *Cardinals*. That colored guy's got *balls*, I tell you that.

By applauding Robinson, a man did not feel that he was taking a stand on school integration, or on open housing. But for an instant he had accepted Robinson simply as a hometown ball player. To disregard color, even for an instant, is to step away from the old prejudices, the old hatred. That is not a path on which many double back.

The struggle seems modest now. What, after all, did Robinson ask? At first, a chance to play. Then the right to sleep in a good hotel and to eat in a clean dining room. Later to fight with umpires and dispute the press. But each step drew great whoops of protest. The Robinson experience developed as an epic and now, not only a national team, the Dodgers were a national issue. Everywhere, in New England drawing rooms and on porches in the South, in California, which had no major league baseball teams and in New York City, which had three, men and women talked about the Jackie Robinson Dodgers, and as they talked they confronted themselves and American racism. That confrontation was, I believe, as important as *Brown* vs. *Board of Education of Topeka*, in creating the racially troubled hopeful present.

One did not go to Ebbets Field for sociology. Exciting baseball was the attraction, and a wonder of the sociological Dodgers was the excitement of their play. It is not simply that they won frequently, brawled with umpires, got into bean-ball fights and endlessly thrashed in the headwaters of a pennant race. The team possessed an astonishing variety of eclectic skills.

One never knew when a powerful visiting batter, "one o' them big, hairy-assed bastards" in manager Charlie Dressen's fond phrase, would drive a terrific smash up the third-base line.

There, squinting in a crouch, Billy Cox, a wiry, horse-faced man with little blacksmith's arms, waited to spring. He subdued hard grounders by slapping his glove downward and imprisoning the ball between glove and earth. The glove was small and black and ancient. Someone accused Cox of having purchased it during a drugstore closeout. With the Whelan glove, Cox was a phenomenon.

Drives to right field activated stolid Carl Furillo. A powerful monolithic man, Furillo possessed an astonishing throwing arm and a prescient sense of how a ball would carom off the barrier. The grandstands did not extend behind right field. Between the outfield and the sidewalk of Bedford Avenue, a cement wall rose sloping outward. It straightened at about ten feet and then fifteen feet higher gave way to a stiff screen of wire-mesh. In straightaway right a scoreboard jutted, offering another surface and describing new angles. Furillo reigned here with an arm that, in Bugs Baer's phrase, could have thrown a lamb chop past a wolf.

Center field belonged to Snider, rangy and gifted and supple. Duke could get his glove thirteen feet into the air. The center-field wall was cushioned with foam rubber, and Snider, in pursuit of high drives, ran at the wall, dug a spiked shoe into the rubber and hurled his body upward. Pictures of him in low orbit survive.

But Robinson was the cynosure of all eyes. For a long time he shocked people seeing him for the first time simply by the fact of his color: uncompromising ebony. All the baseball heroes had been white men. Ty Cobb and Christy Mathewson and John McGraw and Honus Wagner and Babe Ruth and Dizzy Dean were white. Kenesaw Mountain Landis and Bill Klem and Connie Mack were white. Every coach, every manager, every umpire, every batting practice pitcher, every human being one had ever seen in uniform on a major league field was white. Without realizing it, one had become conditioned. The grass was green, the dirt was brown and the ball players were white. Suddenly in Ebbets Field, under a white home uniform, two muscled arms extended like black hawsers. *Black*. Like the arms of a janitor. The new color jolted the consciousness, in a profound and not quite definable way. *Amid twenty snowy mountains, the only moving thing was the eye of a blackbird.*

Robinson could hit and bunt and steal and run. He had intimidating skills, and he burned with a dark fire. He wanted passionately to win. He charged at ball games. He calculated his rivals' weaknesses and measured his own strengths and knew— as only a very few have ever known—the precise move to make at precisely the moment of maximum effect. His bunts, his steals, and his fake bunts and fake steals humiliated a legion of visiting players. He bore the burden of a pioneer and the weight made him more strong. If one can be certain of anything in baseball, it is that we shall not look upon his like again.

As a young newspaperman covering the team in 1952 and 1953, I enjoyed the assignment, without realizing what I had. Particularly during one's youth, it is difficult to distinguish trivia from what is worthy. The days are crowded with deadlines, with other people's petty scoops and your own, bickering and fantasies and train rides and amiable beers. The present, as Frost put it,

> Is too much for the senses,
> Too crowded, too confusing—
> Too present to imagine.

The team grew old. The Dodgers deserted Brooklyn. Wreckers swarmed into Ebbets Field and leveled the stands. Soil that had felt the spikes of Robinson and Reese was washed from the faces of mewling children. The New York *Herald Tribune* writhed, changed its face and collapsed. I covered a team that no longer exists in a demolished ball park for a newspaper that is dead.

Remembering and appreciating the time, which was not so very long ago, I have found myself wondering more and more about the ball players. They are retired athletes now, but not old. They are scattered wide, but joined by a common memory. How are the years with them? What past do they remember? Have they come at length to realize what they had?

Unlike most, a ball player must confront two deaths. First, between the ages of thirty and forty he perishes as an athlete. Although he looks trim and feels vigorous and retains unusual coordination, the superlative reflexes, the *major league* reflexes, pass on. At a point when many of his classmates are newly confident and rising in other fields, he finds that he can no longer hit a very good fast ball or reach a grounder four strides to his right. At thirty-five he is experiencing the truth of finality. As his major league career is ending, all things will end. However he sprang, he was always earthbound. Mortality embraces him. The golden age has passed as in a moment. So will all things. So will all moments. *Memento mori.*

What, then, of the names that rang like chords: Erskine and Robinson, Labine and Shuba, Furillo and Cox. One evening, for no useful reason, I telephoned Billy Cox at his home in Newport, near Harrisburg, Pennsylvania, and said I'd like to drive out for a drink. I hadn't seen him for fourteen years.

"You come all the way out here to visit me?" Cox sounded surprised. "It's hard to get to now. The commuter train from Harrisburg, it's discontinued."

"I'll find my way."

"I'm tending bar at the American Legion Club. You know, it's at the top of the hill. How do you like that, they discontinued the Harrisburg train."

Cox, the third baseman, was above all lithe. Now, at the Legion bar in Newport, he was a fat man. His hair was still black but before him he carried Falstaff's belly. "Hey," he cried when I came in. "Here's a fella seen me play. He'll tell you some of the plays I made. He'll tell you." Three stone-faced old train-men glared from the bar, where they were drinking beer.

"Billy, you were the best damn glove I ever saw."

"See," Cox said to the trainmen. "See. An' this man's a writer from *New York.*"

It was as if New York were a light-year distant, as if Cox himself had never played in Brooklyn. The experience had so diffused that it became real now only when someone else confirmed it. Most of the time there was no one.

"What do you do now, Bill?" I said. "What is it you like to do?"

"Watch kids," he said. His eyes gazed cavernous and blank. "Watch little kids play third. They make some plays."

One thing a writer has, if he is fortunate, and I have been fortunate, is a partnership with the years. In the 1970s, our own confusing, crowded present, I have been able to seek out the 1950s, to find these heroic Dodgers who are forty-five and fifty, in lairs from Southern California to New England, and to consider them not only as old athletes but as fathers and as men, dead as ball players to be sure, but still battling, as strong men always battle, the implacable enemy, time.

Already time has dealt some fiercely. Roy Campanella, the cheerful, talkative catcher, is condemned to a wheelchair; he has been through a divorce like something out of *Lady Chatterley.* Gil Hodges, the strongest Dodger, and Jackie Robinson have suffered heart attacks. Duke Snider, who dreamed of raising avocados, has had to sell his farm. Carl Erskine, the most compassionate of men, is occupied at home with his youngest son. Jimmy Erskine is an affectionate child. Most mongoloid children are said to be affectionate.

"Sooner or later," the author Ed Linn observes, "society beats down the man of muscle and sweat." Surely these fine athletes, these boys of summer, have found their measure of ruin. But one does not come away from visits with them, from long nights remembering the past and considering the present, full of sorrow. In the end, quite the other way, one is renewed. Yes, it is fiercely difficult for the athlete to grow old, but to age with dignity and with courage cuts close to what it is to be a man. And most of them have aged that way, with dignity, with courage and with hope.

"Now entertain conjecture of a time."

R.K.

The Team

THE TROLLEY CAR THAT RAN
BY EBBETS FIELD

I

That morning began with wind and hairy clouds. It was late March and day rose brisk and uncertain, with gusts suggesting January and flashes of sun promising June. In every way, a season of change had come.

With a new portable typewriter in one hand and a jammed, disordered suitcase in another, I was making my way from the main terminal at La Guardia Airport to Eastern Airlines Hangar Number 4. There had been time neither to pack nor to sort thoughts. Quite suddenly, after twenty-four sheltered, aimless, wounding, dreamy, heedless years, spent in the Borough of Brooklyn, I was going forth to cover the Dodgers. Nick Adams ranging northern Michigan, Stephen Dedalus storming citadeled Europe anticipated no richer mead of life.

"Mr. Thompson?"

A stocky man, with quick eyes and white hair, said, "Yes. I'm Fresco Thompson. You must be the new man from the *Herald Tribune*." Fresco Thompson, vice president and director of minor league personnel, stood at the entrance, beside a twin-engined airplane, all silvery except for an inscription stenciled above the cabin door. In the same blue script that appeared on home uniform blouses, the Palmer-method lettering read "Dodgers."

"How do you like roller coasters?" Fresco Thompson said. "On a day with this much wind, the DC-3 will be all over the sky. Perfectly safe, but we're taking down prospects for the minor league camp and a lot have never flown." He gestured toward a swarm of sturdy athletes, standing nervously at one side of the hangar, slouching and shifting weight from foot to foot. "We may call on you to be nursemaid," Thompson said. "Some ball players are babies. Let's go on board. The co-pilot will see about your luggage. We'll sit up front. Might as well keep the airsickness behind us."

Thompson smiled, showing even teeth, and put a strong, square hand on my back. "Come on, fellers," he shouted over a shoulder, and the rookie athletes formed a ragged line. Looking at them, eighteen-year-olds chattering and giggling with excitement, one recognized that they were still boys. The only *men* in the planeload, Thompson indicated by his manner, were the two of us. We had flown and earned a living and acquired substance. We were big league. Entering the DC-3 under the royal-blue inscription I felt with certitude, with absolute, manic, ingenuous, joyous certitude, that the nickname "Dodgers" applied to me. Beyond undertaking a newspaper assignment, I believed I was joining a team. At twenty-four, I was becoming a *Dodger*. The fantasy ("He performs in Ebbets Field as though he built it; this kid can play") embraces multitudes and generations ("Haven't seen a ball player with this much potential since Pistol Pete Reiser back in 1940, or maybe even before that; maybe *way* before"). I strode onto the plane, monarch of my dream, walking up the steep incline with the suggestion of a swagger and dropping casually into seat B2. "What the hell!" Something had stung me in a buttock. I

4

bounced up. A spring had burst through the green upholstery. A naked end of metal lay exposed. "What the hell," I said again.

"Nothing to worry about," Fresco Thompson said. "The people who maintain the springs are not the same people who maintain the engines." He paused and raised white brows. "Or so Walter O'Malley tells me."

"Seat belts," the pilot announced. Fresco turned and counted heads. "Eighteen," he said, "and eighteen there's supposed to be." The little plane bumped forward toward a concrete runway and the seabound clouds of the busy March sky.

In the end, I would find, as others since Ring Lardner and before, that Pullman nights and press box days, double-headers dragging through August heat and a daily newspaper demanding three thousand words a day, every day, day after blunting day, dulled sense and sensibilities. When you see too many major league baseball games, you tend to observe less and less of each. You begin to lose your sense of detail and even recall. Who won yesterday? Ah, yesterday. That was Pittsburgh, 5 to 3. No, that was Tuesday. Yesterday was St. Louis, 6 to 2. Too many games, and the loneliness, the emphatic, crowded loneliness of the itinerant, ravage fantasy. Nothing on earth, Lardner said, is more depressing than an old baseball writer. It was my fortune to cover baseball when I was very young.

From brief perspective, the year 1952 casts a disturbing, well-remembered shadow. It was then that the American electorate disdained the troubling eloquence of Adlai Stevenson for Dwight Eisenhower and what Stevenson called the green fairways of indifference. That very baseball season Eisenhower outran Robert A. Taft for the Republican nomination and, hands clasped above the bald, broad dome, mounted his irresistible campaign for the Presidency. Senator Joseph R. McCarthy rose in Washington and King Farouk fell in Egypt. Although the Korean War killed 120 Americans a week, times were comfortable at home. A four-door Packard with Thunderbolt-8 engine sold for $2,613 and, according to advertisements, more than 53 percent of all Packards manufactured since 1899 still ran. Kodak was rising from $43 a share and RCA was moving up from $26. The New York theatrical season shone. One could see Audrey Hepburn as *Gigi*, Laurence Olivier and Vivian Leigh as *Caesar and Cleopatra*, Rex Harrison and Lilli Palmer in *Venus Observed*, Julie Harris in *I Am a Camera* and John Garfield, who would not live out the year, bearing his special fire to Joey Bonaparte in a revival of Odets' *Golden Boy*. It was a time of transition, which few recognized, and glutting national self-satisfaction. Students and scholars were silent. Only a few people distinguished the tidal discontent beginning to sweep into black America.

> I used to wonder
> About living and dying—
> I think the difference lies
> Between tears and crying.

> I used to wonder
> About here and there—
> I think the distance
> Is nowhere.

On the book page of the *Herald Tribune*, Lewis Gannett called Langston Hughes' "Border Line" "heartbreaking." Hughes was an exotic taste, however, and not yet fashionable. Housewives followed Costain's lastest, *The Silver Chalice*. *Important* books, commentators suggested, were Herbert Hoover's *Memoirs* and *The Collected Papers of Senator Arthur Vandenberg*, adapted by his son, which were said to reveal "secret Roosevelt promises to Stalin at Yalta."

My companion, on the silver DC-3 bucking toward a cruising altitude of four thousand feet, had brought neither important book with him. One can travel for weeks with baseball men and see no books at all. He did carry the latest copy of *Look* maga-zine. Susan Hayward stared hotly from the cover, seductive in soft focus, but Fresco Thompson was concerned with something else. Clyde Sukeforth (*Look* announced), ex-coach of Brooklyn, tells "Why the Dodgers Blew the Pennant."

"I wonder," Thompson said, "if Sukeforth really does know why we blew the pennant, how come he wasn't able to avoid it last October." Thompson smiled, without warmth. "The man worked for the Dodgers for years. We kept him as a coach, paid him a good salary and as soon as he left he turned on us. For what? A few thousand dollars. We didn't blow the pennant. We *lost* it. And to Sal Maglie, Bobby Thomson and a damn fine Giant team. I don't understand people who look for the nega-tives in everything. Baseball is such a fine game. It's such a fine business. Mr. O'Malley says it's too much a business to be a sport and too much a sport to be a business. I came out of Columbia a young fellow and this game has been my life ever since— laughs and a fine living, accomplishments and great friend-ships."

The cockpit door opened and the pilot, a tall, light-haired man wearing a short-sleeved sports shirt, said that the head-winds were increasing. "Flying time might be nine hours to Vero."

Thompson grimaced. "Why don't you hitch this thing to the back of a Greyhound bus?"

"You got a long enough rope?" the pilot said.

Thompson smiled the hard smile. "This man here has to make a game tonight in Miami. In six hours I want you flapping your arms, if necessary."

The pilot laughed and retreated. "Whatever else they say about the DC-3," Thompson said, "if anything goes wrong, you set it down in a parking lot. It'll glide better than some planes fly." Beyond the windows, whorls of cloud spun past. The plane continued bouncing on March winds. "Settle in and enjoy it,"

Thompson said. "There's no place we can go and at least the telephone can't bother us here."

By reputation, Thompson was a wit and he proceeded to fill the morning with a brattle of baseball stories. His voice grated faintly, not unpleasantly, as an anvil moving over firebrick. His delivery was quick, practiced and caustic.

As a ball player, he had been fast, he said, and a good infielder but never an outstanding hitter. He stood five feet eight and weighed 150 pounds. In 1931 he was traded to the Dodgers and assigned a locker adjacent to one given Floyd Caves "Babe" Herman, a mighty batter who occasionally intercepted fly balls with his skull.

"Geez Christ," Herman complained. "They're makin' me dress next to a .250 hitter."

"Geez Christ," Thompson said. "They're making me dress next to a .250 fielder."

He winked at my laughter and continued. Afterward, when he became a minor league manager, a surgeon in Birmingham, Alabama, a man with a bullying voice, became a leading critic. The team played poorly, and one evening Thompson had to guide his starting pitcher back to the shelter of the dugout, after four runs scored in the first inning. "Hey, Thompson," the surgeon cried from a box seat, "another mistake."

"Yes, Doctor," Fresco called loudly in his gravelly voice, "but my mistake will live to pitch tomorrow."

As an executive, Thompson constantly evaluated talent. A skinny pitcher named Phil Haugstad twice backed up the wrong base, and Fresco asked, "What can you expect of a man whose baseball cap is size 6⅛?" Haugstad's matchstick calves were accentuated by the flapping knickers of his uniform. "But it's nothing to worry about," Thompson said. "His legs swell up like that every spring." One minor leaguer, seeking to impress Thompson with his powers at self-analysis, said, "The reason I don't hit better is that I swing an eighth-inch underneath good fast balls."

8

"We'll make you a star immediately," Thompson said. "Simply insert eighth-inch lifts into your soles."

With the longest story, Thompson turned on himself. In Havana once he had scouted Saturnino Orestes Arrieta Armas Minoso, called Minnie. The bases were loaded, with nobody out. Minoso, playing third, fielded a bouncing ball and looked toward home. It might be too late to make *that* play. Minoso glanced at second. The runner was leaping into his slide. Another runner flashed before him and by now the batter had crossed first base. Considering four outs, Minoso had gotten none. He walked slowly to the pitcher's mound, holding the baseball in one hand and scratching his uniform cap with the other. "Right then," Thompson said, "I concluded that this was the dumbest bastard in all Cuba. I caught the next plane home, and when I looked up, Cleveland had signed Minoso and he was batting .525 for their farm team in Dayton. Intellect isn't everything in this game. They say Einstein wasn't much of a hitter."

The torrents of Fresco Thompson's tongue shaped an idyllic beginning. No game is as verbal as baseball; baseball spreads twenty minutes of action across three hours of a day. The pitcher throws. Whsssh. *Klop*. Three-fifths of a second and the ball hits the catcher's glove. It will be thirty seconds before the pitcher throws again. The infielders say, "Attaway! No-hitter. Youkindewitbaby!" The coaches say, "Takes one, only one, let's go, Buck, get a holt of it, Bucko-lucko-boy." Players in the dugout say, "Hey, Ump! In the blue suit! Who taught you to call pitches, Helen Keller?" And in the grandstand, among the beer peddlers and peanut pushers ("Here y'are. Salted right in the shell. Only a quarter and straight from Brazil"), the fan tires the clock with talking. "Lookit that guy in center. He's too shallow. The Duker played it better. He played deep. The way this pitcher moves toward first reminds me of Whitey Ford. Except, of course, he's *righthanded*. I saw a game once kinda like this. You know what the pitcher's doin'. He's letting that batter think. He's got him all set for a curve and he's givin' him plenty of time to think curve so's he can throw the fast ball. What's that? Ball two? Who they got umpiring? Ray Charles? I saw a one-eyed ump one time in semipro. I played semipro two years. Whenever that ump called me out, I'd say, 'What the hell happened, Buster? You wink?' Get it? *Wink?* He only had one peeper. If he winked, he was blind. I was a helluva hitter in semipro."

"I guess I've been talking a lot," Fresco Thompson said.

"No. You've got great stories."

"Well, I've been around the game long enough. I ought to. Say," Thompson said, "isn't it unusual, a young fellow getting assigned to the team?"

"I guess it is."

"How did it happen?"

"A lot of luck, mostly."

"Ah, it can't be just luck that got you on this airplane."

"It's kind of complicated."

"Did you play ball? Or maybe your dad? I'll bet your dad played some ball."

"That's part of it."

"I thought so," Fresco said. He closed his eyes, content, and I let it go. How could I explain that what had gotten me aboard the Dodger plane that morning was nothing more than a succession of miracles?

II

Baseball skill relates inversely to age. The older a man gets, the better a ball player he was when young, according to the watery eye of memory. In the house where I grew up, everyone liked to talk and, as I was growing, my father recalled increasingly what a remarkable hitter he had been. Talk? In that sprawling apartment, talk was bread, air, water, fire, life. My grandfather, Dr. Abraham Rockow, was a dentist who asked a greater fate than probing bicuspids. Gray, handsome and assured, Dr. Rockow would wander from his office—it was the sunny front room of the apartment on the second floor at 907 St. Marks Place—and expound on pinochle, politics and art. Disease was caused by "a focus of infection, often in the gums." Roosevelt was an untrustworthy patrician, "pretending to be concerned about the masses." *Macbeth* (pronounced "Macbaat") was a masterpiece, "but if you think it is a good play in English, you should read it in Russian." Off a long center hallway, Dr. Rockow and I shared a bedroom that overlooked Kingston Avenue and trolley cars that ran by Ebbets Field.

Olga Rockow Kahn, who had majored in ancient history at Cornell, "under Westerman, *the* Professor Westerman," was a slight, forceful woman with smoldering eyes and round red cheeks. "Olga the Opple" they called her at Cornell, and Olga the Opple was a classicist. While teaching English literature and composition at Thomas Jefferson High to pupils named Gotkin, Flaum and Kantor, she longed to live the Athenian Experience. "My God," she complained, "before some silly game with Samuel Tilden the organized cheering in assembly, that shouting 'Tee Jay Aitch Ess,' was Spartan, or perhaps simply animal." She took secret pride in the intellectual level of the TJHS English Department but never relaxed her vigilance for Philistinism. She entertained elegantly, taught five days a week, relished radical theater and feasted on concerts conducted by Serge Koussevitzky, which still left time to exorcise Philistinism from her home. At three I was required from time to time to mount a wicker chair, being careful not to grind heels into the cane, and announce to imprisoned guests, "I'm studying to be a doctor of philosophy with a major in psychology." Many chuckled and a few, but not enough, winced. Although my hands were small and my digital coordination appeared inferior, I began piano lessons at five.

11

The friendly cow
All red and white
She gives us milk and cream.

Now can you play that (said the straw-haired piano teacher) and see if you can make the piano sound a little bit like a cow. How does a cow sound? Mooo-c-under-middle-c-no-that-one-that-one-moooo-hold-the-note-moooooo. Ah, that was *fun*. Olga, he may have real talent. (My mother could pay real bills during the Depression.) Olga would not clutter my mind with vagrant tales of goops or Winken, Blinken and Nod. Instead, she worked bedtime stories into a well-disguised course in Greek mythology. By seven I knew the Lethe from the Styx (if I forget thee, River Lethe, let my right hand lose its cunning), and I knew the Olympians from the Titans and how Hephaestus, son of Zeus and Hera, god of blacksmiths, jewelers, goldsmiths, masons and carpenters, built himself a throne from every different metal and precious stone. Olga was the first of her friends to give birth, which stimulated her pride and overstimulated a sense of destiny. Her son, she said, "might, mind you just might, strike Promethean fire before he's through." There was a history of accomplishment in the family. Her own mother, Emily Rosenthal, had graduated from Medical College in Berne and, about 1900, became one of the first women physicians in Brooklyn. Dr. Rosenthal was slight, her practice was small and it was her misfortune to die before reaching forty. But the brief career appeared brilliant to Olga. "And we may have another brilliant one," she remarked to my father, "if he's given the chance, if only you'd stop that incessant ball throwing with him in the hall."

"Applesauce," said Gordon J. Kahn. "Bosh." He was lying on a blue velvet sofa, his black shoes resting on a cream-colored antimacassar, as he completed the crossword puzzle in the New York *Sun*. "A seven-letter clinical word for lockjaw is trismus," he announced, and turned 45 degrees to go to sleep. Gordon

Kahn taught history at Thomas Jefferson and basic English to adults at a night school, which allowed time for a game of catch, a crossword puzzle and a brief nap each afternoon. His relaxation, like his life, was carefully ordered. His forebears, settled people, came originally from Strasbourg. Usually Jews from Western Europe enjoyed a social advantage over Ostjuden. This was canceled in my parents' case. Not only had Olga attended Cornell, while Gordon worked his way through City College; *both* of her parents bore the title of Doctor. Also, Gordon's father had been a butcher. Olga needed no heraldry to trace sources of persistent Philistinism in the household.

Gordon Kahn, once nicknamed Genghis, claimed to have played third base for City College. He explained carefully that he was a good fast-ball hitter, bothered by curves, and in the field he covered no more than a half dollar. This would seem to contradict my age-ability hypothesis, but it does not. Gordon Kahn was too sophisticated to have claimed stardom. He mentioned weaknesses as well as strengths, even stressing them somewhat in order to build plausibility. He was five feet seven, and horseshoe bald by thirty, but he did have powerful arms— "from hoisting sides of beef," he said, goading Olga—and I saw him hit with power in softball games. Years afterward, when I could have found the City College baseball line-up of 1923 in newspaper files, choosing to believe, I lacked the heart to check.

Gordon Kahn possessed a phenomenal, indiscriminate memory. Snatches of great poetry, subplots from inferior detective stories, mathematical formulae, themes from Brahms, lyrics from a Ziegfeld *Follies,* phrases from political speeches, measured sentences from Jefferson, and the sequence of roads that intersected a Westchester parkway forever were imprinted on his brain. When a loud, abrasive former union organizer struck the format for the radio program "Information Please," he at once consulted Gordon Kahn. My father used his recall as a

13

party trick and to win arguments. "Witch hazel comes from a *shrub* of the genus hamamelidaceous, not from a *tree*. It's explained on the upper part of page 206, in *Croft's Dictionary of Trees and Shrubs.*" Dan Golenpaul, having heard him, asked his help and my father subsequently bent "Information Please" to his own inclination that Brahms, Jefferson, Shelley and baseball could and indeed should fascinate equally. As the program grew, and Gordon stopped teaching night school, our dinners became contentious question bees.

Gordon: Three lines of poetry, please, with the word "light."

Olga: When the lamp is shatter'd, the light in the dust lies dead.

Dr. Rockow: Waat light troo yonder winder breaks?

All: Roger?

Himself: We were sailing along on moonlight bay.

Gordon: Fine.

Dr. Rockow: Waat is daat?

Olga: Not a poem, certainly. And he's not eating.

The delicious attention to the only child, whose hair curled and whose eyes were large and dark, was diluted by the arrival, with the New Deal, of a sister, Emily for her late grandmother, the doctor, very round and very blonde, with a round blonde curl, trained by Elisabeth, a methodical plain-faced broadbodied governess from Austria. The household did not end with resident kin. Elisabeth, brown-haired and taciturn, had been a village kindergarten teacher until Mitteleuropa began to go mad and—bitter lines around the mouth may have told of this or only of bad dentures—she had to come to America, where she kept house for Jews. She was efficient and free of ordinary vices. Her only indulgence was attending the New York Philharmonic Thursday nights. She earned $60 a month, plus board, and idolized Toscanini and Beethoven. Her radio played classical music constantly and she sneered at Olga Kahn's taste. "Your mother likes Koussevitzky only because he is handsome,"

Elisabeth said. "He is not a musician. *Toscanini* is a musician."
When Dr. Rockow opened the bathroom door once, when she
was in the tub, Elisabeth screamed as though scalded. Then she
screamed as though scarred, "Don't look!"

"All right," Dr. Rockow said. "Stop getting so excited."
Later he told Gordon Kahn that if a woman wanted pri-
wacy to bathe, she locked the door before taking off her
robe.

What a house. Two parents teaching. A grandfather pulling teeth. A housekeeper screeching. A sister pouting. A
cleaning woman arriving for "the heavy" work. A radio program, Brahms, sex, poetry, Karl Marx and Freud. The bond
between my father and me was baseball.

First a little toy bat came and we climbed out a rear window that led from the apartment to a pitch roof over a stationery store. "I'm going to show you how to use that thing,"
said Genghis Kahn. "Take your stance. Not that way. Sideways. You're resting the bat on your shoulder. Hold it off the
shoulder. Not that far off. Elbows out. Hands together. Bat a
little higher. Be comfortable! Oops, my fault, a little high.
Oops, try to keep a level swing. Oops, you swung a little
late. Well, that's three strikes, but today I'll give you four.
Oops, hold that darn bat tighter! You could have plunked
me in the shins."

"Gore-*don*." Olga stressed the second syllable and enunciated it as the title of an Oxford tutor. "Bring the child in
immediately. The roof is no place for him to play. He could
fall off."

Gordon Kahn had gray-green eyes that lost their kindness
when he was rebuked. "He can't get the *ball* off it, much
less himself."

"What was that?"

"Nothing." And to me, "Let's go in. It isn't that important
for the moment anyway."

15

"Do you like this playing baseball?" Olga said, with faint, obvious distaste. She and Hephaestus had been kept waiting in the living room.

"I really like playing baseball. I think I'd like to play first base for the Dodgers."

"Oh, God," Olga cried, pressing a hand to one round cheek. "A ball player, is that what we're raising?"

"First basemen have to be tall," Gordon Kahn said with great authority. "With his genes, I wouldn't worry."

"Well, I suppose we'll have to humor him," Olga said, and a few days later brought home a baseball suit, complete with genuine Dizzy Dean insignia.

"Ma! Who wants a suit like that? Dizzy Dean is a Cardinal. I'm a *Dodger*."

"Gore-don, I think you'd better have a talk with him. His manners and sense of gratitude are incomplete."

Although on two occasions Gordon Kahn clipped his firstborn child with righthand punches, he had to be fearfully provoked. Now he simply walked into the hallway and without a word we began to catch. "Other people's feelings," he mumbled presently. "No disgrace in Dean. He won thirty ball games last year. Your mother is a sensitive woman. It's never dull around here. Don't push the ball when you throw. Try to snap it."

When Babe Ruth, drinking through his last days as a ball player, came to Ebbets Field with the Boston Braves, Gordon said that he wanted to take me on Saturday. "Ruth is more exciting striking out than somebody else hitting a home run," he announced at dinner. "And as a historian I can assure you that he is part of American history. He should be seen."

"Wance I umpire," Dr. Rockow said. He was eating buttered asparagus one at a time, pinching the base between thumb and forefinger and swinging the stalk into his mouth. "Firrrst pitch werrry high, but I said strike. Next pitch werrrry good, so I said ball." Dr. Rockow, my father and I all laughed. Olga glared at

16

a stalk Dr. Rockow dangled above his face and said, with great determination, "Is the Boston playing Sibelius' Fifth Friday night?"

"No," Gordon Kahn said. "They're playing the Seventh."

"I just wish," Olga said, "that Sibelius were a little less diffuse."

"Is Ray Benge pitching, I hope, Dad?"

Olga's anti-Philistine glare danced from me to my grandfather and finally settled on my father. "Talk later," Gordon said solemnly. "Eat now."

"And later," Olga said, "if he must talk, encourage him to talk about something of *consequence.*"

Guilt made my father furtive on Saturday morning. Were there any errands he could run for Olga? Could he get something from the Schenectady Avenue library? A new criticism of Whitman? No? Was there enough meat for the weekend? He might pick out a good bottom round? Not necessary? Fine, fine, but he was alive and kicking and if Olga needed anything, she had only to ask.

"Could we have a catch?" I said.

"No. Not this morning. Don't you have schoolwork?"

"Just some junk."

"Homework is not junk. When I was at Boys' High, we had three to four hours of homework a night and we were glad of it. We considered it a privilege to be able to work that hard. And in City College—when I took a course called vector analysis— well, you wouldn't understand."

At two o'clock the old Boys' High homework lover and CCNY vector analyst silently led me onto a trolley at Kingston Avenue and St. Marks Place. After we had ridden three blocks, he began to relax. "Ruth swings upward," he said. "They call that upper-cutting and it's not good for most batters, but Ruth is a special batter. When he rides in an auto, he distinguishes other cars' license plates five seconds sooner than anybody else. That's the sort of eyes he has. In one World Series, he pointed to the bleachers and then hit a home run exactly where he pointed. He could have been a great pitcher if he hadn't decided to become a home run hitter. He's never been known to make a mental mistake. He never throws to the wrong base."

We got off at the corner of Empire Boulevard and Bedford Avenue. Only two blocks away loomed the brownish bulk of Ebbets Field. Babe Ruth did not play that afternoon. Someone said he had a head cold. "What he prob'ly has is a snootful," said a man in a straw hat and suspenders.

"What's a snootful?" I said.

"Head cold," said my father. "A snoot is a nose. With a cold, your nose is full."

"Hey, that's a good one," said the man in the straw hat. "That was quick. You think quick, Mac."

"I do," my father agreed. His voice was normally deep. Now he managed to lower it half an octave.

"Ain't it a shame," said the man, "there ain't more people? Bad times, I guess, but if they'd ever win, they'd draw."

"They'd hit a million," Gordon Kahn announced. His full voice rang among the empty seats behind first base. "Unquestionably they'd hit a million with a serious pennant contender in Brooklyn."

It surprised me that my father had abandoned his reserve as soon as we sat down. That man in the straw hat lacked a front tooth and wore no jacket. "Watcha thinka this team?" he said.

"Need one more pitcher and a shortstop," my father said.

"Nuthin' wrong at third, though."

"Nope, but he's only one man."

"Who plays third, Dad?"

"Jersey Joe Stripp."

"And, sonny," said the man in the straw hat, "he's a professional and don't you ever forget it."

"That's right," said Gordon Kahn. "Never underestimate Jersey Joe Stripp."

18

The two men chattered on and it began to seem less strange, my father talking to a toothless man without a jacket. The Dodgers would finish a poor fifth. The Braves would fire Ruth and finish last. But amid the spellbinding conversation of grown men, these inglorious teams transfixed me. What did it matter, Babe Ruth or Jersey Joe Stripp? If vector analysis was beyond me, I could still watch a ball game. I studied Stripp and Frenchy Bordagaray and Buzz Boyle and Tony Cuccinello. Stripp flagged a line drive backhand. That was something. He dove and reached across his body for the ball and rolled over twice and didn't drop it. My father and I and the straw-hatted man jumped up and cheered together. In the dead sunlight of a forgotten spring the major leaguers were trim, graceful and effortless. They might even have been gods for these seemed true Olympians to a boy who wanted to become a man and who sensed that it was an exalted manly thing to catch a ball with one hand thrust across your body and make a crowd leap to its feet and cheer.

Now the streets beckoned and ball games ruled streets before the automobile pandemic. Interminable, fierce, ingenious improvisations were set on asphalt every afternoon. Stickball is famous. Willie Mays played stickball, and Duke Snider maintains that never, not even the year that he hit .341 for the Dodgers, could he match locals at stickball in his summer neighborhood, Bay Ridge. "I couldn't hit the damn thing with the damn skinny broomstick," Snider says. You needed a stick and a red rubber ball manufactured by Spalding, sold for ten cents and called, no one knew why, the Spal*deen*. The pitcher threw the Spaldeen on one bounce at a manhole-cover home pla.e, and by pinching the ball, "fluking it" we said, he made the bounce eccentric. You could run up and swing the light stick like a whip, but you looked ridiculous if you whipped the stick and the squeezed ball fluked into your chest. A ball walloped to a roof was lost, so on the roof was out. Stickball produced center-field hitters, who had seldom touched a bat, could not recognize a curve, but with broomsticks were murder against fluked Spaldeens.

If there were no sticks, or if the police were running one of their sporadic campaigns against stickball ("Now look, son, you could hurt a *lady* hittin' one hard with a stick"), there was punch ball. The police tolerated punch ball. Somewhere, in the windy heights of Fiorello H. La Guardia's administration, a command decision had been taken. Attention: All Precinct Commanders, Desk Sergeants, Undercover Men. Calling All Cars. Punch Ball is Okay. Legal, even on St. Marks Place, Brooklyn West. But no stickball. Repeat. No stickball. Stickball is forbidden. Be on the alert for stickball players, particularly in the area of St. Marks Place. Be prepared to seize sticks. Use necessary force. A kid could hurt a *lady* hittin' one hard with a stick.

The stick was crucial. Punch ball was not much of a game because you couldn't punch a ball very far without Popeye forearms. Slapball, played in a chalked triangle, was delicate. Girls played slapball. Sometimes, you threw a Spaldeen against the white cement steps of 907 St. Marks. In stoop baseball, a Spaldeen rebounding safely from the steps to the street was a single or a double; a rebound reaching the far sidewalk was a triple. One carrying clear into Mrs. Beale's yard was a home run, but perilous. Mrs. Beale always called the precinct. Attention Cars Eleven, Eight and Four. Proceed at once to Kingston and St. Marks. Boys playing stoop baseball. Spaldeen has landed in Mrs. Beale's privet. Break up game. Confiscate Spaldeen. Be careful of hedge. Watch crocuses, Cars Eleven, Eight and Four. That is all.

In alleys safe from the prowl cars we played pitching-in, the only street game really close to baseball. The hitter held a stick. The pitcher threw a tennis ball, from which the fuzz had been shaved, at a chalk rectangle behind the hitter. A good pitcher made the shorn tennis ball jump, and a killer pitch was the high overhand curve. It passed the batter above the brows, then dropped down into the rectangle for a strike. If the tennis ball struck you, it stung briefly, but no one was afraid of a tennis ball. That was all the difference. Soft dream and hard reality. Once hit by a real baseball, a boy (or man) crumpled.

Bleacher seats at Ebbets Field cost fifty-five cents. You sat in the upper deck behind center field and felt right in the game when you shouted at Goody Rosen, "Come on, Goody, get a hit, get a little *bingle*, next time up." ("Yeah, Rosen," called a black-eyed, black-haired Irishman, "bring home the bacon for Jakey.") Rosen heard. At least he heard the Irishman. You could see Rosen's shoulders stiffen. Then he spat.

If you had $1.10, you bought a general-admission ticket and sat almost anywhere. Weekdays, when crowds were light, you worked your way so close to the dugout that you could glimpse ball players' faces. Goody Rosen had a short pug nose. It might have been flattened in a fight.

Without money, you could still assault the ball park. In the deepest corner of right center field, 399 feet from home plate, the concrete wall gave way to two massive iron doors, called collectively the Exit Gate. The base of the doors did not come flush against the ground. Lying prone on the slanting sidewalk of Bedford Avenue, you looked under a crack, twice as wide as an eyeball, and saw center field, left field and two-thirds of the infield. First base lay beyond the sight line, but if you cared enough, you learned to tell whether the man was safe at first by the reactions of the other players. If a man was out at first base, nobody ran to cover second. You had no choice but to learn the game. A sidewalk position was comfortable, except when wind lifted dirt from the outfield and swirled it under the gate and into your eyes, or a policeman poked a shoe into your ribs and said, "On yer feet. Move." Then you muttered, "Weren't you ever a kid yourself?" And you moved, sometimes to a garage roof across Bedford Avenue. The garageman, an enormous but agile Italian, barred the direct route, so you climbed another building and then, at a height of thirty feet, leaped an alleyway that was four feet wide. I did it once, noticing in flight that the alley was paved in pebbled concrete. From the garage roof you could see the entire infield and a third of the outfield, which would have been satisfactory had I not been nagged by the idea that I was going to have to make that jump again. The alley paving was not merely hard. It was rough. If you fell, pebbled imprints would stipple an entire side of your body. In the fifth inning of a Dodger-Pittsburgh game, I sneaked down the ladder to the garage and, while the garageman spoke with a customer, I fled, hearing behind me, "Go wan, run, ya big-nosed little bastard. Ya sheenies wanna own the world." Anything, even anti-Semitism, was better than trying that leap again, and after a while I made a friend at 200 Montgomery Street. His roof was almost as good a viewing place as the garage, and more congenial.

These adventures helped make plausible the idea of becoming a professional ball player. Ebbets Field was always in reach. There were obstacles—money, the policeman's shoe, a leap, the greasy garageman—but a boy could contend with them and triumph, if he had wit and persistence and a touch of courage. It was easy and absolutely irrational to relate getting to *see* a Dodger game with getting to *be* a Dodger. Which, in the fine irrationality of boyhood, is what generations of Brooklyn children did.

"Find the tennis ball," Gordon Kahn suggested. "Let's catch. You've got a hitch in your throw I want to work on."

We repaired to the long hall.

"Reach back; reach. You want to zip it."

"Gore-don! Is that child playing ball in the hall again? He should be reading."

Olga again was exorcising Philistinism. She thrust forward

Little Stories of the Great Musicians, a large yellow book with "full color" illustrations. "When Franz Josef Haydn conducted at the Court of Esterhazy, he noticed that many of the nobles were dropping off to sleep right in the middle of his symphonies. Well, thought Papa Haydn, placing a hand to his powdered gray wig, I think I shall compose another symphony that will give all the lords and ladies a *surprise!*"

"Hey, Dad. Whosa better fielder? Cookie Lavagetto or Joe Stripp?"

"Comparisons are nefarious," Gordon Kahn said.

"Please, God," said Olga, who aspired toward atheism, "let him become interested in a book. One book. Please. *Any* book."

Her large eyes gazed on the off-white ceiling toward Yahweh. And soon, in His infinite humor, the Lord God of Yisroel placed in my hands a book that enslaved me. *Pitching in a Pinch,* bound in dun, published in 1912, was a memoir written (with help) by Christy Mathewson, who, say the canons of legend, is "the greatest pitcher ever to toe the mound." It appeared one day on a high shelf among botany guidebooks and novels by Frank Norris and Michael Arlen. "A relic of my own boyhood," Gordon Kahn said, and he fetched *Pitching in a Pinch* and displayed a photograph of "Ty Cobb, the Georgia Peach, sliding. Note spikes high." Interested in a book? I was overcome. *Pitching in a Pinch* became my constant companion. No one has ever read a baseball book harder or for more hours of a day or with such single-mindedness. I read nothing else, no Dickens, no Twain, no Swift. Mathewson (with help) created a baseball world that added humor to the earnest and heavy baseball cosmos of my fantasy.

In *Pitching in a Pinch*, Johnny Evers of the Chicago Cubs studied "deaf-and-dumb sign language" after learning that John McGraw, who managed Mathewson and the Giants, was using it to flash signals. But Evers, "no match for McGraw, threw a finger out of joint in a flash of repartee." According to Mathewson, Silk O'Loughlin, "the umpire who invented strike tuh," always kept his pants so perfectly pressed that "players were afraid to slide when Silk was close for fear they'd bump against the trousers and cut themselves." Jinxes caused bad luck and "seeing a cross-eyed lady" brought about a jinx of terrible power. To kill an ordinary jinx, "you spit in your hat," "but when a cross-eyed girl fell in love with one of the Giants and began going to the ball park every day, McGraw told the Romeo to find another Juliet—or go back to the minors." Mathewson's opening to Chapter Ten, "Notable Instances Where the Inside Game Has Failed," was a particular favorite.

There is an old story about an altercation which took place during a wedding ceremony in the backwoods of the Virginia Mountains. The discussion started over the propriety of the best man holding the ring and by the time it had been finally settled the bride gazed around on a dead bridegroom, a dead father, a dead best man, not to mention three or four very dead ushers and a clergyman.

"Them new fangled self cockin' automatic guns has sure raised hell with my prespects," she sighed.

That's the way I felt when John Franklin Baker popped that home run into the right-field stands in the ninth inning of the third game of the 1911 World Series with one man already out. For eight and one-third innings the Giants had played "inside" ball, and I had carefully nursed along every batter who came to the plate, studying his weakness and pitching it. It looked as if we were going to win the game, and then zing! And also zowie! The ball went into the stand on a line and I looked around at my fielders who had had the game almost within their grasp a minute before. Instantly, I realized that I had been pitching myself out, expecting the end to come in nine innings. My arm felt like so much lead hanging to my side after that hit. I wanted to go and get some crape and hang it on my salary whip. Then that old story about the wedding popped into my head, and I said to myself: "He sure raised hell with your prospects."

It is 1936. Gordon and Olga are embarking on a tour of Mexico by boat, leaving the children and housekeeper in care of Dr. Rockow. For one month I am the ward of the continental dentist. "It won't hurt you to be apart from us for a time," my mother says. "And at least you'll find something to do beside playing catch with your father in the hall. But we want you to be happy. We'll leave your grandfather money for tickets to games during August."

"How many games?"

"How many, Gore-don?"

Gordon Kahn pursed his lips. His new mustache had grown in three-shaded, brown and black and like the herring sometimes red. "There are two home stands. One game each should be sufficient."

"Bleacher seats?"

"No," Gordon conceded, "general admission."

"All right, all right, you'll miss your boat," Dr. Rockow said.

On the next day, I sat behind home plate and saw the Dodgers lose to the Cubs. Then I spent an afternoon at stickball. On the day after that, I sat between third and home while the Dodgers lost to the Cubs again. August was three days old and I had exceeded my quota of major league baseball.

"All right, allrrright, if it means so moch to you," Dr. Rockow said, "we can both go Thursday afternoon when I don't practice." I saw four more games before my parents returned, two by myself and two with my grandfather. Dr. Rockow began to root for Johnny Cooney, a very smooth center fielder, and drew from me an oath never to tell my parents about the games or his own rooting. "Don't ee-wen speak too moch of Cooney," he said. "Bahtter these games be jost between us."

It is 1937. The family considers sending my sister and me to camp. The camp director, "Uncle" Lou Kleiderman, visits and asks what I like best.

"Baseball."

"Wonderful," says Uncle Lou Kleiderman, a stocky mustached man who limps and smiles. "We like boys who like baseball." Boys? Baseball? Uncle Lou Kleiderman likes families with two parents teaching and a grandfather pulling teeth, who pay the full tuition in advance. "We have three baseball fields," Uncle Lou says.

"Diamonds," corrects Gordon J. Kahn.

"And"—the camp director is spieling, not listening—"I have pictures of them in this folder right here."

"A hardball diamond," I cry.

"That's right, son," says Uncle Lou, smiling, "and the baseball counselor, Uncle Iz Brown, once had a tryout for the major leagues."

"But hardball?" says Olga. "Won't the child be hurt? Do you have a program in arts and crafts?"

"Maaaa!" Who wants to twist leather into bracelets? You might as well spend a summer in school. "Who did Uncle Iz Brown play for?" I ask Uncle Lou Kleiderman.

"Well, he went to the University of Idaho or Ohio and he can fill you in on the rest." Uncle Lou's smile is beginning to turn.

"Gore-don. Aren't injuries more likely in hardball?"

"We have a full-time physician, Dr. Hy Kogelman, and a nurse." Uncle Lou's face quivers and the smile is gone. Superior medical care is nothing to smile at.

"I dislocated a shoulder sliding once," Gordon Kahn says. "I was stretching a single into a double."

"Good for you," says Uncle Lou, confused by the terminology.

"But I was only out for a few seconds," Gordon says, not wanting to cause a fuss.

"What does Kogelman think of focus of infection?" says Dr. Rockow.

Uncle Lou winces, makes a gastric noise and promises to mail Dr. Rockow a photograph of the infirmary. "First thing in the morning. First-class mail."

"Pip, pip," says Emily Kahn. She is six and she has learned the rule of the house. Whether you have something to say is unimportant. What is important is to make a sound.

"How's that shoulder now?" Uncle Lou says. Gordon explains that the effect is most severe when he serves a tennis ball and he is still explaining when he signs the contract to send us to Camp Al-Gon-Kwit. "A real athletic family," says Uncle Lou Kleiderman. "That's what we like to see." Ooops, wrong coda. Olga's face freezes in horror.

"Would you believe," Uncle Lou says, desperately, "they're some who say Jews are afraid of sports?" But Olga glares him to the door.

Since I will play first base for the Dodgers, my new glove is a first baseman's mitt, big, heavy and, for $2.95, stiff as a shirt cardboard. To soften a glove, you work neats-foot oil into the palm and fingers and when the oil dries into a stain, soft mottled brown on tan, you place a hardball in the pocket. You put one hand into the glove and move the ball up toward the webbing and down toward the heel until you find the spot where the feel is perfect. It is a matter of sensors and quite precise. Being careful not to jiggle the baseball, even a quarter-inch, you slip your hand out, wrap the leather around the ball and tie the glove tightly. Then you leave it alone. Except that in a few days you want to see how the pocket is coming so you untie the glove and toss the baseball underhand and catch it, aware of touch and listening for the sound you want, a deep clean *thwack!* Then you add more neats-foot oil, replace the ball and tie the glove again. After a while, a pocket develops that makes you seem a better fielder than you are. By that time, you have fallen in love with the glove.

I am overwhelmed by the first baseman's mitt and soon we are sharing a bed. Now, in the middle of the night before a train will leave Grand Central Station for Camp Al-Gon-Kwit, I have untied the glove for the penultimate time. It is 11:45 by a radium dial and I am tapping the pocket softly when Dr. Rockow coughs,

27

turns in the other bed and calls my mother's name.

"Pappa? What's the matter?"

"Motter? Nothing is the motter. I have a little cough. But it may be contagious. You had better sleep somewhere else."

I bed down in another room with my sister and my glove, and in the morning Gordon takes us to Grand Central and a black and white sign that says "Al-Gon-Kwit Indians Pow-Wow Here."

What a summer of tragedy. With my stickball swing, I'm not much of a hardball hitter. A baseball bat weighs as much as five broomsticks. I can't pull and I haven't any power. My arm is weak. I would be all right at first base because I've mastered catching thrown balls in the hall on St. Marks Place. But throws can be short, and a hardball bounces erratically off dirt, especially the pebbly, grassless Berkshire soil of Diamond 2 at Camp Al-Gon-Kwit (not depicted in the brochure). I am the third best player in Bunk 4. I am good enough to play the first half of Al-Gon-Kwit's game against Camp Ellis (named for the owner) and to line a single to right field. But Wally Siedman (two doubles) is a better ball player and so is Lonnie Katz, who has long, sleek, veiny muscles and cracks a home run down the left-field line. I am no idiot. I know about Hephaestus and Haydn and about Tinker and Matty and McGraw and I have even, not telling my mother so as not to give her satisfaction, read a little of *Ivanhoe*. If, in my bunk alone, Siedman and Katz are already better, will there be room for me on the *Dodgers?* And first base! In practice, I lean toward a short throw which bounces off a stone and hits the side of my head. It is a minute before double vision passes. "You're a pretty fair ball player," says Uncle Flit Felderman, my counselor, rubbing my head as we sit on an embankment. He is in dental college and understands first aid.

"I'm not crying, Uncle Flit. A hit in the head just makes your eyes water."

"You're all right," Uncle Flit says. "With a little more size, you'll start to pull. But not first base. The outfield."

Hasn't Uncle Flit noticed—*I* have noticed—that I am a terrible judge of fly balls?

"Or second."

I'm not crazy about hard grounders either. "Thanks, Uncle Flit," I say. A week later in batting practice, Uncle Iz Brown throws a medium-speed pitch into my ribs. I spin in pain but keep my feet and rub dirt into my palms. "You want to play the game, *play the game,*" barks Uncle Iz. "Get in and hit, or go to the infirmary."

As the camp train carries us slowly down the Harlem Valley toward New York, I am coughing just often enough to remember the sensation of a baseball striking ribs. On my lap the outsized first baseman's mitt shows the scratches and scars of a vigorous summer.

I cannot tell my father. How can I admit to the old City College third baseman what I have grasped, that I will never be good enough for the Dodgers? "You want to play the game, *play the game!*" My sister? A child, and sometimes vicious. My mother? She wants me to make leather bracelets. That leaves my grandfather, the dentist, the white-haired whizbang continental Marxist toothpuller, wearing a white jacket, out of Minsk, U.S.S.R., Brooklyn's leading battler against foci of infection, Dr. Abraham Rockow, D.D.S.

My mother, the enemy, meets the camp train and kisses me softly and says, "Oh. By the way. We've moved." A taxi takes us to Lincoln Place, near Grand Army Plaza, and a large apartment building of red brick. "We have seven rooms on the top floor," my mother says. She shows me the living room, which leads to glass doors opening onto a tiny terrace. "Those are called French doors," Olga says. "Now would you like to see your name in the *New York Times*?"

"Who? Me? In the *Times*? Yeah, sure." We walk to my parents' bedroom in the strange apartment. I have never heard the household so quiet. Olga reaches into a bureau, a chiffonier, she calls it, and shows me a clipping from the *New York Times*. *Rockow, Abraham, D.D.S., suddenly on June 30.* My name appears two lines lower in the agate type. *Beloved grandfather of Roger.* What he had called a little cough was a massive coronary.

III

The world is never again as it was before anyone you love has ever died; never so innocent, never so fixed, never so gentle, never so pliant to your will. But these are afterthoughts. Generations vie and the young recover swiftly, or believe they do. A few years later in the new apartment there is some horseplay and then Elisabeth, the Austrian maid, makes a lively proposition. "Would you like to watch me take a bath?"

"But." Long indrawing of breath. "What? Sure."

It is Saturday night. Emily is asleep. Olga and Gordon have gone to hear Dimitri Mitropoulos conduct the New York Philharmonic. From the black Air King in my room, the theme of the "Lucky Strike Hit Parade" blares, "All your friends are here to bring good cheer your wa-a-a-y." Then, "And here's number seven, still on the top ten: the Hit Parade orchestra brings you an exciting instrumental version of 'I Hear a Rhapsody.'" That song? In a neighborhood schoolboy joke the druggist jumps a lady customer, who cries out, leading a chocolate malted to comment to the glass on its left, "I hear a rape, sody." That song? That ridiculous song? And now?

"Well?" Elisabeth says. I cannot joke. My throat is dry. I nod. Elisabeth leads the way down a hallway into the kitchen, through a door into her small bedroom, which is tidy and painted white. She turns to face me and removes her dress and slip. She does not wear a brassiere. I stand motionless and gape.

Elisabeth removes her underpants and does not remove her dentures. The body is broad and functional. "Wow," I say, finding my voice. "Wow, Elisabeth, you've got a build."

"Ach." She shakes her head, pleased. "I'm a woman, aren't I?"

She bathes, puts on a rayon nightgown and shoos me off to sleep. In my own bedroom, I can hardly believe my fortune. Age germinates allure, and Elisabeth must be thirty-five. Two weeks later, my parents return to Carnegie Hall and Elisabeth invites me back to her bath. At thirteen I have a steady date. Elisabeth bathes. I watch. In my mind I prepare an arcanum of advances, but I cannot act. At length, out of boredom or bitchery, Elisabeth betrays me. She confesses to Donald the daytime doorman, a tiny man with wisps of white hair running down his neck. Donald wears buff uniforms and shouts at eight-year-olds playing catch in Lincoln Place. *"Ge-radda-here. Go backa shannytown."* Thirteen-year-olds are not assaulted by the war whoop of Donald the Doorman. Most are bigger than he. This undersized tormentor of children not only became the repository of my secret, but with the terrible righteousness of menials, he recounts all that he has heard to Olga. A stormy scene breaks in the living room, between the French doors and the massive ivory-colored bookcases Olga herself has designed. From my bedroom I can hear the tone but only a few of the words. Olga is saying something must be done. Shrill fragments rattle down the hall like shrapnel. "Wastrel. *Pitching in a Pinch*. Dodgers! Baseball! *Sex fiend!*"

I open the door. "Applesauce," Gordon Kahn is saying. "Absolute applesauce."

"Speak to him. You have to speak to him! Before he does something terrible!"

"All right. It's all a lot of bosh, but I'll speak to him."

The next day, Saturday, my father speaks to me about baseballs. Don't I want a new one? Gordon says.

"It's okay, Dad. I got a baseball."

"What kind?"

"A quarter ball." All baseballs were described by price. The nickel ball was worthless. Jerry Surewitz hit a nickel baseball once. It split. The cardboard halves were stuffed with crumpled pages of a Japanese newspaper. The dime ball was better. It was made in America. The twenty-five-cent baseball was really good. You could hit a quarter ball for days and when the cover ripped, you peeled it off, exposing tightly wound yarn. You then wrapped the yarn in black friction tape and you could use the ball for another month, although the tape made it heavy and hard to throw.

"I'm talking about a real baseball," Gordon says. "A fifty-center. Come on over to Levy's Stationery on Nostrand Avenue." My father is a short man who walks with long bouncing strides. Although it is Saturday, he wears a suit and necktie. He has several suits, all from Howard Clothes, all blue or gray, or blue and gray, all herringbone. He explains that two Howard suits are better than one from Saks, but the truth is he does not care about clothing. The radio program, "Information Please," is a national success and he has made one error, one inconsequential error in business, something he does not care about either. He is on salary. He has not demanded a half, a third, a tenth of his brainchild, "Information Please." Dan Golenpaul, the man who came to him for help, owns it all. And as Golenpaul grows rich, his arrogance rises like a miasma and he finds this short, bald, mustached man from Brooklyn, who remembers poetry, Jeffersonian sentences and the sequence in which roads intersect Saw Mill River Parkway, a thorn to conscience but a necessity to the program. No one can prepare and edit so many questions on so many topics so deftly as Gordon J. Kahn. Golenpaul is galled by his dependence, which he denies, and Gordon J. Kahn, still teaching high school, starting at eight each day, travels to Madison Avenue for radio work and Golenpaul's abuse at three. The only sign of pressure is that now, instead of smoking one pack a day, he smokes three, Pall Mall king-sized cigarettes, which one finds "wherever particular people congregate."

"Red Barber is going to be a guest expert," Gordon Kahn tells me, as he lurches toward Nostrand Avenue, a Pall Mall preceding him, an inch of ash suspended at the tip.

"Watch the ash, Dad." Too late. The burnt tobacco congregates with the blue-gray herringbone Howard suit. "You gonna have a lot of baseball questions for him? Have you met him?" (A nod.) "Say, what is he like to talk to? He knows Durocher."

"He's an intelligent man." "Intelligent man" is the highest award in Gordon Kahn's private storehouse. It is his Medal of Honor. "Barber is *extremely* intelligent," he says. "He may make a *living* broadcasting Dodger games, but his *interests* go beyond that. He knows American history, particularly the Reconstruction Period. He likes poetry. His name is Walter Lanier Barber and he's a distant relative of Sidney Lanier."

"Who's Sidney Lanier?"

Gordon Kahn lights a new Pall Mall from the old and says, "When we get back, you are to look up a poem called 'Song of the Chattahoochee.'"

"I thought we were playing ball."

"I mean after that. You might even read the poem. It wouldn't hurt you to read more poetry."

"Aah," I say. "Who has time for stuff like that?" Doubt and pain film Gordon's gray-green eyes.

With the new ball, we drive to Cunningham Park in Queens. Or rather, we are driven by Olga. Gordon Kahn stopped driving one morning four years earlier when, confusing brake and accelerator, he drove a new Studebaker into the glass front of a stationery store. I sit in the rear seat of the new Dodge, thumping the fifty-cent ball into the old Camp Al-Gon-Kwit mitt.

At Cunningham Park, Olga excuses herself to walk. My father and I find an empty diamond, number five, and Gordon says, "We'll start with grounders, then we'll go to flies."

I station myself at first. The grounders skip out hard on two or three bounces. There is no faking on sharp grounders. You put your head down and follow the ball and hope that the last bounce will be true, or at least playable, and not carom into your mouth or groin. Head down is the secret. To follow the ball into your glove you have to keep your head down, but when you do, you leave your nose and mouth and eyes unprotected. "Head down," my father calls. "The ball can't bite." Oh, baseball is a game of subtle terrors. You hope for the last bounce to be high. A high bounce is as easy as a throw. But nobody who understands the game is fooled. One grounder bounces high; and then another. "L. H.," my father calls. "L. H. Kahn."

"What's that?"

"For Lucky Hop. Be ready."

A kind of test is under way. Coming of age at Cunningham Park, Queens. Gordon Kahn is testing to see if his indulged, skinny, quick-tongued son dares show his face to hard ground balls. For once the gabbling is quieted. The bald mustached man, with the thick wrists, who wears a white shirt and bow tie to hit fungoes, and the boy are reaching, sensing, challenging and I suppose loving one another through a fifty-cent baseball, whose cover, even now, is showing spots of grass stain. One bad bounce hits me in the wrist. Another smacks my shoulder. I am not Jersey Joe Stripp, but I keep forcing myself. Head down. Head down. The baseball smarts, but pain passes and I feel a crown of sweat and all sensations are obliterated by pride. I am showing Gordon Kahn that I am not afraid of the ball.

Olga returns from her walk. She is wearing a plaid skirt and sensible brown shoes. "Gore-don. Have you talked yet?"

"Please, woman!"

But the cue for action has been sounded. Olga has com-

manded exorcism of the satyr. After four more ground balls, my
father beckons with one finger. My left wrist is red. My glove
is soft with perspiration. I half-turn, flip it to the fringe of outfield grass, and lope in, knees pumping high, head up. Then I
lean forward, palms on knees, the way major leaguers do when
they are awaiting an artful stratagem from the manager. "You
know," Gordon announces, "women are different from men."

He rests the bat against a hip and wastes three matches lighting a Pall Mall. Then he puffs furiously. I realize. The warm
sweat freezes. I lose my breath. *They know I have been watching the maid.* In the hot sun on the ball field, I cannot envision
the maid naked or any woman naked or myself fool enough to
lust to see. But I *have* wanted, and now I have fetched myself
a retribution. A dozen punishments spin about my brain.
They'll take the radio. That's it. They'll commandeer the black
Air King radio and I won't be able to hear Red Barber and his
sidekick Al Helfer broadcast any more Dodger games.

"Once a month," my father says, "women have a flow of
blood through their private parts. This flow has to do with ova,
the eggs women produce, internally. They produce a new one
every month. The bleeding is called the menstrual period."

"Is that right? I didn't know that. I never heard about that."

"Well, it's true, even so," my father says. "This is called the
menstrual period, although in certain vulgar quarters it is referred to as the monthlies. Nobody we know or would care to
know could possibly refer to it in that way."

"Once a month, they *bleed?* From *there?*"

My father puffs the Pall Mall. "Get out in left and I'll hit some
flies," he says, concluding the only discussion of sex that is ever
to pass between us. I run down fly balls poorly. "You're probably
tired," Gordon calls. "But you weren't bad on the grounders.
Not bad at all." That is the second highest trophy in his storehouse. "Not bad at all" is my father's Distinguished Service
Cross.

35

We rejoin Olga at the gray Dodge, feeling very close. "Did you listen to your father?" Olga says.

"Yeah, Ma."

"Your father's a very sensible man," Olga says.

"He's okay, Ma."

I feel tears welling. "Your wrist," Olga says. "It's all red and it's swelling. Gordon! What have you been doing to that child?"

IV

When the wind blew from the south and the French doors had been opened, the sound of cheering carried from Ebbets Field into the apartment. It was astonishing, to hear cheers from a major league crowd while sitting at home. Over the Air King, Red Barber talked in his wise, friendly way. "Camilli up. Dolph isn't the biggest man in baseball, but there are none stronger. No, suh. They don;t *come* stronger than Dolph Camilli. Down in training camp one time some of the ball players went to visit a zoo. Hold it. Here's Warneke's pitch. A curve down low. There was a gorilla in the zoo and Camilli got to staring at the gorilla and the gorilla got to staring back at Dolph. Warneke's a fast workman. A curve stays wide. Ball two. And they're both a-lookin' at each other and someone, I think it may have been Whit Wyatt, John Whitlow Wyatt of the North Georgia Wyatts, says, 'You know I think Camilli could take him, hand to hand.' Hold it! Camilli swings! There's a high drive to right. It's way up there. Way up! Slaughter's at the base of the wall looking up, looking, but Enos can plumb forget this one. It's *gone*. Over the 344-foot sign. Number 16 for Dolph Camilli. Say, folks, I think Wyatt may have something there." Muffled cheering escapes the Air King. I thrust open the bedroom door. Seconds later an undulating roar, the real cheer arrives, borne by the wind. "That line drive was still *rising* when it went out

36

of sight over Bedford Avenue. Did you see where that one landed, Brother Al?"

"No, I didn't, Red, but where's Canarsie?"

"Hey," I shout. "Camilli hit another."

"That was a real Old Goldie," says Red Barber on the Air King, "and we're rollin' a carton of Old Golds, two hundred fresh-tastin' *real* cigarettes, down the screen to Dolph. We know he'll 'preciate 'em. He's quite a guy."

The Dodgers arose out of the 1930s, the wretched of the earth, armored by the tactical cunning of their new president, Larry MacPhail, Leland Stanford MacPhail, a man who tried to kidnap Kaiser Wilhelm in 1918 and failed but did capture a genuine Hohenzollern ashtray. MacPhail was gutty and brilliant and he rebuilt the team with remarkable trades and with monies cadged from the Brooklyn Trust Company. He put lights up in Ebbets Field, and for the first night game, *the first Brooklyn contest ever under the arcs,* John Vander Meer of Cincinnati pitched his *SECOND consecutive NO-HITTER.* *Double-no-hit Vander Meer!* MacPhail was not only good, he was lucky, and Dodger baseball became a carnival. He hired Babe Ruth to coach, which didn't work out, and signed Leo Durocher to manage, which worked wonderfully, and he brought Barber, the Ol' Redhead, to broadcast. Even if the baseball wasn't really *that* exciting, how could you tell when you listened to that siren-sweet Southern tongue? Red knew his players and his league and his game and how to tell a story and how to let rhythms run. A ball game told by Barber was a drama, with plots and subplots, but going onward, always onward among stories rounding out scenes, and climaxes described with such dramatic restraint that you cried out, "Come on, Red, come on, Old Friend, Companion of a Hundred Afternoons, let go, come *root* with us." And from the Air King: "These Phillies are an *interesting* team. They're in for three days and they're plenty of tickets, heah! Syl Johnson has been

37

to the mound before. That runner on first, Tuck Stainback, won't bother him. Not a bit. Been pitching in the major leagues since 1922. They used to talk about O rare Ben Jonson, Shakespeare's friend, but the Phils have their own rare one in Syl." All right, Red. Great *sportsmanship*. Hurray for all the *Johnsons!* But do you have to tell us when the lousy Phillies are beating us 2 to 1? "There's a second strike on Coscarart. Fine curve ball." *All right, Red. But he's against us.* Crack. Cheer. "Coscarart lines the two-strike pitch cleanly into center field. Base hit." Hey. We're alive! "Plenty of tickets left for tomorrow. Two-thirty game. I'll be looking for you, heah! They're stirring in the ol' pea patch, and with men on first and second and nobody out, here comes the Phillies' manager, Doc Prothro, to the mound, with the potential Dodger winning run at first base."

For six consecutive years, the Dodgers had been clowns. I never remembered them out of the second division. Now in 1939, with MacPhail and Barber and Durocher and Camilli and Hamlin and Hughie Casey, they finished third and drew a million people. "Everything happens in Ebbets Field," Red Barber said, "so it's worth coming out, but still, there are no fans anywhere like Brooklyn fans. Anywhere. No, suh." In 1940 the Dodgers added Joe Medwick and finished second. Then, in 1941, after a beautifully close race with St. Louis, they won the pennant. You knew they had to win after you heard Barber report a game in Sportsman's Park, the only major league ball park west of the Mississippi River. It was one of those rare encounters where two teams match strength so heroically that the verdict, the final score, describes not only an afternoon but a season. Twenty years later participants became excited anew in recollection. Whit Wyatt and Mort Cooper pitched three-hitters. In the fifth inning, the Cardinals put men on second and third with nobody out. Wyatt, master of the outside slider and the inside fast ball, overwhelmed the next three batters. Nobody scored. In the seventh inning Billy Herman and Dixie Walker hit doubles. That was the game: Brooklyn, 1; St. Louis, 0. The Dodgers won the pennant by roughly the margin of that victory.

"You have to give these Dodgers credit," Red Barber confided on the Air King. "They won when they had to win. They weren't afraid. And plenty of credit goes to the fans of Brooklyn, too." Thanks, Red, but credit? Credit for what? We weren't pitching. We were riding the trolley cars for five cents and paying for our tickets or listening to the radio at home. Well, credit for patience, maybe, but mostly that belonged to another generation. The previous Dodger pennant had come during the final days of the Presidency of Woodrow Wilson. "Now there's a team that *was* a team," my father insisted. It was a point of dignity with him not to be caught rooting as ardently or for precisely the same things as I. "You should have seen Zack Wheat, 'Buckwheat' we called him, smack that ball down the right-field line, wobbling his back leg before he swung. You should have seen him, but he finished the year before you were born." Gordon was speaking of Wheat and his boyhood, but he was excited by Camilli and mine. We both knew it in that pennant season. We exchanged quick looks and for the first time we were men together.

That was how the forties began in the Grand Army Plaza section of Brooklyn. There was concern about the Nazi-Soviet treaty, nervousness about the Greater East Asia Co-Prosperity Sphere and horror at Hitler's pogroms. But little Abe Fishbein with the faintly red mustache said the Soviets had been encircled. Gary Lapolla thought he had a point. Gus Simpson seemed pained. Jack Lippman looked uncomfortable. Sol Sherman said that as far as he was concerned Stalin was a Russian Hitler. Nothing else. Or could someone explain if he was any better, how he was? "Dinner," said Olga smilingly, "is served and I don't see how you can equate Stalin with that monster."

"What are we having, Ma?"

"It's impolite to ask."

"Ah, Olga, tell the kid." Abe Fishbein with the beetle-bright eyes.

"Crown roast."

"You're some Stalinist, with your crown roasts, Olga," said Gary Lapolla, all olive skin and suavity.

"Those two son of a guns do exactly the same things, isn't that so?" said Sol Sherman, a thick-chested man with a mustache like Hemingway's.

"It's good, Sol, you teach math," Lapolla said. "If they let you at young people in history, you could do serious damage."

"That's ridiculous," said Sol, shouting.

"What do you think of the Nazi-Soviet pact, Regor?" Gary said. "Your mother thinks you think nothing. She thinks you think of nothing but baseball, which she thinks is nothing. Ergo." The large living room was crowded with bright failed poets and unpublished novelists, now forty-five, teaching or practicing law. "Do you know what 'Regor' is?" Gary said. "It's Roger in a little-known tongue, the obfuscated dialect of Serutan."

I blinked. "Backwards," Jack Lippman said, kindly.

"I suppose there's something wrong, in your cockeyed scheme, with a kid liking baseball," shouted Sol Sherman.

"Aaah," Elsa Sherman said. "Come, Sol. Come, Gary. And you, my dear. Or poor Olga's marvelous crown roast will be cold."

It was hot. The meals were always hot and the meat was always tender. In the dining room, furnished in square walnut pieces, a large mirror contended with Olga's nonrepresentational paintings, and conversation spun from Eliot to Sholokhov, with a touch of Mann, a dash of Auden, a suspicion of Edna St. Vincent Millay. Through each remorselessly intellectual social session, I caught threads. And when the conversation moved to Dixie Walker, I could weave fragments of my own like an adult. That was how the forties began in the Grand Army Plaza section of Brooklyn before, with sickness, heartstorm and most of all with time, the gaiety weathered away.

First, the maid left. After nine years, Elisabeth said she was sick, moved in with a sister in Queens and sent the brother-in-law for her things. "She only stares at the wall all day," the man said, shaking his head in what appeared to be concern. But Olga doubted the story. She regarded the abrupt departure as treason. "Do you know, the bitch saved enough from her pay to buy a small apartment house. She was planning to desert us all the time." Gordon disliked taking sides and by this time he had perfected a diversionary tactic. "I'm having trouble with a question on groupings," he said. "I have the Four Horsemen, the Three Fates and the Sixteen Nines. You should know the last, son."

"The major leagues," I said.

"Amazing," Gordon said. "Now I need a fourth grouping, but not in music. Wendell Willkie is the guest next week and music isn't for him."

"Oh, God, who cares?" said Olga, defeated. "Back-street Annie never gets to meet anyone."

"The Brahms clarinet quintet would be unfair. Levant will miss the show. He and Golenpaul aren't speaking again."

"What is it now?" said Olga, who really did care.

No German governess could be found who would work for what the family could afford. Thereafter the maids were day workers, which rankled Olga. "Information Please" had become successful beyond anyone's fantasies. Olga recognized the glibness of Clifton Fadiman, the memory of John Kieran and the heavy charm of F.P.A. But basically, she said, there would be no program without Gordon. It was Gordon who polished every question. It was Gordon's eclecticism that established the tone. "The awful irony," she said, "is that for all you do, Golen-

41

paul won't pay you enough for us to hire sleep-in help."

Gordon blinked and gazed across the dinner table. "Camilli hit any today?"

"Collared again, Dad. Fast balls, I guess."

"Why don't you speak to *that man* and simply put some of these things to him?" Olga said.

Gordon Kahn, who disliked few things but despised unpleasantness, sputtered, "Woman, please." He could not explain himself. He would not put such things to Golenpaul. (Camilli was finished by fast balls in '43.)

Soon afterward on a soft July evening, in a clapboard summer house fifty miles north of Brooklyn, Emily was stricken with poliomyelitis. In twenty-four hours she journeyed from a life of piano lessons, swimming dates and gossip to an isolation ward in a municipal hospital, where she watched vermin cross unpainted walls and heard meningitis victims die. Within a month she was transferred to a private hospital, but it was two years before she could come home. The quadriceps muscle in her right leg was dead. When at length she was discharged, her walk, once airy, had become a sequence of lurches.

Olga took a leave from the English Department of Thomas Jefferson High School and studied physiotherapy. She would return Emily to grace with her own hands. Gordon grew more silent. In a stricken family, the responses of many years abruptly become obsolete. Olga recognized this and she set out, after a lifetime of teaching, to become mother, nurse, healer, all at once. Gordon persisted in his old responses. "Bosh," he would say, "there's nothing permanently wrong with the child." But the rationale was insupportable and he cast about for a language with which to reach his daughter. Emily responded. Brokenbodied at fourteen, she became a devout Dodger fan. By chance, the vanguard of the great and final Brooklyn Dodgers was beginning to appear.

"Is Furillo a better hitter than Galan?" The speaker at supper was not me, but Emily.

"He seems streaky," I said.

"Galan is past his peak," Gordon said.

"But the good righthanders, Dad. Furillo doesn't hit them."

"Red Barber says he's improving," Emily piped.

"Oh, all the saints," Olga said, her large eyes rolling upward with great drama. "Is there nothing else in this family but the nightmare of baseball?"

The nightmare was polio. Baseball was simply a point where vectors converged. "Yessuh," Red Barber liked to say, "baseball is more than a little bit like life." At carefree times in early boyhood I chose to believe that life was a kind of ball game, but with a mix of years and perception I learned better. The flaw in Barber's analogy was inevitability. A bad game ended and no matter how ardently you rooted for the Dodgers you could snap the sour mood with a good meal. But life in the household of a crippled young girl was permanently embittered. There was no escape or even avoidance. Whenever I came home, disaster rose before me. The distinction between baseball and life was as the transience of the flambeau to the permanence of night.

In retrospect, the Dodgers won the 1947 pennant with a raggle-taggle team and, also from perspective, the quality of that club was insignificant. In the year 1947 Jackie Robinson became the first black man to play in the modern major leagues. After Robinson's remarkable season with Montreal the year before, Branch Rickey, who succeeded Larry MacPhail, assigned Robinson to take spring training with the Dodgers, while still under contract to Montreal. Robinson was so good that Rickey imagined that troops of white Dodgers would demand his immediate promotion. "After all," he said, "Robinson could mean a pennant, and ball players are not averse to cashing World Series checks." If the players asked, Rickey postulated, Robinson's place would be at once secure. Actually, no white Dodger demanded Robinson and, when Rickey himself initiated the promotion, a half dozen players threatened to quit. The law of the wallet proved itself in the converse. Rickey invited the dissenters to quit, on principle, which would also have meant abandoning major league salaries. The most extreme of Dodger racists turned out to be Dixie Walker, but even he asked only to be traded. Rickey sent Walker to Pittsburgh a season later, and he played for two more years without incident or distinction.

Elements mixed in 1947 to make Robinson's challenge an Everest. The Dodger infield was established everywhere but at first base. Robinson, who had never played first professionally, entered the major leagues at an unfamiliar position. There a number of base runners, notably Enos Slaughter of the St. Louis Cardinals, tried to plant spikes in his Achilles' tendon. As a batter, Robinson was thrown at almost daily. Verbally he was assaulted with terminology proceeding from "nigger" up to the most raw, sexually disturbed vulgarity that raw, sexually disturbed men could conceive. In the face of this Robinson was sworn to passivity and silence. He had promised Rickey that he would encase his natural volatility in lead.

Jimmy Cannon, the columnist, spent a day with the Dodgers in 1947 and concluded that "Robinson is the loneliest man I have ever seen in sports." Red Barber, born in Mississippi and raised in Florida, was afflicted with doubts. Prejudices from boyhood, like a cypress swamp, still haunted him. But by May, Barber was captivated by Robinson's ability and courage. One afternoon between innings he made an apparently casual, but touching talk. He, a back-country Southerner, had come to admire Robinson so much, Barber said, "that I hope, I really do, he bats 1.000."

The season turned on a remarkable story composed by Stanley Woodward in the *Herald Tribune*. Rud Rennie, who covered the Giants for the *Tribune*, celebrated his four yearly trips to St. Louis by joining a local band of singing tipplers, which included Dr. Robert Hyland, the team physician of the St. Louis Cardinals. The Giants preceded the Dodgers into St. Louis in the spring of 1947 and, late one night, Hyland told Rennie that it was too bad he wasn't with the Dodgers because one hell of a story would break when that nigger hit town. The Cardinals, he said, intended to strike. Rennie, high, but not drunk, telephoned Woodward, who checked the story with a number of sources, including Ford C. Frick, president of the National League. At length, convinced, Woodward wrote an article describing the projected strike and adding that Frick had already addressed the Cardinals along these lines:

If you do this you will be suspended from the league. You will find that the friends you think you have in the press box will not support you, that you will be outcasts. I do not care if half the league strikes. Those who do will encounter quick retribution. All will be suspended, and I don't care if it wrecks the National League for five years. This is the United States of America and one citizen has as much right to play as another.

The National League will go down the line with Robinson whatever the consequences. You will find if you go through with your intention that you have been guilty of complete madness.

Whether the words were Woodward's or Frick's—eloquence was native only to Woodward—the strikers were put to rout. After that, Robinson's road, although still steep, led from thicket to clearing. He batted well, but not as well as he would, stole more than twice as many bases as anyone else in the league, and fielded adequately. Three times he found himself on base when Dixie Walker hit a home run. Invariably he trotted directly from home plate to dugout, skipping the customary handshake, so as not to embarrass Walker, or risk refusal.

Robinson was competent but uninspired in the World Series, by which time another Negro had begun to play in the majors and dozens were being scouted. The most exciting Series play was a catch made in deep left field by a stumpy outfielder named Al Gionfriddo. The batter who hit the long drive was Joe DiMaggio and, while I was saluting Gionfriddo's genius, as reported by Red Barber, my father suggested that against a hitter like DiMaggio, Gionfriddo should have been stationed far into left, in the first place.

"What do you mean, Daddy?" Emily said.

"Hell," I said. "He caught the ball."

"Good legs," Gordon said, "but he doesn't qualify as an intelligent man." Gordon turned to his daughter and lectured on the basics of positioning oneself in defensive baseball. Her round face lit, as though she were hearing a Philippic. After a while, I excused myself, pleading homework. The Yankees won the Series, four games to three.

Olga was aging softly. She maintained her weight at 105 pounds, and as lines furrowed her face they fell in flowing contours. Wedged between polio and baseball, she became more militantly intellectual. She subscribed to little reviews and no obtuseness could stay her from finishing an essay. Wandering into the living room, I would find *Hudson, Sewanee, Partisan* and *Kenyon* stacked on an end table beside a blue couch. With time, copies became dog-eared. We owned the world's only dog-eared collection of essays by Philip Rahv. Further, Olga acted on the essays seriously. The library, housed in high cases that faced the French doors, grew with new copies of Henry James, Wallace Stevens, Edgar Allan Poe, Yvor Winters, giants of letters and princes of bombast as the season commanded. Abruptly John Keats was "rather quaint."

Gordon consumed himself with work, with baseball talk at his crippled daughter and, when he and Emily were not closeted, with the escapes of crossword puzzle and detective story. I was not interested in the little reviews. I disliked puzzles. There was no place for me in a closet scene. One morning at the age of twenty, I awoke a stranger in the household where I was born.

"It's time seriously to discuss what you intend doing for a living," Gordon said. Then, yielding to his Mahleresque weakness for triteness when most serious, he said, in a portentous bass-baritone: "I think it's time to take stock."

"The idea of sending you to college may have been a mistake," Olga said. "You may not be good college timber and we —I am certainly very much to blame—should not have inflicted so many demands on your intelligence."

After high school, I decided on a semirevolution. I would run away to familiar ground. I prepared preliminary applications for Cornell, Olga's college, mentioning that I intended to major in English. My grades were strong in English, but spotty, and my parents were surprised when an admissions dean wrote an encouraging letter. The problem, Gordon said very tightly, was that the expense of hospitalization and physiotherapy for Emily precluded my going to Cornell. He was sorry, but there was only so much money and, by the way, if I hadn't really decided on a career, he wanted to suggest radio law.

"Radio law?"

"Yes indeed. There's a chap who does legal work for Golenpaul. It's fascinating and he is very affluent. I never thought of affluence as being important but, as you can see, I was wrong." His eyes dropped. I was accepted at the Bronx campus of NYU, where, I told the admissions dean, I intended to pursue a career of radio law.

"Radio law?" the dean said.

The University College of Arts and Pure Science offered compulsory ROTC, clasp-hands-on-desk discipline, an ancient faculty, a persistent strain of anti-Semitism and a kind of justifiable paranoia among cadres of young Jews who craved good marks, but not learning, as they thrashed recklessly toward the common goal, medical school. All the NYU Bronx campus lacked was a balanced curriculum, an intellectual climate and girls. It was not a college, but an anticollege. It was not a place of learning but a theater of memorization. It was an institution where students regarded Lear's catastrophe as insignificant unless it was worth eight points on an exam. During my sophomore year Dr. Theodore Francis Jones, whose history course ranged down a thousand byways from Thebes to Byzantium, summoned me after a lecture. He was bald, with a bird head and bright blue eyes. "I'm surprised to see you're flunking organic chemistry," he said.

"Yes, sir."

"Are you interested in organic chemistry?"

"No, sir."

"What do you want to do?"

I paused. Dr. Jones looked like someone to trust. "Well, sir, I believe I'd like to be a writer."

"A writer!" Dr. Jones spoke so loudly that I blushed. "Then what on earth are you doing at a place like this?"

But in the living room at the Lincoln Place apartment two years later I would not tell my father my longing. We sat in overstuffed chairs, feeling Olga's eyes, and reading disappointment in one another. "You seemed to like journalism, once," Gordon said. "Go to the *Herald Tribune*. Ask for this name. You may be put on a list to become a copyboy."

"Great." The word exploded, like hope.

"If this doesn't work," Olga said, "you should take a trade. It's no disgrace. Not everyone can be an intellectual." We exchanged looks of loathing love.

V

The Dodger DC-3 burst out of overcast near Jacksonville, finding clear air at the border of Florida. "Just like the Chamber of Commerce says," the pilot announced. No one had gotten airsick and I had neglected to tell Fresco Thompson how I found my way to the Dodgers. It was too difficult, too much on the senses, and, besides, it did not seem plausible. "You can see

48

beach and breakers off to the left," the pilot's voice intoned. Minor leaguers lunged to one side of the plane, and the DC-3 tipped slightly. I grabbed both seat arms.

"Don't worry," Thompson said, "ball players haven't over-turned a plane in flight yet, not that there haven't been some crazy enough to try." The late sun lit the cabin. "Slowest trip I can remember. I'm afraid you're going to miss your game."

"I guess I can wait until tomorrow."

"You can afford to. You'll see a ball game every day from now until October." Thompson winked. "You had better like base-ball, young man."

And writing, I thought. At twenty-four, I was passionately fond of both.

Ball players were returning to the Hotel McAllister in Miami when I finally checked in. I recognized Reese, wearing Puck's expression, and the soldier bulk of Gil Hodges, and Carl Furillo with a face from Caesar's legions. It surprised me how many Dodgers I did not know. I had begun to consider the absence of black players—they were not welcome at the McAllister—when someone poked my ribs and cried, "Hiya, Rudolf." It was Harold Rosenthal, who was abandoning the job I would take. He was a round, stooped man of thirty-eight, with crinkly brown hair and eyeglasses, respected at the *Tribune* for deft writing. "You know Vinnie," Rosenthal said. "This is Vin Scully. We'll get a Scotch." Scully had a long-chinned, rather hand-some face, under a shock of red hair. He was the number three broadcaster on the unit which Barber led.

"Into the gymnasium," Scully proclaimed.

"Yes," I said, vaguely. "Hey, Harold. How was the game?"

"Eech," Rosenthal said. He waved his right hand in a de-precatory motion. "Into the gym."

When drinks came to our table near the bar, I tried again. "How did it go tonight?" I said.

"What?" Rosenthal said.

"The game."

"We win, 5–3. Forget it."

"Just an exhibition," Scully said.

I still wanted to talk baseball, to draw out the men.

"Pitching good?"

"Whoop," Scully cried. "There goes one."

"One what?"

"You know why I call this place the gym," Scully said. "You'll see more whores chasing more ball players than in any other place in the world."

"And breaking the New York A.C. record for the sixty-yard dash time after time," Rosenthal said.

"Time after time," Scully sang, in a pleasant baritone voice.

The Miami baseball field possessed some of the gingerbread modernity that characterized the 1939 New York World's Fair. The stadium roof was a cantilevered arch. Tubes of neon served as foul poles. The press box consisted of individual booths where reporters sat glassed in and comfortable. "Wow," I said. "This is going to be all right."

"Now listen," Rosenthal said, "if you're gonna cover this club, there are a few things you better learn right away. First, don't use words like 'wow.' Second, when you get excited, you talk too fast. Third, get your hair cut. This is no place for a Jewish musician."

"Right. I know what you mean."

"You don't know what I mean. Now when there's a night game, you file for the Early Bird by two in the afternoon. Three pages. For the next edition you sub. *'Preacher Roe was on the mound before 8,000.'* You know how to do that? Then you sub-all afterward. You're not down here for the goddamn sunshine."

"Is it very hard?"

"Is what very hard?"

"The pace. Is that why you're giving up the club?"

Rosenthal sighed. His round cheeks puffed and deflated. He had come to the paper in the Depression, he explained, when it was hard for a Jew to get a decent job. He'd been forced to wait years to be hired. "Isn't that something?" he said. "Now I'm walking away from the best sportswriting job in New York."

"Why?"

"I can't bring up a family this way. It's two weeks at home and two weeks on the road most of the year. My wife finally had enough and said, 'What's it going to be, the marriage or the team?' "

Rosenthal's large, sad face hung open for an instant. Then he said harshly, "Come on. Let's go see the Hun-yaks."

"Hun-yaks?"

"The people you're down here to write about. The ball players." He led me under the grandstand, through a door marked "No Admittance" into a dressing room tiled in pumpkin-colored slabs, where Jackie Robinson was standing up and saying, in great excitement, "It wasn't a heart attack. Nothing like that. It was just a muscle strain in my chest."

"Robinson," Rosenthal said, "is not afraid to be dramatic."

"I'm a fan of his," I said.

"That's your problem," Rosenthal said.

"Who's the horse-faced guy in the corner?"

"Cox."

"Bill Cox."

"Billy Cox," Rosenthal said. "Don't go doing that in the paper. It was *Bill* Terry but it's *Billy* Cox."

"Okay," I said, "but please, Harold, not so loud."

"You're talking too fast," Rosenthal said, "and, Christ, remember that haircut."

The players were dressing before lockers that lined the pumpkin wall. "Okay," Rosenthal said, "let's go down the line.

This is Pee Wee Reese," Rosenthal said. "He's the captain. Good morning, Captain. Here's the new fella."

"He won't get anywhere hanging around with me," Reese said. "You told him that, didn't you, Harold?"

"What do you mean?" I said.

"I'm not good copy," Reese said and flickered a smile.

"Look, I'm just glad to meet you. I've been watching you play for a long time."

"Well, I've been playing for a long time." He winked at Rosenthal, whose elbow nudged me to move.

"This is Jackie Robinson," Rosenthal said. "Hey, Jack," he shouted. "You're okay?"

"Yeah," Robinson said. "It was just some muscle pulls. The cardiogram was negative." Robinson shook my hand warmly over a fierce look, a large, handsome and commanding man.

Proceeding, I met Clem Labine ("He's got sense; he won't need the players' pension"), Carl Erskine ("classy guy"), Preacher Roe ("a pitching scholar") and Roy Campanella. "You've got to be a little careful with Campy," Rosenthal said, behind his hand. "Roy kind of exaggerates. He gets carried away."

Suddenly Reese's head was alongside Rosenthal's. On the way to the field he had paused to eavesdrop. "Isn't that *right*, Pee Wee?" Rosenthal refused to be embarrassed.

"Well," Reese said slowly, "let's put it like this: with Campy catching, on a close play at home plate nobody has ever been safe."

After a while we went upstairs and Rosenthal introduced me to an unusual-looking man, whose features seemed a cross of Amerindian and south Italian. Dick Young, of the *Daily News*, was blinking against daylight.

"Young will take care of you till you get set," Rosenthal said.

"Yeah, sure," Young said. "Anything you want." He sat in the press room, stirring a Scotch and soda with a large plastic swizzle stick shaped like a pair of crossed bats.

"Harold," I said, "I'm gonna take care of myself."

"You can't do it right away. Don't you understand? This job is too big."

"I'll give you what you need, kid," Young said.

I shook my head. Vin Scully joined us. He began to talk about a friend who worked in Europe. I'm no goddamn novice, I thought as Scully spoke. "This guy travels," Scully said, "to Florence, Paris, London. Well, we travel, too. *Pittsburgh, Cincinnati, St. Louis.*"

Rosenthal and Young laughed. What's wrong with Pittsburgh, Cincinnati and St. Louis? I thought. The names excited me. I had never been to any of the cities that Vin Scully, at twenty-five, dismissed in a worldly way.

Rosenthal left Florida and the team on Monday, March 25. It was an off day; no game was scheduled. My first problem, then, was to decide what to write. "Today's story," Young announced, "is Clem Labine." The pitcher had developed a swelling on the inside of his right forearm, near the elbow.

"The trainer says it's nothing," I told Young.

"Yeah." I was following him through the lobby of a Miami Beach hotel called Sea Gull, nicknamed Siegal, where the manager gave sportswriters a cabana without charge.

"Well, if the trainer says it's nothing, how can we make it a big thing?"

Young entered the cabana, changed into a bathing suit, pulled a bridge table into the sun and started to type. "Because it's *not* nothing," he said. "You talked to him this morning?"

"Sure."

"Well, so did I. He's really worried."

After a while, I typed:

MIAMI, Fla., March 26—A muscle knot about the size of a small potato cropped up in Clem Labine's forearm today and threw a kink into the Dodgers' plans for the 26-year-old pitcher who is Manager Chuck Dressen's choice as most likely to succeed Don Newcombe as the team's big righthanded winner.

A discussion of Dodger pitching followed. When I finished, Young gave me his story and examined mine. He had written a similar piece, except that the muscle knot, in the *News*, would be "the size of an adult walnut."

Loneliness hit me at night. I had felt the Miami Beach sun, tried the surf outside the Siegal and written my first Dodger story. Now, on a warm, restless March evening, there wasn't anyone to talk to.

"What are you doing?" Someone approached as I stood in the marble lobby. I spun. It was Clem Labine. "How about a movie?" he said.

"Sure. Say, Clem. How's the arm?"

"About the same as it was at 11 A.M."

Labine was a well-built, handsome man, with a pointed boyish face under a careful crew cut. He wore light slacks, a tomato sports shirt, and a pale sports jacket that fit beautifully. "There's something nearby," he said, "called *Moulin Rouge,* about the French painter Toulouse-Lautrec."

Near the box office, Labine pushed in front of me and bought both tickets. "I asked you," he said. For the next two hours, while I watched Jose Ferrer hobble and Zsa Zsa Gabor whirl, while a haunting sentimental song resounded and the astonishing palette of Lautrec brightened the screen, even as Ferrer-Lautrec grown weary but not old lay on his deathbed, I could not forget that at my elbow, indeed my host, was a gentleman whose career I had discussed clinically, as though he were of cardboard, and whose end in baseball I had considered only in terms of Dodger games won and lost, which is to say inhumanely, for the 350,000 daily readers of the New York *Herald Tribune.*

Three days later, Labine was throwing to a catcher in the bullpen of empty Miami Stadium as I walked by. "Hey," he said. "Stand in there."

He wanted me to assume a normal batting stance, to help with his control. I buttoned the cardigan I was wearing, fetched a bat from the dugout, trotted back.

"What's the bat for?" said Rube Walker, the catcher.

"Help me take a normal stance."

"Don't swing now," Walker said. He had no mask.

Walker squatted and Labine threw a sinker. Although Labine was not regarded as very fast, and was complaining about his arm, the ball exploded past the plate with a sibilant whoosh, edged by a buzzing as of hornets. I had never heard a thrown ball make that sound before. The ball seemed to accelerate as it came closer; an accelerating, impossibly fast pitch that made the noises of hornets and snakes.

"That looked all right," I said to Walker.

"Don't turn around, for chrissake."

"Oh."

"And it was outside."

"Stand in there," Labine called. He threw a dozen sinkers, closer to me, and after that began to break his curve. Because of certain aerodynamic principles, a righthanded pitcher's curve starts toward a righthanded batter's left ear. I watched the baseball approach. It closed with me. I was paralyzed. Then, at what seemed the last millisecond, the spinning ball grabbed air and hooked away from my head and over the plate. Labine threw another curve and a third, wincing.

Through a resolute act of will I held my ground. The impulse was not simply to duck, but to throw away the bat and throw my body to the thick-bladed Florida grass. "Bailing out," ball players call this. Resisting was the totality of my strength. I could no more have swung, let alone hit, one of Labine's pitches than run a three-minute mile.

55

"Okay," Clem said to Walker. "Enough." He turned and bit his lip and shook his head. "I just got to," he said to himself. "I just got to."

I passed him, stunned, and said, unthinking, "Hang in." I went upstairs to the press room and drank an early Scotch and then another. I began to sweat, and then the shock of standing in gave way to something deeper. This was not my game, I knew. All the baseball I had played was irrelevant to sinkers that hissed like snakes and curves that paralyzed. What an odd arena for catharsis, the press room of Miami Stadium. This wasn't my game, that the Dodgers played. I didn't want to play this other game. It was too full of menace. It was the knotting of young muscles and killing self-demands.

A fast ball would shatter the human temple.

I didn't want to play this game.

I had never wanted to play *this* game.

"What Labine have to say to you out there?"

It was Dick Young.

"He said his arm still hurts."

Well, thank God, and the hell with it. Now there was a world ahead to write.

CEREMONIES OF INNOCENCE

I

The *Herald Tribune*, toward which I hurried on a biting February afternoon in 1948, had begun imperceptibly to decline, although, as in Hadrianic Rome, existing glories obscured the onrushing dark. By the time the *Tribune* died in 1966 it had become an inconsistent and rather shrill newspaper, most valuable for its modest intrusion on the constitutional monopoly of the *New York Times*. But the *Tribune*, two decades before death, burned with élan, dedication, unpretentious intellectuality, and a sure and certain sense of its own place.

"Here we write," Bob White, a bespectacled, cherry-nosed newspaperman said in the small hours of a Tuesday night. "Up at the *Times* they copyread. We have a newspaper here on Forty-first Street. They have an insurance company on Forty-third. This is *the* writers' newspaper in America." I was sitting beside White on the rewrite bank, near the center of the city room. In a midtown restaurant earlier, fire had sprung from the kitchen, charring tables and threatening after-theater drinkers. White had permitted me to listen on headphones as he took

57

details from a dead-voiced legman. "Damage moderate, mostly to kitchen. No panic. One woman sprained her ankle, and needed first aid. Unidentified."

"Say again."

"She's unidentified."

"Get her name, when we're through, Sid, and call me back."

"It's late."

"I'm here till 4 A.M., Sid."

Like any good rewrite man, White was able to compose a complete reportorial account of six hundred words within twenty minutes. He encouraged me to try the story also, and in an hour or so I handed him three pages. It was 2:15 A.M. Besides White and myself, the working staff consisted of a copyreader who lay snoring on a wooden bench set beside the horseshoe of the main copy desk, two men playing gin rummy on the so-called night desk and a grizzled deskman in the sports department, who had gotten drunk and was muttering and making occasional shouts, "Bitch can't do that to me." White ignored the ambient noise. "I don't know if writing can be taught," he said. "But I don't know that it *cannot* be taught either. I like this late trick. Fellow who had it before me, Ed Lanham, used the slow hours to write short stories. He must have taught himself a lot. He got a contract from *Collier's* and sold one story to Hollywood. *The Senator Was Indiscreet.* I didn't think it was as funny as some other people did. Anyway, try to go lighter on adjectives. Nouns and active verbs carry writing. Or that's what I think. Take this story of yours and try crossing out every adjective, and see how it reads and then, if you feel up to it, try again. It might work better."

"Thanks, Bob," I said, "but you need certain essential adjectives, don't you, like 'hot' and 'cold'?"

"Right, but in this particular case I don't think you need to describe the fire the way you did as hot. As far as we know, it was an ordinary fire and fires ordinarily are hot, aren't they?"

The *Tribune* was rich in teachers, who demanded only that one show an occasional spark, plus an abiding passion to learn. With a litter of newspapers before him, Ring Lardner sent his eldest son, John, to work at the *Trib* once, sharpening native gifts and taking instruction. Teaching techniques varied, to be sure, but the idea of teaching younger men was one unquestioned tradition at the *Tribune*. Another was that the brightest pupils, on pleading for a $5 weekly raise, would be turned down, then leave for *Time* magazine, or the indiscriminate opulence of public relations, or Hollywood.

By 1948 night copyboys earned $24 a week. When I was hired, my colleagues in austerity included an M.A., a prize student at Columbia Journalism and a bustle of B.A.s, including a former Harvard football captain. We reported at 4 P.M. and stayed until midnight, with everyone rotating—myself on the night of the restaurant fire—the shift that spanned 8 P.M.–4 A.M.

We shaped up at a plaster pillar, beside two communal telephones and the wood bench where the late copyreader, who worked from midnight to 8 A.M., had learned to sleep.

On my first hour at work, I tried to catch the eye of the city editor, my father's acquaintance, Joseph G. Herzberg, a frail and deep-voiced man, whose hands shook. Finally, at 5:15, he nodded icily. I bounded past Herzberg's secretary to shake hands and when I reached his chair discovered that one cannot shake a hand that is not offered. I reddened. Herzberg turned very slowly, annoyance in his eyes.

"I just wanted to thank you for hiring me," I said.

"Oh, did *they* hire you?"

"For nights."

"Oh, well, give my regards to your father."

He turned and I walked back the path that I had lunged. Benny Weinberg, a stooped ashen man of forty, the night head copyboy, shook his head and clucked. "You shoul'n'ta dunnit," Benny said. "Mr. Herzberg doesn't like to be bothered by copyboys. Now I'll prob'ly catch it, 'cause *you* spoke to him.''

"It's all right, Mr. Weinberg," I said and almost added that *Joe* Herzberg was an associate of my father's. I held my tongue, but not in resistance to gaucherie; rather, at the *Trib* I was determined to rise or fall entirely on my own.

In the pure performance of his craft, a copyboy carries about pieces of paper on which newspaper stories are written. Most copy went from reporter, or teletype printer, to the foreign, national or city desk, then on to the general copy desk and finally to the night editor's table, a sort of field headquarters. Benny Weinberg described each route and peril in exquisite detail. "Don't come up too quick behind Colonel Ball, on the telegraph desk. He very much doesn't like to be startled. You know not to bother Mr. Herzberg again. The night editor likes you to move quick. Keep alert. You're responsible for answering the two phones. You pick them up and you say, 'Editorial.' Am I going too fast? Don't be afraid to ask questions." Copyboys, M.A.s included, also suffered small drudgeries. We filled paste pots, changed typewriter ribbons and fetched coffee. In one instance a reporter flipped a cigarette to the floor and ordered: "Stamp out that butt." The copyboy glowered but obeyed. For every visible copyboy, two dozen applicants had mailed résumés to the city editor. At the bottom of the *Herald Tribune*, as in a valley of fumaroles, one was conscious of pressure from underneath.

The most frightening figure on the floor was a pale, hairless creature who was named Everett Kallgren and called "The Count." He was night editor. Customarily, we were summoned with the cry of "Copy," which meant a story had to be moved and would someone please do it. Kallgren eschewed "Copy" for the denigration of "Boy!" The Count possessed a ringing, nasal tenor that twanged like a $1.98 fiddle but carried like a Guarnerius del Gesù. "Boy," he twanged on my third night at work, fixing me with eyes of gelid blue, "bring me three-eighths of an inch of copy paper immediately." Someone snickered. Benny Weinberg pointed me toward a green supply cabinet beyond the foreign news desk.

"Got a ruler?" I asked Ben.

"Boy," jeered the Count, meaning hurry up.

"Guess," Weinberg whispered, desperately.

I brought Kallgren his paper. He measured and cried, "Boy." Then he crumpled a superfluous eighth inch, while I blanched.

If a headline displeased him, Kallgren wrote a critical comment in red pencil and cried, "Boy. Take this over to . . ." He would then identify the offending deskman by name. Sensitivity in males excited the Count, and once he found someone whom his notes rattled, the man became a consistent victim. A tall, pale deskman named John Winders actually shook before Kallgren's temper. "Boy," the Count twanged one night, "take this head back to Mr. Winders. Tell him it's wooden. Buy him an ax. Find him a verb. Show him this note." As the copyboy walked the fifteen feet from night desk to copy desk, Winders, an excellent and committed journalist, fainted in his chair.

The *Tribune* was housed in a twenty-story building of buff brick that squatted on the block between Seventh and Eighth avenues, from Fortieth to Forty-first Street. The garment industry ran right to the rear doors and, two hundred yards east on Fortieth, the old Metropolitan Opera House presented a façade of soiled yellow brick. The region was eclectic; in the old *Tribune* neighborhood garment buildings, garages and orange-drink stands mixed into Manhattan drabness. Visitors entered the newspaper offices at 230 West Forty-first Street under bright globes stenciled with the *Herald Tribune* logotype. There was no hyphen between *"Her-*

ald" and *"Tribune,"* which was a good thing for visitors to remember. *Tribune* men cared about such details. It was "the *Journal* hyphen *American,"* they said, but "the *Herald* space *Tribune."*

Production logistics ordered the lower stories. The second and third floors, really one prodigious room, contained eight high-speed presses whose roar, while producing 35,000 newspapers an hour, would have pierced the deafness of Beethoven. When a newspaperman speaks of the music of rolling presses, he is either faking or has had so much to drink that he will next sentimentalize appendicitis. The fourth floor was given to compositors, who set type and made up the pages inside sturdy frames of steel. Editorial—reporters, copyreaders, editors and, for that matter, copyboys—worked on five. Walking into the fifth floor from the Forty-first Street elevator, one passed banks of offices given to editorial writers and executives and random critics. Then, following a wide corridor, one burst upon the newsroom, a huge open pit which was usually but not frequently painted pale green. Reporters sat in banks of desks, extending from the Fortieth Street wall toward the center of the room, where the city editor reigned, surrounded by demigods. The office of George Anthony Cornish, the managing editor, occupied the extreme southeast corner. It was carpeted and contained a bust of Adolf Hitler that had been pierced and chipped by fusillades fired from Garrand rifles.

The path of prose was downward. Stories written and edited on five were cast in lead on four. Mats became plates and were fixed to the presses on three. Finished newspapers, produced, cut and folded by those astonishing machines, rode conveyors to street level. There they were bound and thrown into delivery trucks, which gathered nightly in Fortieth Street, blocking traffic and then fanning out through New York City, tanks setting forth on familiar maneuvers. At the Fortieth Street entrance a sign read "EMPLOYEES ONLY." The word "employee" was a mark of the plain face of newspaper life. A hospital or an advertising agency would have used "staff."

Each day's tension described a parabola. On the fifth floor of the *Tribune*, the curve rose steeply toward 8:30 P.M., the hour at which all material for the city edition was to clear editorial and stories and headlines, locked together with metal clips, clanked down a chute to the composing room. People who had to write the stories and compose or edit the headlines were invariably lifted along the curve. Some, like Kallgren, vented pressure through sadism. Others drank and smoked and, although only Winders fainted, I saw at least two reporters stuck for prose and near a deadline begin to cry.

"It's upsetting like nothing else in the world," Bob White said, late one night, after the first episode of crying. A reporter had sent a copyboy for coffee and pound cake. When the boy returned with coffee and raisin cake, the reporter began a diminishing outcry with a scream. "No. No. No. I don't like raisins. I won't eat the goddamn cake. Why couldn't you do what I said?" And he started to sob. "Not everybody can take the life," White said. "Not everybody should try."

"I've never really seen a place like this, Bob, or people like this either."

"I don't imagine you would have, growing up in Brooklyn. But don't panic. After a while, you'll find good things, like whisky, flow more freely around this place than tears."

The Artist and Writers Restaurant, a handsome, somber establishment with a sixty-foot bar of polished dark wood, attracted most of the business. Leo Corcoran, the head bartender, measured martinis with such precision that a crown rose above the rim of the glass and one did best to lean over to the first sip. The Artist and Writers was called Bleeck's, pronounced "Blake's," for its owner, who had operated a speakeasy and not allowed women into the bar until 1935, at which time a *Tribune* reporter grumbled, "Next they'll be buttering the steaks."

Bleeck's was on Fortieth Street, directly under a garage. With several of Leo's martinis inside him, a baseball writer missed an assignment when he looked out the back window and saw torrents. " 'S rainin'," he said. "I'll write a rainout story at five o'clock," and he returned to the martinis. The day was cloudy but dry. Workmen had been washing cars on the garage roof and the "rain" came from their hoses. Colleagues eventually filled in the man, and the story he wrote on the game he did not see was passable, although poorly typed.

The drinking press was variously furtive, as in sneaking a quick one to "get the damn lead off the ground," gregarious, as when a story was finished and approved, and contentious. Irascibility and combativeness struck people unpredictably when the parabolic tension bottomed, leaving a man adrenalin for which he had no proper use.

The production of an enormous newspaper, Joe Herzberg has suggested, is nothing less than a miracle. "It never ceased to surprise me," he said years later, while bearing the title of "Cultural News Editor" at the *Times*, "that somehow a finished newspaper emerges every day." But the achievement of the *Tribune* then and of the *Times* then and now relies not on divine assistance but on mundane organization. Once lines of copy flow are established, once responsibility for various essentials—page make-up, photo selection, caption writing—is distributed and once the mechanics of production are subdued, the creation of a half million newspapers a night is no more miraculous than one day's output of automobiles at Flint, Michigan. A technological marvel is no miracle.

The immeasurable difference between producing cars and producing newspapers is pursuit of the horizon. A car begins with specifications, that is to say limits, within which production workers succeed or fail. If the front discs are not quite ready for 1972, there is plenty of time. Install them in 1973, or '74 or '75. A newspaper has no specifications. "Nothing ever written,"

F.P.A. observed, "was too good to appear in a paper." The editor planning his news section wants the world in miniature. The reporter starting to type remembers Marlowe's mighty line. Newspaper work, good newspaper work, begins with passionate striving. The rise or fall of newspaper tension is unique.

At the *Trib*, only copyboys were immune. It was no more difficult at 8:20 to walk a story from the wire room to the foreign desk than it had been at 5:15. Sure of ourselves, observing without involvement, we humored Benny Weinberg, took the measure of the people around us and tired the clock with debates.

The newsroom cast was troubling and impressive. A young Hunter College graduate who was assistant women's page editor raised her left arm and snapped fingers when she wanted coffee. Seeing a male obey the wordless order made her smirk. "But I really think," one of the two night copygirls pointed out, "that if she must order coffee that way, she ought to shave her underarms." A chubby Navy veteran served George Cornish as night secretary and wandered among us, an emperor amid clowns. When we ignored him, he drove into conversations, remarking that $240 a week was too much to pay for an editor, whose name he mentioned. He had access to his employer's files, and knew everybody's salary. The police reporter Walter Arm was a hero for his ability to write succinctly and quickly. The foreign correspondent Homer Bigart was a hero because totalitarian governments were always expelling him and, besides, he was said to have been a copyboy for seven years. The ancient columnists, Mark Sullivan and George Fielding Eliot, seemed irrelevant even then, but we admired the radio-TV critic, John Crosby, although he never spoke to us, and the music critic, Virgil Thomson, who was extraordinarily accessible, and Red Smith, whom we never saw. Smith filed columns by wire and expense accounts by mail.

The prettiest girl—newspaper offices are depressingly functional—worked as secretary to the foreign editor. One day the Washington wire teletypist, a volatile man whose hobby was nude photography, summoned his courage and bought her dinner in Greenwich Village. She accepted the meal, but not the donor. A few days later he displayed a dozen pictures of the girl, whose name was Gerry, as she walked about her kitchen, fully dressed. "Goddamn prude," he complained. Later Gerry showed me photographs of herself in a bathing suit, taken while she spent a vacation in the Maritime Provinces of Canada. She was black-haired and trim with an appealing little swell to her belly. In our sudden intimacy, I said I was beginning to weary of fetching coffee whenever a hairy witch snapped fingers. Gerry said I had to be patient. I started to frame a reply, but someone shouted, "Copy, copy, copy," and the music fled.

Mostly, the hours droned in abstract discussion. "Who," asked Willard Hertz, the man from Columbia Journalism, "is the greatest American novelist, and what is the greatest novel? Two parts." Willard was a bulky, bright Clevelander, whose father was a judge. While working as a police reporter in Lorain, Ohio, Willard had eaten an Oh! Henry bar during a police autopsy, he claimed. The literary answers he demanded were Mark Twain and *Moby Dick*. Anything else precipitated argument. "But, Willard," said Henry Goethals, a tall, bony ascetic whose grandfather supervised construction of the Panama Canal, "there isn't any single answer to that sort of question."

"Oh, yes," Willard said. "*Huck Finn* is a fine novel, but *Moby Dick* is unsurpassed."

What was a better war book, *Three Soldiers* or *All Quiet on the Western Front?* Did Thomas Wolfe really hate Jews? Was *Spoon River Anthology* or *Winesburg, Ohio* closer to the tortured heart of America? Was Henry Wallace a populist like Bryan? Would Stalin exploit or respect him?

The debates rang, until someone called "Copy," but they picked up again at once; so that being a night copyboy at the

Herald Tribune was to audit lectures by untitled professors and to attend continuous disorganized seminars of bright graduate students. My own surest area was baseball, and with spring Henry Goethals asked whom I considered the best of hitters.

"Stan Musial in Ebbets Field."

"What about Ted Williams or Joe DiMaggio?"

"Nobody hits like Musial in Brooklyn."

"Would you take me to see him?" Goethals said. "I don't believe I've been to Brooklyn but once."

We met at a YMCA near Central Park. I led Henry to the subway, and after forty minutes we reached the Brooklyn Museum station, where we walked out onto the sunlit mall of Eastern Parkway. "Say," Goethals said, "this is nice." I showed him the main branch of the Brooklyn Public Library and the lot behind the Museum where we had played hardball. He nodded and gazed at long rows of apartment buildings, studying them as one might study Tasmanian vistas. "This must have been an interesting place to grow up," Goethals said.

We entered Ebbets Field through a rotunda, floored in white tile with inlaid designs of crossed bats. "Built in 1912," I said. "Fine place to see a game. You're very close to the field." Our seats were in the upper deck between first base and home.

In the first inning, Harry Taylor mixed a curve and a fast ball and got two quick strikes on the Cardinals' Number 6. Musial then lined a pitch against the right-field wall for a double. He hit the wall again next time up; no Dodger pitcher got him out that afternoon. Years later in a club car Musial recalled the day. "I not only got five-for-five," he said, "I got every hit with two strikes." At the time, the afternoon established me as a man of authority. It was a small step from lecturing the old Harvard football captain on baseball to countering Hertz's claims for Sherwood Anderson with my own for Edgar Lee Masters. *Spoon River* stirred me, and beyond that Masters was a man with whom to identify. A Chicago newspaper had dismissed him once as an inept writer. Long afterward the same paper requested a series of special articles and drew from the poet a thunderous, triumphant "No!"

Each copyboy was permitted to discuss his future with Joe Herzberg semiannually by appointment. You lost all immunity then. Suddenly, sitting in the center of a loud, busy, important newsroom, you had five minutes in which to tell a preoccupied man, whose budget was tight, why you, of all people on earth, were best qualified to join the *Tribune*'s reportorial staff. Naked pleas embarrassed Herzberg. His hands shook more violently when a copyboy approached and he grabbed a newspaper and started turning pages.

"I was, uh, wondering, sir, if there was, uh, any chance of my getting a reporting job?"

"Better come back and see me in the fall." The newspaper he held snapped and rattled. "Go on. Go on. I'm listening. Is that all you have to say?"

"Uh, I see you're looking at the gardening section."

"Yes. It's a fine thing to grow plants. Almost everything human is in flux. There's a permanence to transplanting a tree."

"About my career . . ."

"In autumn. Try in autumn. Nothing now."

"Yes, sir. And I certainly will do some serious gardening between now and then."

After each rejection, we complained about Herzberg. Someone called him "Flowerhead Joe." But we were learning, from him and from the gentler people like Bob White, and just as surely we learned from one another.

Will Hertz could have followed his father into law and comfort in Shaker Heights, Ohio. Goethals, son of a physician at Harvard Medical School, walked his own path. A young man's rebellion is no less determined because it is individual not collective, and as we took the measure of one another, down boisterous newspaper nights, we came to learn styles of rebellion and to sense that the *Herald Tribune* attracted people who longed to fight endemic wrongs, and who sought a life of new experiences rather than a repetition of what was prosperous, time-worn and safe. Exploring one another's lives, while a great newspaper clamored around us, we strode from boyish loneliness and provincialism toward the greater loneliness of what it is to be a man.

If doors were not opened, they could be wedged. Beach Conger, the travel editor, sometimes assigned copyboys to write articles, for $5 or $10, insisting only that the writer really have seen the place he described. This rule became mandatory after a boy named Herbert Zucker sold an article, extolling Waycross, Georgia, as a second Valhalla. Taking Zucker's prose as sterling, another copyboy, Ed Morgan, visited Waycross on a motor trip following his marriage to a daughter of Averell Harriman. "We went far out of our way to get to Waycross," Morgan reported on his return. "Zucker left out that Waycross is hard by Okefenokee. We had to drive miles of bad road through the swamp in 100-degree heat. We kept running into swarming insects so we had to keep the windows closed. When we got out of Okefenokee, we found ourselves driving past thousands of ruined cars. Waycross seems to be the principal auto graveyard in the South." Morgan, tall and restrained, then said, "Nice piece, Herbie."

William Zinsser, the young drama editor, assigned me to interview a female ice skater for the Sunday paper, pointing out that in a few weeks at Madison Square Garden the skater would play before the equivalent of a full year's attendance in a Broadway theater. Zinsser liked anomalies. Later he sent me to an off-Broadway production of *Juno and the Paycock*. "Everyone calls O'Casey the greatest playwright alive," Zinsser said, "but he can't get his stuff on Broadway." Preparing, I read five O'Casey plays in three days, which would have been a semester's worth of work at NYU if NYU admitted that O'Casey existed. *Juno* is not the best, but it ends with the remark, "The whole world is in a terrible state of chassis," one more instance, I wrote, of O'Casey's brilliance. Zinsser printed the first three-quarters of my story, and a day later seven New York newspapers published advertisements for *Juno*, with the legend, "Brilliant—*Herald Tribune*."

The sports department was a world detached, with its own copy desk, its own teletypes and its own tigerish independence. Stanley Woodward, the sports editor, found George Cornish so grievously cautious that he publicly referred to the managing editor as "Old Double-Rubber." Woodward was an enormous, myopic man, who had pitched and played guard for Amherst, where he studied non-Shakespearean Elizabethan drama under Robert Frost. "I didn't care much for their stuff," he said, "and Frost didn't either." Woodward, a scholar and innovator, was called "The Coach." At one standing, he was said to have consumed eleven of Leo Corcoran's martinis, with no other sustenance except salted peanuts, and left Bleeck's vertically under his own power. That was a record, and still endures.

By using what he described as a scouting system, Woodward assembled the finest sports staff in the country. The Coach studied out-of-town papers, and when he spotted a good story, he began a file of the writer's work. If it was consistently excellent, Woodward waited for an opening, then brought the man to New York with talk of "the big time" and possibly a pay raise. He found a remarkable racing columnist, Joe H. Palmer, on a magazine called *The Blood Horse*. Palmer had been a university teacher lacking only a thesis for his doctorate in English. "One leg a Ph.D.," he said of himself. Palmer occasionally composed subheads for his racing columns in eleventh-century English. Woodward calculated that Red Smith, working for the Philadelphia *Record*, was writing 500,000 words a year. "Most was excellent," he said. "I reasoned that if we cut his work load in half, damn near everything would be excellent, which is what happened." He had also attempted to hire John Lardner while the two shot dice in the belly of an aircraft carrier riding into the Battle of Midway. "When this damn war ends," Woodward said, "I want you to be my sports columnist."

"Just roll them, Coach," Lardner said.

"You ought to come off *Newsweek*, Lardner, and come back to honest work. Be a newspaperman." It was early June and stifling. Both men were naked, except for towels.

"I don't want to write every day," Lardner said. "Can't write that well that often."

"You won't have to. I'll use you three times a week."

"Expensive," Lardner said. Actually, he was afraid newspaper work would consume all his writing energies. "I'd need five hundred dollars for the three."

"Fine," Woodward said, but the bargain was canceled by a *Tribune* executive who refused to authorize the salary. "Think of it," Woodward remarked in his seventieth year. "My two regular columnists would have been Smith and Lardner, except for the goddamn zombi who vetoed me." Woodward described the staff he had assembled with great pride submerged in archness. "One made journalism his major at Notre Dame. Another majored in Latin and Greek at Yale. Another came to this country from Scotland as a golf professional. Another was night editor of the Paris *Herald*. Another attended City College of New York and caught on because he did an outstanding job as the paper's correspondent there. Another started as a copyboy. Another was the son of a famous big league player and got the ear of my predecessor because of that. Another was a theatrical press agent. Another was formerly an advance man for Singer's Midgets."

Woodward's cries carried more lustily even than Kallgren's. Once he roared at one of his best writers, "Sir! If you refer to Chicago as the windy city in my sports section one more time,

71

out, Out, *Out!*" Whoever the author, Woodward would not tolerate horrendous clashes of fearsome Tigers and snarling Wolverines, concluded in purple sunsets. He wanted, he said, to present his department "in such a manner that it would be intelligible to the nonsports reader, should one happen to fold back the paper at the wrong place." He liked verbs of action and exact adjectives. He disliked "ding-dong battles, horse-hides, donnybrooks, myriads of colored lights, fetlock-deep mud, net tilts, grid battles, pile-driving rights and the act of rushing people to the hospital."

The Reids fired this wholly remarkable and dedicated man while I was still a copyboy. Various versions ascribe different motivations. Woodward had balked at printing the scores of mediocre female golfers who were friends of the publisher. Woodward had refused to print the scores of mediocre male golfers who bought advertising space. Pressed by Mrs. Reid to list "the two most dispensable members of your department for purposes of economy discharges," the Coach responded, "Stanley Woodward and Red Smith." When the *Tribune* could no longer tolerate Woodward's spirit, its vitality sapped. Newspapers like the *Tribune* and the old *World* attracted creative people and let them flourish. That was their strength, indeed their response to the encyclopedism of the *New York Times*. But with creativity comes unorthodoxy, iconoclasm and passionate, if sometimes misdirected, integrity. The *World,* not long before its death, fired Heywood Broun for attacking the executioners of Sacco and Vanzetti with too much frequency and ardor. Discipline was maintained and the *World* became weaker. The *Tribune* management replaced Woodward with Robert Barbour Cooke, a graceful baseball writer who was tall, poised and had been Whitelaw Reid's classmate at Yale. Cooke, a man of generosity and reportorial talent, did not contest orders from above. Management believed that it was making life easier for itself by promoting Cooke. Actually, the evidence suggests it was inviting death by firing the most gloriously talented sports editor in the United States.

In time, Woodward and I became friends, but as copyboy I was known to him only as one more young man, scurrying to get cigarettes. Woodward tipped for personal services. When he wanted cigarettes, he stuffed a bill into your hand and said, "Buy yourself a pack, too," or, "While you're down at Bleeck's, son, take a minute. Get yourself a glass of draft beer."

"Mr. Marsh?"

I had summoned my courage and approached Irving Marsh, a gentle, white-haired man, Woodward's assistant and now assistant to the new sports editor, Bob Cooke. He was scrawling a headline with his left hand. The sports department occupied a rectangle at the north side of the city room and Marsh sat at a large desk, guarding the entrance, an amiable Cerberus.

He looked up. "Yes?"

"I was wondering if there might be any chance of my doing some string work in sports."

"What have you done?"

"Stuff in drama. I've got the clips right here. And then there are some things I've done with one of the rewrite men, Bob White. He can tell you."

"Well, there's nothing right now," Marsh said.

"Oh." I looked for a route of retreat. Marsh had been generous with baseball tickets; by bothering him for work, I was not only asking the improbable but risking his good will and Dodger passes as well. "Wait a minute, my friend." Marsh looked up with a quick smile. "I didn't say there wasn't anything, *anywhere*. The AP is looking for someone to cover some college football in the fall. Go over in a few weeks and ask for Spike Claassen." He turned quickly to a secretary and began dictating to avoid an outpouring of thanks.

At the Associated Press offices in Rockefeller Plaza the next day, Harold (Spike) Claassen said that if Irv Marsh had recommended me, I could certainly have the job.

"You won't have to supply me with a portable," I said. "I can get my own."

"We don't," Claassen began. Then he sighed and said, "Never mind. Look, call me about September 15. I'll give you your first assignment then."

I drew a game between Wagner and another Lutheran college called Panzer, as in Afrika Korps, which has since dropped its name and become a division of Montclair State Teachers in New Jersey. I was to write 150 words and provide the score by periods. The essentials of Associated Press dispatches are speed, simplicity and artless, necessary organization. Each story is transmitted to hundreds of newspapers. A few may print all. Most carry a fragment. Some publish only the first sentence. The same AP dispatch that runs 150 words in the Philadelphia *Bulletin* may run 75 words in the Camden *Courier-Post* and 50 words in the Hartford *Times*. Readers of each newspaper are equally entitled to coherence. These conditions require a story to begin with the names of the teams, an indication of what sport is in question, a mention of the final score and, if possible, the winning play. One devotes succeeding paragraphs to significant moments, in the order of their importance, and, when space is so tight that real description is impossible, pertinent statistics.

The AP considers that it has beaten rival news services when its dispatch is used, and experience indicates that on a busy Saturday of college football, sports departments select the first story that arrives, regardless of merit. "You should have a finished piece in here," Claassen ordered, "no more than fifteen minutes after the game."

John Keats is said to have written "I stood tiptoe upon a little hill" in twenty minutes. He and Leigh Hunt were holding a sonnet-writing race, which Keats won both in elapsed time and in lyricism. There was no prohibition against lyric writing at the Associated Press. If in fifteen minutes a man was able to compress the facts of a football game into a story that could withstand amputation at any point *and* compose lyrically, he was welcome to go ahead.

The first assignment sent me to Staten Island, where Wagner won in the closing minutes. "A fourth quarter scoring pass," I began, on a shaky Royal borrowed from my father, "from Chris Kartalis to Whitey Drown gave Wagner College a 14–12 victory over Panzer today." By the end of the season, I was writing five-hundred-word stories, and after my eighth weekend Claassen handed me a check for $24. He was a genial, mild man, but frugal.

"That's only three dollars a game," I said.

"Budget," Claassen said, and threw up his palms.

At the AP you learned formula and developed speed. The first is antithetic to creative writing and the second is largely irrelevant, but both are critical to the confidence of every newspaperman. There is never a working day when the guillotine of deadline does not hang above one's neck. It is a comfort beyond prayer to realize that when sweeter muses are struck dumb, one can always write a variation of AP Formula One, "A fourth quarter scoring pass from Chris Kartalis to Whitey Drown," and neither win a prize nor utterly fail.

"What are you doing on Thanksgiving, my friend?" I was a daytime copyboy by now, but still stringing for the Associated Press.

"A football game for the AP, Mr. Marsh."

"Well, if you can get out of it, I'd like you to cover a walking race for us. City Hall to Coney Island. Starts at ten. You can be home in time to have your turkey."

"I've never seen a walking race in my life."

"The clips, my friend. The clips. Can I put you down for it?"

The *Herald Tribune* morgue, opening off the city room, was richly grained with history. More than a century of newspapers were stored there, along with clips—filed clippings—recording a million events in a hundred thousand lives. Did you wonder how critics first responded to *Look Homeward, Angel?* The answer (with limited enthusiasm) lay in the Thomas Wolfe clips. How had the *Tribune* played the signing of Jackie Robinson? One found the date in the Robinson clips, then turned to a bound volume from 1946. The story made page one, but below the fold. A reader passing a newsstand sees only the top half of a full-sized paper; from that viewpoint, a story below the fold is buried. How did the *Tribune* cover the annual City Hall–to–Coney Island walking race? With variations of the AP Formula One lead.

"The stuff seems pretty heavy," I told Marsh.

"Well, there's your opportunity to show us something better." In addition to preparing weekly assignments, contending with daily news conferences and helping put out a daily sports section, Marsh supervised All-Star Games in football and basketball that the *Tribune* promoted for charity and for publicity. Paper traffic at his desk was formidable, but now he paused. "I covered the race myself twenty years ago, just after I got out of City College. Did you get back that far in the clips? No? Well, the year I had it, a Turk won the race, so naturally I wrote, 'The Turk brought home the Turkey on Thanksgiving Day.' "

Later, I telephoned the Transit Authority. Then, Thanksgiving morning, a German refugee led an intense, ragged band of walkers as they ascended the great arc of Hart Crane's bridge. A number of motorists gazed with mild surprise. When the refugee, Henry Laskau, reached a Coney Island bathhouse first, an hour and a half later, he handed out cards. "If you could mention my importing business in the paper," he began the postrace interview, "I would like that." I could not. But thanks to the Transit Authority, I was able to point out in the lead that

Laskau had traveled from City Hall to Coney Island in only twice the time the BMT required and he had been spared jostles, noise and the expense of the new ten-cent fare.

My reward was a by-line, $7 and a personal commendation from Bob Cooke. "I especially liked the part where you said, 'On Ocean Parkway there was heavy traffic and the walkers slowed to a crawl.'" Cooke laughed.

"But I was serious. Runners slow to a walk. Walkers slow to a crawl." Cooke was a big, athletic man who had played hockey at Yale and written baseball with casual wit. "I wouldn't get too serious about a walking race," he said.

Marsh, sitting at the next desk, winced. "I think he means he was serious about his story, Bob."

"Oh. Yes. That's right. You have to be serious about a story, even when it's funny. Especially when it's funny." Cooke winked and turned to his own affairs.

As the department was organized, reporters specialized in distinct sports. Everett B. Morris and Marsh covered the important basketball, Jesse Abramson covered every important fight. The local major league teams, horse racing, hockey, golf, and tennis were individual preserves and each man protected his area according to the territorial imperative. As a result, all that was left for a stringer was arcana. One month, I found myself assigned to the Coast Guard cutter *Tamaroa* "covering" a motorboat race around Manhattan Island.

"Why don't you look up the Circle Line time?" Bob Cooke suggested.

"I don't want to repeat myself."

"Listen," Marsh said, "if one of the speedboats hits a log, someone may be killed. Don't take it lightly." Nobody was injured and the story was difficult, partly because 98 percent of the race took place out of sight. In another month, I reboarded the *Tamaroa* at anchor for a 150-mile motorboat race from Albany to Seventy-ninth Street. In the fall I drew cross-country races, becoming, as I told Marsh, a specialist in writing eyewitness accounts of events that took place out of sight. "Don't be discouraged," Marsh said. "In a few more weeks they'll be walking from City Hall to Coney Island again, and you get to see all of that from the press car."

Then, one perfect day in February 1950, Marsh telephoned. "You want to go on staff?"

"What?"

"Now don't get excited. It's not much of a job. We're starting a new seven-o'clock edition and we need someone to work on the desk from one to nine, sending down racing results, if you're interested. It pays about forty-eight dollars, and of course I'll see that you still get to do as much writing as possible. I don't want you buried on the desk."

For six months, under the careful eyes of Cooke and Marsh, I worked on the copy desk, making type markings on racing results, from time to time writing a headline and acquiring a certain sense of professionalism. I was able to greet some of the sportswriters almost as an equal.

Blustery Everett Morris, retelling a basketball game, roared, cursed, reddened, cheered and expected you to share his emotions. Rud Rennie, forever bemused at damages the copy desk had worked on his prose, complained that, "All of a sudden, copyreading has gotten harder than it used to be." Jesse Abramson, who covered track as well as boxing, tore passion to tatters over a closing burst in the Buermeyer five-hundred-yard run. The pervasive sense, however, was not sports, but literacy.

Al Laney, who covered baseball until the belligerent vulgarity of Leo Durocher drove him to golf, had been part-time secretary to James Joyce for half a dozen years in Paris. Laney, once night editor of the Paris *Herald*, liked sports, which he described with exceedingly long, exceedingly graceful sentences. I collared him one night in the *Tribune* cafeteria; to my surprise, he was anxious to talk about Joyce.

We sat on metal chairs at a little table under fluorescent lights that were too bright, and while a deskman at my right yawned, Laney remembered Joyce in Paris. "He was blind," Laney said. "Did you know that?"

"I knew his eyes were bad."

"They weren't merely bad," Laney laughed harshly. "For much of the time he simply couldn't see. One day Sylvia Beach said, 'Laney. You have a typewriter. Joyce needs some letters typed.' I went to write, but I stayed to read. He would hand me a novel, any novel, that someone had sent him and say 'Begin,' and I would read. Sometimes after just one paragraph he would order me to stop. Sometimes I would read the whole book. Some were in English and some were in French."

Laney was a slim man, who invariably wore a gray fedora. He had a black mustache, a passion for Mozart, and he mumbled.

"Al, did he tell you anything about writing?"

"Some things. It was hard to be certain when he was serious. But Joyce believed, and I heard this often, that once sound and meaning were very close, and that civilization had changed and corrupted language. He wanted to bring sound and meaning together again. You know, there are pleasant words and harsh words and what he was trying to do was to make the existing pleasant words stand for pleasant things, or, if he had to, make up new words, harsh or pleasant."

The copyreader at the table excused himself.

"It was so long ago," Laney said, and his voice trailed into the mumble. "Let's get more coffee."

When we came back to the table, walking past night secretaries, deskmen and a few printers from the early shift, and were seated again before the dirty dishes, Laney put a hand to his forehead and looked beyond me and said again, "It was so long ago, but I'm certain he said this. Yes. I'm absolutely certain he said this. *'When you write you must listen for sounds. And there is a sound that one word makes and there is the sound that one*

79

word makes upon another and there is the sound of silences between words.'"

"What else? Anything else?"

"Without the right sound, writing is worthless." Laney gazed at a cream-colored wall. "He fired me, you know. One day there was an Italian novel and I couldn't read Italian, so he let me go from the job of reading. Joyce fired me from the job for which I was not paid."

After six months I was liberated from the copy desk. The so-called police action in Korea had turned alarming and Everett Morris, a commander in the Naval Reserve, was recalled to active duty. In the shuffle, I was assigned high school sports. During the fall of 1950 all the public school coaches of New York City refused to coach unless their salaries were raised. Technically, this was not a strike—the coaches were teachers and they continued meeting classes. But the effect, from my viewpoint, was the same. I was a high school sports writer with very little school sports to cover.

Irving Marsh talked very seriously. "High school sports may not seem like much, but the job you do is very important. People form their reading habits when they're seventeen or so. If you get people committed to the *Trib* at that age, you'll have won *Trib* readers for life."

"But if this mess doesn't get settled," I said, "what will there be to write about?"

"As you say, the mess."

I traveled to high schools, talked to coaches and athletes and wrote dozens of articles on schools without sports. In the beginning, Marsh asked me to turn in each piece to him. "Come here," he said. "You've written an essay."

"Damn. That's what I was always trying to do in school. Write a decent essay."

"Oh, this is a decent essay all right, but we have this newspaper here and we want news stories." He held the story in one hand and a yellow pencil in the other. "You've left out the time," he said.

"What do you mean?"

"When did you visit DeWitt Clinton High School?"

"Yesterday."

"But I don't believe the word yesterday appears anywhere."

I recaptured three pages, rolled my chair back to my desk and an hour and a half later, on the third try, satisfied him. Marsh walked over to the head of the copy desk, a raucous and unpleasant man. "Here's a pretty fair little piece," he said, and the story was saved from butchery.

With time, I subdued the sports page idiom and Marsh moved me into a higher league. "I was talking to someone up front," he said, "and if you write a good piece for under-the-cartoon, they'll print it." A cartoon ran on the editorial page, and the space beneath it was reserved for long articles supposedly lucid and often thoughtful. United States Senators wrote or signed articles under the cartoon.

"I don't know," I said.

"You'll get twenty-five or thirty dollars if they use it," Marsh said. "Fifteen hundred words."

That was half a week's pay and I said I would try and two weeks later I presented Marsh with a fourth draft of an interpretive article. He put me through two further drafts. The final story was successful enough to prompt the former assistant editor of the women's page, now city desk education reporter, to plant her stocky frame before me and announce, "That piece put a number of decent guys on the spot." Even, or especially, women responded to the territorial imperative.

"I always knew," Robert Frost said one day in his cabin at Ripton. He had been talking about obscure years and how he had held on.

I could give all to Time except—except
What I myself have held. But why declare
The things forbidden that while the Customs slept
I have crossed to Safety with? For I am There,
And what I would not part with I have kept.

I wonder if anyone always knows—you, me, Jackie Robinson, even Robert Frost—that we will cross to Safety. Or is it rather that when we are There, we *think* we always knew? As a full-time *Herald Tribune* sports reporter at the age of twenty-one, I thought I always knew. It had been waiting out there all the time, I told myself, journalism, this marvelous newspaper, these rousing people, the point at which my passion for sports and for writing intersected. But that is comfortable, settled, Calvinist, and I was not (nor am I) any of these. My truth is that I never knew. During the seasons among ferocious Brooklyn Jewish intellectuals and poseurs, I never considered what a newsroom looked like, never envisioned rewrite men with luminary writing wisdom, never knew a man like Stanley Woodward walked the earth. The paper was an intoxicating discovery, and when I found it, I put my Brooklyn past, except for baseball, behind me as rapidly as I could. I bought a car and found a girl. We married and moved into one large room on the ground floor of an old white-stone house, just out of cheering range of Ebbets Field. The Dodgers of 1950, probably the best team in the league, never untangled themselves and finished second. That autumn my wife invited my parents to the one-room flat for a first formal dinner. When they arrived, my father commandeered our principal piece of furniture, a sectional sofa of coral red, and started a monologue. He had lived half a century, he said, and he felt the years sometimes as when caught in a subway crush, but he couldn't be through yet because Joe Herzberg had suggested that he take a job at the *Tribune,* as an assistant to the night editor. He was plainly uncomfortable visiting and combative at the reversal in our roles, with which time threatened him.

"How much for the job?" I said.

"Seventy-five hundred."

"Take it, but the night editor's a pretty rough fella."

Gordon's nostrils flared. "I wasn't asking," he said. "I've already declined."

"I'm sure you have enough problems with your own career without trying to counsel your father," Olga said.

Joan, my wife, chose silence.

"Look," I said, "this is more exciting than anything you know, I'm telling ya."

" 'Telling ya'? " asked Olga.

"I'm flattered," Gordon said. "Oops." He had dropped a cloud of Pall Mall ash on the sectional.

"I'm delighted that you aren't selling shoes," Olga said, "but I'd be more delighted if I could understand what you were writing. God. Touchbacks and what else? You ought to be writing novels. Not that you could. You ought to try."

"Is there any chance," Gordon said, "of your covering baseball?"

"None."

"None?"

"None, Dad."

"Where did you find such unusual green wallpaper?" Olga asked Joan.

"It was here."

"And, Mother," I said, "I can't afford to have it changed."

"The stove isn't very good either," Joan said, "and dinner may be late, but we can all have another drink."

"I can get Dodger passes now, Dad," I said.

"Congratulations, but I can get my own."

When the schoolboy sports season ended, major league baseball came round again, and the editorial board of the *Tribune* decided to introduce a large box in the city edition, with "up-to-the-minute scores of every big league night game, plus pitching summaries and home runs." I was put in charge of the box for a summer, which boiled into a demanding test of my affection for baseball. The gracious mistress turned bitch in summer heat.

Various editions closed through the night, and the editors, particularly the head of the sports copy desk, thought that it was essential that we beat the *Times* by recording in our city edition "nothing for Cleveland in the top of the fourth," while the *Times* city edition recorded only a scoreless tie through three complete innings. The extra zero would be evidence of our superior enterprise. To achieve this beat, a Western Union sports ticker had been installed in the composing room, on the fourth floor. The room was noisy and heated beyond the norm of a New York summer by scores of machines producing the molten alloy that became hot type.

After a snack at seven, I typed the names of all the teams playing night games, and the starting pitcher and catcher, the battery. These were set by machine and presently placed in specified positions within the metal form for the box. The scores for each game were set in monotype: that is, individual pieces of type were used for each inning. A printer hovered over the page and responded quickly to the information I fed.

"Nothing for Brooklyn in the first."

"A zip for the Bums." Using tweezers, the printer fished in a box and came up with a zero. The printer wore work pants and an open work shirt, hanging loosely. I wore a white shirt, open at the collar, but always a necktie. The printer was earning $105 a week. I was drawing $55.

As edition time approached, pressure increased. On Tuesdays and Fridays, when eight games were going simultaneously, the ticker chattered continually, and I was hard put to keep all my records straight. I stood in the heat, perspiring and wilting the collar of the white shirt.

"Two for Detroit in the fourth."

"Two for Detroit in the fourth," repeated the printer.

The ticker noted that Chester Laabs had hit a home run. I penciled rapidly but neatly "Add Browns" on top of a sheet of copy paper, circled "Add Browns" to indicate it was a slug, or label, and then wrote: "Home run—Browns: Laabs."

"How the Cubs doing?" It was Buddy Weiss, who had been a copyboy with me and was now working on the night desk. He had finished closing his pages and had come to visit and root.

"Nothing for the Yankees in the fifth."

"Nothing for the Yankees in the fifth."

"Come on, Cubbies," Weiss said.

"Are you using a dash or a colon after 'home run'? " Sol Roogow, head of the sports desk, wanted to know.

"Dash. Hold it. One for Pittsburgh in the third."

"Well, goddamnit," Roogow said, "why the hell do you have a colon in one game and a dash in another?"

"Sorry. Nothing for Boston in the second."

"American League or National League?"

"The Braves. National League."

"Nothing for Boston Nationals in the second."

"Goddamn, you gotta be more careful," Roogow said.

"Whoop," said Weiss, bent over my ticker. "Randy Jackson just hit one. We're ahead."

I wrote: "Add Cubs: 'Home run—Chicago: Jackson.' "

"You got the dash in the right place this time?" Roogow said.

"Nothing for Washington in the fourth."

"He doesn't know the difference between a dash and a colon," Roogow explained to Weiss.

"Battery change," a young printer cried.

I checked my record of the battery at Cleveland, then wrote: "Sub Cleve batts," circled it and continued: "Feller, Newhouser (4) and Hegan."

"About ready to close up?" Everett Walker, the assistant managing editor, asked.

"I'm waiting for a battery change," I said.

"Close it up," ordered Roogow. Then to Walker: "We're not going to sell any papers in the Bronx on a battery change in Cleveland."

"I guess not, Sol," Walker said.

Across the stone table the printer looked at me and winked. "You know the Braves with their Spahn and Sain and two days of rain," Weiss said. "The Cubs, we've got Rush and Kush and two days of slush."

They laughed. "A lot of fun, huh, kid," Roogow said. He was a joyless man, who suffered from backaches, but whenever Bob Cooke was around, Roogow became avuncular. "I'm teaching the kid a lot," he announced inside Cooke's glass office. "He's got a lot to learn, but he's coming along, getting to learn about deadlines." Curiously, Roogow was right. I did learn about deadlines and more than that, how in the company of men one does best to put forth an unconcerned, brash or even graceful front when under pressure.

It was not until the spring of 1951 that I was permitted to cover baseball. "Do you have some time?" Bob Cooke said. "It's not a regular assignment, and we can always use the college kid, but can you get away and take City College–Columbia? They're playing at 3:30 at Baker Field." I finished a Sunday feature in ten minutes and rode the IRT subway to the northern tip of Manhattan Island and made the field at game time. I wanted to display writing style in baseball, any baseball, even college baseball. I found a seat behind home plate, the better to watch pitching, but with the first out, a pop to left field, I abruptly recognized a shortcoming. I did not know how to keep score of a game.

I jotted, "Ritucci safe pitcher's error," on a large yellow pad, and recorded the rest of the game in longhand, man by man. It was a piercing day, chilly and relentlessly windy. My notes grew bulkier, my fingers froze. College baseball is an inferior game to one raised on the major leagues, and as I watched the two teams struggle, I felt somewhat offended about having to dignify the game with a story. That haughtiness faded toward nervousness. I had never written a baseball story before.

City College won, 4 to 1, and back in the office with still cold fingers I heard Roogow barking, "It's late. Gimme it in takes. Where the hell ya been?" I typed a routine AP Formula One paragraph, giving the teams, the score and the place. Then I started to think: where should the story go from there?

"Come on," Roogow yelled.

Ed Gross, another copyreader, walked over, and said quietly, "Write it well, but hurry up, son. We can fix it in the next edition."

I recorded how each run was scored and supplied the box score just in time for the first edition, a reasonable job performed within forty minutes. But the story was not very good; it was flat.

Two days later, Bob Cooke asked me into his office. "Don't take this in the wrong way," he said, "but that isn't how to write baseball."

"I know, but I don't know what to do to correct that."

"Go to the library," Cooke said. "Get the clips. Read the other baseball writers. Go back a long way. Read Heywood Broun."

"I didn't have to read Grantland Rice to write football."

"This is a different game."

"I've played it all my life."

"That doesn't help you write it," Bob Cooke said. His blue eyes moved about. A strong hand drummed the desk. "Your story didn't have any sense of, of I don't know what," Cooke said. "I mean once I was covering a game and Rex Barney was wild and I wrote, 'Barney pitched as though the plate were high and outside.' That's the way I want to see you write baseball. You can do it. 'Barney pitched as though the plate were high and outside.' "

87

I was promoted to general assignment, which meant that I was relieved of high school sports. Marsh worried that I was moving ahead too quickly. Cooke disagreed and, in a complex of other tensions, the two held their positions even to that day in the following spring when Harold Rosenthal asked to leave the Dodgers.

The phone rang at the small apartment in Brooklyn. "What are you doing Tuesday?" Cooke said.

"Oh. Hi, Bob."

"I'll tell you," he said, and he was excited. "On Tuesday you'll be covering the Dodgers."

"You're kidding."

"Come on in here and then you better pack."

I took a taxi all the way to the office. Cooke briefed me. "Just do what you've been doing. Write what happens and don't take things too seriously."

" 'Barney,' " I said, " 'pitched as though the plate were high and outside.' "

"Attaboy."

As I started out of the department, Marsh was sitting at his desk, looking blue. "Could I have a word with you?" he said.

"I've only got a minute." I sat in the chair where eighteen months before I had been taught to rewrite essays into stories.

"I opposed this," Irving said. "I want you to know that. I think you'll be a fine baseball writer. But not yet. It's too soon."

I set my teeth.

"Which doesn't mean I won't be rooting for you," Marsh said. "Go knock 'em dead."

That was the *Tribune* then, or one touch of the *Tribune*, as it came into my life. I have forgotten as much as I can forget of its last writhing. Late in the 1960s I had occasion to visit the newspaper and the changes startled me, not merely because they were changes. The floors were littered. Apparently economy drives now extended to cleaning women. The new managing editor, Buddy Weiss, was rushing about without a jacket, encouraging people, like a football coach losing by four touchdowns in the final quarter. A third of the desks assigned reporters were bare. The staff was small and desperate. Two or three people asked if I knew of any jobs.

"If you wanna do an article, if you know anyone good who wants to do an article, we can pay *anything*," cried Clay Felker, editor of the *Sunday Magazine* section.

"How much is anything?"

"For the right article, we'll outbid anybody in the country." (And for the Second Coming, I'll go to church.)

I walked into George Cornish's former office. A fat columnist bulged over his typewriter, cursing and reeking of beer. A hungry-eyed columnist sat nearby, squirming in his chair. "Gonna get them fuckers," said the fat man. Between the two, a fat, hungry-eyed secretary slouched on a table, her short skirt hiked high on enormous thighs. "Aren't they wonderful?" she said. "Isn't what they're doing to journalism wonderful?"

"Teach them fuckers to mess with me," said the fat columnist.

Except for the pocked bust of Adolf Hitler, I would not have known where I was.

II

Underneath a patina of professionalism, the Dodgers I joined in 1952 twitched in shock and mortification. No major league baseball club before had been both as gifted and as consecutively disappointing. In 1950 the Dodgers fell far behind the Philadelphia Phillies, caught them on the last day of the season and seemed certain to prevail when an outfielder named Cal Abrams reached second base with no one out in the ninth inning of a tie game. Then Duke Snider singled to center field and

Abrams was thrown out at home by three yards. The Phils defeated Don Newcombe in the tenth, winning the pennant, and the Dodgers dismissed their third-base coach. During August of the following season, 1951, the Dodgers held first place by a lead of thirteen games. In what has come to be regarded as the most exciting of pennant races, the Giants, now managed by Leo Durocher, overtook the team and forced a play-off series. The Dodgers lost in Ebbets Field, then won, 10 to 0, in the Polo Grounds. The second game turned when Bobby Thomson, at bat with bases loaded, struck out on a curve that Clem Labine broke half a foot outside. A day later, the Dodgers moved ahead and went into the ninth inning leading, 4 to 1. Then came two singles and a double. With one out, the Giants had the tying run on base. Dressen telephoned his bullpen. "Erskine is bouncing his curve," Clyde Sukeforth, the bullpen coach, reported. "Labine seems tired." Dressen called on Branca, who threw a low fast ball, then a hand-high fast ball, which Thomson, enacting an antithetic "Casey at the Bat," lined into the left-field stands. The Giants had won, 5 to 4. Jackie Robinson followed Thomson's lope, making certain that he touched every base. Ralph Branca wept. For the second consecutive year the Dodgers had lost the pennant in the last inning of the last game of the season. This time the bullpen coach was replaced.

Defeat, particularly dramatic defeat, confirms our worst image of ourselves. We are not effective, after all, not truly competent, not manly in crisis. We may dismiss a coach, but we cannot elude blame. We have failed. Everyone knows we have failed. We know it ourselves. We stand naked, before an unflattering mirror, hearing hard laughter that includes our own.

After Thomson's homer, mirthless pseudo humor pricked the team. What has two legs, two arms and no guts? Why, that would be famous Dodger righthander Don Newcombe. Did the Dodgers always lose the pennant by one game? No; if necessary they could lose it by ten. How do you frighten a Dodger ball player? You don't have to bother; he's already scared. What, asked Sal Maglie, did a certain Dodger and a certain homosexual have in common? Ha, cried Maglie, they both choke up on the big ones.

Against these attacks toward a seat of manhood, the Dodgers set themselves in belligerence. When Leo Durocher, then married to the Mormon actress Laraine Day, shouted at Jackie Robinson, "My dick to you," Robinson backed out of the batter's box and cried, "Give it to Laraine. She needs it more than I do." On another occasion, Durocher, who was coaching at third, removed his cap and scratched a bald scalp. "Hey, skinhead," boomed a voice from the Brooklyn dugout, "put on your hat before somebody jerks you off."

Like small boys out to demonstrate toughness, the Dodger bench was loud and hypersensitive and defiant. At the same time, a number of players worked shows of unconcern. "Choking up" simply did not exist, they said. It was imagined in press boxes. What was choking anyway? some Dodgers said they wanted to know. "Well," remarked Captain Pee Wee Reese, with a small, sad grin, "when you chew gum and saliva don't come, you're choking."

Athletes, like surgeons and concert violinists, know the dry mouth of pressure. It costs them sleep and shapes their dreams. Baltimore once signed a righthander named Paul Swango, who mentioned, after depositing a bonus check, that he did not like to pitch in front of crowds. Swango disappeared into the deep minors, where attendance is sparse. He was not heard from, or heard of, after that. When Roger Maris hit sixty-one home runs in 1961, the pressure of constant interviews so upset him that he began to lose bristly clumps of hair. He never had another comparable season. But neither Swango's nerves nor Maris' ordeal is typical.

Pressure can stunt an athlete, but evidence argues powerfully that a major league ball player is fully grown. To make the

91

majors at all, a man first survives other pennant races, other play-offs. As he rises, pressures rise with him. A Little Leaguer feels the eyes of his parents and his neighbors and his teammates when he comes to bat. If he wriggles helplessly, he has found something out. High-pressure competitive baseball is not for him. A minor leaguer, driving toward the majors, has coaches and scouts studying him every day. The man who collapses into tremors with men on base dies, as the saying is, in Peoria.

A big league ball player ordinarily performs at a specific level, with crests, called "hot streaks," and dips, called "slumps." Tension plays on him, but, in the imprecision of human behavior, one can never anticipate how. "I didn't want to go in and pitch against Bobby Thomson," Clem Labine concedes. "If you asked me then, I would have said, *'Sure, I'm not afraid of anything.'* But whatever you say, nobody *wants* a spot like that. If they'd asked me, I'd have thrown the best I could and Thomson would have taken his best cut. Who knows, he could have hit me into the *upper deck.*" One day, under pressure against Labine, Thomson whipped himself to overanxiousness. Against Branca he whipped himself toward glory. With Thomson—with almost every big leaguer, it seems to me—choker and hero are two masks for the same plain face.

On the team Billy Cox played dramatically when most was at issue. He hit Giant pitching hard and in two World Series his fielding moved Casey Stengel to grumble, "That ain't a third baseman. That's a fucking acrobat." Cox's attention diffused over a long season. Important games refocused it. Pee Wee Reese played well in many crucial games. Duke Snider tied a record by striking out eight times in the 1949 World Series. In 1952 he tied the Series record for home runs. Carl Furillo batted .353, .125, .177 and .333 in his first four World Series. If one wants to advance the overriding choke hypothesis, he must follow labyrinthine paths through inconsistency, leading finally to the borders of mysticism.

But choking concerned many Dodgers because they heard of it so frequently. Even Carl Erskine, when described as "pebble-game," wondered if the writer were making an obscure reference to swallowing. Erskine could not pitch as often as some others because of chronic arm trouble, which he bore in silence. All the Dodgers' fundamental lacks were physical. When I was with them, they had no overpoweringly strong pitcher. Christy Mathewson of 1905, Tom Seaver of 1969, won the big games, dominated the World Series and carried a team. Without a superpitcher the Dodgers lost some important games. But self-doubt followed failure. It did not cause it.

Wesley Branch Rickey arrived in Brooklyn during World War II fired by two dreams that were to falter. He would build a dynasty to surpass the Yankee empire in the Bronx. He would personally achieve enormous wealth. Rickey became Dodger president after Larry MacPhail responded to the blast of World War II and re-enlisted. MacPhail's Dodgers, assembled under a threat of bankruptcy, could not long endure. Rickey reached Brooklyn thinking in terms of generations, and, as soon as peace came, and manpower stabilized, his Dodgers emerged, formidable, aggressive and enduring. "My ferocious gentlemen," he liked to say. Although Rickey had been banished to Pittsburgh by 1952, every important Dodger pitcher, without exception, had been acquired during his remarkable suzerainty.

Raised on an Ohio farm, Branch Rickey graduated from the University of Michigan, considered becoming a Latin teacher, but chose baseball. Old records indicate that he performed marginally. He caught for the St. Louis Browns and the New York Highlanders—the paleozoic Yankees—doubling as an out-fielder. In four years he batted an aggregate .239. Then he managed in St. Louis, moving from the Browns to the Cardinals. He never brought home a team higher than third. Gruff Rogers Hornsby replaced Rickey in 1925 and the Cardinals won the World Series in 1926. Rickey was forty-five that year, and without great distinction. Then he moved into the Cardinal front office and his life turned around. As an executive, Rickey let his intellect run free; broadly, as Henry Ford shaped the future of the business of automobiles, Rickey shaped the future of the game of baseball. It was Rickey who invented the so-called farm system, baseball's production line. He stocked the sources, a half dozen teams, with young, uncertain talent. As their ability allowed, ball players advanced. In one case in twenty-five, a player proved gifted enough for the majors. It was a bloodless procedure, but effective, and presently the Cardinals dominated the National League. Rickey paid execrable salaries—$7,500 a year was high pay. Considering the attrition rate, he had to curb expenses, but Rickey was also a man of principle. He had a Puritan distaste for money in someone else's hands.

In the mid-1940s he bought minor league teams for Brooklyn and the old Latinist, having organized a Dodger farm system, next created a camp where legions of players could be instructed. He chose an abandoned naval air station, four miles west of Vero Beach, Florida, as the training site. There among palms, palmettos, scrub pines and swamp, he made a world. The old Navy barracks, renamed Dodgertown, became spring housing for two hundred athletes. The mess hall now served not navigators but infielders. Outside, Rickey supervised the construction of four diamonds, five batting cages, two sliding pits and numberless pitcher's mounds, everywhere pitcher's mounds. Pitching excited Rickey. It moved him to melodramatics.

At one meeting of the Dodger command, Rickey lifted a cigar and cried, "I have come to the point of a cliff. I stand poised at the precipice. Earth crumbles. My feet slip. I am tumbling over the edge. Certain death lies below. Only one man can save me. *Who is that man?*" This meant that the Dodger bullpen needed help and would someone kindly suggest which minor league righthander should be promoted? It is a tempered irony that

Rickey's sure hand failed him where he most wanted sureness. He was unable to produce a great Brooklyn pitching staff.

Pitchers, of all ball players, profit most from competitive intelligence. It is a simple, probably natural thing to throw. A child casts stones. But between the casting child and the pitching major leaguer lies the difference between a boy plunking the piano and an artist performing.

A major leaguer ordinarily has mastered four pitches. The sixty feet six inches that lie between the mound and home plate create one element in a balanced equation between pitcher and batter. No one can throw a baseball past good hitters game after game. The major league pitching primer begins: "Speed is not enough." But a fast ball moves if it is thrown hard enough. Depending on grip, one fast ball moves up and into a right-handed batter. Another moves up and away from him. A few men, like Labine, develop fast balls that sink.

The fast ball intimidates. The curve—"public enemy number one," Chuck Dressen called it—aborts careers. A curve breaks sideways, or downward or at an intervening angle, depending on how it is thrown. Branch Rickey regarded the overhand curve as the best of breaking pitches. An overhand curve, the drop of long ago, breaks straight down, and, unlike flatter curve balls, an overhand curve is equally appalling to righthanded and lefthanded batters. The pure drop, hurtling in at the eyes and snapping to the knees, carried Carl Erskine and Sandy Koufax to strikeout records (fourteen and fifteen) in World Series separated by a decade.

Finally, the technique of major league pitching requires excellent control. Home plate is seventeen inches wide; and a man does best to work the corners. A good technical pitcher throws the baseball at speeds that exceed ninety miles an hour, makes it change direction abruptly and penetrate a target area smaller than a catcher's mitt.

Art proceeds subsequently. The artful pitcher tries never to offer what is expected. Would the batter like a fast ball? Curve him, or, better, throw the fast ball at eye height. Eagerness leads to a wild swing. *Strike one.* Would the batter like another? Now throw that public enemy, down and dirty at the knees. *Strike two.* Now he's on notice for the curve. Hum that jumping fast ball letter-high. That's the pitch he wanted, but not there, not then. Sit down. *Strike three called.* Who's next?

The pitchers are different from the others. They work less often, but when they do, they can hold nothing back. Others cry at a loafing pitcher, "Bend your back. Get naked out there." Action suspends and nine others wait until the pitcher throws. All eyes are on the pitcher, who sighs and thinks. "Ya know," Casey Stengel said about a quiet Arkansan named John Sain, "he don't say much, but that don't matter much, because when you're out there on the mound, you got nobody to talk to." Pitchers are individualists, brave, stubborn, cerebral, hypochrondriacal and lonely.

There was so much that Rickey thought that he could do with pitchers. At Vero Beach three plates were crowned with an odd superstructure. This was the strike zone, outlined in string. Pitching through strings, Rickey said, let a man see where his fast ball went. He devised a curve-ball aptitude test. *Hold pitching arm with hand toward face. Grip ball along seams. Draw arm back fully so that ball touches point of shoulder. Now throw as far as you can.* One can throw neither far nor hard. The test humiliates most people, including good major league curve-ball pitchers.

Rickey erred, retrospect suggests, in overestimating the body and in underestimating the insecurity of pitchers. His favorite overhand curve tortures the arm. A line of strain runs from the elbow to the base of the shoulder. An extraordinary number of Rickey's best pitching prospects rapidly destroyed their arms. In trainer's argot, they stripped their gears.

One gentle, soft-featured Nebraskan, Rex Barney, threw

overpowering fast balls, although, as Bob Cooke said so often, he pitched as though the plate were high and outside. Rickey led Barney to the strike zone strings at Vero Beach and commanded, "Please pitch with your right eye covered." Presently he said, "Pitch with your left eye covered." After months of test and experiment, Barney was still wild, and now given to periods of weeping. Rickey threw up his hands and ordered Barney to a Brooklyn psychiatrist. Before he reached thirty, Barney became a bartender. Another major talent, Jack Banta, was finished at twenty-five. Ralph Branca won twenty-one games when he was twenty-one years old. He retired to sell insurance at thirty.

Can each failure be laid at Rickey's grave? No more than one can credit Rickey with Duke Snider's 418 home runs. A model Rickey team played magnificently. A model Rickey pitching staff writhed with aching arms and nervous stomachs.

The first flaw laid bare another. Rickey treated newspapermen with condescending flattery, as one might treat stepchildren, recognizing them as an inescapable price one pays for other delights. In Pittsburgh once he invited me to his box. He was then president of the Pirate team that would lose 101 games. "Good you could come," the master began in a hoarse, intimate whisper, placing a hand on my arm. Bushy, graying eyebrows dominated the face. "I have a question on which I'd value your opinion. What do you think of Sid Gordon?"

"Well, he's slowed down, but he's a strong hitter and an intelligent hitter. His arm is fine and he can catch a fly."

Rickey nodded in excessive gratitude. "How would Sid fare at Ebbets Field?" The gnarled hand squeezed my arm. "On an *everyday* basis?"

"He'd belt a few to left."

"And right," Rickey said. "And right. Don't you think he could clear the scoreboard with regularity?"

"Why, yes. I suppose he could."

Rickey winked. "I appreciate your sharing your views. I don't mind telling you I'm concerned about the Dodgers. So many are my ball players. I'm afraid they may not win it, in which case many will blame bad luck, which would not be the entire case. Luck is the residue of design."

As I left, Rickey remarked, "You know, of course, Gordon was born in Brooklyn." His putative design was altruistic. His real intention was to have me urge the Dodgers to buy Gordon in the pages of the *Herald Tribune*. Publicity is the paradigm of salesmanship.

Balancing this deviousness, which hindered reporting, Rickey offered utter mastery of the phrase. His rolling Ohio-Oxonian dialect was a delightful instrument. Were the Pirates going to win the pennant? I asked once. "Ah, a rosebush blooms on the twelfth of May and does it pretty nearly every year. And one day it's all green and the next it's all in flower. I don't control a ball club's development the way nature controls a rosebush." Was his star home run hitter, Ralph Kiner, for sale? "I don't want to sell Ralph, but if something overwhelming comes along, I am willing to be overwhelmed." To what did he attribute the Pirates' poor record? "We are last on merit." Was he himself discouraged? "My father died at eighty-three, planting fruit trees in unpromising soil."

Once away from the days of this year, Rickey could be quite direct, but in the running of current business he was wed to intrigue. By the late 1940s his relationship with Dick Young and the *Daily News* had become catastrophic.

Where Rickey was rotund, classical and Bible Belt, Young was spiky, self-educated and New York. Rickey was shocked by alcoholism, extramarital sex and the word "shit." Young was shocked by Rickey's refusal to attend Sunday games after a week of misleading reporters. A war was inevitable. Its Sarajevo was bad pitching.

Young began baseball writing in 1943, at twenty-five, and

very quickly stretched the accepted limits of the beat. He wrote not only about the games but about the athletes, giving each of the players a personality. It was traditional to present athletes as heroes. Newspaper readers learned that Babe Ruth, Lou Gehrig and Grover Cleveland Alexander were grand gentlemen and a credit to the games of baseball and life. Young had heroes—Reese and Campanella—but he fleshed out his cast with heavies. He called Gene Hermanski "a stumbling clown in the outfield." Hermanski responded by shoving Young, a compact five feet seven. But Young would not cower. He loved his job, which "a lot of very rich guys would give an arm to have," and relished the power it provided, and worked at it in original ways. He cultivated some players, argued with others, writing hard stories and soft ones, but always defending his printed words in person. If Young knocked a man on Tuesday, he sought him out on Wednesday. "I wrote what I wrote because I believe it. If you got complaints, let me hear 'em. If you want better stories, win some games."

In time Young came to know the Dodgers better than any other newspaperman and better, too, than many Dodger officials. He sensed when to flatter, when to cajole, when to threaten. As far as any lay reader of instincts can say, Young possessed a preternatural sense of the rhythms and balances of human relations.

Conversations with several Dodgers strengthened Young's harsh conclusion that a number of pitchers lacked heart and, after one losing game in 1948, he composed a polemical lead:

"The tree that grows in Brooklyn is an apple tree and the apples are in the throats of the Dodgers."

There is a nice implicit pun here on Adam's apple, but the first thrust is Young's thought. Some Dodgers cannot swallow. They are choking.

Branch Rickey had been schooled on a tame sporting press, easy to manipulate. He could not or would not recognize Young

99

as the centurion of a new journalism. He would not even discuss choking frankly. Instead, he expressed private loathing "for *everything* about that man and what he stands for." In public he patronized Young, who above all things would not be patronized. By the time Rickey left Brooklyn in 1950, he was battling Young, Young's boss, and consequently the most widely read newspaper in the United States. In the *Daily News*, Jimmy Powers, the sports editor, identified Rickey as "El Cheapo." Young ghosted Powers' column ten times a year. The *News* would not mention Rickey's manager, Burt Shotton, by name. Instead, Young lanced the bubble of Shotton as genial paterfamilias by giving him the acronym "KOBS." The letters, forged in sarcasm, stood for Kindly Old Burt Shotton. The Dodgers lost because of, won despite, KOBS.

These assaults did not hurt Dodger attendance, but they murdered egos. When Rickey left, and Walter O'Malley became president, his first order of business was to replace KOBS with Dressen. Then O'Malley appointed Emil J. Bavasi, a warm and worldly Roman, as general manager *de facto* (at $17,500), and vice president in charge of Dick Young.

With time, one comes to regret that two such talented men as Rickey and Young fought so bitterly. Neither, I suppose, was faultless, although Rickey, being older, more secure and less tractable, probably warrants more blame. He went to his grave as a babe in public relations.

On the jacket of his ghosted memoir, *The American Diamond,* Rickey is quoted as summing up: "The game of baseball has given me a life of joy. I would not have exchanged it for any other." That's it. That's the old man exactly, still musing on the game and joy at eighty. But the introduction sounds like Rickey, too. Here, seeking a quotation from a man universally appealing, admired and beloved, Rickey began with five maundering lines from Herbert Hoover.

By the time Harold Rosenthal commended me to Dick Young's tutorship, Young and Bavasi had become friends. In addition, Young respected Dressen and enjoyed the attention and machinations of Walter Francis O'Malley. Coincidentally, he had stopped attacking management. "It is not hard to write scoops like Young does," one of the other writers remarked, "after Bavasi feeds the stuff to you." When Young found a few hours for an orientation lecture in Miami on my third day with the team, he angrily mentioned the accusation.

"You do a good job, some guy who can't do a good job says you're cheating. Have you heard that shit? You heard they feed me stuff?" Young was sipping bourbon, which Roscoe McGowen of the *Times,* who at seventy still paid dutiful visits to his mother, suggested did more for longevity than Scotch.

"I heard that, yes."

Young looked into his glass and began cursing. "I know who told you," he said, "and you're just goddamn dumb enough to believe him."

"Oh, I don't know. I'm not so dumb that I'd say who told me."

Young shook his head. "How the hell did *you* ever get this club anyway? You got pull? What the *fuck* are you doing here? Chrissake. They sent a boy."

"Look. You worry about you and the fucking *News.* I'll worry about the *Tribune.*"

"I'll kill you, kid." Young's face went blank. I wanted to escape his scorn, but sat there without words. "First, though," Young said, "I gotta tell you rules. You know baseball? You ever cover a club? You know what to do or did you go to fucking Yale? Doan matter. I'm gonna take another bourbon. Hey. Another Old Crow. You're a good Jewish boy. Your mother read the *Times.* Well, you can forget that fucking paper. Rocco's a helluva man, but that don't mean a fuck. They wouldn't let him write it the right way if he fucking wanted. I'm not so sure he wants. The old *Times* way is no good any more, if it ever was

101

any good. You following me? I'm only gonna do this once."

"The *Times* is a pretty successful paper." I winced as I heard my words. The *Times* is pretty successful. Jackie Robinson runs bases well. Dick Young is a hard man. I sit in this hotel bar, a half dozen thoughts about my brain. Who the hell are you, Young, illiterate bastard, to talk to me like this? You know what I think of the *Daily News?* My grandfather wouldn't let it in our house. It was a Fascist, Jew-baiting paper. People bought the *News* when somebody got raped. They read the details on page four. And, if by mistake they forgot to throw the paper out, they said, "Hey, look. I found it on the subway." Goddamn right Bavasi feeds you stuff. You wanna scoop me, you go ahead and try (but please, don't make me look too bad).

"It'll catch up to the *Times* the way they do things," Young said. His rage was done. "You like the way the *Times* writes baseball?" The storm had ended.

"Not much. No."

"Our paper has four times as many readers; not brokers and bank presidents, but you know what Lincoln said. *'He made so many of them.'* "

I quoted a *Times* lead I had been reading all my life: "The Yankees drew first blood yesterday and then had it spilled all over them as . . ."

"Yeah," Young said.

The son of a bitch, I thought, doesn't even give points for quoting.

"See, that was maybe okay a long time ago. Not now. I'm gonna tell you how it got to be now, once, like I say. You listening? Shit. You ain't drinking, so you must be listening. There's a lot of games in a season."

"One hundred fifty-four."

"Wrong. You're forgetting fucking spring training and play-offs and World Series. The number changes. It's always, like I said, a lot. Now you're gonna write the games most of the time.

102

Nothing you can do about that and it ain't bad. But anytime, you hear me, *anytime* you can get your story off the game you got to do it. Because that's unusual and people read unusual things. Fights. Bean balls. Whatever. Write them, not the game."

"But most of the time you do write the games."

"That's right, and when you do, you forget the *Times*. They tell you the score, but your real fan knows the score already. When you got to write the game, the way you do it is: 'In yesterday's 3–2 Dodger victory, the most interesting thing that happened was . . .' Get that? Someone stole two bases. Someone made a horseshit pitch. Dressen made a mistake. Whatever the hell. Not just the score. Tell 'em fucking why or make them laugh. Hey. Gimme another bourbon."

Into the heavy silence, I sent forth: "Young's two rules of sportswriting." What he had articulated among curses and assaults was his credo, and a man like Dick Young, who has been hurt by life and who lives behind rings of fortification, is pained on yielding up a credo. It is like a birth. As a laboring woman, he had cried out. Now to his splendid, terse analysis of his job and mine, I had said, in condescension, "Young's two rules."

"There's a third rule, kid."

"What's that?"

"Don't be so fucking sure."

"Hey, Dick. That's goddamn good."

"It isn't mine."

"What do you mean?"

"That rule was made by a *New York Times* sportswriter whose favorite lead—you know, about the blood—you were just making fun of."

After Miami, the Dodgers rode chartered buses to Tampa, where the team played five exhibition games, then joined the Boston Braves, their foils for an agonizing, lucrative journey through the South. In 1952 apartheid flowered in what Stanley

Woodward called the American hookworm belt. Blacks attended separate schools, patronized separate restaurants, drank at separate water fountains, relieved themselves at separate urinals, watched baseball from separate sections of the grandstand, bought Cokes at separate soft-drink concessions and, at the end of the wearying way, were eulogized in black churches and interred in cemeteries for colored only. "We like our nigras," said white people who described themselves as moderates. "They like us. We all like the way things are. Say, y'all oughta heah 'em sing."

That time seems simpler than today, but mostly because the past always seems simpler when its wars are done. Jackie Robinson was a focus. At big, dark Number 42, forces converged: white hatred for his black pride, for his prophetic defiance and simply for his color, contested with black hope, the same black hope which Southern whites said did not exist. *Man, a little music and some coins is all them pickaninnies want.*

Before anything else, however, Robinson was used commercially. His visit to a Southern city stirred scuffles for reserved seats among whites. Black crowds lined up early on the morning of each game, struggling for places in the narrow colored section (reserved seats not available). When you barnstormed the South with the Robinson Dodgers, you always covered sold-out games. And if you were inclined toward economics, you realized that Jack was doing something other than reordering baseball. He was earning his annual salary, which never exceeded $40,000, before the season began.

We boarded Pullmans in St. Petersburg. The Dodgers and the Braves leased private cars and a roomette became one's movable home. We all dozed on the Pullman sleepers, ate in the Pullman diners and drank in Pullman club cars. The players would shower in ball park clubhouses. Reporters shared the toilet next to a hotel press room, which the Dodgers rented in each town at a day rate of $6 or $8.

After winning an exhibition from Cincinnati in Tampa, the team thundered into the dining car at St. Petersburg. "Players first," cried Lee Scott, the traveling secretary. He was a slight, fastidious man with a pencil-line mustache. "They worked hard. Let the workers eat first."

Ignoring Scott, Young, who had worked hard, joined Carl Furillo. The two talked intensely over shrimp cocktail. At another table Robinson sat with Erskine. At a third Campanella ate beside Labine. Although I did not know it then, Robinson had ordered the blacks "spread out. Don't sit together at one table. Mix it up. Eat with the white guys. You all sit at one table, you look like a spot."

I obeyed Lee Scott and drank and read, and ate with a man from the New York *Post*, and went to bed, but not to sleep. Our train was a world (I thought) free and independent in the racist South. If you chose to draw the shades, you could pretend that there was no racist South. Certain older reporters did just that. Hell, a ball game was a ball game anywhere, wasn't it? And afterward the club bought beer. Then there were cards. On a barnstorming trip you could play poker very late every night for two straight weeks. Other reporters, including Young, had seen the South before. They accepted apartheid with a brief, angry grunt, the way they accepted a cramped press box, or a sinewy steak. Hurtling due west, our train transversed the Florida panhandle. It was odd, I thought. We wrote about the games, the players and the prospects. But, here in a wounding land, no one would report or could report the horror all about —racism. It was legal, even controlled, to be sure, but outside my roomette window stirred nameless, unreasoning racial hate threatening then as it threatens now to shatter the country. I wish I could figure a way, I thought, punching at a tiny Pullman pillow, to get beyond the ball games and to get the real story into the paper.

105

There was a glue factory in Mobile, someone said. Whatever, the clear morning smelled. We rode taxis out of the railyards to the Admiral Semmes Hotel and breakfasts and showers. Fairly clean, at one o'clock I hailed a taxi along with Bill Roeder, a reserved, round-faced man of thirty, who composed airy pieces for the New York *World-Telegram*.

"Ball park," Roeder said.

"Hartwell Field?" the driver asked. He turned, showing a square face and spectacles.

"How many ball parks do you have?" Roeder said.

"Oh, we got plenty," said the driver, starting the cab. "Say, you guys goin' out to see the coal?" Roeder and I sat in separate silences. "We comin' to where I grew up," the driver said. He turned into a street of gnarled trees and clapboard homes. "Coal now. The coal is taking over. How do you like that? Where I grew up there's all these fucking cannibals."

"All right," Roeder said.

"We got to stop these cannibals 'fore they eat us. Gonna be a lotta cannibals out today, see that nigger Robinson."

"Just drive, will you?" Roeder said.

"Does this happen all the time?" I said.

Roeder stared sullen out the window. After a while, a green wooden grandstand rose in front of us. "You get out," Roeder said. "I'll pay him."

"Fucking niggers want to take over baseball, too," said the driver.

"Go on ahead," Roeder said. In a minute I heard the driver shout. Roeder had paid the meter but withheld a tip. That was our social protest, emancipation through nontipping. We'll straighten out this country yet, I thought. And if we meet a kleagle, you know what? I'm not going to buy him a drink. Surely I *wanted* to protest, but I rejoiced in the luxury of sportswriting and, instead of ripping the meter out of the cab, or citing John Stuart Mill or doing something wise, I hurried away from the taxi to see how Hartwell Field looked, and where the press box was, and whether Western Union facilities would be satisfactory.

Most of the old grandstand was reserved for whites. It was crowded, but not yet full. Two strips, at the end of each foul line, were open to blacks. The black humanity of Mobile stood and squatted and bent and sat wedged two to a seat.

Twenty minutes before game time workmen rigged ropes from the black sections to the outfield. Armed Mobile police and Alabama troopers took patrol positions. Then the cattle car of a stand was opened and the black mass spilled onto the field. The people ran. There was no reason to run. There was ample space for everyone behind the ropes. But they ran in jubilation and relief, and as they hurried, the black mass diffused and ceased to be a mass and became individual men and women who were running, and who wore bright red and yellow and green. Someone in a yellow shirt was limping. A woman was carrying a baby and leading a small boy. These were people and that was a hard thing to face, and rather than face it I asked Young what the ruling would be on balls hit into the black crowd.

"Double."

"Getting a two-base hit in every inning." In a needling little game we composed parodies of the hoary lead, "scoring in every inning."

"Wordy," Young said.

"Doubling in every inning."

"Better."

Jackie Robinson was the third man to bat. Vern Bickford's first pitch to him broke wide, and when the scoreboard showed "ball one," the blacks, who ringed the entire outfield, cheered in triumph. Robinson fouled the next pitch, hopping in an awkward follow-through. A roar went up from the whites. In the end, to a *tutti* of enthusiasm and disappointment, Robinson hit a short fly to left. He played an unimportant role in this exhibition. Both teams used other blacks. But to the crowd, Sam Jethroe and Roy Campanella were ball players who happened to be colored. Then there was Robinson, the threatening, glorious black.

"Does that bother you?" I asked at dusk, as our sealed train moved slowly on a single track among low pine trees.

"What?" Robinson said.

"That noise about everything you do and the way the fans get pushed around."

"If I let *that* shit bother me," he said without emotion, "I wouldn't be here."

"I mean—"

"Gotta play cards," Robinson said.

But one way or another, Robinson always answered a question. At Pelican Field in New Orleans we began to chat while he threw with Pee Wee Reese along the third-base line. "Writers think I should thank them when they do a good story about me," Robinson said, "but aren't they just doing their job?"

"You get on a writer when he knocks you."

"That's right." Robinson moved about as he caught. "If I think he's wrong, I blast him. Why shouldn't I?"

"Well . . ."

A cry rose from the stands and at once defined the scene. Robinson whirled. "Goddamnit no," he shrieked. "Don't cheer those goddamn bastards. Don't cheer. Keep your fucking mouths shut." A barrier was coming down at Pelican Field. One small section of unoccupied seats in the white section was being opened to blacks. White policemen had opened the gates and the blacks were cheering in joy.

"Stupid bastards," Robinson screamed. "You got it coming. You're only getting what's coming. Don't cheer those bastards, you stupid bastards. Take what you got coming. Don't cheer."

He threw down his glove and walked in a little circle.

108

"You come to catch, Jack?" Reese shouted.

"Shit," Robinson said, and picked up his glove and resumed warming up.

In a minute he walked into the dugout and slumped down by himself. "I'm sure it doesn't mean a damn, Jack," I said, "but I just want you to know I think that racist shit is a disgrace."

"Then write it."

"I will."

"You'll be the first."

"This must be hell," I said to Jackie Robinson.

"Never been there."

"I mean knowing that you can't get off the train, that if we had to stop overnight in any one of these towns, you wouldn't have a place to stay."

"Are you kidding?" Robinson's high voice grew shrill. "Any town down here, any one, I could be a guest of the most successful Negro family—the lawyer, the banker, the doctor. I could be their house guest. I'm not stuck like you. I don't need any fucking salesmen's hotel."

Sportswriters reigned at the salesmen's hotels. The Jeff Davis with its Urban Room in Montgomery. The Biltmore ("Lions Meet Here") in hilly Nashville. And the Read House, where Broad and Chestnut intersect in Chattanooga (package store, meeting rooms, pets limited).

I found Chuck Dressen in a suite at the Read, sitting on a flowered sofa, sipping a Scotch and black cherry soda. It was almost noon. "I want to talk about pitching," I said.

"Was you in an incubator?"

"No. Not that I know of."

"Well, if a pitcher is a incubator baby, he can't go nine. The incubator weakens 'em. Ya didn't know that, did you? College ain't nothing in this business, kid. Ya wanna drink, kid, ya drink, doncha?"

"I've got to write."

109

"It's good to take one, 'fore you write, ain't it, Jake?"

A coach had been sitting at the rainy window. "Yep," Jake Pitler said. He was fifty-eight, Jewish and retained, some said, primarily to absent himself on Yom Kippur, publicizing Dodger Semitism without hurting the starting line-up. Now Pitler moved quickly and made a Scotch and soda. "Ya oughta try it with black cherry, kid."

"I'd better stick to just plain soda."

"There's tricks to this game," Dressen said. "Ya can't just worry about the next play. Ya gotta worry about two plays, or three." Dressen was a short and thick-bodied man full of hypotheses and advice. He had been born in Decatur, Illinois, in 1898, the son of a railroad man, and played for the Staleys, the professional football team that evolved into the Chicago Bears, and after that major league baseball. By reputation he was a man of shrewdness, a master stealer of signs and a grand tactician. "You get blowed, kid?" he said.

"No. No. I don't know anybody here."

"Well, don't do it. Don't get yourself blowed. Getting blowed makes you sweat in hot weather. You can't do the job, pitching or writin' good stories, when it's hot if you let them go down on you."

"I didn't know that."

"And watch out for pickpockets, right, Jake?"

"Right, Chuck."

"At the 1933 World's Fair in Chicago, a pickpocket damn near got my dough. Now me, I got small nuts, but even so I felt his hand. I got small nuts but sensitive. Right, Jake? Whoop. Yep. Good-bye, Dolly Gray." Dressen whistled and winked.

"I wanted to ask about pitching."

"Too many incubators and too many guys that get blowed."

"It's kind of hard to write that in the paper, Chuck."

"What? Whoop? Yup. I see what ya mean."

"Well?"

"Water seeks its own level," Dressen said.

So my grandmother had told me once in Brooklyn. Chuck Dressen had a small pinched face. He began to remind me of my grandmother.

"Charlie's goddamn right," Pitler said.

"Ya pitch 'em and pitch 'em," Dressen said, "and they eliminate theirselves. The pitchers eliminate theirselves and the hitters seek their level like water."

"Charlie's right," Jake Pitler said.

"Water seeks its own level," Dressen said. "A .220 hitter will hit .220 if you play him long enough and a .320 hitter will hit .320."

"Like Stan Musial," I said.

"Aah, Musial," Dressen said. "I gotta way to pitch to Musial."

"How?"

"A slow curve. That's public enemy number one. The curve. A slow curve breakin' in on Musial tit-high."

"Have you tried it?"

"Nah."

"Why not?"

"The pitchers won't listen to what I say."

"Who's your best pitcher?"

"Newcombe, but the Army got him."

"Who would you say is your best ball player?"

Dressen winked. He had small eyes that darted.

"Not to write," I said. "I'm just asking, Chuck."

"Not to write?"

"I heard you promise," Pitler said.

"Robi'son," Dressen said, "is the best ball player I ever managed, anywhere."

"Color doesn't matter?"

"Lookit," Dressen said. "I know about that Klan. I don't go to church, but my folks was Catholics and them Klan bastards burned crosses where I grew up. I never got much schoolin', but

111

I know a lot of things. Now on this team there's some guys, they don't like Robi'son, or none of 'em. But that don't mean shit because we're gonna win the pennant and when they see it's Robi'son getting them World Series money, he's gonna look awful white awful fast."

We had another drink and I asked about Joe Black, who had pitched well that day in Mobile. "Might," Dressen said. "Dunno. Ain't afraid. College guy. Maybe. Does he get blowed? Dunno. Maybe in relief."

There was no privacy with the team and very few secrets. That night on the Pullman rolling toward Virginia Joe Black hailed me from his roomette. "Hey, man. Sit down. Ya wanna talk a little? I used to teach in school. I'm not a dummy. Hey. How you like the South?"

Black was six feet three and very dark, with fine features and a bull neck. "How do *you* like the South?" I said.

Black grinned. "I can't tell you," he said. "They won't let me in."

"You take your family to Vero Beach?"

"That's what I mean," Black said. "There aren't any colored in Vero Beach. They got a whole separate town for colored, called Gifford. You been to Gifford? No? I don't believe that town has running water."

Black looked out the window. The train was hurrying through bare Piedmont Hills. Spring had not advanced beyond Tennessee. "Hey," Black said, gazing with large, soft eyes, "am I gonna make this club?"

"How do I know?"

"You talked to Number 7."

"That's right."

"He like that game in Mobile? Six good innings. Hey. I can give better than that. And I'll protect them. And I don't walk many. And I hum it pretty good. You know what Campy says, 'Ah hums that pea.' "

I put a hand on Joe's huge arm. "I'll see if I can find out a little more," I said. "You really want to make this ball club, don't you?"

Black dropped his drawl. "If I could express myself as well as Shakespeare," he said, "I still couldn't tell you how much."

From town to town the Main Streets had their sameness. Drugstores by Rexall, king of condoms. Drygoods by Stern & Fein, or Fein & Stern. Movie houses playing something closed in New York City.

SEE SHELLEY WINTERS!
THE BLONDE BOMBSHELL!
MEET DANNY WILSON!

The weather turned raw. Labine's arm continued to ache. Black pitched three shutout innings. Everyone caught cold. The Vick Chemical Company shipped cartons of nose drops to the home offices of the team. Charlie Dressen said Preacher Roe would pitch opening day. We reached Washington. We were out of the South. We played in Baltimore. I asked Dressen if he felt he had to win a pennant to keep his job.

"Nah," he said. "That fellow before me won eighty-seven. Last year I won ninety-seven. The way I look at it, I'm ten games ahead. Get it?" He whistled, winked and squeezed my arm. "Write it that way," he offered. "I'm a friend of Bob Cooke. We'll be home tomorrow. I'll be talking to him."

Fala died. The Philharmonic played *Elijah* with choirs singing from four scaffolds. Ralph Ellison's *Invisible Man* was published. We were home.

"Okay?" I said to Cooke on the telephone.

"Fine. You showed something. Only one thing. Call them 'the Dodgers.' Don't call them 'the Brooks.'"

"Okay?" I said to Marsh.

113

"You didn't hear from me, did you? When you do hear, that's the time to worry."

III

Between the conclusion of spring barnstorming and the opening of the season, the Dodgers played three games with the Yankees at Ebbets Field. Even in sour years the Dodgers did well in this series, after which they began to lose while the Yankees stormed Olympus. "We're better than the *Yankees*," I had complained to my father long ago. "Why can't we beat the Cubs?" Gordon Kahn always answered with apothegms: "Spring training proves nothing. The Yankees have learned the trick of winning when it counts."

"Will you be covering the Yankee series at all?" my father was asking now on the telephone, after the team and I returned to New York.

"No. I'm getting three days off."

"That's a pity. Those games are often interesting."

"Spring training proves nothing," I said.

"Oh, I wouldn't be too certain of that."

"Besides, the Yankees have learned the trick of winning when it counts."

"That's true," my father said, "but remember this: Change is a hallmark of baseball."

He wanted to see me about a number of matters, he said. I suggested Bleeck's, my home arena, and the day before the 1952 season began I wrote a thousand words on what to expect of the Dodgers and went to the bar. Gordon Kahn walked in, wearing a sports jacket over a sleeveless blue sweater, a clip-on bow tie and rumpled pants. He nodded and said with grave affection, "So it turns out you do know how to spell."

That warmth and Leo Corcoran's martinis melted conten-

114

tion. "I always had a difficult time explaining baseball to two people," Gordon Kahn said, "one of whom you know particularly well."

"Mother."

"The other was Clifton Fadiman. Whenever I wanted to use a baseball question on 'Information Please,' Kip announced, 'I know nothing at all about baseball!' "

"Did he know baseball?"

"No. It was true. But he said it with so much pride, he sounded as if he wanted an award."

"The Clifton P. Fadiman Baseball Ignorance Award, Olga Kahn, donor."

"Hey."

"Sorry."

Gordon looked at me and said, "How did you like the beat? How did you find it? Were you surprised?"

"Jesus, yes. You can't believe the goddamn South. You wouldn't have believed Mobile. I'm telling you those Southern creeps will start a riot at a ball park before Robinson is through."

"You know we had Robinson on 'Information Please,' and when I asked him how he did at school, he said he ran track and played basketball, football and baseball for UCLA and got Cs and was darn glad to get them."

"Jack? Said 'darn'?"

"Or something of the sort."

"This guy is under assault every minute of every game, and he has to fight for every breath and he doesn't say things like 'darn' or 'heavens to Betsy.' "

"Profanity is superfluous to English," Gordon Kahn insisted.

But you have inverted reality, Father. English is superfluous to baseball profanity. I choked down that response. I did not want to tell my father that. Here he had been imagining major league baseball for fifty years and now his son, not yet twenty-five, had found out the imaginings were fluff. He knew tech-

niques and final scores, but of the rough reality of baseball life
(I could have argued) Gordon Kahn knew as little as the award-
winning Clifton P. Fadiman. To make that argument to this
gentle Victorian, I would have had to cite Dressen's sex counsel,
to repeat dialogues in true language; in short, I would have had
to be willing to be cruel. "I guess so, Dad," I said, "but the fellers
curse more than either of us would have figured."

"But there are men on the team of real intelligence."

"Well, Erskine is very bright and Preacher seems to know a
lot, but look, I've only been with them for three weeks."

"I wanted to talk to you about the ensuing months," Gordon
said, in abrupt formality. "How is your wife?"

"Fine." She had begun working as a guidance counselor in
the then obscure ghetto of Bedford-Stuyvesant. Our separate
ways would converge again only when a first son was born. But
I did not want to discuss forebodings of divorce. "She's working
hard," I said.

"Your mother and I are somewhat concerned about the specific ambiance where *you* work."

"What? Now wait a minute. Look at this bloody bar." At 6
P.M. Bleeck's was crowded with *Tribune* and garment people.
"There are probably more good writers here now than you two
have known."

"And of course you include yourself in that modest evalua-
tion."

"Maybe."

"I was referring to the dugout anyway. You know you have
to work at writing and you have to work at reading, and your
mother and I feel it would be sensible if you joined us in weekly
readings of *Ulysses*. That presumes you are still interested in
Joyce. What we have in mind are readings aloud, and then
discussions, on Tuesday nights."

"Tuesday nights are night games."

"Wednesdays then."

116

"I guess that would be all right. I'll check at home."

"We should try and see one another more often."

"Right," I said. "We should. Let's get a bite."

"No. Nope. Can't do that. Always eat at home. It's almost 6:30, and your mother doesn't like to be kept waiting."

He walked out of Bleeck's and I returned to the martini. Reading Joyce aloud on Wednesday nights in Brooklyn. That would be something to tell Dressen, Robinson and Young.

"Hey, Kahn. You the sportswriter?" a stout man was asking.

"Yeah."

"Well, who's a better pitcher, Erskine or Roe?"

"Apples and pears."

"Who do you like better?"

"They're both good."

"If you had to pick one for a big game?"

"All right," I said, forgetting Joyce and marveling at my own authority. "Erskine."

"You're full of shit," said the stout man, "and I'll tell you why."

The team broke astonishingly well. That April Clark Gable was divorcing Lady Ashley and Rudolf Friml was marrying his secretary and for the first time a live picture of an atomic explosion lit television screens throughout the country. "Atomic bomb blast in Nevada," the *Tribune* announced airily, "tops two on Japan." I was disinterested. For me the month was Jackie Robinson batting .478 and Roy Campanella, Carl Furillo and Billy Cox hitting close to .400. Except for a loss to Sal Maglie, the team appeared invincible. "Hodges ain't hittin' for beans," Dressen said. "When he starts and Reese, we'll beat anyone, even Maglie. There's tricks to this game, kid."

"What about Labine? Is his arm getting better? It's been pretty cold."

"I remember when I was with St. Paul," Dressen said. "We

trained in Fort Smith, Arkansas. We had this pitcher Howard Merritt who had a bad arm near the elbow like Labine. It was so cold in Fort Smith there was ice on the field every morning. One cold day Merritt was standing around and the manager yelled, 'Go in and pitch.' In that cold Merritt worked the trouble out of his arm and he won twenty games that season."

"That's right," Jake Pitler said.

Five years later when the *Baseball Encyclopedia* was published, I looked up Howard Merritt. He had never pitched in the major leagues.

Early May portended struggles. Robinson's hitting fell off. Roe's arm seemed frail. The team began to lose, and on May 4, a few hours after Harry Truman concluded a televised tour of the White House by fingering a passage from Mozart's Sonata Number 9, the Dodgers fell to second place. Dressen, desperately concerned at losing another pennant and with that—for all the bravado—his job, mentioned on a train to Pittsburgh that, "Maybe we really ain't got a chance."

Charlie had offered a variety of confidences to me because I was careful about what I used and also because that was his nature. Now his simmering indiscretion erupted. "Goddamn," he said. "They ain't tryin' in the front office. Last year, I wanted Shuba, they gimme Russell. Now they're stickin' me with two outfielders who ain't major leaguers."

"Jim Russell is gone," I said.

"I mean Thompson and Williams."

"But Thompson's a helluva fielder and Williams can do a lotta things."

"They ain't major leaguers."

"I don't understand, Charlie. Doesn't Walter O'Malley want to win? Doesn't Buzzy?"

"They got a whole organization. They gotta worry about Montreal and St. Paul and them. When I was in Oakland, I worked for a *good* owner. Brick Laws. He said to me, 'Charlie, do what you want.' He let me run it." Oakland, then a modest franchise in the Pacific Coast League, lived as Dressen's Eden, free of snakes. "I wisht we did it here the way we did it when I was in Oakland," he said. "That's where we really knew how to do it right."

I slouched out of Dressen's drawing room toward my roomette, trying to piece out his meaning and unable to understand that what he said had no meaning at all. He was worried and casting about. But our young relationship, illiterate *Meister* and ingenuous student, made me freight all his words with importance. Further, I shared his concern. As Stanley Woodward foretold, I was as much Dodger fan as newspaperman. Going to sleep that night, over the clatter of a Pennsylvania roadbed, I thought of poor Dressen and his Dodgers, who were also my Dodgers, undermanned, a second Light Brigade. It would be a disgrace (I thought) if mismanagement at the top cost the team first place yet again. The next day, at the conclusion of my account of the game, I reported: "Charlie Dressen says that he may not win the pennant as long as he's stuck with two ball players who, he says, 'ain't major leaguers.'" I did not mention Don Thompson or Dick Williams. I was furious only at the front office.

As soon as the *Tribune* appeared, Buzzy Bavasi telephoned Dressen and said that he, Walter O'Malley and Fresco Thompson were agreed that personnel matters should be discussed only within the ball club. "It isn't a good idea for a manager to second-guess the front office to a writer, any more than it's a good idea for a front office to second-guess a manager at contract time. Isn't that right, Chuck?" Bavasi said. "I'm not blaming you, or blaming anyone, but you ought to know that Walter's pretty sore."

Dressen sought me out at Forbes Field the next afternoon and said, "Why did you write that?"

"Why shouldn't I have?"

"You got Buzzy and them mad at me."

I slammed a palm into my hip. "Goddamn, I didn't think."

"It's okay," Dressen said.

"Goddamn, Charlie. Sorry. I didn't know."

He turned, embarrassed by my apologies, and scuttled to the water fountain in the dugout.

"If I'd known," I said, blushing.

"Kid," Dressen said.

"Yeah?"

"They ain't givin' me the best pitchin' either."

The Dodgers, loud in victory, were raucous in defeat. Dick Williams, who reasoned that he would be thrown off the bench for calling an umpire "motherfucker," cogitated and found a solution. "Hey," he'd shout. "Ump. You're a mawdicker." That satisfied Williams and drew a blank look. Dressen was more direct. An umpire named Frank Dascoli called plays with sweeping gestures. "Hey, adagio dancer," Dressen bellowed. "Call the pitches right." The hardest needler that May was Jackie Robinson. When Robinson becomes excited, his high voice rises and, from his position at second base, he maintained a running commentary on umpiring. One afternoon when Forbes Field was uncrowded, I sat next to the field and took longhand notes during one base on balls.

"[Ball one] Oh, no. Ball shit. Don't worry. Bear down, Ralph. Where was it? Where was the pitch? Goddamnit, ump, do the best you can. Don't let him bother you, Ralph. Bear down. [Ball two] Good pitch. Goddamn good pitch. Where you looking, ump? Stay in the game. Bear down, Ralph. Don't mind him. [Foul ball] There's one he didn't blow. Bear down. [Ball three] Oh, no; oh, shit. Where was it? Where the hell was it?" He trotted to the mound, said something to Ralph Branca and walked slowly back to second base. "Play ball," the plate umpire shouted. "What?" Robinson was moving to his normal fielding depth. "Wait'll I'm back. Don't mind him, Ralph. He can't hurt us. We already *know* where he stands. Attaboy. Good pitch. [Ball four] Hey, ump, what the fuck you trying to do?"

On May 13, with the Dodgers back in Ebbets Field, the National League president, Warren Giles, issued a memorandum that called on "all Dodgers and especially Jackie Robinson to strive for courtesy in their address to umpires."

"The son of a bitch," Robinson yelled in the clubhouse. "He singled me out. Now I wonder why the son of a bitch would do that?"

"Must be your soft voice, Robi'son," Reese said.

"Shit," Jack said, but he grinned. Pee Wee could always make him grin.

"Do you think it's because you're colored?" I said. The words sounded elephantine.

"Is it because I'm colored?" Robinson repeated. "Ask yourself a question. Does Giles make public memos about Stanky, about Durocher?"

A few days later Giles appeared at Ebbets Field to present Roy Campanella with an award as the Most Valuable Player of 1951. Giles interrupted his routine remarks. "And right here in Brooklyn," he said, "let me say that the National League and I are proud of Jackie Robinson and the prestige that he has brought to our league."

I watched Robinson's face through binoculars. He seemed to chuckle and his smile was hate.

A third child and second son, named David, was born to the Robinsons on May 14 and Jack responded with a triumphantly aggressive game that brought the team back to first place. The Chicago Cubs led Preacher Roe, 1 to 0, when Willard Ramsdell hit Robinson with a knuckle ball. That loaded the bases in the fourth inning. A walk and ground out scored two runs. Now Robinson led away from third as Roe, whose lifetime batting average was .110, stepped in to bat.

As Ramsdell wound up, Robinson charged as if to steal home. After ten strides he stopped dead, his spikes swirling dust, and retreated. The pitch was low. Ramsdell wound up again. "There he goes," shouted someone on the Dodger bench. Robinson charged still farther in another challenge. The second pitch was wide. A knuckle ball is hard for catchers to handle and Robinson's rushes were not only distracting to Ramsdell but forcing him to eschew his best pitch. With the count three balls and one strike, Robinson burst for home and did not stop. Ramsdell's hip-high fast ball had him cleanly beaten. Robinson sprang into a slide; it seemed as though he would crash into Bob Pramesa, the Cub catcher. But that was a final feint. As Jack slid, he hurled his body *away* from Pramesa, and toward first base. Only his right toe touched home plate. Pramesa lunged and tagged the air. "Goddamn," screamed Willie Ramsdell. "Ya shoulda got him." Then Roe singled and Ramsdell had to be taken out. The Cubs did not challenge after that.

During batting practice the next afternoon, Robinson cried shrilly, "Hey, Will. Why'd you hold the ball so long?"

Ramsdell glared and turned. "So you could get your goddamn picture in the paper."

I was coming to understand how quickly moods and circumstances varied in baseball, where in early season each game is a new beginning, and I was teaching myself to listen with particular care to what players said and the tones they used, the bars of music that made the men. On May 21, the day John Garfield died, the Dodgers scored fifteen runs in the first inning against Cincinnati; the final was 19 to 0. That was a story to be handled lightly and understated. A game in Philadelphia three days later was more challenging. Roy Campanella chattered consistently before games, and this evening he put a strong square hand on my shoulder and indicated two vitamin pills in his other palm. "You'd be amazed," he said, "at all the power that's in them little eggs."

"Who told you that?"

"I know it," Campanella said.

Ridiculous, I thought. Campy went out and hit two home runs, one with bases full.

"Hey," he cried in the clubhouse afterward, "maybe you oughta get them eggs yourself. Maybe they're the onliest thing that could help you."

Campanella stood five feet eight inches and weighed 205 pounds, and whenever Red Smith saw him, he liked to remark, "Baseball is a game for small boys and old colored gentlemen." But the old gentleman's roundness, like the outward geniality, was deceptive. When Campanella took off his uniform, there was no fat. His arms were short and huge up toward the shoulder. Fat housewives have arms like that, but Campy's arms were sinew. His thighs bulged with muscle and his belly was swollen, but firm. He was a little sumo wrestler of a man, a giant scaled down rather than a midget fleshed out. He had grown up in a Philadelphia ghetto called Nicetown and he made you laugh with his stories of barnstorming through Venezuela with colored teams where (he said) you always had to play double-headers and meal money was fifty cents a day. But he would second-guess a manager and then deny what he had said. He accepted no criticism and his amiability was punctuated by brief combative outbursts. Still, it was difficult to resist him. "How'd you start catching?" I said in the clubhouse. "How'd an intelligent man like you end up with a dirty job like that?"

His broad brown face became very serious. "In high school in Nicetown, the onliest thing was to play for the baseball team. The coach drew circles in the gym, different circles for different positions. When I got there, the pitcher's circle was filled and the circles for infielders and outfielders was pretty crowded. But the catcher's circle. There wasn't nobody there. So I got in that empty circle to have a better chance of making the team. I stayed in the catcher's circle because I was the onliest one there." He pretended outrage at my grin.

Black-haired Carl Erskine, who never raised his voice, never cursed, seldom drank and was not stuffy, defended Campanella against all detractors. We were coming to know one another slowly; knowing Erskine was finding depths. "It's the two faces, Carl," I said. "If you want to be a happy-go-lucky guy, fine. But if you're angry at society, which colored guys have every right to be, then let it show."

"We probably all have a lot of faces," Erskine said.

"Well, nobody ever told me to watch out on quoting you."

The dark eyes grew bright. "Meaning?"

"That you stand behind what you say."

"Well," Erskine said, "with me and Campy there is a special closeness. You know. He's my catcher."

On the mound at Ebbets Field, Carl appeared to work harder than any other pitcher. Erskine was a well-built man of normal size—five feet ten and 165 pounds—but small for a professional athlete. When he pitched, one became aware, as he himself was, of Ebbets Field's short fences, and Erskine seemed never to throw easily. He wound up, eyes always toward the plate, rocking back and then firing straight overhand. As his arm whipped into a follow-through, the sheer exertion moved him into a little forward hop. He invested all his strength in every pitch.

With Willie Ramsdell again cast as straight man, Erskine pitched a no-hitter against the Cubs on June 19. He might have pitched a perfect game, one in which no one reached base, except for an early threat of rain. In the third inning, with the Dodgers leading, 1 to 0, Dressen looked at the sky and scooted to the mound. Willie Ramsdell was the batter. "Hurry up," Dressen ordered. "Get this guy. We got to win before it rains." Erskine threw four fast balls in great haste and walked Ramsdell. Rain delayed the game for forty minutes anyway. Erskine retired everyone else.

At the conclusion of each home game, a rotund show-business

character called Happy Felton interviewed the "star of the day from each team." Felton paid each star $50. In the ninth inning, Ramsdell, who had pitched passably and been the only Chicago base runner, waited in a little studio under the stands as Erskine got first one out, then another. The final Chicago batter was Eddie Miksis. This posed a hard ethical problem for Ramsdell. If Miksis singled and broke the no-hitter, *he* would become the Cubs star. The team would be spared the indignity of the no-hitter. Conceivably they might even go on to win the game. Ramsdell, however, would be out $50. The decision-making process was instantaneous. "Come on, Ersk," roared the Chicago starting pitcher. "You can get this bum." Miksis bounced out, and that was how Carl Daniel Erskine got his no-hitter and Willie the Knuck Ramsdell got his $50.

An oracular baseball writer named Dan M. Daniel sometimes growled across generations, "The road'll make a bum of the best of 'em." Then he added with slow malevolence, "And, kid, you ain't the best."

The road with the Dodgers was a lonely, thrilling chaos, at once seductive, free and wild. There were no telephone bills to pay, no relatives to meet, no office to visit and no planning to suffer when you were on the road. Your life was prearranged. The Dodgers reserved rooms, train space and airline tickets. The *Herald Tribune* paid for them. The clubhouse man looked after baggage. The men who devised the National League schedule planned your days. You had only to be: *be* in Chicago for the start of a three-game series Tuesday; *be* at Wrigley Field by noon; *be* outside the Players Gate at 5:15 Thursday, chartered bus leaves for Union Station. Being and writing. The road asked nothing more. But with time—with very little time—the sense of freedom ebbed. First, the wonders of transportation ceased. Packing and unpacking became a nuisance. Next, shuttling between time zones grew disconcerting. Then the apparent independence of baseball travel revealed itself as a kind of tyranny. You *had* to be in Pittsburgh on September 8 because that was what the schedule-makers decreed, just as surely as you had to be in Cincinnati on September 9. Ultimately the road was like its women. In the dark bar the girl appeals with blonde hair, a soft face and a fresh mysterious voice. But in the morning glare the hair is straw, the face a wreck of lines, and open-mouthed the naked lady snores.

When the team played at night, you wrote eight hundred words for the first edition. This feature story would not last the evening. For middle editions you wrote so-called bunk leads and running accounts of the game. "Preacher Roe was seeking his fifth victory tonight when he took the mound for the Dodgers at Sportsman's Park against Gerry Staley, 2 and 4, for the Cardinals." With eight hundred words of that done you wrote your final and most important story at the conclusion of the game. The work was neither easy nor debilitating if you were young. Weariness vanished in an exhilaration of having subdued a third deadline, and now ardent hours of night awaited, if it wasn't too late.

You covered a team better on the road. You lived with the ball players, and their lives mixed with yours almost naturally. As the second Western trip began on board the Twentieth Century Limited, I felt a sense of leaving behind all threats, all uncertainty, all danger.

Allan Roth, the team statistician, was a witty Canadian, with an astonishing arithmetical mind. Branch Rickey had found him in Montreal, where Roth invented statistical analyses for hockey, and convinced him to go south to baseball. Now Roth recorded each pitch of every game on a sheet of graph paper and tabulated his data in a cross complexity of techniques. He knew what George Shuba hit, what George hit against lefthanders, what George hit against lefthanders' curves and what George hit against lefthanders' curves on odd Tuesday nights in Cincinnati. He knew how often Clem Labine threw his curve wide, how often he threw it for a strike, how often it was hit to right field by righthanded batters and, through another series of steps, how often it was lined to left by lefthanded batters on Sunday afternoons in St. Louis. Rickey had hired Roth to supply information to the manager. If Shuba never hit lefthanders' curves, then sit him down against Ken Raffensberger.

Dressen regarded Roth and his bodies of facts as threats. "I got my own way of figurin'," he said. Dressen soared on intuition and probably feared that figures might wither his expertise. By 1952, while Dressen followed whim and inspiration, Roth was flooding the working press with data.

Unlike many statisticians, who glow with all the warmth of Franklin Pangborn as bank examiner, Roth laughed at his own work when it was finished. Indeed, he invented the game of Silly Records.

The idea, he explained in his roomette, as the Limited rolled north of Peekskill, was to create real records that had no meaning. "For example, most one-handed catches of easy throws in one inning by a first baseman."

"Three," I said.

"Eh?" Roth said. "Three. Very good. Very good. But *who*, schlemiel?"

"Active player?"

"Active righthand fielder. Give up? Good. I'm invincible at this. Joe Adcock."

"All right," I said. "Most times touching knees righthanded pitcher, one game."

"Robin Roberts. And by the way, he does that to slow down."

There really was no beating Roth at Silly Records. When harassed, he moved Big Bertha into position. "Either league," he roared. "Roommates with shortest names."

"Dunno."

"Roe and Cox. Six letters." Then over a happy grin, Roth mimicked Dressen, "There's tricks to knowin' this game."

In another roomette Bill Roeder and the man from the New

York *Post*, Sid Friedlander, were working the game of Barton
MacLane. Here you mentioned the name of an established film
actor who had never given a good performance. The participants made a jury. If you had seen Barton MacLane in a performance you honestly considered good, you spoke up, and
both the actor and the man who nominated him could be dis-
qualified. Economy was the beauty here. A single name evoked
a dozen inept acting efforts recollected in high merriment.

"Adolph Menjou," Friedlander said.

"Definitely," Roeder said. "Hall of Famer. Bruce Cabot."

"I don't know," Friedlander said. He was a gentle, white-
haired man, who spoke softly. "I'm trying to remember *King
Kong.*"

"At the end," I said, "Bruce Cabot says, ''Twas beauty killed
the beast.' "

"Objection withdrawn," Friedlander said.

"Diana Lynn," I said.

"Johnny Weissmuller," Roeder said.

"As an entry," Friedlander said, "with Buster Crabbe."

"Don't forget the goddamn monkey," I said.

"Name," Roeder said. "And no profanity."

"Irving."

"Five seconds," Roeder said.

"Cheetah!"

"New man shows promise," Roeder said.

"If Mr. Roeder will pardon the profanity," Friedlander said,
"let's get the fucking ball club to stand for a fucking drink."

In another roomette, Jack Lang of the *Long Island Press* was
fleecing Roscoe McGowen at gin rummy. As Pee Wee Reese
said, it was no trick to take McGowen as long as you didn't drop
your damn hand right on the table. McGowen lost angrily,
always blaming luck, and now, $8 down, he was struggling for
dignity by telling Dick Young that any writer could learn by
reading Shakespeare.

"That right, Rocco?" Young said, politely.

"Listen," McGowen said, and quoted:

" 'When my love swears that she is made of truth, I do believe her though I know she lies.' "

"Hey," said Young, "that's a kind of pun."

"Shakespeare liked puns, Dick," McGowen said.

Young's eyes darted. "Say that thing again." Lang tapped cards on the table and McGowen repeated the quotation. "Sheez," Young said, in unconditional approval, "that's a helluva line."

It was pleasant with the writers, but it was magic among the ball players. In the aisles, outside their roomettes, you could hear ball player talk that was alive and rich and angry and grim and funny.

"If that son of a bitch Maglie throws at my head again, I break my bat across his fucking dago head." (Carl Furillo)

"So I says to Augie Guglielmi, the little ump, 'Augie, I ain't spoke to ya in two months, but I just want ya to know I still think you're horseshit.' " (Preacher Roe)

"Couple years ago he's in a jam and got Kiner up and he throws three of the wettest spitters you ever saw. And do you know what Kiner said after he fanned? He says good and loud, 'Your curve gets better every year.' Ol' Ralph never even winked." (Carl Erskine)

"Get me some money, gonna fix up my house. You know what I'm gonna put up? A goddamn fence. Fuckit." (Billy Cox)

"When I was in Oakland, *there* was some ball players. . . ."

Someone started to sing. The voice was twanged but warm. In the car you heard it resound:

. . . From the fields there comes the breath of new-mown hay;
Through the sycamores the candle lights are gleaming,
On the banks of the Waa-bash
    Far
      A
        Waaaay.

By one o'clock voices had grown weary, cards tiresome, eyes heavy. Soon all the ball club was asleep, rocketing at more than eighty miles an hour somewhere west of Albany and east of Buffalo.

Chicago was a favorite town; there were no lights at Wrigley Field. For day games, you only had to write one story and everyone was finished with work by dusk. Instead of the glaring bright lights of a ball park, the evening offered various bright lights downtown. "I know a good spot with real lookers that dance right on the bar," Dick Williams said. He was single and a free spirit. "There's one called Sharon's supposed to be terrific."

"How do you know?"

"One of the Cubs told me."

The Gaiety Bar, never a cover charge, king-sized drinks, catered to itinerants with a little pocket money. A band blared, led by a strident cornet. "Night Train" was what the band was playing. The rhythm accelerated toward a boom and then retreated, then repeated, rooting out thought.

"Beer," Williams said.

"Gimme a Scotch." My drink came with a plywood swizzle stick.

"Two bucks a drink, a bucka beer," announced the bartender.

I only had $24 with me. I sipped the Scotch. It tasted of plywood.

Two girls moved through the dark and started dancing on the bar. They were built well, with long thighs and flat abdomens, but they were vacant-eyed and both their mouths looked hard.

"I didn't know your grandmother was working, Dick," I said.

"Christ," Williams cried, and clapped a hand over his glass.

"What's the matter?"

"She got a crab in my beer."

130

We bought more rounds. Williams, with $10, was even poorer than I.

A girl with tawny hair and tawny skin was dancing now. I tried to catch her eye. "Take it easy," Williams said.

"She's all right."

"She'll be here later."

We retreated to a leathered booth. Williams started a joke. The two girls who had danced earlier sat nearby. The music hammered ears. Williams finished three jokes before the tawny girl, now looking collegiate in a skirt and white blouse, moved toward our table and sat down. "I've got to drink if I'm going to sit with you," she said.

"Drink slow, baby," Williams said.

"Sure."

"You want a double Scotch, Sharon?" a waiter asked.

"Single."

The waiter walked off shaking his head.

"How many Scotches can you drink with all that dancing?" I said.

"None."

"What do you mean?"

"It's tea," Sharon said. "They just charge you for the Scotch."

"Tea and soda," Williams said. "Eech."

She was an art student, Sharon told us, and a wild baseball fan. She knew a lot of the Cubs and she liked to go to Wrigley Field.

"I'll leave you a ticket for tomorrow," Williams said.

"Well, I was supposed to go to art class, but okay. Leave two, one for my friend."

"When are you through tonight?" Williams said.

"Two o'clock."

"Son of a buck. And we got a curfew."

"What?" Sharon said.

131

"The manager. Dressen. He runs a check at midnight to make sure we're all in our rooms."

"Oh, that don't matter," Sharon said. "I couldn't see you anyway. My boy friend's over there. He plays cornet."

When Sharon left, I said to Williams, "The second ticket was for the goddamn musician."

"Can't make out," Williams said. "There must be something wrong with me. Last five girls I screwed, two was Filipinos, one was Spanish, one was colored and one was a Jew." Williams stopped. His mouth fell open. I was a Jew. The awareness choked him.

"But you know something," he said, recovering. "The Jewish girl was the best lay."

That evening's bill came to $17.

The team split in St. Louis, after a smooth ride down the Alton Line. A chartered bus carried the whites to the Chase Hotel, a comfortable and seemingly gracious white-stone building, where the room clerks greeted us by name. The blacks rode black taxis to the Hotel Adams. "It doesn't bother me," Robinson said. "I get treated like a hero at the Adams. They give me anything I want there. *Anything.*" (Two years later when the Chase agreed to accept Negroes, provided "they eat in their rooms," certain blacks rejected these conditions. Robinson said the terms were acceptable; it was a wedge anyway. Presently hotel officials lifted all barriers and someone told Robinson that he should consider himself as just another guest. After that the other blacks followed. When Robinson said he didn't want the Chase, he spoke in the voice of wounded pride.)

Still in first place, the team won a night game from the Cardinals, and at one the next afternoon, Robinson telephoned me and said, "It's started again."

"What's started?"

"The Cardinals have started racial shit. I've been in the league for seven years and I don't think I have to put up with it any more." The night before, while Robinson played second, several players in the St. Louis dugout continually shouted "Nigger." Someone else yelled, "Hey, porter, git my bag." Another phrase he had heard was "black bastard." Finally, Robinson said someone, he didn't know who, had held up a pair of baseball shoes, shouting, "Here, boy. Here, boy. Shine."

"I've got to write that."

"That's what I thought you'd say. I think if people knew what was going on, they'd want it stopped."

I hung up and dialed the Cardinal office and asked for Ed Stanky, an old hero. In 1945, Stanky, a mediocre hitter, drew 148 bases on balls. He battled and won games and once, on accepting an award from baseball writers, he said, "Thank you for recognizing my intangibles." He was a poor boy from Philadelphia, hard-eyed, Polish and bright.

"What's on your mind?" he said. "You need an early story?"

"I got an early story. I want to check it."

"A newspaperman checking out a story. What are you, some kind of Bolshevik?"

"I'm trying to be fair."

"I'm just kidding you," Stanky said. "Go ahead."

I told him Robinson's accusations.

Silence.

"What I'm asking, Ed, is did this really happen?"

After another pause, Stanky said, "I heard nothing out of line."

"Are you denying it?"

"I was right there," Stanky said. His voice was rising. "I'm telling you I was there and I heard nothing out of line. And you can quote me."

"Okay. I'm just trying to get both sides."

"Will I see you tonight?"

"Sure."

"Don't let yourself become Robinson's little bobo," Stanky said. "That's free advice."

I wrote a conventional story in which I quoted Robinson's charge and Stanky's denial and tried to give each equal space. I telephoned the piece to the paper, then joined Clem Labine in the lobby. "I was in the bullpen," Labine said. "I couldn't hear what was going on in the dugouts. But nobody was talking about stuff like that later. I don't think it's much of a story anyway." Clem clenched his right fist and considered his forearm. "Look," he said, "maybe if someone called me a French-Catholic bastard, I'd tell him to go fuck himself. I wouldn't come crying to you."

"It's not the same thing."

"Why?"

"Because in Mississippi they're not lynching French-Catholic bastards, only niggers." Labine winced and then he nodded.

At the ball park, I reported Stanky's denial to Robinson, as he was getting ready to take batting practice. He made a circular gesture, and his strong, black hands come to rest on the gray uniform shirt. "Do I need publicity? Do I want racial unrest? I wouldn't have told you what I told you if it wasn't true."

With a sudden stab, I understood. Stanky had played me for a fool. I had followed the textbook maxim, consulting both sides (but been lax in gathering neutral opinion) as if there were two sides. I had been misled. Now the first edition of the *Herald Tribune* was on the streets of New York, circulating my misleading story.

In the dusk I charged toward the St. Louis clubhouse and Stanky's office, angry, confused and in a queer sense hurt. A St. Louis newspaperman lounged in Stanky's office. "Well," Stanky announced. "Here comes Robi'son's li'l bobo."

He was sitting behind his desk, a square man, with strong arms and burning eyes. A bat rack stood in one corner of his office. I stopped beside it.

"Are Robi'son's feelings hurt?" Stanky said. "Are they black and blue?" I could not speak.

"Don't you get it?" Stanky said. *"Black and blue."*

"I get it." My voice was high. "I want to clear up that matter of last night."

"It's all cleared up," Stanky said.

"Robinson swears he heard those things."

"I was right there," Stanky said, "and I heard nothing out of line. I heard 'black bastard.' I don't happen to consider that out of line." He half-rose in his chair. His lips and the bridge of his nose had gone pale.

"What?"

" 'Black bastard' and 'nigger' are not out of line," Stanky said. He was standing up, ready. I grabbed a bat. If he charged, I was going to use a bat. Or try to use a bat. I was going to club at an old idol. Suddenly Stanky grinned. "Maybe you aren't Robi'-son's bobo. Maybe you're Charlie Dressen's. That's all right. Don't take it all so serious."

Later in the high press box, I typed a substitute story very quickly:

"Ed Stanky, manager of the St. Louis Cardinals, today confirmed charges by Jackie Robinson. . . ." I recounted what happened and filed a story, feeling that if I had been naïve in the afternoon, I was enterprising by night. The scoop would reform no bigots, but at the least it would discomfit some. And it would set down the record accurately.

The press box rose in tiers. White reporters sat in the front row. The few Negro sportswriters were confined to the rear. Now, I trotted up the stairs, going from white to black, wreathed in virtue, and fetched myself a beer. I was not thinking of the segregated press box or of the pennant race, when the teleprinter by my side began to clatter:

NOTE TO KAHN: HERALD TRIBUNE WILL NOT BE A SOUND-ING BOARD FOR JACKIE ROBINSON. WRITE BASEBALL, NOT RACE

By the conclusion of this mortifying trip, June had arrived, the Dodgers narrowly held first place and it was time to sail further on the voyage with *Ulysses*, as navigated in the Grand Army Plaza section of Brooklyn by Olga Kahn. Come rain, come losing streak, come headache, come relief, on Wednesdays, when in town I read. These nights, begun with a formal opening statement and concluded with coffee, had shown us Stephen Dedalus rising, teaching, walking, Leopold Bloom meditating and lunching, but in an ambiance of humorless intensity I had not yet grown as fond of *Ulysses* as I was of *Portrait*.

"Good evening, Professor," said Gordon Kahn at the door of the old apartment. He led me through a foyer. "Your mother's on the phone. Why can't they get a bigger lead?"

"Furillo isn't hitting."

We reached the living room. My father sank into his red Cogswell chair. "It's nonsense," he said, "when some boob describes Furillo as 'The Rock.' He always throws to the right base. There's something there."

"He doesn't have much actual learning."

"And Dressen. It isn't fair to patronize him. He's doing an excellent job."

"Yeah."

"Managing a baseball team is one of those things that looks easy when someone else does it."

"Look. You know what happened in one town last trip? The team was losing, 5 to 2. They go out on the field in the last of the eighth and Dressen says, 'Hold 'em, fellers. I'll think of something.' "

Gordon Kahn's eyes showed shock. I wanted that. I had no stomach to be quizzed on my bobbling of the Robinson story or on the *Herald Tribune*'s sudden censorship.

"Were you on the field to hear that?"

"Reese told me."

"Has it occurred to you that Reese might want to manage?"

"Boy. Absolutely wrong. You don't know the club at all."

"Ah," said Olga, returning from the telephone. "The chapter tonight is about Hamlet and simply full of puns." She was carrying the red-covered Modern Library *Ulysses*. "In Dublin on June 16, 1904, it is two o'clock in the afternoon." She slipped onto her chair, a flowered wingback. "The scene symbolizes the classic Scylla and Charybdis."

"Don't oversimplify human relationships," Gordon said.

"What's that?" Olga cried.

"He's talking to me," I said from the blue couch.

"About *Ulysses?*"

"About Dressen."

Olga said, "Oh, dear," looked upward and began: " 'Urbane, to comfort them, the Quaker librarian purred: And we have, have we not, those priceless pages of *Wilhelm Meister?* A great poet on a great brother poet . . .' "

"I think that's enough, for this evening," Gordon said mildly after two hours of communal reading.

"Yes," Olga said. "We all know Joyce believed that in *Hamlet*, the ghost, not the prince, was Shakespeare himself. Coffee is waiting."

"If he wasn't kidding," I said.

"Who?" Olga said.

"Joyce."

"Joyce didn't kid," Gordon said. "Is there a good game this week? I haven't seen one in some time."

"Tomorrow," I said. My mind flew between England and Ireland. Shakespeare as a ghostly father.

My father's basso drew me back to Brooklyn. "Thursday is bad. How about Saturday?"

"Phillies." I wondered whether Al Laney knew if Joyce were kidding.

"Declining team," my father said.

"Dad, the way it works is that two games a week are damn good. Two are fair. Three are one-sided." My own guess was that Joyce was serious.

"Well, then."

"Do you want to sit behind first or watch the pitching?" What was the difference which one truly was Shakespeare? I thought. Joyce had looked at genius as a genius. That was the exciting thing. "We'll have a drink afterward," I said at last unthinking to my father.

The Saturday game was one-sided, but not with the weight of Dodger power. The team's pitching collapsed and the Phils won easily, 9 to 3, enabling me to start my story during the eighth inning. Twenty minutes after Andy Pafko flied to short right center field for the final out, I joined my father in a deserted section near first base. We had sat there together fifteen years before. "Come on up to the press room," I said.

He rose, a Pall Mall dropping a quarter inch of ash. "The pitchers couldn't keep the ball low," he said. "In a ball park this size you have to keep the ball low."

"I know. They call that wild high."

"I certainly wouldn't suggest that this is a great team."

"Nobody looks good getting beat by six."

We walked toward the elevator that rose in the southwestern corner of Ebbets Field. Dressen was waiting at the elevator gate. His small eyes rolled about. His lower jaw twitched.

"So this is your boy," he said, after I made introductions.

"Yes, sir," Gordon Kahn said. He beamed and ashes fell.

"I take good care of him. Ya gotta watch these young guys." Dressen winked at my father. "But I set you straight," Dressen said to me. "Ain't that right?"

Fellatio equals perspiration, I remembered. "You're a helluva head counselor, Chuck."

The author's father

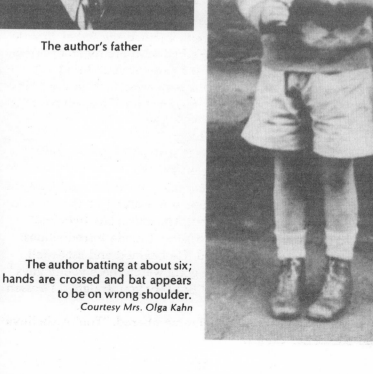

The author batting at about six;
hands are crossed and bat appears
to be on wrong shoulder.
Courtesy Mrs. Olga Kahn

Robinson in an early year
at Brooklyn
Sport Magazine

Leo Durocher as a young manager
Sport Magazine

Pee Wee Reese, who spanned two
eras in his prime *Sport Magazine*

Perhaps the most exciting of all moments in baseball: Jackie Robinson stealing home *Barney Stein*

Duke Snider, slugger and
center fielder
Sport Magazine

Joe Black, the first black pitcher to
win a World Series game
Sport Magazine

Carl Erskine, master of the overhand
curve   *Sport Magazine*

Snider batting in Ebbets Field under a full moon *Barney Stein*

Some of the boys of summer in rare informal picture near the batting cage at Ebbets Field. From left: Reese, Furillo, Robinson, Erskine, Hodges, Newcombe, Snider, Campanella *Sport Magazine*

Roy Campanella, who caught them
Sport Magazine

Billy Cox, the great glove at third
Sport Magazine

Carl Furillo, emperor of right field
Sport Magazine

Andy Pafko, briefly the left fielder
Sport Magazine

Preacher Roe, master of the
discreet spitball
Sport Magazine

Opening day at Ebbets Field, 1952. Black, Pafko, pitcher Ben Wade, Robinson and the rest. Managing the Giants, Leo Durocher *Barney Stein*

"Aaah," Dressen said, pleased, and the elevator arrived.

We rode up silently, my father and Dressen eye to eye. As we entered the press room, Gordon said, "I'm sorry the game didn't turn out more satisfactorily, Mr. Dressen."

"Huh?" Charlie said. "The way them cocksuckers played? The fuckers din' deserve to win. They played like pansies. Shit. Know what I fuckin' mean?"

My father nodded solemnly. Dressen started gulping his Scotch and White Rock black cherry. I whispered to my father, "I'm sorry about the language. He's a little, uh, coarse."

"Nonsense," my father said, his deep voice overloud. "I can tell at once that he's an intelligent man."

It was the hottest July anyone remembered. According to the New York Weather Bureau, the daily maximum temperature averaged 86.9 degrees, the second highest in the annals. Heat was everywhere in our travels from St. Louis to New England—heat squatting over the ball parks, making pitchers sweat through shirts, heat pent in drab hotel rooms with sheets that crackled as you went to bed, heat rippling the heavy air beyond train windows, soiled by splashes from a thunderstorm that had suddenly broken somewhere weeks ago. Between New York and Boston, coves curled toward the railroad tracks, and the pale-blue water speckled with sunglint and sail. On the longer ride to Pittsburgh, hills humped upward, green Eastern hills of maple, birch and elm. Farther, in Indiana and Illinois, in Ohio and Missouri, farmland lay in curving furrows, and houses clustered into all the Winesburgs. So summer came, tempting and hot, but of all the new scenes what compelled me most strongly was the crowded and drab clubhouse under the right-field grandstands in Ebbets Field. It was not air-conditioned as clubhouses are today; ventilation came from narrow windows ten feet above the ground. In 1937 I had watched from across Sullivan Place as teen-agers shouted insults at the Dodgers until someone heaved a bucket of water through the windows. Now, I myself could go inside.

The clubhouse was a long rectangle, with a trainers' room and a corridor to Dressen's office opening on the west. Old metal lockers ran around the walls. Reese, as captain, was assigned the first locker along the outside wall. This came with a battered metal door, a rough symbol of eminence since no other locker had a door of any kind. A small electric heater stood nearby. Reese reclined in an old swivel chair someone had found for him once. The other ball players sat on three-legged milkmaid's stools.

Hodges, Snider and Robinson dressed close to Reese. Campanella's locker stood in the center of the room near a locker used by Billy Cox. On other teams, black players dressed together, so that there was a kind of segregation within the newly integrated sport. The Dodgers dressed according to seniority and according to importance. Robinson would not have had it any other way. Reese was inclined to agree.

In the stark clubhouse players assumed roles, repeated day after day with variations. On the field they won and lost before a nation; the clubhouse was sanctuary, and once inside you tried to relate public performance with private role. Small, sharp-faced Billy Cox, the possessor of phenomenal hands and a strange disquiet, discouraged personal conversation. Preacher Roe said he and Cox talked mostly baseball. Cox could take a drink, and Roe imposed one condition on his roommate: "When I say, 'Come home, Billuh,' you got to come along."

The players called Cox "Hoss." Some shouted, "Hey, Hoss. Hey, Hoss Cox," then burbled laughter.

Cox responded with a strange gesture. Holding his right hand at the hip, and extending the index finger, he thrust the finger outward and said, "Fuckit." He was always making extraordinary plays at third base, and after a while the Dodgers responded with derisive cheering, a harsh professional compliment. Cox had begun the finger waggle in response, along with a sidelong cry of "Fuckit." Afterward the waggle was enough. Leap. Stop. Assist. "Yah, yah, yah," from the dugout. Putout. Finger waggle. "Fuckit." Cox was a kind of punctuator of scenes.

By late July the lead was seven games. The team was winning and suspected that it was going to win. Pee Wee Reese stood in front of his locker holding his uniform pants. "I wonder," he said, "how many times I've put these things on and off."

"I wonder," Duke Snider said, "how many times you've added figures to your bankbook."

Reese made Cox's motion for "Fuckit" and dropped into his chair. "Look at those legs," he said. They were strong and straight, downed with light hair but rutted by cuts and scrapes and scars. "Spikes," Reese said. "By the end of the year my legs look like a road map."

"Tell us about it, Pee Wee," Snider said. He turned away, losing interest.

"I never realized that," I said.

"What do you think happens around second base?" Reese said. "They come at you and come at you and the spikes are not made of rubber." Reese leaned back. The chair made a grinding noise. "I remember when I used to think that playing baseball was the easiest thing in the world. I don't think so any more."

"When you were a kid," I said, "you dreamed about this?"

"No, sir," Reese said. "I did not dream about the lights. There were never any night games in my dreams. I'm thirty-three years old and after a night game I'm all worked up—hell, you don't calm down right away—and I have trouble falling asleep and the next day I dread the game. I ought to run before I play, to get my legs loose. Sometimes I hit a bleeder first time up and I have to break from the plate in a hurry. You can pull a muscle if you haven't loosened up, but if you're tired enough, you won't run before a game because you have to save your strength. So

141

maybe you pull a muscle. Fuckit." He got up and began putting on his pants.

Dressen sent Labine to St. Paul for several weeks to pitch his arm back into shape, and Labine gathered his possessions shortly after dawn and left without saying good-bye to anyone. He felt humiliated. Robinson was worried about his wife. She had to undergo surgery for a growth which proved benign. Three days later Robinson, still overwrought, protested an umpire's call by kicking his glove thirty feet.

"Yer outa here, Robinson," bawled Augie Guglielmo. Dressen moved Bobby Morgan to third and sent Billy Cox to replace Robinson at second. "He was right to do what he did," Cox muttered.

"What was that?" Guglielmo said.

"I said, 'Fuckit.' "

"Yer outa here, too, Cox. Git outa here."

Still the team won.

Campanella was hitting poorly. He had chipped a bone when his throwing hand struck a bat as he tried to pick a man off third. The lead reached eight games. Dressen drove the team, and in the rage of summer, geniality began to fade.

On August 15, Robin Roberts of Philadelphia won his nineteenth game, beating the Dodgers, 8 to 3, at Ebbets Field. The Dodgers smacked flies to the base of the wall in left field, long drives that center fielder Richie Ashburn caught in stride, and numerous two-out singles. Roberts controlled a game without appearing to dominate it. Recounting this frustrating evening, I wrote:

The Dodgers got their final run in the eighth inning when George Shuba hit his fifth homer of the year. But indicative of the "fighting" spirit this hot night was the fact that after Shuba circled the bases and got the customary handshake from Andy Pafko, he walked to the water cooler and sat down in the dugout, untroubled by further handshaking, or by back-slapping and applause from his teammates.

Campanella waited in the clubhouse the next day. "Hey," he shouted. "I saw what you wrote. I can't clap. My hand's broke."

"I didn't mean just you," I said.

A number of heads turned. Snider looked on curiously. Shotgun Shuba laced a shoe.

"What do you want me to do?" Campanella said. "Jump up when he hits one and knock my head against the top of the dugout? Is that what you want?"

"That's not what I want."

"How can you, sitting up there," Campanella shouted, "see if we got spirit down here?"

"Roy," I said. "Would you do me a favor?"

"What's that?"

"Stop reading the *Tribune*. Try the *Times*."

"I would," Campanella said, " 'cept the *Tribune* is the on-liest paper I can get delivered in time for me to read it in the shithouse in the morning."

"I'll remember that when I write about you."

"Sheet," Campanella roared, and paraded naked and stately to the trainers' room, where he would soak his sore hand in a whirlpool bath.

Reese was grinning from the swivel chair. Hodges gazed solemnly into his locker. Across the corridor, Preacher Roe sat cross-legged puffing a corncob pipe. No one spoke. I was the only man wearing street clothes, the only civilian, in the Dodger clubhouse. I retreated.

Later on the field, Robinson motioned to me. "What you wrote," he said, "was silly. Some guys thought it was anti. But you were right to stand up to Campanella." A few hours later the story was forgotten. The Dodger fighting spirit came around nicely. The team defeated the Phillies, 15 to 0.

"You shouldn't rile Campy," Dressen suggested over drinks. "He's worried about himself."

143

"Well, I'd figured that he's an intelligent guy who'd respect my right to write."

"What? What's that? What's that word? Starts with a 'I.'"

"Intelligent."

"Yup. That's it. All ball players is dumb."

"All?"

"And outfielders is the dumbest."

"Why do you say that?"

"I wisht they was all Reese and Robi'son. But that Shuba, that Snider, that Furiller. *That* Furiller. He can't even bunt."

Carl Furillo was suffering a frightful season. Grit lodged in a cornea restricted his vision, which no one knew, and he listened to a variety of useless suggestions from Dressen without heeding them. "Skoonj," they called him, and Skoonj, good year or bad, was a ball player who walked his own way. "How'm I gonna bunt if I can't bunt?" he said. "Anybody ever ask fucking Dressen that?"

To bring Furillo into the Brooklyn organization, Larry Mac-Phail purchased the franchise at Reading in the Interstate League following the 1941 season. War had made the franchise inoperative. "Worthless," MacPhail explained, "except for two assets. A bus in good condition and Carl Furillo."

During my seasons with the team, Furillo had a mean batting average of about .300. The first year he hit .247. The second year, after eye surgery, he hit .344. He was solid, handsome, dark, with short curly hair, and a Roman nose that had been broken many times. Women who saw him in dungarees and T-shirt were stirred. Some men felt envy.

Furillo's responses to people and situations were intuitive. He sized me up, carefully, when I joined the club, considered my 140 pounds and quickly named me "Meat." By August he had decided to trust me with his thoughts. "Hey, Meat," he said. "You know what I'm gonna do when I'm all through? Open an Italian restaurant in Vero Beach."

"You really think that would work?"

"Look, Meat. You give good food, spaghetti, it's gotta work."

"But I don't think there are many people around Vero in August."

"You give good food," Furillo said, "it don't matter where you are. People will come."

"But why Vero? Why not a bigger town?"

"Look, Meat," Furillo said. "When I open this place, you come down to Vero and you'll get a free meal. On the house. And that's a promise."

"Well, thank you, Carl," I said.

For mysterious reasons, he felt antipathetic toward Bill Roeder. "That Roeder thinks he's smart," Furillo said.

"Well, he is pretty smart," I said.

"Yeah, but he don't know everything. Nobody knows everything, except Him." Furillo jerked a thumb upward, signifying God. "Hey. How many feet in an acre?"

"I think it's two hundred by two hundred."

"Let's ask Roeder, Meat. He'll get it wrong, and that'll show you. He ain't as fucking smart as he thinks."

Furillo liked to fish and work with his hands. In right field, in front of the short wall and tall screen, he was an emperor. He knew the angles of the wall and the scoreboard that jutted out and how a ball would carom. No one ruled that field as he did. He threw out dozens of runners at second before people stopped challenging him. Charging apparent singles, he was said to have thrown out a half dozen men at first. "This man," wrote Roscoe McGowen of the *Times*, "is armed."

Once in Boston Sid Gordon, then with the Braves, slapped a long line single to right. Ed Mathews, a swift rookie, broke from first. Furillo ran toward the foul line from right center, caught the ball on a bounce, whirled and loosed his throw. For a remarkable instant you could see the baseball and Mathews racing on converging paths. The ball bounced fifteen feet from third base, as Mathews dipped into a slide. The ball accelerated with the bounce, spin biting dirt, and skipped low over Mathews' legs. Cox whipped the Whelan's glove and in one motion caught the ball and made a tag. Furillo trotted to the dugout, apparently unimpressed by his own play, seemingly emotionless.

I saw the other side in the clubhouse. One hot afternoon Bob Rush of the Chicago Cubs threw an inside fast ball and Furillo could not duck. He threw up his left hand and the ball glanced off his knuckles and smashed into the bridge of the Roman nose. Furillo fell, without a sound, and lay without moving. He was borne from the field on a stretcher.

In the trainers' room, I found him on a white table, supine and still. Dr. Harold Wendler, an osteopath, had placed an ice pack on his face. It ran from brow to nostril and covered both eyes.

"How is he?" I whispered.

"Severe impact," Wendler said. "We'll need X-rays."

I took Furillo by the hand. "Hey, Carl. It's me. Meat. Doc Wendler says you're going to be fine."

The palm was curiously soft. Furillo clutched my hand weakly, like a child.

"Meat?" he said in a small voice. "Who's that?"

I said my name.

"Rog," Furillo said, as he lay in darkness. "Am I gonna be okay?"

"Sure, Carl, sure. You're doing fine." My own voice was not strong. I was shocked at the anomaly of a man in a full Dodger uniform—they had not even taken off his spiked shoes—so terribly stricken.

"You wouldn't lie to me?" Furillo said.

"Shit, no. You're fine."

"Hey," he said, pulling at my hand. "Tell me the truth? Am I blind?"

I saw Dressen later. "You gonna tell Joe Black to get Rush?" I said.

"Aaah," Dressen said. "Fuckin' dumb outfielder."

"What?"

"Furiller shoulda ducked. An' Snider is just as dumb."

Watching Duke Snider turned Bill Roeder sardonic. The Duke could run and throw and leap. His swing was classic; enormous and fluid, a swing of violence that seemed a swing of ease. "But do you notice when he's happiest?" Roeder complained. "When he walks. Watch how he throws the bat away. He's glad." Roeder would have liked to have Snider's skills, he conceded. If he had, he believed he would have used them with more ferocity. Snider was living Roeder's dream, and so abusing it.

Edwin Donald Snider was the full name, but Duke suited. His hair had started graying when he was twenty-five, but his body bespoke supple youth. As Duke moved in his long-striding way, one saw the quarterback, the basketball captain, the Olympian. *Yours is the Earth and everything that's in it.* "If" was a perfect poem for the Duker. He and Kipling would have been to one another's taste.

While trying to become a man, Snider suffered periodic sulks. His legs were not really steel springs; they ached sometimes like anybody else's. His model swing was useless when he lunged at a bad pitch. In a hurt boyish way, he saw forecasts of his golden future as pressure. Why can't I be ordinary? he said. When his hitting wavered, he brooded and fielded sloppily. Portnoy's hero was an only child. A confrontation with Dressen was inevitable and fierce.

The final Western trip began with a train ride to Cincinnati on Sunday night, August 17. I decided to fly and remember packing two books. I was having difficulty finishing *Crime and Punishment.* I had seen notices for Bernard Malamud's *The Natural*, a mysterious account of a flaming, gifted ball player,

147

a super-Snider, who came to a bad end. "What *The Natural* demonstrates," John Hutchens wrote in the *Herald Tribune,* "is problematical, except that Mr. Malamud is quite a card and nothing seems safe any more, nothing at all."

I was starting a story on the real Snider, who was slumping, that Monday when a call came from the Dodger office to report that Dressen had decided on a benching. "Indefinitely," said Frank Graham, Jr., the publicity man. "This is Snider's first benching since he became a regular in 1949. He's gone twelve games without a homer and he has only nine hits in his last forty-six times at bat."

"Anything else?"

"You miss the game yesterday?"

"I was off."

"There was a short fly to center. Some of the fellers say he should have had it but he loafed."

"Well, Duke says Dressen ripped him in front of everyone the other day."

"Is that right?"

I compounded the elements into a story, in which I tried to balance objections. Snider had a point. The stronger argument was Dressen's.

At twilight Tuesday, after a three-hour flight, I walked onto Crosley Field in Cincinnati and someone went, "Pssst." Snider was standing by himself in a corner of the dugout, while the rest of the team worked out. His long face was somber and white.

"Hiya, Duke. Sorry."

"It probably won't do any good," he said, "but if either Mike Gaven or Dick Young comes on the field tonight, I'm gonna punch him in the mouth."

"Well, it won't do any good. I can tell you that."

"They got no right to write what they did."

"Duke, the club announced yesterday that you were benched. Everybody had to write it. It was news, and because there was no game, it was big news."

"Maybe I should be benched. It's okay to write that. But Young did a whole piece saying that I was a crybaby and Gaven said my salary was gonna be cut by 25 percent no matter what I did from now on."

"How do you know that?"

"Because Beverly called me up from Bay Ridge and read me the stories. She was crying."

After a while, I said, "Okay, but don't start hitting people. You outweigh Young by fifty pounds, and Gaven's an old guy. You might kill him."

"Where you going?"

"To the press room. Let me see what I can do."

"They won't listen," Snider said. "They're too busy lapping up the sauce."

Gaven, a porky man with great jowls, was eating. "I can write anything I want," he insisted without interrupting the rhythm of his chewing. "Maybe I got private information you don't have that his salary *will* be cut."

"Well, if you go on the field, he says he'll hit you."

The chewing stopped. "He better not," Gaven cried. "If he does, every Hearst newspaper in the United States will be on him." But Gaven stayed off the field.

Talking to Young, who arrived later, I watched the jet eyes harden. "As if I fuckin' benched him," Young said. "As if I fuckin' loafed on that fly ball." After the game, Young sought out Snider in a bar and said, talking quickly, "Hit baseballs, Duke, not writers. Then I'll be able to write good things about you."

"Yeah. Maybe."

"Don't get down on yourself."

"I was sore, Dick. Maybe your story was okay." Young turned away. Snider sipped at a Canadian whisky and ginger ale. His eyes became enormous and sad. "Stop thinking so much, Duke," I said.

Three days later Snider was back and for the rest of the season

149

he played brilliantly. Dressen's impersonal brutality worked. I don't know what was more disturbing, that or the way Snider, while hitting at a .400 pace, continued to discard his bat jubilantly when walked, joyous, as Roeder had observed, not to have to face another challenge.

Malamud's first novel downed quickly. One of the pitchers saw me with it as we were leaving Cincinnati for St. Louis and I lent it to him. "I like that book," he said, the next day, "as far as I got. I liked it when he screwed that brunette and they describe her muff."

"Well, stay with it because he's gonna make it with a blonde and redhead and Malamud describes the pubic hair each time."

"Goddamn."

"What's the matter?"

"I left your son of a buck of a book on the fucking train."

Without thinking, I bore *Crime and Punishment* into the St. Louis dugout, along with my scorebook. "Hey-yup," Dressen cried. "What you doing with that book?"

"It's a helluva book, Charlie," I said.

The ferret face softened. "Ya know something? I never read a book in my whole life."

"Not even in school?"

"I only went a few years. But I can read good. Newspapers and magazines and them. But I never read a book. Ya think I should?"

I was instant ambassador from culture to the dugout. They were all behind me as I stood on the old boards, Shakespeare and Southey, Dante and Hardy, Olga Kahn, Shelley, Hemingway, Housman and, in my right hand, Dostoyevsky. "Sure, Charlie," I said on behalf of literature. "It would help your vocabulary. You'd learn new words. You'd make better speeches and all." I was addressing a major league manager as one might speak to a truant boy of ten.

150

"Ah, fuck," Dressen said. "I got this far without readin' a book. I ain't gonna start now."

We flew from Chicago, with the team seven games in front, on a flight that ended in a literary way. One of Harold Rosenthal's favorite jokes consisted of composing the headline and the story that would appear in the *Tribune* if a plane carrying the Dodgers crashed. He prepared rough drafts, after which Allan Roth and I made suggestions. The result looked like this:

ALL PERISH AS DODGER PLANE HITS ALLEGHENY PEAK
REESE, ROBINSON, DRESSEN VICTIMS
TEAM HAD JUST COMPLETED 7-AND-3
WESTERN TRIP; PITCHING IMPROVED

BRADFORD, Pa., September 1 (AP)— The entire Brooklyn Dodgers baseball team was killed tonight in the flaming pyre of a United Airlines DC-4, which crashed into a hillside four miles west of this northern Pennsylvania town. Tomorrow's scheduled game against the Braves has been postponed.

My contribution was one sentence, concluding the eight-hundred-word story. It read, in full:

Nine sportswriters also perished.

Black humor roots within its creators' brains and makes them victims. By September I'd had enough of airplanes, and on this final flight, aboard a DC-4, relief flooded me when the pilot said, "Uh, folks, we're in a hold. It's a little foggy up around New York. We're going to circle Allentown for a while." Allentown lies east of Allegheny peaks, I thought. But the descent stretched on. Ten minutes. One cigarette. The honking noises came from the hydraulic system, but the creaking had to be the wings. What was it a pilot once told me? "A DC-4 in weather will snap twice as many struts as a Constellation." Twenty minutes. As we dropped toward the city of skyscrapers, visibility was zero. Plane lights blinked. The fog glowed red. Otherwise everything was black. How would it be, the brilliant red death of exploding wing tanks, or sudden, utter, inconceivable dark?

"Hey," Carl Erskine said. "Do you like poetry?" He had slipped into the seat beside me and meant to cheer me or himself, or both.

"Sure, Carl. I majored in English."

"Ever hear of a poet named Robert W. Service?"

"Right."

"A poem called 'The Cremation of Sam McGee'? Well, would you like to hear me say it?" And he was off:

> *There are strange things done in the midnight sun*
> *By the men who moil for gold;*
> *The Arctic trails have their secret tales*
> *That would make your blood run cold;*
> *The Northern Lights have seen queer sights,*
> *But the queerest they ever did see*
> *Was that night on the marge of Lake Lebarge*
> *I cremated Sam McGee.*

Erskine's eyes sought me. I nodded.

> Now Sam McGee was from Tennessee, where the cotton
> blooms and blows,
> Why he left his home in the South to roam 'round the Pole,
> God only knows.
> He was always cold, but the land of gold seemed to hold him
> like a spell;
> Though he'd often say in his homely way that "he'd sooner
> live in hell."

Over five more stanzas the Arctic cold killed Sam. His body was placed in a furnace, where coals blazed. After a long time the door was opened to see if the cremation was done.

And there sat Sam, looking cold and calm, in the heart of the
    furnace roar;
And he wore a smile you could see a mile, and he said: "Please
    close that door!
It's fine in here, but I greatly fear you'll let in the cold and
    storm—
Since I left Plumtree, down in Tennessee, it's the first time I've
    been warm."

Robert Service's envoi and our landing coincided. Carl
winked. I said, "Good going." And we went our separate ways.

By September 3 the Dodger lead over the Giants had
dropped to five games. In almost empty Braves Field, Boston
moved five runs ahead; then the big hitters rallied, tying the
score in the fourth inning. Dressen called for Joe Black, and
watching the big man stride in, you could tell. There would be
no more easy scoring for Boston today.

Black had come on slowly and irresistibly. He possessed only
a fast ball and a small, sharp curve. Dressen liked pitchers with
varied weapons and he was reluctant to believe that Black
could win with just two pitches. But Joe pitched strongly in
Chicago. He won in Pittsburgh. "It isn't all that hard," he said.
"When they say pitch high, I pitch high, and when they say
pitch low, I pitch low." His control was superb, but what probably won Dressen was a game when the Cincinnati bench sang
a soft, derisive "Old Black Joe."

Black neither responded nor changed expression. He simply
threw one fast ball each at the heads of Cincinnati's next seven
batters. "Musta been some crooners in the lot," he said. "That
stopped the music." Dressen admired Black's unpretentious
toughness. By mid-season, Black became the principal reliever
on the team.

Now in September in New England, he overpowered the
Braves. The game stayed tied until the eighth inning. Then

Robinson hit a grounder which the Boston second baseman threw wildly. Robinson never broke stride, and slid safely into third. That was his way—stealing the extra base when it mattered. Furillo bounced out and Robinson had to stay where he was. Snider bunted at Ed Mathews, the third baseman. Mathews charged and Robinson charged with him, staying one step behind. Mathews gloved the ball. He glanced back at Robinson, who stopped short. He threw to first. As Mathews released the baseball, Robinson sprinted home. He scored the winning run, with a long, graceful slide.

"Helluva play," I said in the clubhouse.

"No," Robinson said. "Just the play you make in that situation. As long as I'm a step behind him, he can't tag me. He can't reach that far. And he can't catch me. I'm quicker than he is. So he can do two things. He can hold the ball. Then I stay at third and Duke is safe at first. Or he can throw. Then I go home. But there's no way they can get an out without giving up the winning run."

The next night Dressen summoned Black into the seventh inning of a tie game. Joe held off the Braves until the eleventh. Then he tired and, allowing his first run in ten tense innings of relief, he lost. The next morning Dressen ordered Black to fly to New York. "If he's around again," Charlie said, "I might use him again, and I want to save him for them Giants. There's one guy ain't afraid of them Giants." Without Black the Dodgers lost the final game and the evening train ride down the coast of southern New England was a cortege. No one spoke poetry.

A day later the team lost a double-header to the Giants. The Giants had come to within four games, and they would play the team three times in the next two days. If the Giants swept, momentum would carry them to another pennant.

"I gotta think," Dressen said in the clubhouse at the Polo Grounds. "Gotta get me a pitcher for tomorrow."

"Is that the most important decision of the year?" I said.

"Yeah, kid. I gotta go home. I gotta think."

Near midnight Dressen decided to start Preacher Roe, although the Polo Grounds, with its short foul lines, emphasized Roe's wounding flaw. He threw home runs. "Ah don't know why people git on me 'bout my hitting," he said. "Ah takes care of things the other way. Ah've *throwed* some of the longest balls in history." Elwin Charles Roe, an Arkansas doctor's son, had been to college and taught high school mathematics, but the role he liked to play was hillbilly. "Hillbilluh" he pronounced it.

His face was angular and his body was bony and he liked to puff a pipe. "You ever been in the Ozarks?" he asked once.

"What's down there?"

"Hills," Preacher said, "and hillbilluhs. Some say it's quiet, but we like it."

"What do you do?"

"Hunt. I got me some real fine pointers. You know about Mr. Rickey's dogs after I had mah first real good year? Nineteen forty-nine, I believe it was, I won fifteen and lost only six. Led the league in winning percentage, I do believe.

"Well, that winter, I got back home and told myself, 'Preach, you sure are a pretty good pitcher. Now it's time you made pretty good money.' So I set there, awaitin' for Mr. Rickey to send me my contract. And each day I waited, I thought I ought to have a little more. When that ol' contract finally came, I was gonna look for a comfortable sum.

"Contract never did arrive in the mail," Preacher said. " 'Sted, down the road one sunny winter day come Mr. Rickey himself, driving a station wagon and makin' a lot of dust. He pulled up and climbed out and joined me on the porch. The two of us set there a while, just rockin'.

"Then Mr. Rickey says, 'Preacher, you're a fine pitcher. You're a wonderful pitcher.' I thank him, and we're still rockin'.

155

" 'Now, Preacher,' Mr. Rickey says, 'I don't know what to do. I'm so proud of you, it's like you were my own son.' I thank him again. 'Preacher,' he says, 'what should I pay you? It's like paying my own son. But, look, I bought you a present.'

"Just then a couple of hunting dogs jump out of the back of the wagon. 'They're for you, Preacher,' Mr. Rickey says. I sets to admirin' them, and Mr. Rickey gets up, and reaches in a pocket and hands me a paper. 'By the way,' he says, 'here's your contract. The figure's blank. Fill in what you think is right, *son*.'

"After he'd gone, I commenced thinkin' what a fine thing he'd done and how much trust he put in me and I took that original figure I had and knocked a thousand dollars off it. Day or so later I go hunting. I run the dogs up and down the hills and bagged me a mess o' quail. Got back, thought some more. Knocked off another $2,500.

"Went hunting again. Had the best day ever. Brought the dogs into the yard, locked the gate and went out on the porch and commenced more thinkin'. All the great huntin' an' the great dogs and Mr. Rickey's trust made me ashamed to be greedy. I took that contract and filled in a number $10,000 under my original figure. I got up offa the porch and walked down to the corner and put the signed contract in the mail.

"When I got home, those two huntin' dogs had jumped the fence and taken off. They didn't stop running till they got back to Mr. Rickey's house in Brooklyn."

Roe underplayed his talents. "I got three pitches," he said. "My change; my change off my change; and my change off my change off my change." In essence: slow, slower, slowest. But he could throw hard and, after watching for a while, one saw in this sharp-nosed, bony, fidgety man an absolute master of guile. Even his fidgeting was planned. It was an essential to his spitball.

When wetting a pitch, Roe touched his cap and his sleeve,

tugged his pants, dabbed his brow and, as his fingers rested at the forehead, he spat quickly into the heel of his hand. Then he pretended to pull his belt with his pitching hand. In the process fingertips touched wet heel. Now he was ready to throw the spitter.

We watched him from the press box through binoculars. In fidgeting, Roe *always* went to his forehead and belt, so we never could tell just when he "loaded" the ball. Nor did we know how he was doing it. Plate umpires, urged on by batters and opposing managers, sometimes demanded to see the ball. Whether it was wet or not, Preacher nodded and carefully rolled the ball the sixty feet to home. The evidence always dried in the dirt.

In the first inning at the Polo Grounds, Roe seemed more nervous than usual. He could not stand in one place. Through binoculars you could see his lips moving. He was chattering to himself. Alvin Dark doubled. Whitey Lockman singled sharply, and for all Roe's wiles, the Giants were ahead, 1 to 0.

But the team, whose courage was so frequently maligned, refused to die. In the second inning, Gil Hodges, pale with tension, stepped into one of Sal Maglie's curves and hit it into the upper stands in left field. An inning later Reese slammed a line drive into the lower field seats. Shuba and Cox hit home runs in the seventh. And Preacher, having made two early mistakes, made no others. He showed the Giants fast balls at eye level, and broke arching curves around the knees. When they waited for the curve, he slipped hard sliders under their hands. When they set for spitters—his spitter dropped—he'd loose the fast one and break their timing. He faked a hundred spitballs. Perhaps he threw ten. Or perhaps five. Muttering, fidgeting, always two thoughts ahead of the batter, Roe did not give the Giants another hit until the ninth inning. The Dodgers won, 5 to 1. The lead was again back to five. The next afternoon Dressen tried another lefthander, Ken Lehman, who had recently completed two years with the U.S. Army in Korea. Lehman was fair-haired, handsome and very bright. "I think," he said, "I'm gonna sit next to Preacher, rub against him. Maybe some of that stuff will rub off on me." But he was gone after one inning and two runs. Black relieved, expressionless and fierce. This day he did not back Giant hitters from the plate. Instead, he flattened them. At least three Giants barely ducked under fast balls. The Giants lost poise and power; behind Black's ferocity the Dodgers pulled far ahead.

This was Durocher's game, destroy the enemy, sow salt in the infield, and he was losing it. "Come on. In the ear. The big pitcher. Forty-nine. We're gonna get him." In the seventh inning, a Giant reliever threw toward Black, and missed. Black was backing away at the windup. His response an inning later was to deliver the single most terrifying pitch I have seen.

The object, supposedly, is to frighten, not to maim. Against a journeyman white outfielder named George Washington Wilson, from Cherryville, North Carolina, Black drew the perfect line. Wilson, who batted lefthanded, dug in his spikes, cocked his bat, and Black powered a fast ball at the body, shoulder high. Wilson ducked, in absolute if understandable panic, pulling his head down with such force that his baseball cap came off. The pitch sailed through narrow daylight, no more than a foot, between the cap and cranium of George Washington Wilson. He got up quickly, utterly ashen, and popped up the next pitch, with a quarter swing. The Dodgers won, 10 to 2. The pennant was sure. The Giant tide, like the questioners of the team's courage, had at last been properly dammed.

On a Sunday afternoon in Boston, Joe Black, starting for the first time, overpowered the Braves and the Dodgers clinched a tie for the pennant. Five hundred fans met the team at Grand Central Station. They cheered as the players appeared through a runway and waved signs in the air. One read: "FOR PRESIDENT, JOE BLACK, MOST VALUABLE PLAYER."

The Dodgers secured the pennant in their next game, on Tuesday night, September 23, by defeating Philadelphia, 5 to 4. The starting pitcher, a slight, handsome righthander named John Rutherford, threw a grand-slam home run, but Shuba homered for the team and Snider, magnificent since the benching, drove in the winning run with a long double. My story cited the charges that the team never won big games and commented: "Perhaps. But they sure won a lot of little ones."

"Hey," Duke Snider shouted, as he sipped champagne in the clubhouse. "How was that goddamn perfect swing? How'd you like that one?"

"What was it you hit, Duker?"

"I hit a sinker, but it didn't sink." We laughed. "And in the World Series I'm gonna hit a screwball that doesn't screw."

"Whoop," cried Campanella, wrapping an arm around my chest. "How's that for fighting spirit?"

"We'll take those Yankee bastards," Robinson shouted.

"Son of a buck," Carl Erskine said, with shining eyes.

Billy Cox waggled his finger and said, "Fuckit."

A day later nine bottles of Scotch appeared in the press box, one for each man who covered the team. Joe Black had sent them with a note: "I know I threw the pitches, but the things you fellows wrote about me sure helped. Thanks." The brand of Scotch he chose was important to him. Black and White.

Bob Cooke gave me three days off, dispatched me to a weekend football game at West Point and asked how I felt about writing the principal story on World Series games. "It goes outside," he said. "Page one."

"I'd like the lead on the games in Brooklyn."

Behind eyeglasses Harold Rosenthal's eyes looked merry. "Might as well find out now," he said, "if the kid chokes."

"What the hell does that mean?" I said. "And I can always write an AP lead."

"Not for this paper, you can't," Cooke said.

"None of that 'paced by the six-hit pitching,' " Rosenthal said.

"Yeah," said Sol Roogow. "Rest in pace, get it?"

"The Series is nothing to worry about," Cooke said. He began drumming his fingers on his desk, and looking about. "We've gone with you all year." The fingers played a piano exercise. "The stories have to be eight pages long. Can you write an eight-page story in an hour?"

"And in English?" Roogow said.

Cooke's drumming was making me nervous. "Yes," I said. I wanted to get up and walk. "It's no big deal."

"No," Rosenthal said heavily. "Front-page pieces are no big deal at all when you're twenty-one."

"Twenty-four."

"Look," Cooke said. "Don't be fancy. Just lead with the most important things."

Joe Black won the first game of the World Series, 4 to 2. Robinson, Snider and Reese hit home runs. No Negro had won a World Series game before, but I had learned the *Tribune*'s curious definition of importance. "Home runs and Joe Black," I began a conservative story, "the combination which brought a pennant to Brooklyn yesterday . . ." I was confined to writing hits and errors.

The Series built through climaxes. Erskine, assigned to pitch the second game, stood tiptoe on a ladder to peer through a clubhouse window, at the weather and at the excited people outside. He lost his balance and fell, striking his head against a radiator. He fainted, revived, but was knocked out in the fifth inning. The scene shifted to the Stadium. Roe outpitched Ed Lopat. The Dodgers led, 2 to 1, in games. Then Allie Reynolds struck out ten and beat Black, who allowed only three hits, and the Series was tied.

There are no free tickets to a World Series game. Six hundred places are assigned to working journalists (most of whom really work), but everyone else—players' wives, visiting baseball men and the Commissioner of Baseball—pays for his seat. That is a message I had to learn by heart. No sooner did the Dodgers win the pennant than telephone calls started. Someone had known me as a high school sophomore; someone else was a casual acquaintance ten years before. The brother-in-law of a girl I knew and the brother of a girl who had declined to go out with me and, inevitably, Dan Golenpaul of "Information Please" telephoned. Each call began in praise and ended in supplication. "I really enjoy reading you in the morning." Pause. Inhale. "Say, do you think you can get me a pair for the Series? I'll *pay* for them."

"There are no free tickets to a World Series game."

"Oh? Well, even so, I mean, could you help an old friend?"

I bought a pair for each game, at $6 a ticket, spending a total of $84, which was $12 more than my weekly salary. Then I offered the tickets to friends who had not called. Both strips were gone in a day. All Brooklyn panted for my tickets, but as it did, I made a modest economic discovery. Once $84 is removed from a checking account, to be repaid in multiples of $6, it is gone. Friends gave me cash and checks, but the small installments always dissipated. It was months before my account recovered. Whatever the arithmetic, $6 times 14 never equals $84.

I reserved Sunday tickets for my father and, with this grinding Series tied, telephoned to offer suggestions for his viewing. "I don't know your exact location, but it's somewhere behind the plate. Erskine's going. Watch his change-up, but mostly watch that overhand curve."

"I doubt if that will stop the big Yankee hitters."

"When Carl is right, nobody hits him."

"He's small. Small pitchers tire."

"We'll see about that," I said, without confidence.

Sunshine lit the concrete mass of Yankee Stadium on Sunday. Sunshine splashed across the infield and warmed the outfield grass. The crowd, which would number 70,536, arrived early. At first World Series audiences are weighted with people who have come to be seen by columnists, or to sell a client something between innings, or to make a deal while men lead from first and third. But the 1952 World Series, played entirely in New York City, had lost its novelty by Sunday. As Erskine snapped overhand hooks during warm-up, his stuff drew cries of admiration from the stands. It looked, someone remarked, as if the hucksters and the actresses had all gone off together. Today we had baseball fans. The noise they made, like sunshine, lit the scene.

The Dodgers peppered the Yankee starting pitcher, Ewell Blackwell, who had long since lost the edge of his sidearm fast ball. Snider lined a 420-foot home run. By the fifth, Erskine led, 4 to 0.

So quickly that there was no time to consider what had gone wrong, the Yankees scored five times. Erskine allowed a single, walked a man and gave up two other hits. Then Johnny Mize, a 220-pound man from Georgia, with astonishing wrists and cat eyes, lifted a home run into the lower stands in right. The Yankees led by 5 to 4.

Dressen walked to the mound, one hand in a hip pocket, scratching. He shook his head and took the ball from Erskine. He shook his head again and gave it back. Erskine ended the inning, and the Dodgers tied the score in the seventh when Snider slammed a long double to right center field off Johnny Sain.

Pitching very hard, playing very bravely, Erskine and the team held off the Yankees at the Stadium. In the second inning, Andy Pafko, a thick-legged, earnest man who never seemed entirely comfortable as a Dodger, had sprung beside the low right-field barrier and caught Gene Woodling's drive in the glove webbing. Pafko's timing prevented a home run. Now when Yogi Berra drove a long fly to right center, Snider sprinted across the sheep meadow of an outfield, leaped, hung in the air and caught the ball. "I made it harder than it was," Snider said years afterward, "by losing track of the damn wall. Actually, I was shyin' as I jumped." But that nuance went unobserved amid the excitement of the time.

In the eleventh inning, Snider singled home a run. The Dodgers led. Erskine retired Mantle on an easy grounder. Now seventeen Yankees had gone out consecutively. Mize was the hitter. He cocked his bat and squinted. Erskine threw two pitches. Mize lined the third to right, where Carl Furillo had replaced Pafko. Furillo placed his right hand on the barrier and hurled his heavy body into the air. Furillo's glove was nine feet high when he caught the ball and saved this remarkable game.

Afterward I greeted my father at the entrance to the press box, pumping his hand. "I said watch the pitching, but I guess the great thing today was the outfielding. Did you ever see three better catches in your life?"

"The pitching was fine, too. He does have an excellent curve, except once in a while he didn't keep it low."

"That's what set up the great catches."

Gordon nodded, curiously restrained. Leaving Yankee Stadium, we passed Row T, in Section 2, where he had sat. It was fairly high, and one had to look down row upon row. The press box, hanging from the mezzanine, cut off the view from the top. One could see no more than the fringes of the outfield. One could not see sky, nor could one possibly have seen a fly ball and an outfielder in pursuit and the thrilling confluence of vectors—ball and running, leaping outfielder. My father was not commenting on the catches because he hadn't seen them.

"Sorry," I said. "That's how the Yankees are."

"Nonsense. Enjoyed the game very much. I really found your

163

friend Erskine an excellent little pitcher."

It now seemed right not only for the Dodgers to win, but for the Yankees to be beaten. Their organization was both aloof and deceptive. Taking my check for $36 a week earlier, the fourth highest Yankee executive had said, "We don't usually take care of rookie writers with such good tickets. You're an exception. You're pretty lucky to get tickets at all." The third highest executive, after three martinis, said he would never allow a black man to wear a Yankee uniform. "We don't want that sort of crowd," he said. "It would offend boxholders from Westchester to have to sit with niggers." Just as the humanity of the Dodgers burst past the limits of a ball field, so did Yankee arrogance. The most popular sports comment that autumn was: "How can you root for the Yankees? It's like rooting for U.S. Steel."

But a day later Berra and Mantle hit home runs in Ebbets Field. Although Snider hit two homers, the Yankees won, 3 to 2. The Series was tied for the third time. October 7 broke clear and brisk in Brooklyn. For the seventh game Joe Black said he felt strong and ready. The Dodger season was ending with the team's best pitcher at work. That is how any season should end.

From the high Ebbets Field press box, I had seen Black pitch two dozen times. This day I saw him labor. The small, sharp curve, the cobra at the knees, kept biting dirt. It was harmless, a bad pitch. Nothing more. The fast ball wandered. He had to push it. Starting a third game in seven days, after two months of pitching relief three times a week, he was worn down, not strong at all, but weary. Woodling and Mantle hit homers. Black left in the sixth inning, losing 4 to 2. His head hung. His arm ached. He was deaf to an ovation joining thirty thousand throats.

In the seventh, the Dodgers loaded the bases with one out. Casey Stengel, out of first-liners, called on a tall, toothy left-hander named Bob Kuzava, who lost as often as he won. He struck out Snider. Now Kuzava was left to confront Jackie Robinson. It was always coming down to the best men. The count went to three and two. Robinson fouled off four pitches. The flags of Ebbets Field flapped in the wind. Robinson lifted an ordinary pop fly to the right side. The base runners ran. No Yankee moved. It seemed that the pop would bounce and that two runs or more would score and the Dodgers would win their first World Series. Who hits after Robby? Maybe we'll get six. What will I use for a lead? Billy Martin, the Yankee second baseman, sprinted, reached, lunged and gloved the pop fly when it was no more than two feet from the ground. It had been the first baseman's ball. No matter. Martin, an Oakland roughneck, had rescued the forces of U.S. Steel. The Dodgers never again threatened. The Yankees had won their fourth consecutive World Series. Next Year, the Messianic Time when the Brooklyn Dodgers become the best baseball team on earth, had not yet arrived. "Every year," I angrily began the page-one story, "is next year for the New York Yankees."

In the old apartment, a week later, Leopold Bloom was preparing to gaze in rising lust at the underclothes of Gerty MacDowell, but he was delayed by Olga Kahn, again speaking on the telephone.

"In a sense," Gordon said, "this was next year for you. I thought you proved a number of things."

"But damn, it was disappointing."

"The Dodgers have been disappointing me, in more ways than I can count, for forty-five years. I started rooting at the age of six."

"I rather suspected that you had."

A barrier built between us, between boy and man, between pretense and candor, was down. "Now where," Gordon said, lighting one Pall Mall from another, "could you possibly have gotten an idea like that?"

IV

Wicker furniture, February dankness persisting through March twilights, plasterboard walls and suites like hutches were the Dodgertown barracks at Vero Beach. Here, in the second spring of my Assignment Brooklyn, Buzzy Bavasi poured Grasshoppers from a pewter cocktail shaker, his moon-face intent on filling my paper cup to the brim. "Crème de menthe," Bavasi said, "brandy, cream and ice I ordered from the kitchen. Sip, don't drink. That's the way. Like it?"

"It tastes like a mint-flavored malt."

"Son of a buck. One year with the club and you're getting like the rest. A wise guy." Bavasi's mouth turned down. "Well, I was gonna tell you why we traded Pafko, but I won't."

Emil J. Bavasi, *de facto* general manager of the Dodgers, attended DePauw University with Ford Frick, Jr., whose father, once Babe Ruth's ghost writer, became Commissioner of Baseball in 1951. Bavasi's family owned a large newspaper distribution company on Long Island, and by the time he entered college he knew that he was free to choose a field, without total fealty to income. He liked baseball. Given a boost by Ford Frick, Bavasi entered the Dodger organization at Valdosta, Georgia, sixty miles west of the old copyboy's Valhalla of Waycross. He understood the game and studied the body of extralegal rules that govern it and advanced to Nashua, to Montreal and then to Brooklyn.

With his quick, questioning mind went a love for the Byzantine. If Bavasi disliked a story, he approached a reporter obliquely. "I didn't read it myself, but some people in the office are upset with what you wrote about yesterday's game." *I didn't write anything unusually rough, Buz.* "I didn't say you did. I just said some people were upset. I don't know. I told you I haven't read it myself."

A quantity of impersonal lying swells dialogue between ball club and press, whenever both sides are playing hard. Reporters invent rumors. "I hear Pee Wee Reese is for sale." *Nonsense. Where did you get that? I hear your newspaper is for sale.* At worst the reporter now has a story to shelter him through a rainy day. "DODGERS CALL REESE SALE REPORT FALSE." At best, he strikes a richer lode. *The Cubs offered $200,000, but we said no.* "DODGERS SPURN CUB GOLD FOR THEIR PEE WEE."

On the other side, executives interrupt negotiations for a pitcher to deny that a trade is possible; they proclaim that team harmony is like a melody that's sweetly played in tune after fining a catcher $250 for threatening to slug the manager, and they swear that their franchise is as fixed as Gibraltar, while investing in new ball-park bonds in another city fifteen hundred miles away. The serious ethics, lightly stated, are: "Lying to get a story is not dishonesty but glorious trickery" (S. Woodward) and "Lying to a newspaperman is blessed by the angels without fear of fall" (A. Doubleday, *et al.*).

Although some writers resented Bavasi, I found him a pleasant, generally admirable man. If he misled me, why, then I had allowed myself to be misled. There was no more malice to the deed than there was in raising (and getting away with raising) a poker hand on a pair of threes, eight high.

The press room sprawled behind the Dodgertown kitchen, with a small busy bar at one end, chairs and work tables along the walls, a large round table in the center and a screen door leading outside. Two men sat at work tables typing. The bulk of one in a wicker chair and the swelling back reminded me of someone, but I advanced on the bar, where Mike Gaven was telling a story about a team called the Newark Ironbounds, which he said he had managed, many years before.

"We used to play these colored teams, and when they hit a home run with bases loaded, all you'd see around the base paths were legs and eyes. A little brandy, please," Mike said.

When the bartender handed him a pony, Gaven performed

a curious routine. "Mike," I said, "why dip your cigar in brandy before you light it?"

"Brandy brings out the flavor of the tobacco."

"Then, why do you throw the pony out?"

"Tobacco ruins the flavor of the brandy. Say," Gaven said, "you know who reads your *Herald Tribune?* Stockbrokers who went to Dartmouth and secretaries who want to impress their boss. Why doncha work for a paper somebody reads?"

The flat Newark voice carried, and the bulky man in the chair turned and cried in a tenor growl, "Why don't you write some-*thing* somebody can read, Mr. Gaven?"

"Coach!" Stanley Woodward had gone to work as sports editor of the Miami *News.* "Hiya. How are you, Stanley?"

"Trying to conserve considerate pride." Woodward was typing a story about the outlook for the Philadelphia Athletics, who trained in West Palm Beach. "I was there yesterday. Can you give me a hand here when I'm done?"

Changes in Woodward shocked me as we talked toward the end of a night. At dinner he was vigorous and amusing. "Living at the heel of the Great American Hookworm Belt is a trial," he said. "It's ninety degrees in the summer, all day and every day. Rosy-fingered dawn is ninety degrees. We live in a part of Miami called Coconut Grove, which is a mistake. Miami is a mistake. The mangroves should rise in protest. The gnats already have. Whenever the wind blows from the Everglades, gnats mass in close formation. They have evolved with a genetic understanding of screens. Each biting adult gnat is a micron smaller than the holes in the mesh. We are their feast. I can endure that, but the maid who keeps our house has a bad time. She's used to the North and she thinks that if she steps outside by herself, the Klan will murder her, which is a possibility. So she stays in the house all the time, and the gnat bites make her cry."

After steaks, back in the press room, I tried to provide Woodward with a column. Poker chips clattered at the center table. Billy Herman, Roscoe McGowen, Bavasi and a few others bid and raised. Walter O'Malley's bull voice was loudest. "I'm afraid I have to raise you again, Mike."

"Bad thing," Woodward said, quietly, "for a newspaperman to play poker with a millionaire. Bluff you out of your life. What's going on with this club?" I tried to describe what I knew. Chuck Dressen had begun spring training on March 1 with a talk on the theme of hate. The team had won a pennant, so everyone hated them, he said.

"You wrote that?"

"Sure."

"Good boy. But I can't follow you a week. Is something fresh?"

Reese was an exceptional story. He seemed selfless. John Griffin, the clubhouse manager, said sometimes when he was short of help, Reese, the team captain, helped carry bags of bats.

Woodward yawned.

"Pee Wee says team spirit is ridiculous. What exists is money spirit. You help other players, bunt or hit-and-run and they help you, not for a team, but for themselves. You both want money."

"I want money," Woodward said. "Can you get me another martini?"

"Reese's great hurt is that he has only a daughter. He wants a son. He told me the other morning, 'I guess I'm shooting blanks.' "

"I don't have any sons," Woodward said.

I brought more martinis. Behind thick lenses, Woodward's eyes were wet. He breathed heavily. "Asthma," he said. "The swamps make my asthma worse."

From the center of the room, Walter O'Malley cried, "Three kings haven't beat a straight yet."

"Shit," said Roscoe McGowen.

"Bad," Woodward said, suddenly very sick and very drunk.

"No good here. New England man. Moved out of my place. Not fair." Tears ran out from under the thick lenses. "Son," Woodward said, clasping my shoulder in a mighty grip, "shouldn't they let an old man finish in New York?"

The only limits to the speed of change in his time and in ours, Ernest Hemingway said, is our ability to comprehend speed. I sunned myself in Florida. George Jorgensen became Christine and Clare Boothe Luce became Ambassador to Italy. Dwight Eisenhower declined to commute the death sentence of Ethel and Julius Rosenberg and the Zenith Company announced that there were now more TV sets than bathtubs in the city of Chicago. Stalin collapsed. Trygve Lie quit the United Nations. Russian doctors applied leeches to Stalin's head. Chuck Dressen said the rookie Jim Gilliam was so good, "he ain't missed one yet. The worst he's done when he swings so far is ticked it." From Moscow came a physician's bulletin. The heart of Stalin had stopped beating. Where would Junior Gilliam fit into the Dodger club?

Dick Young scooped me decisively. After five years at second, Jackie Robinson, thirty-four, was going to become a third baseman, Young reported. Gilliam would play second, opening day. And Billy Cox, the best third baseman since the dawn of baseball, was now an extra hand, utility man. Each day's papers were flown from New York to Vero Beach. "Charlie," I said, holding a *Daily News* before the manager, "is this true?"

"What you write yesterday?" Dressen said.

"About the new pitcher, Russ Meyer's screwball."

"I think you wrote the wrong story."

"But how can you bench Cox?"

"We ain't benchin' him. We're makin' him utility. He don't like to play every day anyway."

"But he'll like it less when you tell him he *can't* play."

"Mebbe. But he won't mind when I see he gets an extra

thousand dollars to make the switch." Dressen said he wanted
to even matters and that he had another scoop. "Kid, I'm gonna
make Joe Black into a helluva pitcher."

"He is a helluva pitcher."

Dressen made an impatient gesture. "Needs more stuff. I'm
gonna show him a change and a screwball and a big curve.
There's your story."

I found Black in the barracks, writing a letter. "Yeah," Joe
said. "The day I got here, he didn't even say hello. Right off he
said he was going to show me a big curve, but look." Black
extended his right hand. The index and middle fingers angled
downward. "Tendons that lift them aren't right. I was born that
way. It does something to my grip. That quick little curve is the
only curve I can throw. I tell Number 7 and now he says I got
to throw a fork ball. You know. Throw with the ball shoved up
between the fingers. It gives you a kind of change."

"Can you?"

"Man says I got to, I got to. Hey, you know what worries me?
That sophomore jinx. I'm not gonna let that bother me."

I rechecked with Dressen. He knew about Black's malform-
ity. But he remembered another pitcher who had lost a half-
inch off his middle finger. "Threw the livest goddamn fast ball
you ever saw."

"Have you talked to Cox yet?"

"What's that?"—whistle—"Yup. Whatcha doin', getting like
them?"

"Who's them?"

"Lang. Roeder. Every day they say have I talked to Cox yet,
have I given him his thousand? Well, they can't tell me how to
run my club. I ain't gonna talk to Cox until they stop askin'. Get
it, kid? Write Black's gonna win twenty. I'll worry about Cox
and them."

Jim Gilliam was a black deer, lovely to behold as he turned bases, elbows wide for balance, reaching, a dark arrow, toward a backhand stop. He was twenty-four then, but his face had not a single line and his body glistened, lean and dark. Bobby Morgan, a sandy-haired utility infielder, was the first ball player who offered an oblique comment. "Hey," Morgan said, indicating a black player wearing a St. Paul uniform. "How come he ain't a Dodger? He's dark enough." A reserve outfielder said, "Yeah. They're gonna run us all right outa here."

Dressen was always experimenting with line-ups, as a good manager must, and it was a camp joke that each spring the Dodgers tried five new third basemen before rediscovering Cox. But Gilliam to certain players was not a joke. There existed in 1953 what John Lardner called the 50 percent color line; that is, it was permissible for a major league team to play only four black men out of nine. The ratio, five whites to four blacks, substantiated white supremacy. But to have five blacks playing with four whites supposedly threatened the old order. No straight paths lead from Bedlam or racism. In camp during 1953 was one Edmundo Isasi Amoros, a black outfielder from Matanzas, Cuba, who had played twenty games the year before and, according to coach Billy Herman, had miracle wrists. Change-ups fooled Miracle Wrists and he batted .250. But he might improve. The team was uncertain in left field. A 1953 line-up might include Campanella, Black, Gilliam, Robinson and Amoros in left. Five out of nine would be black. As the reserve outfielder said, "They're taking over."

Actually, by this time the Dodgers were exceedingly cautious crusaders. They dispatched Amoros to Montreal, where he batted .321, and the 50 percent color line was not tested until a full year later, when it vanished without trace and without protest. But in that uncertain spring of 1953, when Senator Joseph R. McCarthy challenged the fitness of the political centrist Charles Bohlen to be Ambassador to the new Soviet Court of Georgi

Malenkov, the possibility of five black Dodgers playing at one time threatened uncertain men.

When March was two weeks old, we left Vero Beach for the McAllister Hotel and a series of exhibitions with the Chicago White Sox. On the night of March 19, after a long, tedious game, I hurried back to the hotel, my head aching, and tried to sleep and failed and decided to order tea and toast in the coffee shop.

Harsh lights and soiled tabletops welcomed me. The room was almost empty. From a distant table, Billy Cox made a small wave.

"Hey," he said when I joined him. "What the fuck is goin' on?"

"I got a headache, Will. The center-field lights shine right into the press box and kill your eyes."

"Don't kid around. You know what I mean. I hit. I field. I'm fucking fired."

"Billuh's real upset," Preacher Roe said.

"What do you think of Gilliam?" Cox said.

"Helluva ball player."

"How would you like a nigger to take your job?"

A waitress came, a chubby bored blonde, with mottled skin, and I gave my order.

"You heard me," Cox said.

"I guess I wouldn't like a nigger to take my job."

"Ya see," Cox said, to Roe.

"Can Robinson play third?" I said.

"I don't mean Jack," Cox said.

"Robi'son's one hell of a man," Roe said.

"I mean the nigger, the kid," Cox said.

"They got as much right to play as anyone else," Roe said, "but now they're pushin' Billuh around."

"The ball club's doing it, not Gilliam, not Robinson."

"I don't know," Roe said. "It's pretty fucked up."

"It sure is," I said.

173

"Ah," Billy Cox said. "Fuckit. But what the fuck they want a guy to do?"

Upstairs I found two aspirin. What an infinitely barren ending for the Robinson experience if Dodgers called other Dodgers "niggers." Bobby Morgan's nastiness meant nothing. Vituperation is the natural speech of bit players, beyond the earshot of stars. But Cox and Roe, roommates with shortest names, were magnificent athletes, real Dodgers. No game was scheduled for the following day. I had both space to place and time to plan a story. I wandered around the cramped hotel room remembering Fred Allen's joke about a Philadelphia hotel room so small that even the mice were hunchbacked. I turned on the television set. A straw-hatted white tenor appeared, singing:

> She took my arm,
> Up in ol' West Palm,
> Where the oranges grow
> On tree-ees.

He swung a cane and tried to dance. No sense of rhythm.

If I wrote a racial story, would the *Tribune* print it? I had not been permitted to set straight the nasty incident between Robinson and the Cardinals. If anything, this was nastier.

I turned and looked about. Why do all hotel rooms display the same poor copies of Dufy's racetrack and Van Gogh's sunflowers? The story would force Dressen and Buzzy and O'Malley to face what was going on. That would be a good thing. But assuming I were able, somehow, to slip the story into a newspaper which was made nervous by race, was my motive really to do good—as Frost said, to do good well? Dick Young had just beaten me badly. Now I would not be appalled to beat Young's brains out on this one, would I? Did a sense of justice impel me, or was it envy? I did not know. Cox and Roe might not speak to me again. I valued their acquaintanceship. Long after the straw-hatted man had faded into a minister telling me to put not my trust in princes' gold and the reverend become a flag and then a test pattern, I stopped questioning my motives and decided on a course of risk. It was a fine thing to be a newspaperman and I wanted very much to be a good one.

In bleary morning, I rode northwest to Miami Stadium and a workout and to interview several other players. Then, with great intensity and haste, I composed a cryptogram of a story. I had to mask my principal point from *Tribune* segregationists, who preferred Bobby Morgan to Jackie Robinson and had the power to censor. But I had to state my point clearly enough for sensitive readers to understand it. Eventually, the *Tribune* published the cryptogram without a single stroke of editing.

MIAMI, Fla., March 20—While Chuck Dressen fiddles with his Brooklyn infield, Billy Cox burns. The deposed third baseman hoards his words, but he isn't free with his job, either, and today, after the Dodgers' morning workout, Cox stood before his locker shaking his head.

What Billy will do next is a question serious enough to prompt Buzzy Bavasi, the Dodger vice president, to change his plans and fly here from Vero Beach tonight. The morale problem created by the switch of Jackie Robinson to third base is delicate now and may grow worse.

Dressen is working with one goal—he wants to field the strongest possible team. And right now he thinks his strongest team must use Junior Gilliam at second, Jackie Robinson at third and Cox as utility man. Cox, first informed of the utility scheme by newspapermen three weeks ago, was a little disturbed then. He is very disturbed now.

Dressen's Explanation

He has not been told the reasons for Dressen's switch and it isn't hard to see what's behind his headshaking. For years now, he's been told he's one of the greatest fielding third basemen in history. He's a .260 hitter on a club that boasts great power. He's out of a job.

Dressen explained his position this way: "Billy isn't going to get hurt and he ought to realize that. He's making good money now and he'll still make it as a utility man. This will give him more years in the big leagues.

175

"He's a .260 hitter," Dressen continued, "and he isn't going to get any better at thirty-four. This is the best thing for the club and the best thing for Billy."

But Dressen was explaining to a newspaperman, not Cox. When he announced that Cox was to become a utility man, Dressen said he was going to talk to Billy. He has not talked to him about the move, and he doesn't want to, now. Charley thinks Cox should realize the reasons behind it and respect them.

Resentment Noticeable

But Cox himself is only a part of the problem, perhaps the easiest part. When Don Hoak and Bobby Morgan worked out at third, nothing was said by other players. When Gilliam moved to second and Robinson to third, resentment grew. The reason is near the surface and remarks passed by some Dodgers in the clubhouse and at their hotel indicate that the problem of Negroes in baseball has still to be finally resolved.

Perhaps it was consciousness of this that moved Joe Black, a serious and deep-thinking man, to remark last night: "I'll miss Billy's glove at third. That was a big help."

And certainly it was consciousness of this that moved Black to point toward Gilliam and add, "I hope this doesn't get the other guys upset."

At 3:15 I telephoned the story to a *Tribune* recording operator. When no one had called back to argue by six, I drove to the Sir John, the premier black motel of Miami. The two-story buff quadrangle rose around a small pool. I saw Robinson and Black sitting in lounge chairs. A cornet warbled. Black musicians, working Miami Beach hotels, had to live at the Sir John.

In fading light, Robinson read my story quickly. "Is your paper going to print this?" he said.

"I guess."

"Well, it's your story and you've got to stand behind it yourself. I won't say anything more than what you got in it."

"Jack's right," Joe Black said. "But, say, there might be a little excitement tomorrow."

"Are you coming to the clubhouse?" Robinson said.

"I got to."

"Walk easy," Joe Black said.

The Associated Press picked up the story and a brief version ran in the next morning's Miami *Herald*. But Woodward, revived in his full *Tribune* vigor, printed boldface excerpts in the Miami *News*. Stanley pierced my indirectness and wrote a story charged with his white rage at the South, saying that racial tension could tear apart the Dodgers. That night, the New York *Post* dispatched the columnist Milton Gross to write a series called "The Roots of Bigotry." Bavasi telephoned and said, in a hard tone, "You better tell me who it was that talked to you."

"I can't tell you. It wouldn't be fair."

"Is it fair this way? You protect one or two guys and make everyone a suspect."

"I'm sorry, Buzzy. I didn't mention names in the *Tribune* and I can't tell you."

"Well, I'll find out," Bavasi said. He made a list of five Dodgers that he decided might have spoken to me and summoned them individually to his room.

"In this morning's *Herald Tribune*," he told each ball player, "there's a story about some stupid bigoted remarks. The story says you called Gilliam a nigger. I don't care what you think and neither does Charlie or Mr. O'Malley, but you've got to learn to keep your goddamn mouth shut."

"Hey, Meat," Carl Furillo roared as I walked into the Dodger clubhouse at 6 P.M. "You got it wrong. You loused it up. Who are you, Roeder?"

I walked to him quickly. "You got nothing to do with this story, Skoonj."

"Five, six years ago, maybe I didn't know about them colored guys. That was then. This is now. Know what I mean?"

"You're not in the story."

"Bavasi says I am."

177

"Honest, Carl."

He jabbed my arm. "You're still okay," he said.

Billy Cox reared up in silence, holding a bat and grinning a hard smile. "Goddamnit," he said. "Next time let me see what you write before you print it."

I stepped back. Cox winked and lowered the bat. Then he turned and started toward his locker.

"Billy," I said. "Your name isn't in the story. I wouldn't use your name after a private talk."

Cox dropped to a stool. He sat facing the locker, and the pumpkin-colored wall beyond. He looked around. The horse face was expressionless, but the eyes showed huge and sorrowful. "It don't matter none," he said.

"I didn't quote you, Bill."

The large eyes gazed. Cox had been hurt in war and hurt by life, and although he played third base with glorious courage, the other part, the hours off the field, were forever wounding him more deeply. They made him afraid. So he kept his distance, held his tongue and drank his beer. "It's all right," Cox said. "Don't worry about it."

"I wouldn't do a thing like that."

Sure, Cox told me with his eyes. Say what you want. One night I let my guard down and look what happens. But it don't matter none. You're a writer, no worse, no better than the rest. That's how things are, that's things and people. Abruptly, Cox said loudly, "Okay!" Then he extended his right index finger and made the gesture. Fuckit. He had had enough truck with humanity. The best third baseman on earth folded his small black glove into his pocket and hurried toward the safety of the field.

Bavasi issued a statement that "reports of dissension have been exaggerated." Jackie Robinson said in a burst of diplomacy, "I'm the one who should be upset. I'm being forced out of my position." Carl Erskine said, "Race relations on the team are a model the whole country could learn from." The story had cut clean. Dressen's utility plan worked perfectly. That season Cox played a hundred games, mostly at third, but also at short and second, and batted .291, the highest average of his major league life.

In April a bakery hired Admiral Byrd, the Antarctic explorer, to push sales of frozen bread. J. Fredd Muggs, a chimpanzee clothed in rubber pants, made his debut on Dave Garroway's dawn television program. And in Washington, D.C., Charlie Dressen canceled plans to remake Joe Black, the pitcher. "I told him," Charlie said, after an exhibition game with the Senators, "to pitch like he did last year."

"But what about the screwball and the fork ball and the change-up?"

"He don't throw none of them any good."

The classic flaw of Dodger management—manipulating pitchers toward ruin—gaped again. I sat beside Black as the team flew to La Guardia Airport. "Sophomore jinx," he said glumly. "It's got me."

"You don't believe in jinxes."

"How else can you figure it? I pitched, right? Did everything the man said. Fast ball high. Curve ball low. Ask Camp about my control. Now I been throwing so many damn things I don't know if I can control anything."

"It'll work out," I said. It never did. A man needs touch, concentration, poise, confidence as well as strength, if he is to be a great pitcher, and Joe Black was a great pitcher in 1952. To all these elements, Dressen added doubt, like a solvent of lye. The saddest spectacle of the 1953 season was watching Joe Black recede. The outward mansion never changed. The man remained warm, perceptive and fiercely determined to do well. But now his fast balls moved to the center of the plate and became high doubles, and the small, sharp curve, breaking at

179

belt level, was driven on a long, low line. Clem Labine became premier relief pitcher, and in the autumn of 1953 Joe Black, last year's proud gladiator, pitched one inning during the World Series. It was the last inning of an already lost game. He allowed a run.

This season the Dodgers came of age. Carl Erskine won 20 games. Every regular batted higher than .300, except for Cox (.291), Gilliam (.278) and Reese (.271). As lead-off man, Gilliam drew 100 bases on balls, only 5 fewer than Stan Musial. He hit 17 triples, and led the league. Reese, now thirty-five, stole 22 bases. Duke Snider hit 42 home runs. Roy Campanella hit 41. The Yankees of 1927, with Ruth, Gehrig and the rest, a benchmark of batting power, scored 975 runs. The 1953 Dodgers scored 955. The Dodgers were measurably superior in the field. They completed 38 more double plays and made 77 fewer errors. The Dodgers of 1953—not the pitching staff but the eight men in the field—can be put forth as the most gifted baseball team that has yet played in the tide of times.

Curiously, the season began with stumbling. Dressen experimented with his pitching staff and the Dodgers lost as often as they won, and Walter O'Malley called a press conference and said that he expected the team to win consistently. "In the past," he said, "sentiment has entered into decisions made by this office. Such will no longer be the case."

Dressen squirmed and perspired at O'Malley's side, but by the end of June the Dodgers had seized first place by defeating the Milwaukee Braves, 11 to 1. Julius and Ethel Rosenberg were electrocuted at Sing Sing. Elizabeth II was crowned. President Eisenhower sent Fleur Cowles as his representative and Mrs. Cowles wore a plain dress, she said, "so as not to detract from the Queen." Someone marketed a vodka containing chlorophyll, "to take your breath away and fool your wife." Although Senator Robert A. Taft died at sixty-three and Lavrenti Beria was condemned at fifty-five and Senator Joseph R. McCarthy continued to rage, it did not seem to be a troubled summer. By late July the Dodger lead was seven and a half games.

There was no hazard now, except for memory. The Dodgers still remembered the Giants and 1951. Then one day in August, Dick Young asked Charlie Dressen about Leo Durocher's team.

"The Giants is dead," Dressen said.

Young wrote a one-column box, and "The Giants is dead" became a familiar quotation. Young beamed, but Dressen grumbled. "I coulda give it to him the other way," he said. "I can say, 'The Giants are dead.' I know that, too. And next time that's what I'm gonna do."

Through the hot months, the Dodgers played phenomenal .800 baseball. They clinched the pennant in Milwaukee on Saturday, September 13, when Erskine defeated the Braves, 5 to 3, in a game punctuated by three Milwaukee errors. Dave Anderson, a young reporter who had succeeded Harold Burr on the Brooklyn *Eagle*, wrote the best lead. "The Milwaukee Braves," he began, "died with their boots."

"Two-to-one they change it on you," Young said.

"If not the deskman, then the printer," I said. "I've tried to get 'cerebration' into the *Tribune* four times this season and it's always come up 'celebration.'"

Anderson grinned, but turned less cheerful when he saw a copy of the *Eagle*. Someone indeed murdered his pleasant pun. His published story read, "The Milwaukee Braves died with their boots on." *On*. Not even Dante conceived an inferno for sodden copyreaders.

No Dodger team before had won two pennants in a row. No National League team before had clinched a pennant so early. That bright September even the McCarthy wickedness waned. Lucille Ball confessed that she had registered as a Communist during the 1936 elections to please "my radical grandpa." No one seemed to care very much, and "I Love Lucy" persisted as the most popular program on television.

Sal Maglie never hit Carl Furillo in the head, but another Giant pitcher, Ruben Gomez, plunked his wrist. Furillo trotted to first, paused and, ten seconds later, charged at Leo Durocher in the Giant dugout. Durocher met him and the men rolled on the ground. Furillo clamped Durocher's skull in his right arm. The top of the bald head turned purple. Monte Irvin, Jim Hearn and several other husky Giants pulled Furillo off Durocher. One of them stamped Furillo's hand, cracking a bone. Furillo could not play again until the World Series. He had been hitting .344. His average stayed there and he won the batting championship. In this Brooklyn season even the injuries were advantageous. At last, not next year but now, the Yankees were ready to be taken.

In the first inning of the first game of the World Series at the Stadium, the Yankees knocked out Carl Erskine and scored four runs. A day later, Mickey Mantle walloped a two-run homer off Preacher Roe and the Yankees led, two games to nothing. A number of writers composed leads around the theme: "It looks like Chuck Dressen's Dodgers is dead."

My father telephoned after the second loss and began: "Somehow your friends have the unerring knack of playing bad baseball when they most need to play good baseball."

"I didn't figure Roe would lose. I don't understand it."

"Who's pitching tomorrow?" Gordon asked.

"He has to come back with Erskine."

My father grunted concurrence. "And you'll be on the front page?"

"That's the rules. We're back in Ebbets and I write the lead story in Brooklyn."

"Well, try to spell Erskine's name correctly."

"O-i-s . . ."

"The 'oy' is silent," Gordon said, then—citing a line from some forgotten vaudevillian—"like the cue in billiards."

"I'll talk to you tomorrow."

182

"Good luck, son."

Erskine set a World Series strikeout record in chilly sunshine the next day, October 2, 1953. I sat between Rud Rennie, a courtly man who professed boredom with all things but pretty women, and Red Smith, who approached sports with resolute, professional irreverence. In passionate silence, I rooted for Carl. During the eighth inning, with the World Series, the ball game and the record still in doubt, a number of spectators left. My stomach was knotted. As I made notations in the scorebook, my hand shook. "Why in the world," I said, trying to keep my voice low and steady, "would anybody leave a ball game this exciting right now?"

"Numerous reasons," Rud Rennie said. "Their feet may be cold. Mine are. They may want a drink of something more than beer. I think I'd like a highball. They may want supper. Did you think of that? It's getting pretty close to suppertime. Or, somewhere they may have a young lady waiting."

I bit a lip. Here I was the junior man, the lead-story writer to be sure, but the junior man, and I had to play the kid. I stretched, in contrived nonchalance, and placed my chin against a wet palm as the ninth inning began.

Red Smith called my name. "Would you pass me a piece of copy paper, please," he said. A stack of yellow Western Union paper already stood before him.

"Huh? Oh, sure, Red. Here."

Holding his hands at eye level, Smith used the paper to wipe sweat from his palms. "This," he announced, "is a brute of a ball game." Rud Rennie gazed toward center field, eyes filmed as by a nictitating membrane.

I had perhaps forty minutes to compose a story. It came quickly:

Back from the dead yesterday came Carl Erskine, Jackie Robinson and Roy Campanella. Erskine blazing his way to a strikeout record,

Robinson and Campanella supplying the punch and the revitalized trio driving the Brooklyn Dodgers to their first 1953 World Series victory, a bitterly earned 3-to-2 triumph over the New York Yankees.

A crowd of 35,270 fans, largest ever to squeeze and elbow its way into Ebbets Field for a series contest, came to see a game the Dodgers had to win. They saw much more. They saw a game of tension, inescapable and mounting tension, a game that offered one climax after another, each more grinding than the one before, a game that will be remembered with the finest.

It was a predominantly Brooklyn crowd, which was fitting because it was a Brooklyn day. Robinson, the power behind the first two runs, and Campanella, who powered home the winning run with an eighth-inning homer off Vic Raschi, made amends for weaknesses in the first two games. But Erskine, unable to last beyond the first inning in the first game, held center stage and the Erskine role was most dramatically enacted.

Fans Mize for Record

The soft-spoken twenty-six year old Hoosier, a twenty-game winner for the Dodgers this season, struck out fourteen Yankees, a record, snapping by one the standard set by Howard Ehmke, of the Philadelphia Athletics, when he beat the Chicago Cubs in the first game of the 1929 World Series.

Four times Erskine struck out Mickey Mantle, the Yankee center-fielder and most-advertised star. Four times he struck out Joe Collins, the Yankees' first baseman. Once he struck out Johnny Mize, the home-run slugging pinch hitter, and once was enough. That was in the ninth inning and that was the strikeout that broke the record.

The Dodgers won the next day, tying the series, but after that content fled from Brooklyn. The Yankees won the fifth game, when Mantle, batting lefthanded, lined a screwball into the upper left-field stands. Casey Stengel's Yankees became the first team to win five consecutive world championships on October 5 at the Stadium, when Billy Martin, who had saved the '52 Series, slammed one of Clem Labine's good sinkers on a low line up the middle for a single in the last half of the ninth inning. Gil McDougald had straightened past third and was nearly home. Snider stuffed the ball into his hip pocket and ran from the field, his head bobbing. Long afterward he thought, "I should have thrown. Suppose McDougald had fallen down."

The Dodger clubhouse was sepulchral. The men sat in front of the strange lockers in the large alien carpeted dressing room. Reporters and photographers burst in. If you knew the players and saw them silent, humiliated, it was like crashing into a sick room. Photographers popped bulbs. Reporters hurried to Carl Furillo, who had tied the game by rocking a home run off Allie Reynolds in the ninth. "I showed 'em," Furillo said. "I showed 'em I could come back after breaking that hand." This black-haired powerful man was dominated by his private triumph. Five minutes after losing the Series, he was issuing victory statements. Everywhere else the men, with whom I had traveled for two years, and whose vitality I so enjoyed, were motionless and sorrowful and waxen.

"Nice try," I said to Reese, who sat head down on a three-legged stool. There was no swivel chair for him at the Stadium. Reese looked up, recognition in his eyes and hurt. "That's all it was," he whispered and lowered his head again, foreclosing conversation.

"Good to see you hitting," I said to Robinson. Jack had taken off his gray uniform shirt. A roll of fat collared his neck. He shook his head. Jowls stirred. "I'd trade every fucking hit if we could have won."

Labine had removed his baseball cap and slumped on the locker stool, head between his arms, with only the light-brown crew cut visible. His chest moved oddly, and when I came closer, I heard sobs issuing from this man who above all things was proud of his poise. Duke Snider caught my eye. "I still say we're the better team," he said.

"I know." I felt cheated. "That's the hell of it. That's the

185

rottenest thing in this life, isn't it? The best team doesn't always get to win."

Jesse Abramson, the skilled hard-boiled boxing writer, said my dressing-room story showed excessive emotional involvement. Bob Cooke and Irving Marsh agreed. The transpontine madness had me in thrall. "Take a week off," Cooke said. "Get some perspective."

I read the newspapers. Nigel Bruce, the great Watson, died at fifty-eight, deserting his confederate, Rathbone-Holmes. Kathleen Ferrier, who made men weep as she sang Mahler's *Kindertotenlieder,* died of cancer at the age of forty-one. After Herbert Brownell, Jr., Attorney General to President Eisenhower, investigated the personal finances of Joe McCarthy, he cleared the Senator of breaking criminal statutes. That Wednesday night, as ever, I visited my parents for a resumption of *Ulysses* according to Olga Kahn. We tried the chapter in which Joyce describes the birth of Mina Purefoy's baby at 10 P.M., on June 16, 1904, the progress of the language and the development of the embryo coinciding in laborious labor. We drove through it for a listless hour, after which Olga prepared coffee.

"Well," Gordon said, "at least you can't complain that it was an uninteresting baseball season. Your assignment certainly wasn't dull."

"No, but in the end I felt flat."

"Maybe you'd enjoy covering another club next year."

"I've got good sources on the Dodgers. I don't know if I could build up others as good and, anyway, going through the whole thing again would probably bore me."

"Suit yourself, but isn't twenty-five early to worry about boredom? By the way, the Erskine strikeout piece wasn't a bad story, not a bad piece of work at all." We both felt tired. After coffee Gordon saw me to the door. He was smoking a Pall Mall behind a long, bent ash. His gray eyes were soft, but the deep voice grated from a cold when he said, "Good night, chief."

The next day's newspapers broke the remarkable news that Charlie Dressen was through. Ruth Dressen had written a harsh letter to Walter O'Malley, demanding a three-year contract and O'Malley immediately invited Charlie to the team offices, at 215 Montague Street. He slapped Charlie's back, indicated a chair and said through a cigar, "Is what Ruth says what you feel you've got to have?"

"Yeah," Dressen said, averting his eyes.

"Then I think we should call a press conference for tomorrow morning. The policy here, as you know, Charlie, is one-year contracts. At the press conference we can announce together that you're leaving." Dressen blinked and shook his head. "Me and my wife got to have security," he said.

"Of course," O'Malley said. "I wouldn't try to hold you."

O'Malley dismissed Dressen and summoned Bavasi and Fresco Thompson. Bavasi recalls that he was willing to argue for a two-year contract, but that Dressen and wife wanted three years or none. Thompson, who could anticipate O'Malley's moods, lately had lost enthusiasm for Dressen. "It isn't Hodges' bat or Erskine's arm that makes us win," he had been saying. "It's Dressen's brain. We're thinking of having it sent to the Hall of Fame, collect."

O'Malley told Frank Graham, Jr., his publicity man, to announce a "very important" press conference for ten the next morning.

"What about?" Graham asked.

O'Malley placed a finger to his lips. "He was tired of Dressen," Graham says. "I knew there was some resentment of Charlie's manner and all the publicity he got for himself. But I didn't suspect what was coming."

The following morning O'Malley presided suavely. "I appreciate Charlie's views," he said. "Many of his colleagues are getting long-term contracts. However, the Brooklyn club has paid more men not to manage than any other club. The one-year contract is our policy here, and if it weren't, I'd *make* it our policy."

"My wife and I," said Dressen, co-eulogizer of himself, "gotta have security."

That quickly it was done. A fresh set of realities assaulted me. It was harsh, rather than pleasant, at the top of the baseball business, as it is harsh at the top of any business: survival depends not only on successful striving, as a manager pouring the totality of his being into a pennant winner, but also on avoiding missteps, and so on caution. To Dressen, success made one more strong, and he grew heedless. He did not realize that success, breeder of envy, simultaneously increases vulnerability. He saw himself as the heroic leader, who had managed the Dodgers to successive pennants. He did not see himself as the overbearing, semigrammatical encyclopedist whose indiscriminate chatter with the press, whose innate bluntness and whose blossoming pride made him an irritant to his employers.

I called Dressen on the morning after he was fired. It was Friday, October 16, cloudy but pleasant, and I was assigned to write the follow-up story. "Don't worry about me, kid," Dressen said. "I'm in real good shape. Thanks for callin'." Sitting in his hotel apartment, he assumed that I was offering condolences.

"Bob Cooke wants me to write a story. Will you help me out?"

"Sure. Look. I wanna ride around. Come over."

All Dressen's friends had preceded me into his paneled suite at the Hotel Granada. There was Red the Florist, short, sharp-featured and with eyes as furtive as Dressen's. Jerry the Stockbroker, square-faced, guttural, seemed strangely ominous. Herbie, the balding wire-service photographer, would beg Dressen to put on a cotton-picker's hat during spring training "so we can get a caption about you weeding out rookies." Invariably, Dressen obliged.

The hotel living room was furnished in neat, nondescript, overstuffed pieces, covered with flowered patterns. Dull prints hung on the walls, but there were no photographs, no trophies, no plaques, no sign that any person, any couple, lived here.

"Where's Ruth?" I said.

"In the bedroom," Dressen said, "brushing the little poodle's hair. Baby. That's the name of the little poodle."

"You gonna write a story about O'Malley?" Jerry the Stockbroker said. "That's what we got you here for."

"We're gonna tell you some things," Red the Florist said.

"Put them in your paper," Jerry said.

"The car's downstairs and Charlie wants me to drive," Herbie, the bald photographer, boasted.

The Granada Hotel stood at an edge of downtown Brooklyn, between the creeping wasteland of Bedford-Stuyvesant and still lively Flatbush Avenue. Across the street rose the Brooklyn Academy of Music, dun-bricked and massive, where Olga Kahn had heard Serge Koussevitzky propel his Bostonians through Sibelius. Now Koussevitzky was gone, dead for more than two years, and the B.S.O. had been passed on to Charles Munch.

"Get this fucking O'Malley," Jerry ordered, as we crowded into Herbie's car.

"Show us somethin'," Red the Florist said. "Charlie will tell ya. All you gotta do is write it."

Each of these men, a pretender to Dressen's friendship, was urging him to attack Walter O'Malley, one of the most important men in baseball. Three fight managers were shoving a middleweight into the ring against Rocky Marciano, crying, "Slug him, punish him, deck the bastard, baby." There was a survival instinct in Dressen, as well as pride and lunatic optimism, and on this one autumn morning he held his tongue. "The guy in Oakland, Brick Laws," he said. "I got a job with him. I'm gonna manage Oakland next year.

189

O'Malley offered me forty thousand dollars. The deal in Oakland is the minors again, but it's maybe gonna pay more. I got some attendance bonuses and like that."

The photographer drove out of downtown Brooklyn to Eastern Parkway, and then to Interboro Parkway, the oldest of New York City's expressways. The Interboro rolls narrowly from Brooklyn toward Queens, winding among cemeteries. Outside the windows soldiers' headstones freeze sergeant and private in perfect formation, equal now and tidy in death, except where frostheaves have broken ranks. Elsewhere marble angels look toward no one's home. Mausoleums, obelisks and smaller stones cramp one against the other until a man remembers death defined as joining the majority.

"You *have* to keep driving around here?" I said to Herbie the photographer.

"Charlie likes this highway," Red the Florist said.

"You're the only reporter in the car," Jerry the Stockbroker said.

"You oughta be grateful, not complainin', the story we're givin' you," Red the Florist said.

What an end, I thought. Three years of a man's life, the wine of press conferences, two pennants, the exultation of two million fans, come down to driving nowhere with strange men, scowling and cursing among gravestones.

"You'll be all right with another manager, kid," Dressen said, suddenly. "At least you ain't no pallbearer. You didn't like to see me beat. You'll be all right."

"I guess." Dressen punched my knee, and it struck me for the first time and very hard that the team as I had known it was no more; it was broken up now, history with the tombstones. Whoever managed it, and however well, it would not again be this small-eyed, thick-bodied man, who had never read a book and had mixed his Scotch with black cherry soda and had been boundlessly generous to me.

190

"Two of 'em called," Dressen said. "They wanted me to stay. You can guess."

"Who?"

"Reese, and the best ball player I ever managed, Robi'son."

"Well, stay, goddamnit."

"Nah. I got this here deal in Oakland."

Back at the *Tribune*, I looked up records for the Oakland franchise. In 1952 the Oakland Oaks had finished seventh. Over the entire season they had drawn 135,784 fans, a good four days of Giant games at Ebbets Field. Charlie's attendance bonus looked like a promissory note from Willie Sutton.

I wrote a thousand words, describing Dressen's plans deadpan and suggesting that he would be back in the major leagues with another pennant winner before very much longer. (He never was.) I wondered if this was the last story I'd write about him. Against that possibility, I took pains to recast all his remarks in good grammar. I knew Charlie would appreciate that.

At home in my small apartment on Clinton Avenue in Brooklyn, I poured a drink and turned on the radio. A newscaster was talking about an espionage ring within the Signal Corps, "still operating, according to a close friend of Julius Rosenberg, executed atom spy." I didn't care. I looked forward to bouncing the Dressen experience off my father, who, for all his scholarship, shared Charlie's vital lunatic optimism. It would be cloudy tonight, the announcer said, with a low of 55 degrees. The Dressen experience, as I considered it, sounded like a title for a tract. The whole thing, the Dodger loss to the Yankees and the mousetrapping of their manager, possessed, it seemed as I poured a second drink, certain elements of tragedy.

The telephone rang. It was 6:35. "Are you sitting down?" my sister Emily began.

"Which one?"

"Dad."

"What? What's that? Was it at least quick?"

191

"They think so. He died on a sidewalk. There wasn't any doctor. They think it was a heart attack. Can you come over to Kings County Hospital? I'm taking care of Mother. They want someone to identify the body."

I drove down dark streets at reckless speed. The sidewalk was a rotten place to die. Pebbled cement scrapes a twitching face. A man deserves privacy at the end, and anesthesia. Surely my father had earned that for a gentle life. Myself, ungentle, now must stand and call the corpse my father. Would they have stripped him naked? My father's final day on earth I spent with Charlie Dressen. The dying gasp and grimace on cement. Oh, I hope someone has had the kindness to close the mouth.

Corpse consigned to a licensed mortician, municipal codes conformed to, the $7.52 Gordon had been carrying received and signed for, I guided my mother and sister back to the spacious apartment. We sat in the living room with the French doors and blue-gray walls. The apartment was too large now. Everything had shrunk: books, sounds, paintings, carpets, people. My father's supper waited in the dining room. A half grapefruit had been cut and sectioned. His blue water goblet had been filled.

"There shouldn't be a rabbi," Olga said. "He should have an agnostic's funeral."

"Sure," I said. But what the hell was that?

Olga's dark eyes bulged. She chattered ceaselessly. It was hard to comprehend that this small iron lady, my mother, was babbling.

"I want a cremation," she said.

That was sensible, Roman, un-Catholic and sensible. Olga sat on the blue couch, legs crossed, circular face normal, except for the eyes. "My father was cremated," Olga said. "He was your grandfather, you know. Why don't you ever talk about your grandfather? Or write about him? He was a remarkable man. Many people would be interested in the story of his life. That is what you might write, instead of baseball, if you can. Papa's story. I want the two ashes, both urns, Daddy's and Papa's, side by side."

"I'll see about a cremation," I said.

"How can you cremate Daddy? Don't you know his favorite joke? When he died, he wanted to be cremated. Then, when a lover came to call some icy night, he said, I could scatter his ashes on the ice, so that my lover wouldn't fall and hurt himself." My mother's hands went to her face. The fingers spread and I saw, without hearing, the hands that once played simple Mozart duets with mine.

Joe Blau, an old associate of my father's, who taught religion at Columbia, and led an Ethical Culture group, said he would handle the eulogy, asserting neither that there is a God nor that there is none.

"That's about where we are, Joe," I said.

"I suppose you're full of his favorite quotations."

"Sure." But I was not. I thought for a long time. Applesauce, he had said, and something about Dressen coming back with Erskine and something from *Caesar:* It seems to me most strange that men should fear, seeing that death, a necessary end, will come when it will come. But that was Shakespeare swelling a scene. "What I remember, Joe, is that he really liked the second movement of Beethoven's Seventh."

"I can think of many quotations," Joe Blau said with rabbinic solemnity. "Why don't you console yourself with one from Socrates? 'To a good man no evil can come either in life or after death.' "

When a father dies, a son buys a coffin, entering the mercantilism of mourning. Coffin salesmen are specialists at turning guilt into profit and as Simenon writes, "When someone is dead, you feel guilty, even if for a smile you did not smile."

A deluge of Gordon's frightened friends, thirty years older

than I, and glad to have been spared, decided that lawyers should accompany me to the mortuary. Several lawyers vied for the place as, at certain parties where a girl is stricken, rival doctors contend to make the examination. Two lawyers prevailed. Intense, affluent Jack Lippman played good tennis and once at a lake of summer asked me, "Pitch in a few." Lippman wore eyeglasses and his swing was awkward. After he missed five times, I threw medium-speed high outside pitches. Lunging, he drove some to right field. I would never have thrown that way to my father; he'd have lined the ball back into my teeth. Silent, sorrowing Gus Simpson was a Socialist who had lost an eye in physical combat with followers of the Jew-baiting priest, Charles Coughlin. I drove to the mortuary with two men, physically flawed but living while my father, who could see perfectly and hit a baseball hard, lay wreathed in the faint odor of embalming fluid.

In brilliant, mild weather, I guided my pale-green car through the twisting roadway inside Prospect Park. The mortuary, a modest red-brick building, stood near the southwest corner, between a roller skating rink and the ball fields of the Parade Grounds which stretched for five hundred yards.

It was the morning of October 17. An expressionless man, wearing a dark suit, waited inside the mortuary door. "My office is this way," he said. He acknowledged the two lawyers. "Are these your uncles?"

"They're lawyers," I said.

"Burial is a private matter."

"We're here to talk price," Jack Lippman said, in a high, dry voice, "and we don't have very much time."

The mortician looked at Lippman. "Prices range up from four hundred dollars. The price of the coffin is the determining factor. Use of a chapel and one limousine are included. Was the deceased well-off?"

"No," Jack Lippman said.

"I'm buying the casket," I said.

"Yes," the mortician said to me. "We have excellent coffins for men of reasonable but not necessarily extensive means. Something with a copper lining for twelve hundred fifty will last for centuries. With that we include artificial grass, so that the area around the grave is consistent green."

"He's being cremated," I said.

"Where is this four-hundred-dollar coffin?" Lippman said.

"We'll take the twelve-fifty coffin," Simpson said. He fixed Lippman coldly and said to me, "Gordon was a wonderful man. He deserves the best."

The mortician led us into a softly lighted showroom in which an air conditioner whined. Coffins stood everywhere on sturdy bases: dark, carefully rubbed fruitwoods, with white cloth lining; dull, handsome copper; plain pine for Orthodox Jews. The prices, except for the plain pine, exceeded $1,000.

"Where's the four-hundred-dollar one?" Lippman said.

The mortician pressed his lips and sighed. He opened a door and walked into another room. Here coffins were tightly stacked on shelves. "That," he said, indicating a coffin covered with gray cloth.

"We'll take it," Lippman said.

I walked to the cloth coffin and touched it. This was my father's coffin; then at last, I had come to the coffin one removed from my own. I withdrew my hand. The cloth beneath was darker. The shade was sensitive to moisture, touch, life. Five hundred people coming to the funeral and I had bought a coffin of chameleon gray.

"No," Gus Simpson said. "That just won't do."

I walked toward a fruitwood coffin marked $685. "This one," I said.

"Do you wish time payments?"

"I've got the money."

"Shall I notify the newspapers?"

195

"I've taken care of that."

I followed the mortician back to his office, and while Jack Lippman and Gus Simpson ignored each other's glares, I signed a funeral contract, which I discovered two weeks later included $15 extra for artificial grass. Was it artificial fescue? I wondered. Was Merion more?

Outside the summer sun was taunting. I walked to the car, a lawyer at each elbow, wholly alone. The wrongness of things seized me. At the Parade Grounds boys were throwing footballs. It was that season; baseball would come again. The team was broken up and with my father dead there was no one with whom I wanted to consider that tragedy, and because there was no one I recognized that the breaking of a team was not like greater tragedy: incompleteness, unspoken words, unmade music, withheld love, the failure ever to sum up or say good-bye.

INTERLUDE I

It was not, as Eugene McCarthy remarked of his decision to challenge Lyndon Johnson for the Presidency, like St. Paul falling off a horse. The metaphysic of conversion is said to have thrown Paul from saddle to roadside, where, for several verses, he sat basking in Christianity. My own decision to find and live again with the Dodgers of my youth proceeded slowly and, so to speak, against the grain. When the idea had developed to embryo and I exposed it to an editor, I found myself being put down, which is rather a different occurrence from being unhorsed.

"Those Dodgers are no more special than, say, the Boston Red Sox of 1948," said the editor, whose name is Otto Friedrich. "You only think they're special because you covered them. They're only special to you."

"And that Wessex stonemason was special only to Hardy, but *Jude* came out a pretty good book." Overkill, but with editors, critics and witches foul is fair.

Friedrich shuddered and reached for his Cinzano. A maître d' refilled our glasses. Possibly because we were sitting in Toots Shor's restaurant, under the cubistic rendering of a runner sliding home, Friedrich persisted in discussing baseball. He had grown up on a farm in New Hampshire, he said, where his

197

father, Professor Carl Friedrich, the Harvard political scientist, lived and played the cello; when New England atmospheric conditions were suitable, young Otto fled his own ritual piano lessons for a radio which carried the voice of Red Barber. "I remember those broadcasts distinctly," Friedrich said. "Am I mistaken or was Barber truly excellent?"

Friedrich was editing the *Saturday Evening Post* then, about as well as any man could edit inside a sarcophagus, but he possessed a transcending sense of privacy, which sometimes collided with his craft. Those things about which he felt most personally were a priori barred from the mass middle-brow magazine he was trying to make. Indeed, when Friedrich composed a touching memoir of his Paris days, his words were published not in the *Post*, but in *Esquire*. Thinking that I was suggesting a magazine article on the Dodgers for the *Post* (which I was not), and remembering the team with other lost saints, Friedrich shook his head and sipped Cinzano. Leaving, I remembered the virgin queen who at last made love and then inquired if serfs did the same.

"Yes," said her paramour.

"But it's too good for serfs," the queen protested.

And I added one more secret Dodger idolator to a list by then ten years old and numberless as sand. I left the *Tribune* for magazines in 1954, following what was then the common ladder of journalism. When young, one toiled at a paper, later proceeding to *Collier's* or *Coronet*, where supposedly expense accounts allowed for renting convertibles and buying steak dinners, after which one wrote *Of Time and the River*, or at least *Other Voices, Other Rooms*, and became an author rather than a writer. The distinction was said to be immortality and $50,000 a year.

For $9,500, a private, carpeted office and an expense account which did allow for rented sedans and London Broil blue plates, I joined *Sports Illustrated*, during the first summer of its life. It was also the first summer in which Walter Alston managed in the major leagues. His experiences and mine were equally confusing.

A maxim at the *Tribune*, and at any good newspaper, commands: "Do not preconceive." If you go to the ball park, or to the concert hall or to a political campaign, thinking, "Things are probably going to go about like this," you, writer not author, are going to invent lead paragraphs to describe imaginary events. It is a writing reflex. Then the Phillies upset the Dodgers or Heifetz chooses a slow tempo or John Lindsay slurs a speech and you find yourself the prisoner of preconception. "The Phillies made their first mistake at high noon today, which is when they showed up at Dodger Stadium." The sportswriter who remembers, or who thinks he has invented, this lead at breakfast, knows pain at 4:20, when a weak fly to left concludes the Phillies 11-to-2 victory. The writer may reverse the joke, which will then not make much sense, or he can expunge the breakfast lead from thought and try to write about what happened. By the time I left the *Tribune* I had been trained, both by colleagues and by the exciting unpredictability of sport, not to anticipate. That was one important aspect of professionalism. Another was sitting quietly in the press box, despite the rising impulse to bellow, "Come on, go get 'em, Oisk."

The problem at *Sports Illustrated*, as at all magazines covering news, is that not every story can be built in a day. A number of technical considerations—sophisticated layout and production schedules—demand anticipation. Magazine management must prepare for contingencies. Horse Wins Race. Horse Loses Race. Jockey Throws Race. Lightning Strikes Jockey. The science is imprecise, but it is important to reserve pages and to prepare treatments covering all the likely eventualities. My specific problem at *Sports Illustrated* was that my immediate superior, John Knox Tibby, insisted that we calculate, not all likely contingencies, but the right one. I was his handicapper.

199

I moved out of the stark *Herald Tribune* newsroom into a carpeted office without a window, but within shouting distance of the managing editor's suite. "You're doing fine judging by where they put you," someone told me on my first day at *Sports Illustrated*. "No view, but a very high-rental area." I sat for a few afternoons, telephoning friends, who were out covering ball games. Then on Thursday I heard myself being asked, "Who's going to win that big Yankee-Cleveland double-header this Sunday?"

"I don't know, Jack, I don't know the American League that well, and even if I did, I couldn't be sure."

"You're covering it," Tibby said. "It's our lead story." He spread blank pages on his desk and sketched rapidly. "Here we have a picture, over this whole page, that says baseball. Here we run a smaller picture that says crowd. Here's the head and story. And here"—he printed in large block letters—"is your by-line. Now, who's going to win?"

"I still don't know."

We drank double martinis at the English Grill. We drank single chocolate malteds at the Cromwell Drugstore. "What you really care about is poetry," Tibby said. "I can see you years from now, forgetting the slider pitches, and happy"—here he paused portentously—"as poetry critic of *Time.*"

"Well, I don't know," I said again and began to think of interviewing E. E. Cummings, T. S. Eliot, Wallace Stevens and Robert Frost.

Toward dusk, worn down, I confessed that I thought the Indians were ready to take the Yankees. Tibby was sophisticated, persuasive and besides, professionalism has a stop. Underneath, we really do think we know.

"Most people here would disagree. They say the Yankees are Olympians."

"Yes," I said, bounding apoetically from Greece to Deutschland, "but we're about to see 'The Twilight of the Gods.'"

200

"That's it," Tibby said with soft certitude, and on Sunday night after Early Wynn and Bob Lemon had swept the Yankees, he was jubilant. My story needed revision, but the Wagnerian baseball headline was fine.

"It's an accident that it worked out," I said.

"You're being modest."

"No. If I really knew who was going to win, I'd bet. I'd tell the DA. Or something. On the *Tribune* we learned: never anticipate."

"That was the old *Trib*," Tibby said slowly. "This magazine is something entirely new." Then, yet more slowly, "You and I, we may be Donner, having crossed the pass without realizing we were doing it."

I thought about that for a while and, when I had begun to quiver, I called on Richard Johnston, the assistant managing editor, and said that, what with the idle days, my own rhythms as they had developed at the *Trib*, the demand for preconception and problems in diction, communication and attitude, I thought I was going to have to quit.

"And do what?" Johnston said.

"Go to dental school."

"All right. Some of what you say may make sense. Some doesn't. Some of your newspaper work was fine. Some I would have laid a heavy hand to. Meanwhile, I've been invited to a small private party for a ball player and his wife. Would you join me?"

"Who's the ball player?"

"Joe DiMaggio."

"You know something, Dick? I've never met DiMag."

Joe DiMaggio did not appear at the party. Marilyn Monroe stood, gloriously blonde, in the center of a mirrored room, wearing a translucent bodice that outlined rouged nipples, and a black skirt that curved with her buttocks. She stood in the center of the room and she stood in each mirrored wall and Earl

Wilson, the columnist, pointed a camera and said, "Bend forward, Marilyn, so I can get some cleavage."

Marilyn made a little cry and bent, pulling her bodice up in a gesture of modesty, that showed more nipple still. "And who are you?" said a press agent.

I blurted my name and muttered at Marilyn that I knew some baseball players myself.

"What?" she said, smiling vacantly.

"I used to travel with a ball team."

"Oh," she said. "I don't know very much about that."

The press agent concluded that I was neither Leonard Lyons nor Arthur Miller and elbowed me toward a corner where Dick Johnston stood mute, gazing from mirror to mirror.

"Why didn't you help me?" I said. "It isn't exactly easy to make conversation with somebody like that."

"Well," Johnston said, still looking about, "I started to talk to her, but my tongue got stiff."

Sadly, it was no go at the magazine. *Sports Illustrated* was improving and I was growing, but along divergent roads, and when I found myself assigned to ghost-write the football articles of Herman Hickman, my patience snapped and I resigned. At almost the same time, Buzzy Bavasi was selling Preacher Roe and Billy Cox to Baltimore, using the money to sign "a strong lefthanded pitcher named Koufax." I thought to go back to newspaper work, but I had seen carpeted offices and Marilyn Monroe. Newspaper days were forever behind me, like games of stickball.

In 1955 the Dodgers, past their prime, finally won a World Series. I sat as spectator while John Podres beat the Yankees in game seven, helped by Sandy Amoros, squat eraser of the 50 percent color line, and a change of pace that Charlie Dressen had loved to teach. "Reach back there, kid, like you're throwing the fast one and when your arm gets to here"—almost fully extended—"pull down like you're pulling down the window shade. It spins like the hard one, but it's got no speed." Alston managed the 1955 team with calm and skill, and after Podres' victory, 2 to 0, something that could happen only once had come to pass. The Brooklyn Dodgers had won their first World Series. The exultant cry rang. "This year is next year." Then a season afterward, when the Yankees won again, humiliating Don Newcombe, the old joke had a wooden stake driven through its heart. "Ah," comics suggested, "wait till last year." Robinson retired in 1956. The ball club moved in 1958. The Jackie Robinson Dodgers were no more. In Los Angeles one could see the Walter O'Malley Dodgers, possessed of Koufax, Drysdale and another world championship by 1959. But they were not the team.

I went to work as Sports Editor of *Newsweek*, a position then freighted with obscurity, and began selling articles on sports and other phenomena to a variety of magazines. I was trying to move away from baseball, but my journalistic identity, such as it was, lived with the *Tribune* stories on the Dodgers.

Maturity tugged at me. Farewell, a long farewell, to the first marriage. Farewell to Brooklyn, dining cars and teams. But at parties, among the actresses who wanted to look like Marilyn, when anyone recognized my name, it was always the same. "Say, aren't you the one who covered the Dodgers?"

"Yes, but I write other things as well."

"Look, was Billy Cox really all that good?"

"Did you see the piece I sold to *Saga* magazine on the agony of Jonas Salk?"

"And Preacher; how did he hold the spitter?"

"Or the one in the *Saturday Evening Post* on the troubles and promise of Art Carney?"

"What's George Shuba doing these days?"

"Pardon me. I want to talk to that girl over there."

I suppose it was Robert Frost who brought me to my senses. Although the old *Saturday Evening Post* pursued a policy "of discouraging stories by writers about other writers and most especially about other writers who have not published in the *Post*," I insisted that a conversation with Frost, an unpublished *Post* author, might be as interesting as one with Jack Webb, Karl Mundt or Arthur Godfrey. At length, I was commissioned to call on the poet.

He greeted me in his weathering cottage, on the shoulder of a Vermont hill, and after some fencing said, "So you're a sportswriter."

"Yes, but I write a few other things as well."

"Of course," Frost said. It was the dawning of September 1960. He wore a ragged gray sweater over a white shirt. "Nearly everybody has to lead two lives. Poets. Sculptors. Nearly everyone has to lead two lives at the very least." Frost put a mottled hand to his large brow. "When I was young," he said, "my family worried all the time that I was going to waste my life and be a pitcher. Later they worried that I would waste my life and be a poet. And they were right."

The next year I returned at his invitation and found him walking down a reach with two small dogs. He waved and called across a hundred feet of grass, "Did Lefty Tyler pitch in a World Series?" (George Albert Tyler, who grew up in Derry, New Hampshire, where Frost taught school, pitched ten good innings to no decision in the 1914 Series at Boston, and later split two Series decisions for the Chicago Cubs.) To me the poet was saying not merely "hello," but "I know who you are."

It was then, in Frost's last decade, that I began to consider the Dodgers not as baseball players but as baseball-playing men, as some are poetry-writing men, or painting men or men who make decisions of state. The experience of traveling with them was not something to dismiss, nor to let anyone dismiss in arrogant ignorance. It had become part of myself; it was something to be proud of.

Not ten years had passed, but already the boys of summer

were aged. Frost could compose with wit at eighty-six; they slumped in hitless decline at thirty-five. As the first longing to seek them stirred, one thought settled on me like a headstone. If they were old, why then I was old myself. One judges age by one's contemporaries. So this long journey, which did not end in sorrow, began with the memory of a poem written by a Japanese, Saigyō, a thousand years ago, which still, in Donald Keene's translation, pierces the heart:

> Did I ever dream
> I should pass this way again
> As an old man?
> I have lived such a long time—
> Nakayama of the Night.

BOOK TWO

The Return

These were the 'Wing'd-with-Awe,'
   Inviolable.
Gods of the Wingèd shoe!
With them the silver hounds,
   sniffing the trace of air!

EZRA POUND

CLEM AND JAY

After great pain a formal feeling comes.

EMILY DICKINSON

According to the United States census of 1970, the city of Woonsocket, Rhode Island, on the Blackstone River, harbors 46,465 souls. Twenty years earlier, the population exceeded 50,000. Preparing for the drive to Woonsocket, where Clem Labine made his retreat in 1962, I tried to imagine this poised, impeccable man reaching middle years among decay. Woonsocket lies on a rough line between Boston and New York, but growth, like the interstate highways, has passed the city by. There are pockets like that in New England and the South. Turn right at a paint-flecked sign, proceed six miles and leave the present.

"Be glad to see you if you want to make the trip," Labine said on the telephone, in a voice that sounded strong, assured and impersonal.

"Are you still designing clothing?" He had sketched sports jackets during his pitching days.

"No. I stopped that even before I went to the Mets—and got

dropped. I'm general manager up here now. We manufacture Deerfoot brand team jackets."

"You're successful, then."

"In a way."

"Do you still throw?"

"Snowballs at telephone poles. Come up and we can have lunch at my club."

To find Woonsocket, you drive north and east from New York, on broad highways probing ugly and alien, into New England. For a time IS 95 runs near the coast of Connecticut, and on a clear, late-summer morning Long Island Sound dazzles the eye, a glinting blue dappled with white. That is an instant difference driving northeast from New York. The air clears. A man sees sunshine. He realizes how New York has grown more dirty and more dark. When last Labine snapped curves at Ebbets Field, the city was a cleaner, lighter place.

Everywhere New England bears its special markings: Indian names, nineteenth-century factories and individual local shrines. At Bridgeport, where the Poquonock River dawdles toward the Sound, I saw my first factory of red brick. Thirty miles farther, at New Haven, Yale Bowl gaped, an empty Coliseum. One comes abruptly on Hartford and its Great American Insurance obelisk, Travelers Tower, reaching 527 feet high. North, along Highway 15, open green country rises and falls, and you cross into Massachusetts at Mashapaug and ride past Sturbridge, where entrepreneurs have built a replica of a colonial farming village among the ridges.

Highway 15 feeds the Massachusetts Turnpike, where traffic floods toward Boston, but near Worcester, where Bob Cousy, the famous basketball player attended Holy Cross College, I turned off, away from the main line and followed a slow truck down a two-lane road for fifteen miles. It was 1:05. I stopped to telephone him at a roadside booth.

"Where are you?" Labine said.

210

"Massachusetts. Route 146."

"Okay. Stay on 146 a good way, toward Woonsocket. There'll be a big foreign-car place. Triumphs and Volvos. I'll meet you there."

"I'm driving an undependable brown Citroën."

"Well, have *you* gone French? My boss's name is Finkel-stein."

After I left the Dodgers, Labine established himself as an excellent relief pitcher. In relieving, you are almost always correcting someone else's mistakes, or trying to, and never opening scenes on your own terms. The records show that Labine saved ninety-six games other men started, and won only seventy-seven himself. But during the 1956 World Series he pitched a heroic ten-inning shutout against the Yankees. He was thirty then, and at the peak. In 1960 the Los Angeles Dodgers sold him to Detroit, where he lost three games, and the Tigers shipped him on to Pittsburgh, where he rallied. But by 1962 he was discarded to the original New York Mets, perhaps the poorest baseball team to play in the major leagues. No matter. The Mets released him, and a few months before his thirty-sixth birthday Clem Labine, pitcher, was out of business.

Had he grown fat? With days of glory done, bone-weary athletes are inclined to shun exercise. Working pitchers sweat their beer. Retired pitchers sprout bellies. Labine had worn his hair close-cropped. "Chop-top," Dick Young called him. Beyond his forty-second birthday, would he still sport a crew cut?

Labine was waiting inside his car, a large, buff hardtop, in the Triumph dealer's lot. He waved and I followed him for two more miles until we climbed a ridge and reached a sign that said "Kirkbrae Country Club."

"Lock your car," he called.

"This isn't New York."

"Lock it. We have trouble with teen-agers, too." He stepped

out, agile, his build unchanged. He wore a pale V-neck sweater, over a white turtleneck, and when he walked, he held his forearms angled down and away from his body, an odd mannerism that had lasted. We shook hands and he led the way into a stone clubhouse, then toward an airy dining room with a window wall facing fairways. People nodded. He seemed a comfortable country-club man.

"You want to play, Clem? Eat in a hurry?" A motherly waitress hovered at our table.

"No," Labine said. "We want to take our time."

"Straight up?" the waitress asked.

"On the rocks," Labine said. "What'll it be?" he asked.

"Scotch and soda."

The face across the table—even features with deep eyes, under arching brows—was youthful, but no longer looked boyish. Small lines converged at the mouth. The skin itself looked worn. Time was beginning to walk across the face.

"Still crew cut," I said.

"That's right," Labine said. "I used to be a conformist and wear a crew cut. Now I'm a nonconformist—and wear a crew cut."

He always made a passable phrase. "Harold Rosenthal used to say you were one ball player who wouldn't have to worry about a pension."

"I liked Harold," Labine said. And the drinks came. He drank his vodka martini hard and quickly.

"It all seems real still," he said, "and alive, and I can remember things and pitches I made and the hitters. Do you know I got Stan Musial out forty-nine times in a row? Somebody counted and told me. I'd curve him and jam him with the sinker. Then there was Henry Aaron. I never got him out. I was no superstar, never a Feller or a Koufax, but I could get the job done.

"Someone in high school here said I had a curve like a left-

212

hander. That was my pitch. Once Warren Spahn asked me how I threw it. I bent my thumb under a little. Cheating, they call that; cunny-thumb, but, hell, all the good curve-ball pitchers cheat.

"I tried spitters in Caracas once. Someone showed me and I worked on it and the first time I threw it, I hit the catcher in the throat. I had no spitter. I'm not talking about morality. I don't have to. I couldn't control the thing like Preach."

My glass was low. The waitress had been watching. Fresh drinks came promptly and again Labine drank hard.

"It flashes before my eyes like a lifetime," he said. "The kid with the curve. That was in 1945. Then, I blink twice and I see myself through with the Dodgers, one blink for all those years. Being traded is a hard thing. It's knowing you're not wanted any more and adjusting to a new environment, and you tell yourself, like I did with Detroit, Al Kaline and Norm Cash can really help a pitcher. You're better off. But where are all the guys? Where's everybody you've been playing with? You're not in the fraternity any more. That's one of the hardest things."

"I would have thought that losing that World Series game in 1953 was hardest, when Billy Martin hit you, remember?"

"Goddamn right I remember."

"I would have thought that would have been harder."

"No. I broke down a little, but I learned. After that, when I lost a big one, I asked myself two questions: Did I do my best? Hell, yes. Do I want sympathy? Hell, no. Looking back, it was good I learned about losing. In 1951, were you with the club then? I pitched the shutout against the Giants in the play-off. Ten to nothing, it finished, but when the game was still close, Bobby Thomson came up and the count went to three-and-two. The bases were loaded. I threw the curve, and it must have broken a foot wide. It would have forced in a run, but Thomson swung, and I had a strikeout. The

213

next day I was sitting out in the bullpen and there were three of us. Erskine, Branca and myself. You remember?"

He told again how Newcombe had tired and the three of them—Branca, Erskine and himself—had thrown and how Dressen called on Branca and how Thomson lined the second pitch—a hanging spitball some say it was—into the grandstand. Like that, in the flash of one line drive, the Dodgers lost the pennant.

"There was a bench," Labine said, "where we sat in the bullpen. If you can find it, you'll see a chunk of wood is missing. That's where I took a bite. And Erskine. Carl said, 'Well, Clem, that's the first time I ever saw a big fat wallet flying into a grandstand.' That's what it was. Thousands lost."

"The baseball writers," I said, "made up a song for their dinner that winter:

> Turn back the hands of time.
> Where, oh where, is Clem Labine?
> Give me the lead that once was mine.
> Let's do it over again."

"I heard about that."

"You had that great attitude. The bigger the challenge, the more you wanted to take it on."

"I *said* I had that great attitude. But you don't think I wanted that spot, do you? Or that Ralph did? Or Carl? Nobody wants a spot like that. You get older and you can face those things. Come on. Your glass is empty. Peggy! Another round!"

Sunlight slanted into the room. The age lines around his mouth seemed softer; talking about younger days can do that to a man, make his face actually look youthful. "In World War II, I volunteered for the paratroops. Because I was a hero? Hell, because I was eighteen dumb years old. All this talk about guts. The first time I ever relieved for the Dodgers I got bombed. I mean I was awful. And Dick Young wrote, here was a new fireman, whose best weapon was gasoline. That's fine. I may not like being made a joke of, but he's got a right to comment any way he wants. But then there was one game in Philadelphia. I relieved with bases loaded. The hitter bounced the ball back to the box and I was going for two and I never did this, not even in high school, ever, except for this one time. Going for two, home to first, I threw the damn ball over Campy's head and all the way to the backstop. That got us beat. There was a little bar near the Warwick Hotel and that's where I went after that game. I was standing with Dick Williams, who was trying to cheer me up, when Young came over. He said, 'Clem, now don't feel bad. That was a mechanical error and I've seen the greatest and the greatest make mechanical errors.' I said thanks and bought him a drink and he asked me if I liked being a relief pitcher. I told him, hell, no, I wanted to be a starter. All right. I was dumb. I shot off my mouth.

"We got back to Brooklyn a few days later and the barber I used in Bay Ridge had a clipping to show me. It was a story by Young. He'd written that I lost in Philadelphia and I would always lose close games in relief because I wanted to start so badly. Subconsciously, or whatever, I was going to blow all the big ones in relief." Labine's right fist clenched. "Did Young have any right to do something like that?"

"Young had demons in him sometimes. Don't make me defend it."

"I've got no bitterness," Labine said, bitterly. "I'm here and he's still in New York with his column. I remember when the Mets dropped me. I deserved it. Still, it was the end. All Young could say, he'd known me thirteen years, was this. He said, 'That's the way it goes.' "

Golfers clattered in. Someone called a greeting. "Big man in Woonsocket, though," Labine said. "Woonsocket is Indian for Thunder-mist. This is a strict Catholic mill town, or was when I was a kid. There are a lot of Italians here and Poles and then

215

there are the French Canadians like me. My father was a weaver. I spoke nothing but French until I was seven years old. Then the kids I started running with were Italian and they made fun of me for being French and I didn't like that much, but I didn't much like being French either. That's what prejudice does. It makes you ashamed of yourself. I was raised a good Catholic like everyone else. Go to school, go to church. Work hard in the mill and when it's over you get a good spot in the Cimetière du Précieux Sang."

"But you were different," I said. "You could pitch."

"And play hockey," Labine said. "And halfback in football. But what does that mean? I had coordination and some strength. But I didn't understand *anything*. Then I came out of here into the Dodger organization, the best in baseball, and I'm playing in the minor leagues and at one club, I'll never forget, there was a girl who shacked up with everybody excepting this catcher who was dumpy and kind of ugly, like the girl. Do you know what happened? The catcher fell in love with her. All the other fellers on the team wanted to tell him that he had fallen for a nymphomaniac. But we couldn't tell him. He *loved* her. And they got married. We made a trip and the new bride threw a party for the other wives. Maybe six guys were married. She asked all the other women over, including the manager's wife, understand. And they all came and this nymph shows them in, and opens the dining room doors. Wham! Inside there are seven guys. The nymph has gotten all the other wives dates."

"What happened?"

"The catcher finished that year in another league."

We laughed, and then there was a pause.

"You look fine," I said. "And pretty damn young."

Labine motioned for another martini. You can drink for joy or for idleness or to get drunk, but sometimes there are other reasons. "You heard about Jay?" Labine said, suddenly.

"Who's Jay?"

"My son. Clement Walter Labine Junior. You think I look pretty damn young? You should have seen me a year ago. I looked much younger then, before Jay, that's my son, stepped on a mine in Vietnam and blew his leg off."

There is no dining room in the Woonsocket Motor Inn, which has large rooms and wooden-postered beds, a generally excellent motel. For breakfast you walk to the supermarket next door, where, at a small dining counter, fresh orange juice, two scrambled eggs, home-fried potatoes, toast and coffee cost eighty-four cents. Woonsocket has its own newspaper, the *Evening Call,* established in 1892, but at breakfast one depends on the larger Providence *Journal.*

I was to meet Labine at Sports Apparel, Inc., "that modern plant in Woonsocket," at eleven o'clock. There was time to read the *Journal* and to cruise. The Mets had won in New York City before a "roaring throng" of fifty thousand, more persons crowded into one ball park than lived in this entire city.

Woonsocket spreads from the Blackstone River, which flows southeast and long ago cut a narrow valley. Streets called Social and Main twist away from the river. Some still are cobblestoned.

The Sports Apparel factory, sprawling and red-brick, stands near the river on Singleton Street, with two other mills nearby. These are the kind of buildings that have been abandoned throughout New England, their old proprietors fled south where nonunionized whites and blacks hired out cheaply. But Woonsocket mills are still alive. Factory windows (Vachel Lindsay wrote) "are always broken, somebody's always playing tricks." As I pulled into the small crowded parking lot outside Sports Apparel, every window I could see was whole.

"Mr. Labine," I told the receptionist.

"Do you have an appointment?"

"Eleven o'clock."

217

Clem appeared a few minutes later. "You're all right?" he said. He was wearing another handsome sports ensemble. "I thought we'd have lunch with Elliott Finkelstein. Would you like to see the plant? My father worked like hell. This plant is where he was a weaver."

On the back wall of Labine's spare office, a map of the United States was divided into five sections. "The pins are my salesmen," he said. Labine handed me a copy of the gold and white *Deerfoot Sportswear Catalogue*. The first page proclaimed: "Managed and Directed by Clem Labine, Former Major Leaguer." Next to a picture in which Labine was wearing a Brooklyn cap and smiling, a caption added, "One of baseball's pitching greats. From 1950 to 1960 a star of the fabled Brooklyn Dodgers. Still a sports enthusiast and for many years an executive of Sports Apparel, Inc., Clem is now recognized as an expert in the styling of athletic apparel. Feel free to write to him at any time."

"Who writes you?" I said.

"Coaches. Athletic directors. We sell to teams from schools and colleges."

Sports clothing—golf jackets and team coats, and plaid shirts, jog suits, alpine coats and blankets—hung from pipes over an iron-grated floor. The colors were purple and navy and blue and white and green. "This is an assembly line," Labine said. "It looks confusing, but we have what we call speed-rail movement of the garments. Efficient and logical. We have quality-control check points along the way." He led me to a room where a man was cutting patterns in leather. "How are you, Jim?"

Labine's perfect grooming bounced against Jim's overalls. "Jim's trick," Labine said, "is to get as many pieces from a given piece of leather as possible."

"That's right," Jim said, "kind of a jigsaw puzzle. You want to use as much and waste as little as you can."

"Thank you, Jim."

The tour continued. We saw design rooms and lofts filled with flocking, nylon, Naugahyde and wool. Labine explained how materials were fed into the line and that the various processes in jacket manufacture were carried on by expert technicians.

"Hello, Marie," he said to a woman sewing linings.

"Hi, Mr. Labine."

"After you design the jacket and cut the basic patterns, then it's a repeat. But the physical work goes on—the sewing and the stitching and putting on designs, like a team symbol. On wool we attach designs; with nylon we supply silk-screen printing. I think," said Clem Labine, the smooth, assured executive, "that this is an impressive, modern plant."

Lunch took us fifteen miles toward the main line of the New Haven Railroad, and a restaurant a world away from pattern cutters and seamstresses. The 1776 house was all wood walls and copper ladles, like a number of warm colonial restaurants in the suburbs of New York. Elliott Finkelstein, Labine's boss and closest friend, turned out to have graduated from the City College of New York, in the 1930s, with plans to become a chemist. But to a City College Jew during the Depression, any job at all was a benediction. "So I came here," Elliott Finkelstein said. "Part of my family had started out here in the rag business. There's nothing glamorous about garment manufacture. And I stayed, and maybe my friendship with Clem is the finest thing that's happened since."

In my compound with Labine, dark, stocky, bright Elliott Finkelstein was an unexpected element: not an athlete, but a fan, growing older.

"Is the game what it was?" Finkelstein said. "It doesn't seem as exciting since Clem left. He was some pitcher."

"I hung some curves," Labine said. We were seated in a booth.

"You guys never knew what you had down in New York. You sportswriters were lucky to have a man like this to write about."

"We got along."

"Well, how does he seem to you now?" Finkelstein said.

I knew what he meant, without wanting to know, and I calculated an answer, unready to hear so soon again about the maimed boy. "Pretty good. Listening at the plant, Clem, I was thinking how different everything is with you now, even the language. Elliott, he could ream an umpire."

"Bad language is part of being a ball player," Labine said. "The animal is different on the field."

"He's very good at our business," Finkelstein said. "He isn't there because he was a pitcher. He knows style. He works with people. He's a fine executive, and listen, there's something about him you may have missed. Clem can't stand intolerance of any kind. He never laughs at racial stories.

"Woonsocket is a kind of cradle of ball players. Napoleon Lajoie, the old second baseman, and Gabby Hartnett, the old catcher, were born here. Three major leaguers from a city this size isn't bad. But Clem. You should have come up to see him before the tragedy."

"It is a tragic story," Labine said, "but there isn't anything tragic about my son, Jay."

"How do you feel about the Vietnam War?" I asked Labine.

"First I guess I was a hawk. Then I was a dove. Then Jay went over and I went superhawk. Atom-bomb those Northern bastards for my kid. Now that he's back and we're working things out, what do you think? I'm superdove."

"Where he belongs," Finkelstein said.

He was through at the factory by 4:30. "Let's see more of the town," he said. He drove the hardtop down Singleton, which runs beside the narrow Blackstone. "It flooded once," he said. "There's a casket factory a few miles upstream. I was in spring training and I picked up a paper and there was one headline I'll never forget: 'Coffins Floating in Woonsocket.'"

He turned down Social Street, then out a narrow road of frame houses. "Not much, I guess, compared to what you're used to." After a while, as the road bent, a great angel rose in stone, guarding an ornate cement archway. This was the Cimetière du Précieux Sang. Labine did not slow, but I could see monuments, high crosses, small angels, a prosperous imposing Catholic necropolis in this poor town.

"There are some Labines in there," he said, not looking. "Have you been up here before?"

"Never. I didn't know about the French colony."

"Most people don't."

"You get down to New York?"

"Once in a while. I liked Bay Ridge okay, although it was kind of suburban, not really New York. I'm only a small-town guy, I guess. They called me from some ad agency in New York to help make a commercial for Mayor Lindsay. He seems okay, am I right? I went. I didn't see much. In and out. But I remember that excitement of the city."

He pulled the hardtop down a street and parked. "The Woonsocket High School field," he said, pointing, "where I played football. I went to a skating rink in California once with a few ball players who knew I'd played high school hockey. Bam. If I fell once, I fell three times. And they looked at me like *Yup, you played hockey. Oh, sure.*" Boys were indolently kicking a football in front of us.

"Jay never cared for the sports I did," Labine said. "I'd take you over to see him, but there's a little tension now. I'm on him to finish accounting school and he says that I never got past high school myself.

"These days, I suppose I'd go to college. Then there were scholarship offers, but I was a weaver's son, offered a contract by the *Dodger* organization. It's hard for Jay to understand what that meant.

"We had fights. Clement Walter Labine Junior wanted to be

different from me and he is different from me and maybe I wanted him to be the same.

"We had lots of these fights and one day he said, 'Fuck you, Dad, I'm joining the Marines.' Whenever we used to have fights, three days later we'd make up. Now three days later he had enlisted." The deep voice choked. "He couldn't take that back.

"So Jay was gone and he went out on a patrol doing his job, he's a good boy, and stepped on the mine and we're lucky, he's lucky, he's alive. The Marines sent a car to our house. Barbara was away. I was out playing golf. My brother-in-law saw this Marine car and went over and said, 'Is this about Jay, Clem Labine, Jr.?' The Marine officer was very polite. He said who was he talking to and my brother-in-law said he was Jay's uncle and the Marine said that under the rules he couldn't say anything. Next of kin only. And my brother-in-law got excited and said couldn't he say one thing, couldn't he say if Jay was alive? The Marine looked at him and said, 'I can only speak to next of kin,' but the Marine nodded his head. So when they came and got me off the golf course, the first thing they said was, 'Jay's been hurt, but he's alive.'

"He wasn't much for baseball. But he liked to go over to Diamond Hill and ski. He got to be a fine skier. And he liked diving. Now he's learning over again, how to be a skier and a diver with one leg.

"He wrote me a letter from the hospital. It was so calm and matter-of-fact. It wasn't as if he was describing how his leg had been blown off. It was more like a letter from camp—he went to camp—that said, 'Dear Dad, I fell and cut my knee.'"

For the second time in my life, seventeen years after the 1953 World Series, I saw Clem Labine's eyes full of tears.

"If I hadn't been a ball player, I wouldn't have been away all the time. But the traveling cost me all of it, Jay growing up. If I hadn't been a ball player, I could have developed a real relationship with my son. The years, the headlines, the victories, they're not worth what they cost us. Jay's leg.

"Everything they told me in church and Sunday school I believed. God looks after you. God looks after me. God looks after Jay. He's a helluva kid, but I've learned something out of this myself. I think things through. I'm not swallowing the church line. God in His infinite wisdom. Heaven is waiting, just beyond Cimetière du Précieux Sang. Maybe. But now I'll have to see Him to believe it. Since this thing happened to Jay, I've become agnostic."

Labine looked at his watch. "Hey. I better get you to your car. It's a long way from here to New York, isn't it?"

A day later, I telephoned Marine headquarters in Manhattan and asked how badly a man had to be hurt in Indochina for his family to be notified personally instead of by wire.

A sergeant named Mike Burrows called back. "In this war," he said, as though reading, "next of kin are notified personally not only in the event of death but for any wound, however slight. We dispatch a telegram of confirmation, but an individual, frequently an officer, always precedes the telegram."

"The luxuries of a small war," I said.

"Did you have anyone particular in mind?"

"It's the son of a former Dodger pitcher, Clem Labine."

"Hey, I remember Clem. Good curve ball. How's he holding up?"

"He's all right. His boy has lost a leg."

"No," said Sergeant Mike Burrows of the Marines, no longer reading. "Isn't that a goddamn lousy war?"

THE BISHOP'S BROTHER

Pozehnaj nas pane a tento pokrym ktory budeme pozivat, aby sme sa zachovali v tvojej svatej sluzbe. Amen.

Bless us, Lord, and this food we are about to take that we may keep ourselves in Your holy service.

Slovakian mealtime prayer

George Thomas Shuba, the second ball player who ever pinch-hit a World Series home run, had been wholly different from Clem Labine. He was a blunt, stolid athlete, a physical man mixing warmth with suspicion, a bachelor living alone and apart from most of the other players. His abiding love was hitting. All the rest was work. But touching a bat, blunt George became "The Shotgun," spraying line drives with a swing so compact and so fluid that it appeared as natural as a smile.

"Not yet," he said early in 1952, when I suggested a Sunday feature on his batting.

"Why not?"

"I haven't got enough hits."

A month later he approached and said, "Now."

"Now what?"

"I've gotten enough hits. Write the feature." It sounded like an order, but after the story appeared George said thank you for several days.

Joining such disparate people as Labine and Shuba was baseball's persistent encouragement toward self-involvement. "What did *you* throw?" reporters asked. Or, "What did *you* hit?" "How is *your* arm, *your* knee?" And, *"You* pitched a nice game" or, *"You* really stroked that double." Even the converse from fans—*"You're* a bum, Clem; hey, George, *you're* bush"— focused a man's thinking on himself. During the prime of Clement Walter Labine and the boyhood of Clement Walter Labine, Jr., baseball was always pulling the father away on road trips and involving the father with his own right arm rather than with his son's cares. It is the nature of the baseball business, and Shuba, through an episodic eight-year career in the major leagues, had decided privately, with no hints at all, to wait for the end of his baseball life before marrying. Now he had written:

It will be a great pleasure to have you visit our home in Youngstown. The wife and children (3) are waiting to meet you. I'll make a reservation for you at Williams Motel. Leave the Ohio Turnpike at Exit Seven. I put the Postal Inspectors there. As you know, I work for the Post Office.

Went to the last two games of the 1967 World Series at Boston. Saw the 1969 All-Star game at Washington. Drive carefully. See you soon.

On a long day's journey from Manhattan to Youngstown, one follows the appalling new American way west. You escape New York through a reeking tunnel that leads to the New Jersey Turnpike, where refineries pipe stench and smoke into the yellow air above grassless flats. It is three hours to the hills along the Pennsylvania Pike and your first sense or hope that mankind will not choke to death in another fifteen years.

The country levels as Pennsylvania meets Ohio, and the first Midwestern flatlands open toward prairies. Youngstown, 170,-000 people strong, produces pig iron, steel, lamps and rubber, in a dozen factories along the Mahoning River, which bisects it.

The Williams Motel, on the southern outskirts, turned out to be a brick rectangle, open on one side and comfortable but not lavish. Unlike the nearby Voyager Inn, it offers neither sauna baths nor pool. "We have your reservation," a lady said behind the front desk, a strong-featured woman who wore glasses with colorless plastic rims. "Mr. Shuba made it for you. Are you with the Post Office?"

"No."

"I thought maybe you were with the Post Office. Mr. Shuba puts the postal inspectors here."

"I'm not a postal inspector."

"Twenty-six," she said, losing interest and handing me a key.

I telephoned the main Youngstown post office and George came on, the voice plain, pleasant and tinged with a heaviness from East Europe. I knew then that George's father had been an immigrant. One never thought much about such things when traveling with the team. Black and white, not Slovak or Italian, was the issue.

"Is your room all right?" Shuba said.

"Fine. What are you doing?"

"Just finishing up."

"I mean what do you do at the post office?"

"Clerk-typist," Shuba said. "I knew the room would be good. I put all the inspectors in the Williams Motel. I'll be by soon as I finish. We've got a dinner you'll like."

"I haven't eaten much Slovakian food."

"It's lasagna," George said, sounding very serious. "Didn't you know? I married an Italian girl."

Unpacking, I remembered George on the day he had joined a radio engineer and myself batting a softball in Forest Park, St. Louis, and how, taking turns pitching, we worried about upsetting George's timing. "Just throw," he said, "just throw." He pulled low liners one after another in the park and that night did the same against a Cardinal pitcher called Cloyd Boyer. And then a year later a certain quickness went from his bat, and he was not a fierce hitter, although still dangerous, and outside the Schenley Hotel I saw him carrying a lightweight portable typewriter.

"What's that for, George?"

"Oh," he said, and looked around, as though afraid to be overheard. He winked. He had a plan. "I'm not gonna be through at thirty-five, like some. Maybe I'll be a reporter. Some of those guys go on working till seventy. Look at Roscoe McGowen. So I'm teaching myself how to type."

"George," I wanted to say, "to write, you have to read and know the language and how to organize and, damnit, spell." Thinking that, I said, "Could be a pretty good idea."

At the door leading into Room 26 at the Williams Motel, Shotgun Shuba, now a 46-year-old male clerk-typist in the U. S. Post Office in Youngstown, Ohio, appeared heavier. The face, a study in angles, sloping brow, pointed nose, sharp chin, looked full. The middle was thick. But the sense was of solidity, rather than fat. I hadn't remembered him as so powerful. "You could still go nine," I said.

"Ah."

"Or pinch-hit."

"I got no time for that stuff. Come on. Dinner's waiting. We'll have some red wine. You like red wine? I'll drive."

In the car Shuba mentioned an old book I had written and a recent article. "About student rebels with long hair," he said, "or something like that."

"About the SDS coming apart in Chicago."

"Yeah. That was it. Why do you waste time writing about *them?*" There was no harshness in his voice. He simply did not understand why anyone who was a writer, a craft he respected, would spend time, thought and typing on the New Left.

"I try to write about a lot of things. It keeps you fresh."

George considered and turned into a street called Bent Willow Lane. "Kind of like exercising your mind, isn't it?" he said finally. "Yeah. That must be it. Move around. Do different things. Sure. Keeps up your enthusiasm." We had entered a middle-income neighborhood, of tract homes and roads that twisted, so drivers could not speed, and hyperfertilized lawns of brilliant, competitive green.

"I thought Youngstown had mills, George," I said.

"Over there," he said, indicating the northeast. "You won't see any mills around where *I* live." He pulled up to a gray split-level, saying "This is it," and parked in an attached garage. "I finished this garage myself. I'm a home guy now. Wait till you meet my wife. She's taking courses at Youngstown University."

As we walked into her kitchen, Katherine Shuba, nine years younger than George, said a warm hello and called Marlene, Mary Kay and Michael, nine to four, who greeted me solemnly over giggles. Mrs. Shuba turned off a large color television that dominated the living room and placed the children at a kitchen table. We sat promptly in the dinette. It was six o'clock. Old ball players pursue the pleasures of eating with lupine directness. Suddenly George bowed his head. Katherine clasped her hands. The children fell silent.

"Bless us, Lord," George said, beginning Grace. Then, in almost apologetic explanation he said, "My father said Grace in Slovakian every day of his life. He died when I was pretty young, but I've never forgotten it."

"Well, it's something to remember."

"Ah," George said and we proceeded with an excellent Italian dinner, lasagna and salad, lightened, as George had promised, with red wine.

"So you don't play any more or coach?"

"I watch the kids. Maybe umpire a little. I don't coach small kids. It doesn't make sense to. With small kids, up till about fifteen, let 'em have fun. You know what's damn dumb? A father getting on a small kid, telling him this or that, stuff he can't use much yet. All the father does is spoil the fun."

"Somebody must have coached you."

"It was a different time, and nobody coached me that much anyway. My father, from the old country, what could he teach me about baseball? What did he know?"

"Your swing was natural."

"I worked very hard at it," Shuba said.

Katherine guided the children back to the living room, which was carpeted and comfortably furnished, but showed no sign that Shuba had hit for pennant winners or even that he had played professionally. "Oh, I've got some equipment still," he said. "Maybe after we finish the wine, if you like, we can have a catch."

He fished a half dozen gloves from the trunk of a car and we walked to the back of the house. Shuba's home shares three acres of greensward with other houses, framing a common play area. "If my little guy wants," Shuba said, "he can do some hitting here."

The dusk light held as we started to throw. Shuba did not have an outstanding major league arm. Scouts described it as uncertain, or weak. Now he cocked that arm and fired easily. The ball shot at my Adam's apple and I knew, with a clutch of anxiety, that I was overmatched.

In *Gamesmanship*, Stephen Potter describes that clutch seizing you on a tennis court when an opponent's service turns out to be overwhelming and you return it forty feet beyond the base line. "Cry, 'Where was it?' " Potter recommends.

" 'Where was what?'

" 'My shot, of course.'

" 'Why, it was out. It went over the fence back there.'

" 'Very well. In the future please indicate clearly whether my shots are in or out.' "

The Shubas of Youngstown live removed from English drollery and there was nothing clever or sensible to call at George.

Weak or strong, he had a major league arm, and I knew what I would have to do, and hoped I could. Aim at face height and, while appearing to work easily, throw hard by snapping the forearm as I released the ball. That way there could be a rhythm to the catch, a kind of exchange. A good catch is made of sight, sensation, sound, all balancing from one side to the other. The ball is in white flight. Red stitches turning, it whacks a glove; it is back in flight and whacks the other mitt. You can tell quickly from the sound and the speed of the throws and even from the spin what is going on, who has the better arm.

George took my throw and returned it, again hard. My glove felt small. You try to catch a ball in the pocket, so that it strikes the leather at a point slightly lower than the webbing between the thumb and forefinger of the hand within the glove. There is control there without pain. Catch a baseball farther down and it stings. Catch it farther up and you lose control. When you catch a ball in the webbing, you may not realize that you have made a catch. Each point of impact creates a different sound: thin at the webbing, dull toward the heel, resonant and profoundly right in the pocket. Sound tells when you are playing catch, how the other man is grabbing them.

Shuba delivers a heavy ball; it smarts unless caught exactly right. Mostly he threw waist-high, moving the ball from one side to the other. I caught mindlessly, ignoring slight stinging to concentrate on my throws. They sailed true, but after ten minutes a twinge raked the inside of my right elbow. We caught in silence, communicating, as it were, with ball and glove. George was studying me and I could feel his eyes and it was a warm evening and I was wondering about my arm and beginning to sweat.

"You've got good body control," Shuba called.

"Hey. You've made my day."

Ebullient, I relaxed. As soon as the next throw left my hand, I knew it was bad. The ball sailed low, but fairly hard to Shuba's backhand. Nimbly, angrily, he charged, scooped the ball on a short hop and fired at my face. The throw thwacked the small glove, low in the pocket, burning my hand.

"What are you trying to do," Shuba said, "make me look bad?"

"No, George." Then very slowly: "That's the way I *throw.*"

"You're trying to make me look bad," Shuba said, pressing his lips and shaking his head.

"George, George. Believe me." All the years the other writers had made jokes—"Shuba fields with his bat"—had left scars. *They* should have played catch with him, I thought.

Half an hour of light remained. "Come on, George," I said. "Show me the old neighborhood."

"What for?"

"I want to see where you started playing ball."

"I don't know why you'd care about something like that," Shuba said, but led me back to the car.

Fernwood Street was where he lived when Bent Willow Road was part of a forgotten farmer's pasture. Wooden frame houses rise close to one another on Fernwood. Each one is painted white. "This neighborhood hasn't changed in forty years," Shuba said.

"Mostly Slovakians?"

"All Slovakians."

His father, John, or Jan, Shuba, left a farm in eastern Czechoslovakia during 1912 and settled in Youngstown, where other Slovak Catholics had come, and took a job in a mill. George does not know why his father left Europe, but the reason was probably economic. Before 1930 Slovakian emigration was coincident with crop failure. Since then it has been political, to escape Hitler or Soviet Communism. Slovakians have contending symbols. The *drotar* is an itinerant tinker, never anxious to settle down, unable to make use of the resources of the soil. A cry rang through old Slovakia: *"Drotar* is here; have you something to repair?" Slovakians say that *drotari* were the first to emigrate to America. After the long journey, nomadic longings spent, *drotari* settled into jobs in mines and mills. The old itinerants then built fixed, unchanging neighborhoods. The other symbol is based on the historic figure Janosik, who fled a Slovakian seminary in the seventeenth century. Slovakia still was feudal and any lord had power of life and death, but Janosik became a bandit, along the lines of Robin Hood. Caught at length, he was hanged. Disciples of Janosik were called *zbojnici*. When *zbojnici* and their idolators found the relative freedom of the United States, they turned against the romance of roguery and, like Shotgun Shuba, stood strong for law, obedience and the Church.

"We like to keep things the way they were," Shuba said. He parked on Fernwood, in a dead-end block. All the houses rose two stories. "Here's where I first played," he said. "In this street. Day after day. Three on a side, when I was little. That's good baseball, three on a side. Each kid gets a chance." Tall maples made borders at the sidewalks. "We played so hard, when we were kids, you'd have thought we were playing for money.

"It was a big family. My brother John is a steel worker in a mill. Ed is a photographer for the Youngstown *Vindicator*. You know about my brother Joe. He's doing very good in the Church as a monsignor, in Toronto, Canada. I'm proud of him. Counting the ones born in Czechoslovakia there were eleven of us. I was the last. Some died over there. I had one brother died here. He got the flu. They didn't have fancy medicines. My mother gave him a lot of soup. Soup was good for the flu, but that brother died."

We were walking down Fernwood toward ball fields. "This is Borts Park," Shuba said. "Mrs. Borts gave it to the city. When I got older, instead of playing in the street, I played in Borts Park. I was a second baseman."

"Your father must have been proud of you."

We continued under the tall maples. "You don't understand the way it was. My father was forty-five years old when I was born. He never saw me play. Old country people. What did they care for baseball? He thought I should go and work in the mills like him and I didn't want to. I wanted to play."

The nearest diamond at Borts Field was bare; patches of grass had been worn off. "Boy, did I play here," Shuba said. "I had that quick bat. One year there was a Dodger tryout. It was 1943. I was seventeen, not in the mills. I was working in a grocery store. And at the cemetery on Sundays I'd pack black earth to fill around the graves. They could plant flowers in it. I'd get ten cents a box for the black dirt.

"The Dodgers didn't come to sign me. They wanted a pitcher. Alex Maceyko. They had me playing third. I had the quick bat, but Wid Mathews, who Rickey liked, was the scout and he signed somebody, Alex I guess, who never did much, and I went home, and forgot about it. Then it was February. I remember all the snow. Somebody come to the house on Fernwood and said, 'George, my name is Harold Roettger. I'm with the Brooklyn Dodgers. I want to see you about a contract.'

"I let him in and we sat down and he said he was going to offer me a bonus of $150 to sign. But I'd only collect if I was good enough to stay in baseball through July 1. I thought, hell, wouldn't it be better, a big outfit like the Dodgers to give $150, no strings or nothing? But that was the offer and I took it."

Night had come. Borts Field was quiet. "Well, George," I said, "your mother must have been proud."

"Ah," Shuba said. "You know what she told me. 'Get a job in the mills like Papa. There's lots of better ball players than you up there.'"

The night was warm and very still. "All right. I'll drive you to another part of the neighborhood," George said. It was so dark that all I could see were house lights and a bar with argon and neon signs advertising beer. George angled the car toward a corner grocery. "Dolak's," he said. "Where I worked. I loaded potatoes, fifty pounds to the bag, down in the basement, and carried them up. Years in the minors, they didn't pay me much. I was a ball player, but I still had to come back winters and load bags of potatoes for Dolak."

The signs in the store window were hand-lettered. "SPE-CIAL," one read, "HALUSKI."

"Like ravioli," Shuba said. "I delivered for Dolak, too, while I was in the bush leagues. Three miles from here is the cemetery where I packed the black dirt. I worked here and I walked to the other work and in the cold it was a long way. A long way a long time ago."

When we returned to the split-level on Bent Willow, Katherine was studying a text on the psychology of preschool children. She is a full-faced woman and she looked up with tired eyes, but cheerful to see people, and closed the book.

"We're going downstairs to talk," George said.

"Can I bring you anything?"

"Bring the V.O."

George loped downstairs. The large cellar was partly finished. A table and two chairs stood in one corner. Files had been pressed against a wall nearby. Farther along the same wall old uniforms hung from a clothing rack. Across the room was a toilet, which George had not yet gotten around to enclosing. The floor was linoleum, patterned in green and white squares.

I walked to the rack; all the uniforms were Dodger blue and white. Across one shirt letters read "BEARS," for the Mobile farm team; across another "ROYALS," for Montreal. The old Brooklyn uniform bore a large blue Number 8 on the back.

"Let me show you some things." Shuba opened a file and took out scrapbooks. He turned the pages slowly without emotion.

"They started me at New Orleans, but I wasn't ready for that, and I came back to Olean and led the league in home runs that first year."

"So you kept the $150."

"Yeah, but they shoulda risked it."

Katherine came with the drinks. "Then to Mobile," George said, "and they moved me to the outfield. They were thinking of me for the major leagues and I didn't have, you know, that major league infielder's glove. But I knew about my bat and one day in Montreal a year or two later, the manager says to me in batting practice, where everyone was supposed to take four swings, 'Hey, Shuba. How come you're taking five?' I told him, 'Look, let somebody else shag flies. I'm a hitter.'"

I laughed, but George was serious. Nothing about hitting amused him. I told him Arthur Daley's story of a catcher chattering at Charlie Gehringer at bat. Finally Gehringer turned and said, "Shut up. I'm working."

"I'm in Mobile," Shuba said. "It's '47. I hit twenty-one homers. Knock in 110 runs. Next spring at Vero Rickey says, 'George, we're sending you back to Mobile. Fine power but not enough average. We can't promote you till you're a .300 hitter.' I shorten up. It's '48. I bat .389. The spring after that he sends me to Mobile *again*. 'Nice batting,' Rickey says, 'but your power fell off. We need someone who can hit them over that short right-field wall in Ebbets Field.'

"What could I say? As long as he could option me, you know, send me down but keep me Dodger property, Rickey would do that so's he could keep some other guy whose option ran out. Property, that's what we were. But how many guys you know ever hit .389 and never got promoted?"

"There's no justice in the baseball business, George," I said.

The high-cheeked, Slavonic face turned hard. "The Saints want justice," he said. "The rest of us want mercy."

"I thought you had some fun," I said.

"It wasn't fun. I was struggling so much I couldn't enjoy it. Snider, Pafko, Furillo, they weren't humpties. I was fighting to stay alive. To play with guys that good was humbling. And I was kidded a lot about my fielding. In 1953 I went out to left field in Yankee Stadium for the second game of the Series. They're bad shadows out there in the fall. You remember I took you out and walked you around to show you the shadows and the haze from cigarette smoke.

"I went out and in the first inning someone hit a line drive and I didn't see it good and kind of grabbed. The ball rolled up my arms, but I held on to it. With two out, somebody else hit a long one into left center and maybe I started a little late, but I just got a glove on it and held it. When I came back to the dugout, Bobby Morgan said, very loud, 'Hey. I think they're going for our weak spot.' "

I laughed again. "Hey," Shuba said. "That's not funny. What he should have said was 'Nice catch.'

"Now something *funny*, that came from an usher. I wasn't going good, and by this time all the bosses, O'Malley, Bavasi and Thompson, are Catholics, and my brother gets promoted to monsignor and word gets around. It's real early and I'm not hitting at all. Some usher hollers down, 'Hey, George. It's a good thing your brother's a bishop.' "

George smiled and sipped.

"When did it really end?" I said.

"All the time Rickey's keeping me in the minors doesn't do me any good and one year in Montreal I rip up my knee ligaments. That's where it started to end. When I made the club to stay in '52 that knee was gone already. It just kept getting worse and worse. Around 1955, I was only thirty-one, but the knee was so bad I couldn't do much. So I quit. That's all there was.

"I tried the sporting goods business. Up and down. So I went to work for the Post Office, steady and safe."

"Does all the excitement and the rest seem real to you now?"

"Oh, yeah. It's real." George was drumming his fingers on the wooden table.

"What do you think of it?"

"Doesn't mean much. When somebody would come up and

ask for an autograph, I'd say, 'Is this for a kid?' And if it was, I'd give it to him. But if he said no, if it was for a man, I'd say, 'Ah. Don't be foolish. What does a grown man want something like that for?' I had my laughs. One day against the Cubs, Hank Sauer was on first and Ralph Kiner was on third and neither one could run. I hollered, 'Look for the double steal.' But what does it mean? Ruth died. Gehrig died."

The glasses were empty. He called and Katherine came downstairs and looked hopefully at George, wanting to be invited into the conversation, but Shuba has a European sense of a woman's place. "Why don't you come upstairs and sit with me?" she said.

"Because we're talking," Shuba said. "Men's talk."

"There was this time," he said after fresh drinks had come, "in the World Series when I pinch-hit the home run."

"Sure—1953. Off Allie Reynolds."

"That's not what I'm talking about," Shuba said. "It was the first game of that Series and Reynolds was fast and the fellers were having trouble seeing the ball and he's got a shutout. I come up in the fifth and he throws that first pitch. I never saw it. It was a strike. If it had been inside, it would have killed me. Reynolds was in sun and I was in shadow. I never saw the ball. The next pitch he curved me. I only saw a little better. I was swinging, but I went down on one knee." Shuba was a formful batter, always in control; slipping to a knee was as humiliating as falling flat. "Now the next pitch. I still wasn't seeing the ball good, but I took my swing. My good swing. I hit it and it went to right field and I knew it would be long but maybe the right fielder could jump and as I trotted to first base I was saying, 'Hail Mary, get it up higher. Hail Mary.'

"Only the second time in history anybody pinch-hit a home run in the World Series," Shuba said, his face aglow. "But it wasn't me. There was something else guiding the bat. I couldn't see the ball, and you can think what you want, but another hand was guiding my bat."

"I don't know, George. Birdie Tebbetts was catching once when a batter crossed himself. Birdie called time, and crossed *himself*. And he told the hitter, 'Now it's all even with God. Let's see who's the better man.'"

"I don't care what Tebbetts did. Another hand was guiding my bat."

"Do you remember Ebbets Field, George? Now, if you close your eyes, can you see it?"

"Ah. That don't mean nothing."

"What means something?"

"The Church."

"I mean in this life."

He sprang up, reaching into a top drawer in the nearest file. "Marks in school," he said. "Look at Marlene's." He put one of the girl's report cards in front of me, then opened a notebook in which he had recorded her marks from term to term. "She had some trouble with arithmetic here in the second grade, but my wife talked to the Sister and worked with Marlene at home. Then Mary Kay . . ." He talked for another ten minutes about the way his children fared in school and how he, and his wife, kept notebook entries of their progress. He was still talking about the children when Katherine came downstairs again and without being asked refilled our glasses. "All that baseball was a preparation," Shuba said. "You have certain phases in your life. Baseball prepared me for this. Raising my family."

"Which is more important?"

"This is the real part of my life."

"So all the rest was nothing?"

"Not nothing. Just not important. You do something important. Write. But playing ball." He jerked his head and looked at the beams in the cellar ceiling. "What the hell is that?"

"You might not understand this, or believe me, but I would

have given anything to have had your natural swing."

"You could have," George said.

"What?" I said. "What do you mean I could have?" And I saw, again, George standing in to hit as I first saw him, in 1948, when I was twenty and a copyboy and he was twenty-four and trying to become a major leaguer. It was a very clear, bright picture in my mind, and I could not see the pitcher or the crowd or even whether it was day or night. But I still saw Shuba. It was late in the year, when they bring up the good youngsters for a few games. He balanced on the balls of the feet as he waited for the pitch, holding the bat far back, and there was confidence and, more than that, a beauty to his stance. My father said, "What's this Shuba's first name? Franz?" But I was trying to understand how one could stand that beautifully against a pitcher and I did not answer and Shuba hit a long drive to right center field on a rising line. At a point 390 feet from home plate the ball struck the wire screen above the fence. It was still moving fast, thirty feet up. "Pretty good shot for Franz," I said, but now my father, impressed, had fallen serious.

In the basement, Shuba said, "What did you swing?"

"Thirty-one, thirty-two ounces. Depends on the speed and the shape I was in."

"Here's what you do," Shuba said. "Bore a hole in the top of the bat. Pour lead in it. Ten ounces. Now you got a bat forty-one or forty-two ounces. That's what you want, to practice swinging. Builds up your shoulders and your chest and upper arms."

"I couldn't swing a bat that heavy." I sipped the V.O. The cellar had become uncomfortably hot.

George was standing. "You take a ball of string and you make knots in it," he said. "You make a lot of knots and it hangs in a clump." He walked from the table and reached up toward a beam. A string coiled down and suspended, the base multiknotted into a clump. It was waist-high. "That's the ball," George said. His eyes were shining.

A large-thewed arm reached toward a beam. "I got some bats up here." He chose two signed "George 'Shotgun' Shuba." Both had been drilled and filled with lead. He set his feet, balancing as he had when my father joked about Franz Shuba, and he looked at the clumped string and I rose and drew closer, and he swung the bat. It was the old swing yet, right before me in a cellar. He was heavier, to be sure, but still the swing was beautiful, and grunting softly he whipped the bat into the clumped string. Level and swift, the bat parted the air and made a whining sound. Again Shuba swung and again, controlled and terribly hard. It was the hardest swing I ever saw that close.

Sweat burst upon his neck. "Now you," he said, and handed me the bat.

"I've been drinking."

"Come on. Let me see you swing," he said. Cords stood out in Shuba's throat.

I set my feet on green and white linoleum. My palms were wet. "Okay, but I've been drinking, I'm telling you."

"Just swing," Shuba ordered.

I knew as I began. The bat felt odd. It slipped in my hands. My swing was stiff.

"Wrist," George commanded. "Wrist."

I swung again.

"You broke your wrists here." He indicated a point two-thirds through the arc of the swing. "Break 'em here." He held his hand at the center. I swung again. "Better," he said. "Now here." I swung, snapping my wrists almost at the start of the swing. "All right," he said, moving his hand still farther. "Snap 'em here. Snap 'em first thing you do. Think fast ball. Snap those wrists. The fast ball's by you. Come on, snap. That's it. Wrists. Swing flat. You're catching on."

"It's hot as hell, George."

"You're doing all right," he said.

"But you're a natural."

"Ah," Shuba said. "You talk like a sportswriter." He went to the file and pulled out a chart, marked with Xs. "In the winters," he said, "for fifteen years after loading potatoes or anything else, even when I was in the majors, I'd swing at the clump six hundred times. Every night, and after sixty I'd make an X. Ten Xs and I had my six hundred swings. Then I could go to bed.

"You call that natural? I swung a 44-ounce bat 600 times a night, 4,200 times a week, 47,200 swings every winter. Wrists. The fast ball's by you. You gotta wrist it out. Forty-seven thousand two hundred times."

"I wish I'd known this years ago," I said. George's face looked very open. "It would have helped my own hitting."

"Aah," Shuba said, in the stuffy cellar. "Don't let yourself think like that. The fast ball is by the both of us. Leave it to the younger guys."

5

CARL AND JIMMY

> Congenital malformation . . . in which the child has slanting eyes
> . . . a large tongue and a broad, short skull. Such children are often
> imbeciles.
>
> Mongolism, as defined by Webster

In the comedian's story, Carl Erskine has been having difficulties throwing strikes. Someone scratches a single. Two men walk. Now with nobody out and bases loaded, that paradigm of constancy, the archetypal Dodger fan, rises in Ebbets Field. "Come on, Oiskine," he bellows. "These guys stink."

A curve breaks low.

"Don't worry," the fan shouts. "I'm witcha."

A curve is wide.

"Hang in there," calls the fan. "You can do it, Oisk."

A fast ball sails high. Ball three.

"Go get 'em," the fan shouts. "We love ya, Oisk, baby."

A final fast ball is inside. The batter walks, forcing in a run. "Hey, Dressen," screams the constant fan, "take that bum out."

I had all but forgotten the story, a specialty of a comic named Phil Foster, until Erskine, replying to a letter, signed himself "Oisk." He lives where he was born, in Anderson, Indiana, amid oaks, sycamores, Hoosiers and memories that resound in Brook-lynese.

When I last saw Erskine, he had shouted from a taxicab near Madison Avenue and Fiftieth Street in Manhattan. That is an epicenter of the advertising world and finding Erskine there was like encountering a poet in a television studio. Not impossi-ble but incongruous. "What are you doing here?" I demanded, climbing into the cab.

"It's complicated," he said. A shirt manufacturer had asked him to take executive training and then direct a band of retired athletes selling sportswear. "How much is a house in Westches-ter?" he said.

"Better figure thirty-five thousand, and up," I said. It was 1960.

He winced. He had lost some hair. "That's what other people told me."

"How do you feel about leaving Indiana?"

"Mixed. This is challenging."

"How are the children?" I said.

"Fine. There are three now. And Betty's expecting again."

The cab stopped in traffic. I had somewhere to get to. I scrib-bled my number. "It'll be great having you back."

"I'll really call you," Erskine said, but never did.

Later Ralph Branca explained that the Erskines' fourth child had been born mongoloid. "A lot of people thought he ought to be put in an institution," Branca said, his dachshund face more sorrowful than usual. "But Carl and Betty wanted to bring it up themselves. So they took off. They're gone." Erskine had stopped house-hunting in Westchester. He had quit his position with the shirt manufacturer. He had brought Betty and all the children back to Anderson. There he felt native and believed he stood a chance to make Jimmy Erskine as fully human as a mongoloid can become.

Near Toledo, I left the Turnpike for Highway 24, which fol-

243

lows the Maumee River southwest through Ohio towns called Texas and Napoleon and Antwerp. It is a pretty road winding into back country. When you have driven turnpikes too long, you develop a variety of fears. What would happen if, at seventy-five miles an hour, a tire exploded; or if the trailer ahead should lose a wheel; or if suddenly you sneezed with blinding violence? These are, of course, distant possibilities, but the fear is immediate. It is as if the human organism, controlling a vehicle for hour upon hour at the speed of a cheetah in full spring, asserts a protest by exaggerating dangers. Turning onto a country road, and having to cut the speed in half, one is flooded with relief. The road is respite.

"If you want to git to Interstate 69," a boy said in a gas station at Milan Center, Indiana, "jes' keep goin'."

"That the way to Anderson?"

"Where's Anderson?" To the boy at the pump, Milan Center and the village of Leo, sixteen miles north, were the world.

IS 69 leads down from Huntington County into Grant and on to Madison, through farmland mixed with stands of wood: thick oak, luxuriant maple, hickory, birch, ash, beech. Indiana trees are a deep-rooted, towering breed. The state was forest before man assaulted it with axes and with plows.

Anderson, Madison County seat, is an expanding industrial community, 69,923 strong according to the 1970 Census, up 42.5 percent since 1960 and, some demographers predict, the heart of a one-million-population area when A.D. 2,000 arrives. The city begins four miles west of IS 69, and as I turned, the sky glowed orange. It had been a long day's journey and, remembering the Shubas' V.O., and the Erskines' earnest baptism, I stopped on Arrow Avenue, and bought a bottle of Scotch from a back shelf. Anderson is a blue-collar town; men there drink blended whisky and Canadian.

The Erskines live on West Tenth in a two-story red-brick building with a modest front yard like ten thousand private homes in Flatbush. "Well, it's about time. We're getting hungry." At the doorway, Carl, who was forty-three, looked grayer than I had anticipated. His features were sharp. But the body still held trim. It surprised me when he walked to see him limp.

"You look well." Betty Erskine, a round-faced comfortable woman, appeared not to have changed at all. She smiled and we sat for a moment in their living room, spacious, nicely furnished and carpeted. On a spinet, against one white wall, a music book stood open to Chopin. Susan Erskine, blonde and fifteen, was studying piano. Looking at Susan, you knew, without asking, that she was a cheerleader for Anderson High. "And Gary," Betty said, "our second son, is finishing college at Texas. The Dodgers have already drafted him. Danny is rugged, and he plays football for DePauw at Greencastle. And this is Jimmy."

Jimmy Erskine, nine, came forward at Betty's tug. He had the flat features and pinched nostrils of mongolism.

"Say, 'Hello, Roger,' " Betty said.

Jimmy shook his head and sniffed.

"Come on," Carl said.

"Hosh-uh," Jimmy said. "Hosh-uh. Hosh-uh."

"He's proud," Carl said, beaming. "He's been practicing to say your name all week, and he's proud as he can be." The father's strong right hand found Jimmy's neck. He hugged the little boy against his hip.

The Erskines' den extends square and compact from the living room. The walls are busy with plaques and books. "Would you like to drink the present you brought?" Carl asked. It was after dinner. He went to a cabinet under a bookcase and produced three scrapbooks, bound in brown tooled leather. "Some old fellow kept these. We didn't know anything about them until I came back here to live.

"I was looking beyond baseball, beyond a lot of things and I enrolled in Anderson College as a thirty-two-year-old freshman." Erskine tells stories with a sense of detail. "All right," he said. "Monday morning. Eight-o'clock class. The start of freshman English. I get to the building. I got these gray hairs. It's two minutes to eight when I walk in, a little scared. All of a sudden the room gets quiet." Erskine grinned. "They thought I was the professor.

"I got in about sixty-five credits before Dad died and for a lot of reasons I had to quit. Heck, I wasn't only a thirty-two-year-old freshman. I became a thirty-six-year-old dropout."

Betty went for a Coke and a drink, and the ceremony of scrapbooks began. "Here's one of yours," Erskine said. "How does it read?" He had opened to the World Series strikeout story:

A crowd of 35,270 fans, largest ever to squeeze and elbow its way into Ebbets Field for a series contest, came to see a game the Dodgers had to win. They saw much more. They saw a game of tension, inescapable and mounting tension, a game that offered one climax after another, each more grinding than the one before, a game that will be remembered with the finest.

"John Mize," Erskine said, "was some hitter. But he had a pretty good mouth, too. All afternoon I could hear him yelling at the Yankee hitters. 'What are you doing, being suckers for a miserable bush curve?' Then he's pinch-hitting in the ninth and I get two strikes. Wham. John Mize's becomes the strikeout that breaks the record."

"On a miserable bush curve?"

"A sweet out."

"Here's the Scotch," Betty said. "And a Coke for you, Carl."

"But I wasn't out of it," Erskine said. He was sitting forward on a plush chair, his face furrowed with thought. "After Mize, I had to pitch to Irv Noren. I walked him. All right. Now here comes Joe Collins. I forget the record. All I can think is that the right-field wall is 297 feet away and Collins is a strong left-

handed hitter who has struck out four times. Baseball is that
way. One swing of the bat. He hits the homer. He scores two
runs. He goes from goat to hero. He wins it all. Collins had the
power and I'm thinking, 'Oh brother, he can turn this whole
thing around for himself.'

"That's in my head. What I didn't know is over on the Yankee
bench Mize and the others have been kidding Collins. They tell
him the World Series goat record is five strikeouts. One more
and his name goes into the book forever.

"He goes to the plate entirely defensive. He's choking up six
inches on bat. He's using it like a fly swatter.

"I get two strikes on him real fast. Still, I have this fear of the
short porch in right. The last.pitch I throw is a curve and it's a
dandy. It snaps off and it's about ankle-high. So help me, he
swings straight down. He beats it into the ground and gets
enough of the ball to nub it back to me. I get my record. Think
of the two minds. It ends with me scared to death of the long
ball and Collins scared to death of striking out. He doesn't get
to hit the long ball and I don't get to strike him out." Erskine
grinned and refilled our glasses.

"A great thing about our family comes ten years later. It's
1963. Sandy Koufax goes out and strikes out fifteen Yankees.
We're living here then, but we see it on television. And one of
the boys, looking real blue, says, 'Don't feel sad, Dad. You still
hold the record for *righthanders.*'

"All of the kids give pleasure, in different ways, the older
boys, Susan, Jimmy. It's hard for some to understand that Jimmy
is fun. Heck, we had an Olympics for all the retarded kids of
Madison County and Jimmy won a big event."

"What event was that, Carl?"

"Ball bounce. He bounced a basketball twenty-one times."

Erskine sipped at his Coke. "You wonder, of course. You look
for guilt. When was he conceived? Was somebody overtired?
Did you really want him? A few months along in pregnancy

Betty got a virus and ran 103. Did that affect Jim? Whose fault is it? We've talked to scientists and doctors and you know what mongolism is? A kind of genetic accident. There's an extra chromosome there that can come from mother or father and no one has any idea why, except that illness or being tired doesn't seem to have anything to do with it. You establish that, a man and his wife, and go on from there. You're not alone. Jimmy isn't alone. There are three thousand retarded children just here in Madison County, and when we came back to live here, there wasn't any place for them. I'm on a committee. We've set up schools. We're making beginnings."

Easy in his den, sitting against his louvered bookcases, the son of the Middle Border let his mind range. "The Erskines are Scots. It would have been my great-great-great-grandfather who settled in Virginia, and then moved on to Boone County, Indiana. That's sixty miles west. I remembered my Scottish background once in the Ebbets Field clubhouse when a lady wrote me a letter. She lived in Scotland and had seen my picture in a magazine. I must be Scottish and a relative of hers. I looked just like her Uncle Willie."

"Willie Erskine?"

"Or something."

"How do Presbyterian Scots become Indiana Baptists?"

"Easy. The Baptists take anybody."

He got up and brought in a dish of nuts and picked up his story. "When my father was very small—Dad, if he were living, would be eighty-six years old—near the end of the nineteenth century, the Erskines left Boone County and moved here. Anderson was a center of glass-blowing, and there was a natural-gas industry. My family had swampy farmland in Boone County they'd gotten for twenty-five cents an acre. Now it's been drained, and it's really valuable. But there are Scots and there are Scots. My family sold the land for twenty-six cents an acre, or maybe twenty-four.

"The auto industry came to Anderson long ago and General Motors tied in with an electrical company called Remy Brothers. And that was Delco Remy, spark plugs and electrical systems. There are seventeen local plants. There's no one who's been here any time who hasn't worked part of his life—a year, a month, a week—for Delco Remy.

"My Dad was real interested in baseball, and I guess I had the most promise of his three boys. At night at the side of the house, there'd be four or five congregated for catch. It got to be quite a thing for these older people to play burnout with me. You know. Step closer and closer, keep throwing harder and harder. I'd hang in and end up with a bruised hand. At nine, I was pitching from sixty feet.

"It was Dad who showed me a curve. First he taught what *he* had: the old barnyard roundhouse. You threw it sidearm and it broke flat. No break at all, except sideways. When I was eleven, Dad bought a book on pitching. We're in the living room. Dad has the pitching book in his left hand, held open with a thumb and he has a baseball in his right hand. He's reading, and very engrossed. The arm is carried back. The wrist is cocked. At this position you come forward with a snap and a spin of the fingers. He goes through the motion, staring at the book. He releases the baseball. The ball goes through the doorway to the dining room and into a big china cupboard with a glass front. It breaks the glass. It breaks the dishes. We stand there. Dishes keep falling out. My mother comes in." Erskine's eyebrows rose in merriment. "Maybe a year afterward my father said that was the best break he ever got on a curve."

It was the sort of boyhood Booth Tarkington memorialized with a romantic *Saturday Evening Post* glow, but Erskine is an existential man. "I guess there wasn't any money," he said. "I needed a mastoid operation and for a long time I'd keep bringing laundry to the doctor's house. My mother was paying the surgeon by taking in his wash.

249

"Around 1930 there was a lynching thirty miles north in a town called Marion. The day after it happened, Dad drove me up and showed me where it was. Two Negroes had been taken out of the jail and hung in the jailyard. The bark was skinned off the tree where they were hung. I can still see that naked branch. There had been a scramble. People had made off with things as souvenirs. But there was a piece of rope. I saw a lynching rope before I was ten." His soft voice carried controlled horror.

"One Negro boy grew up in my neighborhood, Johnny Wilson. We played grade school basketball together; he made all-state in high school and went on to the Globetrotters. He's a high school coach today. Jumpin' Johnny Wilson ate maybe as many meals at my home as he did in his own. With a background like that, the Robinson experience simply was no problem. It was really beautiful in a way.

"Somewhere Jack said he appreciated help from some white teammates in establishing himself, but to me it goes the opposite. It's 1948. The Dodgers want me from Fort Worth. I'm twenty-one and scared. I don't know anybody on the big club. I cut their names from the newspapers when I was a kid. The team is in Pittsburgh. I walk into the Forbes Field dressing room carrying my duffel bag. Just inside the door Jackie Robinson comes over, sticks out his hand and says, 'After I hit against you in spring training, I knew you'd be up here. I didn't know when, but I knew it would happen. Welcome.' "

Erskine's face lit. "Man," he said, "I'd have been grateful if anyone had said 'Hello.' And to get this not from just *any* ball player but from Jackie Robinson. I pitched that day and won in relief.

"Whenever Jack came to the mound, he always gave me the feeling he knew I could do the job. He just wanted to reassure me. Whatever words he used, the effect was: *There's no question about it. We know you can do it. Here's the ball. Get it done.* Times when I wasn't sure I could do it myself, he seemed to be.

"Now here's what bothers me. He wins a game. We go to the next town. We're all on the train, a team. But leaving the station, he doesn't ride on the team bus. He has to go off by himself. He can't stay in the same hotel. But I didn't do anything about it. Why? Why didn't I say, 'Something's wrong here. I'm not going to let this happen. Wherever he's going, I'm going with him.'

"I never did. I sat like everybody else, and I thought, 'Good. He's getting a chance to play major league ball. Isn't that great?' And that's as far as I was at that time.

"Now I hear people putting him down. Black people. To Stokely Carmichael and Rap Brown, he's a period piece. When I hear that, I feel sorry for *them*. Carmichael and Brown can never understand what Robinson did. How hard it was. What a great victory.

"But he can understand them. He was a young black man once, and mad and hurt. He knows *their* feeling, and their ignorance must hurt him more."

In the little Indiana den, it is the old story of the father and the son, a startling sunburst over autumn haze, expressed by a father whose own son is robbed of expression.

Anderson, Indiana, site of the annual Church of God Camp Meeting, thirty thousand strong gathered within and about Anderson College's Styrofoam-domed amphitheater, dubbed "The Turtle" by undergraduates, is a community that takes pride in its parks. "There are thirty-eight in all," said Carl Erskine, the morning go-getter. He had risen early, driven Jimmy to school at the Methodist church on Jackson Street, phoned the insurance brokerage in which he is a partner and stopped off at the First National Bank of Anderson, of which he is vice president.

"I thought I'd show you a little of the town," he said at 10:30. "Then we can pick up Jimmy after class and the three of us can go to the Y." We crossed Dwight D. Eisenhower Memorial Bridge, fording the White River, and leading downtown. The old masonry structures of Anderson are yielding prominence. "That new one with the glass front is the bank. Next to it is the San Francisco Restaurant. This isn't San Francisco, or New York, but it isn't all that sleepy either. Now we'll head out toward the college."

A large library, donated by Charles E. Wilson of General Motors, stands near the Turtle. "I do a little radio sports show from here once a week, and I coach baseball," Erskine said.

"How do you move around?"

"You mean the limp? It's more embarrassing than anything else. When I was through with ball, I began to develop pains in my left hip, the hip you land on when you throw righthanded. The pains got worse and worse. My arm hurt every day for ten years, but *this* was agony. Finally I went to a local man and he said I'd damaged a bone in the socket and the thing to do was to ease up. No running. No handball. I love handball. All right, I'm thirty-nine years and through, because the kicker is that he tells me if I do ease up, I only put off the wheelchair a few years. Whatever, a wheelchair is just ahead.

"When I was pitching and I had the constant arm pain, I went to Johns Hopkins and a famous surgeon said something was gone for good and I should pitch sidearm. But the only way I could get velocity and a good break was to come straight over. Saying pitch sidearm was really telling me don't pitch. I kept pitching overhand and it kept hurting, but I got a dozen years in the big leagues.

"This wasn't pitching. This was walking. I flew to the Mayo Clinic, and one of the surgeons there had worked out a procedure for rotating the bone in the hip socket. He said I could keep the pain and look all right. Or he could operate and stop the pain and leave me a limp." Erskine smiled as an irony stirred. "All the time I had bad pain, nobody knew. Now that I have the limp people keep coming up and asking if my leg hurts. With that limp they figure it must hurt bad and"—a thin, swift smile—"it's painless."

As we reached the Jackson Street Methodist church, boys and girls straggled out a doorway. The class for retarded children was letting out. One boy's head shook from side to side, flapping straight straw hair. A girl of eleven squinted through thick glasses. Someone was snorting. Jimmy Erskine saw his father and broke from the flagstone walk.

"Hello, Jim. Want to go swimming? Want to swim?"

"Ihmin," Jimmy Erskine said. "Ihmin." He jumped up and down with excitement.

A few blocks off, at the YMCA, Erskine put on gym clothes and dressed Jimmy. Carl and I shot baskets for twenty minutes. Erskine took one-hand set shots, as Indiana schoolboys did in 1945. Jimmy found a ball and bounced it. He bounced it three times, four times, five times. When he bounced it longer, he shouted with joy. Carl played a round of handball, his limp suddenly more noticeable. Jimmy sat next to me watching. "Hosh-uh," he said, and climbed into my lap. "Ihmin, Hosh-uh. Ihmin."

There were only three of us in the Y pool, warm, green and redolent of chlorine. Carl swam with a smooth crawl. Jimmy splashed about, making little cries. "Swim, Jimmy," Carl said. "Show how you can swim."

Jim fell onto his stomach, thrashed his arms and floated for three strokes. Then he jerked over to his back and showed a wide grin.

"Attaboy, Jim."

"Hosh-uh," Jimmy said.

"Watch him jump in," Carl said. "Jump, Jim. Show us how you can jump into the water."

The little boy hurried to a ladder. His foot slipped at the lowest rung. Carl put a strong hand to Jim's right buttock and pushed. Jim stood by the side of the pool, took two deep breaths and jumped into a kind of dive. He struck the water hard, chest first.

"Good goin', Jim," Carl said.

Another grin split Jimmy Erskine's face. Praise delights him. He waded toward the ladder and, climbing for a second time, held a support with his left hand. Then to show his father that he knew how to learn, he placed his right hand on his own buttock. What Jimmy Erskine had learned, from his father's boost, was that one leaves a pool with a hand placed on a buttock.

After leisurely dinner at the San Francisco Restaurant, Carl asked, back in his small, warm den, if I remembered the World Series of 1952. The sun of October flooded my memory and I saw again the blue crystal sky and the three-colored playing field and shrill, excited people thronging to Yankee Stadium, and my father's walk, lurching with expectancy.

"I had first-class stuff," Erskine said. "Not much pain. The curve is sharp. We go into the fifth inning ahead four runs. Do you happen to remember the date? It was October 5. That was my fifth wedding anniversary. My control slips. A walk. Some hits. Mize rips one. I'm behind, 5 to 4. And here comes Dressen.

"I'm thinking, 'Oh, no. I got good stuff.' I look at Dressen coming closer and I think. The numbers are against me. October fifth. My *fifth* wedding anniversary. The *fifth* inning. I've given the Yankees *five* runs. Five must be my unlucky number.

"Charlie says to give him the ball. You weren't allowed to talk when he came out. He was afraid you might argue him into leaving you in, and you had to wait on the mound for the next pitcher, so's you could wish him good luck. Now Charlie has the ball. I'm through. The fives have done me in. Suddenly Dressen says, 'Isn't this your anniversary? Are you gonna take Betty out and celebrate tonight?'

"I can't believe it. There's seventy thousand people watching, as many as in all Anderson now, and he's asking what I'm doing that night. I tell him yes, I was planning to take Betty someplace quiet.

" 'Well,' Dressen says, 'then see if you can get this game over before it gets dark.' He hands me back the ball. I get the next nineteen in a row. We win in eleven. I took Betty out to dinner and we celebrated the first Series game I ever won."

"What do you think," I said, "your life would have been if you hadn't been a pitcher?"

"I don't know. It's like asking what my life would be without Jimmy. Poorer. Different. Who knows how?"

"But you always knew you wanted to play ball."

"Except I never recognized myself as having extraordinary ability. Now we did have a coach at high school, Charles Cummings, who made sure we played with a National League baseball. During World War II those balls were hard to come by, but Mr. Cummings saw something and he made a terrific effort to see that I pitched with a ball that later, someday, maybe, if I was lucky, I'd make a living with.

"The nearest Dodger scout was Stanley Feezle, who had a sporting goods business in Indianapolis. He'd come around from time to time and look at my glove. 'Hey, that's a little tacky,' he'd say, and hand me a new one. I wasn't signing anything, but soon enough I wanted to play for the Dodgers.

"In service the Navy stationed me in Boston. I worked out with the Braves, and Billy Southworth, their manager, said I reminded him of Johnny Beazley, and if I signed with Boston, I'd be in the majors inside two years. Organized baseball had a rule against signing servicemen. Remember that. It'll be important.

"I'm nineteen and up in the Braves office and John Quinn, the general manager, is pressing me to sign, but I'm thinking I want to be a *Dodger*.

"I tell him I can't sign because I'm a minor. He says that's all right. The All-Star Game is going to be played right here in Boston, in a week. He'll arrange for my parents to be his guests at the game, send them Pullman tickets and everything, then I can sign with my dad.

"I get out of there and call Stan Feezle. Nothing is changed, he says. My dad and mom *are* going to the All-Star Game, but not as guests of the Braves. They'll be guests of the Dodgers.

"A week later, my mother, my father and I sit in a big parlor in a suite of the Hotel Kenmore. And who's with us, puffing a cigar? Branch Rickey."

In the den in Anderson, graying Carl Erskine fires the Kenmore scene to life. Rickey, bushy-browed, prolix, grandiloquent, leaned back in his chair and told the Indiana Erskines about his own farm boyhood in "Oh-hi-yuh." The father and mother were overwhelmed. Carl, in Navy bell-bottoms, felt proud and nervous.

"I understand," Rickey said, "that the Boston club is after you, young man." Rickey puffed, allowing suspense to gather. "I don't know what they've offered and I don't really care. The Boston club has never been able to sign someone *we* wanted. And I want you, young man. Just how much should you get to sign with Brooklyn?"

The parents were speechless. "Well," Erskine said, "Boston has offered twenty-five hundred. Would three thousand be all right?"

Rickey waited. Six eyes sought him. "Carl," he said, "we won't give you three thousand." Pause. "We're going to give you a bonus of three thousand, five hundred. What do you think of that?"

Erskine thought that Branch Rickey was even a bigger man than he had heard.

Erskine pitched nine games for Danville in the Three-Eye League, named from the states through which it spread: Illinois, Iowa, Indiana. He struck out fifty-two men in fifty innings—one strikeout an inning is a remarkable pace—and returned cheerfully to Anderson, where he was startled to find himself declared a free agent. Someone—Erskine suspects a Boston official—reported to Albert Benjamin "Happy" Chandler, the Commissioner of Baseball, that Rickey had signed a serviceman, and Chandler invalidated the contract. Rickey protested, and then asked if the ruling meant that he could get back the $3,500 bonus from the Erskines. (He could not.)

Four other teams sought Erskine. The Boston Red Sox offered $10,000. The Phillies offered $11,000. Still emotionally a Dodger, Erskine telephoned Feezle and said, whatever the other bids, he'd sign a new Brooklyn contract for $5,000.

A quarter century later, Erskine laughed at himself. "I got the five thousand," he said, "which makes me the only man in history to collect two bonuses from Branch Rickey, but what I didn't know was that the second time, instead of settling for five thousand, I could have gotten thirty thousand."

"Did you have the great curve then?"

"No. That came later. Let me ask you. How do you throw your curve?"

"Break the wrist and snap the fingers."

"Snap," Erskine ordered. "Which finger do you use? The middle one. But when you throw a curve, you snap it off the index finger. Most people do. I had a good year in Danville my second season there. I won nineteen and two more in the play-off. But Jack Onslow, who managed Waterloo and later the Chicago White Sox, explained that I was tipping the curve, by kind of tucking the ball against my index finger before I threw it. 'I'm only telling you this 'cause you'll be out of this league next year,' Onslow said. 'But with that curve you got, you may not go all the way.'"

In Havana, where he played winter baseball in 1948, Erskine began throwing a curve off his middle finger. For weeks he could get no speed on the ball, nor any significant break. Gradually over months, the new curve snapped off the middle finger, became faster and sharper. But whenever he pitched a game, he reverted to the relative safety of the old curve that had worked in high school and at Danville, Illinois.

By February he came to a decision. He had to use his new curve in a game. He had to throw it in the first inning and every inning. It had to be his only curve. Otherwise, he would never rely on it and never become the pitcher he should be. Against a team called Almendares, Erskine mixed the new pitch with fast balls and pitched eight shutout innings. Then Dee Fondy, who later hit .300 in the major leagues, opened the ninth inning with a triple.

Erskine paused. A shutout meant a $25 bonus and he was earning only $325 a month. He was ahead by two runs. His infield would play back for the out, rather than close, to prevent Fondy from scoring. The old curve still seemed harder and better than the new one. Erskine set his teeth and considered in the open privacy of the pitching mound. The question he decided was truth versus $25. He would *not* go back to the old curve. He threw five of the new curves in the next ten pitches and got his shutout, his $25 and the ball game. He never threw the old curve again.

Wooden shutters stand open behind Erskine's chair. Memories have poured, but night claws at the window. "Old Campy," Erskine says. Nine hundred miles away, Roy Campanella is sitting in a motorized wheelchair, with shriveled arms and withered stumps for legs.

"The worst thing I can imagine is what happened to Campy,"

Erskine said. He gazed at the ceiling. "Real intimacy develops between catcher and pitcher. You work 120 pitches together every few days, after a while you think like one man.

"All right. Campy is hurt over the winter of 1957–58. That's the same winter the team moves to California. We start out playing in a football field, the Coliseum, with left real close, a China wall. You know how Campy used to hit high flies to left; as soon as I see the China wall, I think, 'Son of a buck, if Campy was well, he'd break Ruth's record, popping flies over that dinky screen.'

"We start badly. We get to Philadelphia. I'm supposed to pitch. It rains. Campy was born in Philadelphia. Whatever, I start thinking about him with his broken spine and I don't tell anybody anything, but I go to the station in the rain and take a train to New York. I find a cab and go to University Hospital. They say I can't see him. I persist. At last, okay.

"Now I'm the first person not family to visit, the first man who's come from the team.

"I get to his room. I'm still thinking of the short fence and Ruth's record. I open the door and there's a shrunken body strapped to a frame. I stand a long time staring. He looks back. He doesn't see just me. He sees the team. He starts to cry. I cry myself. He cries for ten minutes, but he's the one who recovers first. 'Ersk,' Campy says, 'you're player representative. Get better major medical for the guys. This cost me. Eight thousand dollars for just the first two days.'

"I say, 'Sure, Campy.'

" 'Ersk,' he says, 'you know what I'm going to do tomorrow? I'm working with weights and I'm going to lift five pounds.'

"I go there thinking of him breaking Babe Ruth's record, he's thinking of lifting five pounds. But he's enthusiastic. He starts to sound like the old Campy. He wants to know when I'm going to pitch. He's got some kind of setup where they turn the frame and he can watch TV. I'm going the next day in Philly if it doesn't rain, and he gets real excited. They'll be televising that one back to New York. 'I'll be watching you, Ersk,' he says. 'Make it a good one.'

"I get out of there. By this time I'm pitchin' with a broken arm, but this one I got to win. I got to win it—I don't care if it sounds like a corny movie—for Roy.

"The next day I go out with my broken wing. I pitch a no-hitter for five innings. I end up with a two-hitter. I win it for Campy. That was the last complete game I ever pitched in the major leagues.

"I could look back and say I should have pitched a few more years. My arm doesn't hurt now. The game looks easy on television. But in 1959 I walked into the office of Buzzy Bavasi and told him I'd had enough. I was thirty-two years old and my arm was 110. It ached every day. Some of the time I could barely reach the plate. Buzzy said he'd put me on the voluntary retired list, and he went out to get his secretary to draw up the papers.

"I thought, '*This is it.*' And all of a sudden in Buzzy's office in Los Angeles I'm seeing myself in the Kenmore Hotel room with Branch Rickey thirteen years before. I can see it clear as my hand. I can see my Navy bell-bottoms. I see Rickey puffing smoke. I see the way Dad looked. I hear the sound of Rickey's voice. That's the beginning. And here, I think, in Buzzy's office is the end.

"I say to myself, '*Wait!* I don't want this to end. Shouldn't I go for one more start?' And then I say, 'No. I don't want one more start. I've given myself every opportunity. At thirty-two, after 335 games, I'm worn-out.'

"I say to myself, 'Remember the way you feel. Burn this in your mind. *Strong!* Five years from now when you're back in Indiana and you start saying, the way all old ball players start saying, I could play another year, conjure up this feeling you have now.' "

"Have you had to do that, Carl?" I said.

"Only about five hundred times."

Erskine turned out the lights. He went upstairs and looked into Jimmy's room. The little boy breathed noisily in sleep.

6

THE SANDWICH MAN

Gentlemen, we have just traded for the pennant.

Anonymous Dodger official after acquiring
Andy Pafko on June 15, 1951

On the telephone, Andy Pafko said that it would be nice to get together, but that he didn't belong in a book about the team. "I wasn't in Brooklyn long enough," he said. "I don't rate being with Snider and Furillo. I wasn't in that class."

Across seventeen major league seasons, Andy Pafko batted .285, hit 213 home runs and fired every throw and ran out each pop fly with the full measure of his strength. Certain athletes who grew up in the Great Depression played that way, the mongrels of poverty tearing at their calves.

Pafko is proud to have been a good, hard-working ball player, but he regards his year and a half with the Dodgers as a failure. The season in which he came to Brooklyn as pennant insurance reached its climax with Pafko positioned at the left-field wall of the Polo Grounds, shoulders pressed against cement, wanting to run deeper, but helpless, a spectator in uniform as Bobby Thomson's home run carried the pennant to the New York Giants.

The roads north from Anderson run straight and flat. State Route 32, and Federal Highway 41, among trees, farms and near Noblesville, Indiana, a town of 8,500, pass the anomaly of a Rolls-Royce dealer on the plain. Two Dodgers, Pafko and Joe Black, have settled in Chicago. Like Shuba, Pafko descends from Middle Europeans who made their way in the American Middle West. "But we're Lutherans," he said, "not Catholic, and we were farm people. I still get out in the country. I scout for the Montreal Expos. Look"—the thick voice lightens—"put me in, but don't make it a big thing. I never felt I was a Dodger star."

Before lunch, he waited in the parking lot of a Skokie steak house called Henrici's, standing straight and rather stiffly, his hair still thick and black.

I told the captain, "Reservation for two." He stared at Pafko and said, "Don't I know you?"

"Andy Pafko."

"Milwaukee Braves," the captain cried. He seated us in a booth and sent for drinks.

"You see," Pafko said. "They don't really know me any more and if they do, they think I was a Milwaukee player. Nobody remembers I was a Dodger."

I remember how he hit Dodger pitching. He was one of those few ball players—Mickey Mantle and Willie Mays were others—who made the playing area of Ebbets Field seem too small. He hit line drives against or over all the walls and with Chicago in 1950, when he hit thirty-six home runs, he was always beating the Dodgers out of games they should have won. A year later, Buzzy Bavasi sent the Cubs Joe Hatten, an outfielder, an infielder and Bruce Edwards, a catcher who couldn't throw, for the contracts of Johnny Schmitz, Rube Walker, the catcher, Wayne Terwilliger and Pafko. Terwilliger, a skinny second baseman, played thirty-seven games for the Dodgers, but had his moment. In Philadelphia a frog-voiced fan called out

Dodger names from his scorecard, with a pointed basso comment for each one. "Aaargh," he roared, "I can see it now. Yer name in lights. A lotta lights. Wayne Terwilliger." The deal was for Pafko, an all-star outfielder who could play third.

"This is gonna sound crazy," Pafko said, "but even though it looked like the Dodgers was gonna win the pennant, I was disappointed to be traded. My home was here. Chicago. I had five years with the Cubs. I could hit .300. That wasn't bad for a kid from the farms up north.

"Funny about the Cubs. I got in a World Series with 'em in 1945, but after that they didn't win. Hell, they got Durocher and they still don't win. But I belonged. The day before the trade, Don Newcombe beat us at Wrigley Field. I went home and at six o'clock the phone rang and Wid Matthews, the general manager, said, 'Andy, I am sorry to have to inform you that we have traded you to the Dodgers.' I didn't have a winter to adjust. Next day it was the same ride, only to the other side of Wrigley Field.

"I got my belongings and moved them over to the visiting clubhouse. Preacher Roe came over and said, 'Andy, we're glad to have ya.' Still I was a stranger. All right. You bounce around in baseball and that day I hit a home run, but they beat us, 4 to 3."

"Who's us?"

"The Dodgers."

"The 'us' changes that quickly."

"Your team is who you're playing for. The Dodgers get thirteen games ahead, but we started to lose the lead. The trade made it a bad year. I have this feeling something worse is going to happen. In the first game of the play-off I hit a home run first time up. But Jim Hearn won for the Giants. The next day I'm noticing Labine. I'm *really* noticing. He's got a great curve. Thomson couldn't hit it with a fan. My wife Ellen is staying back in Chicago.

"Last game we're ahead in the ninth. They get some hits. A run in. They tell me Sukeforth said Branca was throwing good. But I was wondering. Why not Labine? Branca walked by me in left field. I hit him in the back. 'Go get 'em, Ralph.' But I was doubting. Branca threw a ball. Then came this shot. I started back. In Ebbets Field I might have gotten it. In the Polo Grounds it was gone. Give him credit. It was my biggest letdown ever.

"Back in Chicago, Ellen has a taxi waiting to take her to the station. She hears the hit on the radio and calls out the door, 'I'm not going.'

"The cabbie says, 'What do you mean?'

"Ellen says, 'Just forget it.'

"Then she cried. Forget it? That's one year I'll never forget. I have to leave the Cubs. I lose the play-off. Ellen loses the trip.

"The three biggest disappointments of my life. Well, that was the worst. Ever since things have been getting better."

During 1919, the Pafkos came from Bratislava, peasant farmers, and settled with relatives in Minneapolis. By the time Andy was born in 1921, Michael and Susan Pafko had borrowed money, bought a dairy farm near Boyceville, close to a fork of the Hay River in northwestern Wisconsin. They kept chickens, and hogs, and grew alfalfa and oats. Andy, called Pruschka, was the third of six brothers. As late as 1942, his third season in professional baseball, he was still helping pay off the family farm.

"Ol' Handy Andy Pafko," Red Barber used to say. "Pow'ful wrists. He strengthened them as a boy milking cows on his daddy's farm."

"Sure," Pafko said over a club sandwich, "I milked the cows. And not only that. I chopped wood. I fetched well water. You had to be strong, and you had to take discomfort, too, if you know what I mean."

"What?"

"No plumbing. In the winters it hit thirty below. Some fun going to the outhouse." The large, square face split in a smile.

"Ted Williams was my idol. He played for the Minneapolis Millers. It was 1938. He was skinny, but he must have hit forty homers. They called him 'The Splendid Splinter.' Later Joe D. was my idol, but then it was Ted. Some coaches encouraged me and my brother John encouraged me and I heard there was gonna be a tryout down in Eau Claire and I went, but my mother didn't want me to. She wanted all of us to stay together. My mother said she would be happy if when we grew up, all of us lived within fifty miles of Boyceville.

"I went to the camp anyway. They signed me and a while later sent me home. It was cut-down time and they had no place for me. I asked Ivy Griffin, the man who signed me, 'Hey, what should I do?'

" 'When you go home,' he said, 'play as much ball as you can.'

"I went back to the farm and did what Ivy told me. I played softball once a week. But I was twenty years old then and I was thinking it had been some crazy dream, Pruschka Pafko playing with Ted Williams and Joe D.

"Now there was only a month left in the season. It was harvest time. A shiny car pulls up. My mother thinks it must be someone selling tractors. But the man says, 'Where's Andy?'

" 'He's workin' in the field.'

" 'I want to talk to him.'

"Someone at Eau Claire had gotten hurt. It was Ivy Griffin in the car. They needed me. The hell with the harvest. I got signed for seventy-five dollars a month. Four years later in the major leagues, I was able to buy a car myself."

Pafko sipped beer and shook his head. "Baseball was a tough life. I didn't hit much in Eau Claire but then a good year at Green Bay. Then down in the Sally League, I tied Enos Slaughter's record with eighteen triples. Then to the Pacific Coast

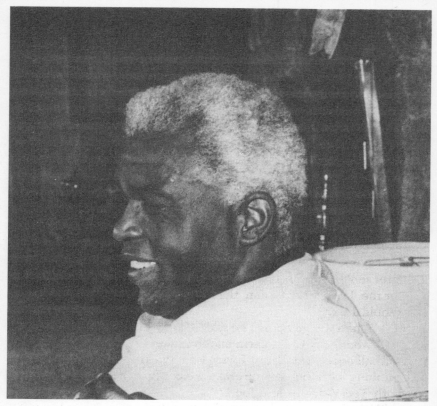

Gordon Kahn II

Jackie Robinson

Clem Labine

Carl and Jimmy Erskine

Preacher Roe

Joe Black

Pee Wee Reese

Andy Pafko

George Shuba

Duke Snider

Roy Campanella

Carl Furillo

Billy Cox

Gil Hodges

Walter O'Malley

League. I won the batting championship with .356. Then, in '44, I had my first year with the Cubs.

"Telling it here doesn't make it sound hard, but it was hard. I never *had* played baseball, only softball, but there wasn't a guy, not one, who helped me. Nobody helped anybody. The minors was a jungle. Other guys were jealous. I had to figure everything out for myself. I started standing way back from the plate and stepping in. As I moved up, I had to crowd the plate. The higher you get, the better outside curves you see.

"After the Cubs won in '45, they started downhill, but now my life *was* getting easier. I liked Chicago. They knew me everywhere. I played the outfield, third. I was liked. I was crowding the plate, getting my hits.

"Wham. Over to Brooklyn. Now every time I come up, somebody's throwing at my ear. Day after day, those pitchers flattened me. I'd been brushed, but I never knew what it meant *really* being thrown. You know what Durocher says. 'Don't stir up weak teams.' Nobody bothered me with the Cubs. But Brooklyn had this murderers' row. Hodges. Campanella. Snider. Furillo. Someone ahead of me hits a homer. The next pitch comes at *my* head. That wasn't fun. Those Dodger-Giant games weren't baseball. They were civil war."

He had downed the sandwich. He said he didn't want more beer. "Ginger ale," he told the waitress.

"You remember when Robinson was signed?"

"It didn't bother me none. There was a great pitcher on the Cubs, Claude Passeau. He came from Mississippi. He'd get on Robinson. Throw at him. So would some other guys. Now it's 1948, and I'm new at third and Robinson hits a triple and bowls me over. I always had a good glove, but I was feeling my way as an infielder. He really crashed me. I thought, 'Next time—there'll be a next time—I'll get even.'

"Sure enough that same game he hits another line drive and here he comes again. I get the relay and tag him pretty good.

I give him the ball and some fist and the left elbow. He gets up and looks. He starts walking off, looking back, challenging. I don't want to fight, but I'm ready. I look higher. All I saw in the stands was black. I thought, 'Uh-oh. I don't want to start a race riot.' But I *admired* him, you know what I mean?

"To do what he did, the way they threw at him, I had to admire him. But that doesn't mean he had any right to bowl me over. I had to stand up for myself and for my fans.

"I loved associating with the fans. That was the best part of the time with Brooklyn. Ebbets Field was so close you could hear 'em all. One day: 'Andy, you're a bum.' Next day: 'Andy, you're my boy.' In Ebbets Field I heard 'em talking all the time. Say, you must be in a hurry?"

"Hell, no."

"That catch I made for Erskine in the World Series. Gene Woodling hit the ball. I put my hand on the right-field barrier in Yankee Stadium and pushed off and jumped as high as I could. It was a line drive. A shot. I got it near the webbing and it knocked me backwards into the stands, and when I'm falling over, I hear 'em shouting, even though it's Yankee Stadium, 'Hold the ball.' "

"You did."

"And that January, the Dodgers sent me to Boston. Walter O'Malley wrote a letter and said someday he'd explain why. I was starting to wonder. Two trades in three years. I don't know. Is something funny here? I ended up better off. Boston moved to Milwaukee, back in Wisconsin. I was going home.

"I was through in '59. The Braves had me coach three years. Then I went down to manage at Binghamton, New York, and West Palm in Florida and Kinston, North Carolina. That's farm country, but not like where I grew up. There were hills near our farm and lakes. Kinston is flat country; they grow tobacco. We won a pennant in Kinston in '67. I worked out while I was managing. I pitched batting practice five times a week. I was traveling secretary and the part-time trainer, and their adviser. Some made it. Ron Reed, the pitcher, from La Porte, Indiana. Mike Lum, an outfielder from Hawaii. Handsome kid. I tried to help them all, remembering how nobody ever helped me."

Pafko's gnarled hand drummed on the table. "It was like I was a substitute father, but I don't get the way everything's changed. The boys are different from the way I was.

"I call a workout at ten A.M. At ten they start putting on their uniforms. When I began, it was *Don't wait.* If he says ten, be there at nine. In uniform. Ah." He brushed hair back from his forehead. "Do you get it?"

"Well, there aren't so many growing up any more on farms without plumbing in cold corners of the country."

"The kids from Southern California were the worst, most spoiled. I had the hardest time working with them," Pafko said."Did you ever think of this? Baseball is losing young people to football. Boys with good bodies. And to industry. Baseball, the greatest game there is.

"I put in nineteen years, sixteen as a player, three as a coach. God's let me live; my pension, $780 a month, began on February 25, 1971. And it was fun. We sold the farm. My mother's dream didn't work out. We're all living in the cities. I've got security because I was a ball player. That anyone can understand, but I can't put in words how much I loved it, playing in the major leagues."

Three waitresses had approached silently, listening to the halting, passionate summation. When Pafko paused, one, no more than twenty-five, said, "Sir?"

"Yes."

"The captain says you're Andy Pafko, who used to play for the Milwaukee Braves."

"And the Dodgers," I said, "and the Cubs. He was the best ball player in Chicago."

"We wondered," the girl said, "if we could have your autograph."

Pafko smiled and asked each girl her name and signed for them all.

"Now for me," I said.

"Don't kid me," Pafko said. "It's just nice being remembered."

"I'm not kidding." I had been traveling with a glove, a Wilson A-2000, huge, $50 retail, more elaborate than any glove that had been designed when Pafko played in Brooklyn. "I'm asking everybody on the team to sign it, for a souvenir."

Pafko looked at some signatures. Then he turned the glove over and wrote his name on the back. "I don't belong with those others," he said. "Thanks for a good club sandwich. Maybe I saved you a little money, huh?

"Furillo, Snider and guys who could play like that, you oughta buy them the steaks."

7

BLACK IS WHAT YOU MAKE IT

The flame of the lamp turned so low that it sputtered on the wick like the old man's breathing. "Learn it to the younguns," he whispered, fiercely.

RALPH ELLISON, *Invisible Man*

Irony ringed Joe Black's life in baseball. He appeared without acclaim, determined and fearless, and quickly became the strongest pitcher on the team. Then, with success, came dread. These afternoons as hero might vanish as suddenly as they had come. He had longed to succeed. Now nightmares warned of a sudden end. All of Joe Black's dreams came true, the good ones and the bad. Five years after his brilliant Dodger season, he was dropped by the Washington Senators, a last-place ball club. His baseball skill was spent. At thirty-three, he would have to make a new life and find another dream.

I saw him two years later one sweltering afternoon at Yankee Stadium, still looking enormous and powerful. A ragged mix of children chattered behind him. "Hey, man," he said, "you still typing?"

"For *Newsweek*."

"Oh, that's why I don't see your name; but how are you gonna get well known typing if nobody sees your name?"

271

His insights were quick and accurate. "What are you doing now, Joe?" I said.

"Getting my master's at Seton Hall. Me and Doris been divorced. I'm back in Plainfield, New Jersey, where I started teaching and coaching at the junior high school. These are my team. I come to introduce 'em to the manager."

He meant Casey Stengel, who was leaning on a strut of the batting cage, surveying line drives stroked by Mickey Mantle and Roger Maris. "Hey, Skip," Black called from a box seat railing. "You got a minute?"

Stengel turned and approached in a rapid limp. "Yes, sir, yes, sir. I remember ya. Good fast one. What's all that ya got behind ya there?"

"This is my team, Case. They're having troubles. They've lost sixteen out of eighteen games and I wondered what the old master thought I ought to teach 'em."

"Lost sixteen out of eighteen, you say?" Stengel scratched his chin. "Well, first you better teach 'em to lose in the right spirit."

Long afterward Black left the Plainfield ghetto and went to work for the Greyhound Corporation in Chicago. Now he had written that he was married again, owned a small house on Yates Street, and that the new Mrs. Black, Mae Nell, made excellent roast beef. "So when you get to Chicago, we'd like you to try some."

I found Yates Street on the Far South Side and Black's home in a row of neat, buff modern homes, each showing a picture window to a house across the street. Walking up the steps, I saw Black in silhouette holding a baby at one shoulder. He opened the door and greeted me and grinned. He had put on weight at the middle. He must have gained fifty pounds, over the 220 he weighed as a pitcher. Against his bulk, Martha Jo, two months old, cuddled. Her torso was hidden by one hand.

"Well, come on in. This is Mae Nell." A trim, pretty woman said hello. "She's from Houston. The house isn't really set up yet. We haven't been in it that long. Sit down and make do with what we have." On a table in the long narrow living room, Black's old glove stood, bronzed. "That's the glove I used when I became the first black man who ever won in the World Series. One nine five two. You saw it." Black was forty-six, divorced, relocated, but, except for the weight, he had not changed much. The face, the manner were the same, and at once the mood on Yates Street became what it had been in the winter after the World Series, when we played three-man basketball in a Brooklyn gym, Joe always taking care not to trample smaller men, and afterward we drank malted milks, to get back strength, and talked about the funny and exciting things that had been happening, and that lay ahead.

Martha Jo began to cry. Black rose. He was wearing a loose shirt, as heavy people will. He paced the room, making deep, soft sounds to his daughter.

"Before the World Series of 1952, I walked Chico—Joe Junior—who was the same age. I had no idea that morning I was gonna do something special. I was going out to pitch a game. I'd pitched a lot of games. I beat Allie Reynolds, 3 to 2, and when I get the last out, they all come round. Reese, Hodges, Robinson. They're all slapping me on the back. Then it hit me. I didn't worry about a thing before, but going back to the clubhouse, I'm all butterflies.

"The first time Charlie used me in relief was here in Chicago; I went an inning and I reared back and fired and nobody touched me. Afterward Dizzy Dean showed up and said to Dressen, 'Hey, that big colored guy throws as hard as me.' And then at the end of that season, I'd relieved forty-five times, Dressen gave me a start. It's a two-thirty game and here it was two-twenty and I kept sitting in the dugout. 'Hey,' Dressen said. 'You're starting. How come you're not warming up?' I told him I wouldn't know what to do with ten minutes' warm-up. In the bullpen I'd warm up with twenty throws. I took seven minutes. I won easy."

He was twenty-eight then. He felt so strong he believed he would pitch until he was forty. As rookie-of-the-year he accepted a contract for only $12,500 to pitch in 1953. "It was going to be a progression, increasing each time. In ten years, 1963, I'd be making forty thousand. But ten years later I was long gone. The thing about the colored players then was that we couldn't make the majors early enough. All of us, we had to wait for Jackie."

Black grew up in an integrated neighborhood, on the west side, the wrong side, of the railroad tracks in Plainfield. The Trianos and the Petris were Italian. There were Polish and Jewish families whose names he has forgotten. It was the 1930's, and people begged, Joe Black remembered over roast beef, with Brussels sprouts and salad. Streets went unpaved and everyone was poor. His family had moved north from Virginia and Joe's father had made himself a mechanic. He was a big man with strong hands and he could fix a Ford or a Dodge runabout as well as anyone. But Joe was born in 1924, so by the time he became aware of things, his father was no longer repairing cars. In the Depression a black mechanic was fortunate to sweep in a factory one day a week.

Joe's mother supported the family, cooking in other people's kitchens and scrubbing other people's laundry. A picture survives of Joe at six standing before a little frame house wearing tattered shorts and a shirt and no shoes. "That," he says, "was my Sunday best."

After the election of Franklin Roosevelt, Black's father dug ditches for the WPA and, as Joe remembers it, earned not money but certificates. Each was good for a different staple. One of the three children got into a line where the certificate was good for a loaf of bread. Another got into line for stew. That was how the family fetched dinners, until 1937 when Joe was a freshman in high school, and times improved and his father found a job.

At nine, Joe began selling newspapers. Two years later, in the autumn of 1935, he had picked up his quota at the offices of the Plainfield *Courier* when he noticed a crowd standing outside on Church Street. "Hey," he asked a circulation man, "what are they doing, hanging around here?"

"They're keeping up with the World Series." The newspaper posted inning-by-inning scores in a window. "The Tigers are beating the Cubs."

"Mister," Black said, terribly impressed, *"I'm* going to play ball when I'm older. All those people are going to keep up with *me.*"

From that day, baseball commanded his dreams. All he had was a sponge ball, but he threw it for hours, so he could learn to pitch. His bat was broken. It was only half a bat. He swung it over and over again to learn to hit. He heard that major leaguers wore spikes on their shoes. Once he jammed his feet into tin cans and hobbled. He wanted the feel of metal underneath him. His mother worried. "Joe, what are you wasting all this time with ball games for? You got a good mind, Joe. Get an education so's you'll have it better than me and your father."

"I'll have it better. I'll play ball."

In the sixth grade, Joe entered Evergreen School, a Georgian structure set in a middle-class neighborhood, and suddenly became aware that he was different from some children. "Not different black," he says. "Different poor." His mother had time to wash her children's things but had to leave them rough-dried. Joe taught himself to use an iron. He wanted to be neat. When he began at Evergreen School, he changed shirts every day, rotating the two he had. Boys taunted him. The collars he ironed for himself were frayed.

For two months Joe endured teasing about old shirts, patched trousers, ruined shoes. Then, after school, he selected one of his tormentors, and knocked him down. A day later he chose another victim. The teasing stopped.

He believed in God and thanked Him for his powerful athlete's body. Sports came easily. At Plainfield High he played varsity football, basketball and baseball. He could play anywhere on the diamond. He could hit for power, run and field and throw. At home, he filled a scrapbook with pictures from the Plainfield *Courier*. He liked Lou Gehrig and Mel Ott, who played up in New York, and Paul Waner, who played in Pittsburgh, and Paul Derringer, who pitched out in Cincinnati. His special team was the Detroit Tigers. They captured him during the 1935 World Series when they defeated the Cubs, four games to two. His second-favorite Tiger, Charlie Gehringer, played second base with beautiful agility and once batted .371. His absolute favorite was Henry Benjamin Greenberg from the Bronx. The year Black was fourteen, Hank Greenberg hit fifty-eight home runs. Only Babe Ruth had done better. Black decided he would be a first baseman because Greenberg played first base, and two years later when Greenberg switched to left field, Black decided that he too would be a left fielder.

"No," said the coach at Plainfield High. "Pitch, Joe, and play short."

In April of Black's senior year, the coach asked about plans. Joe said he expected to become a ball player. He was team captain. The coach nodded and said something about a college scholarship, but Joe meant that he wanted to be a ball player in the major leagues. That May, a big league scout, who doubled as local umpire, offered contracts to three Plainfield schoolboys. Black was puzzled. "Hey," he said to the scout, "how come you sign up all these guys and don't sign me?"

The scout blinked. "Colored guys don't play baseball."

"What? You crazy? You've seen me playing for three years."

"I mean Organized Baseball."

"This is organized. We got a coach and uniforms."

"I mean there's no colored *in the Big Leagues*."

Joe felt that something had struck the back of his neck. There was no pain, only shock. The private hope on which his life was built stood stripped, not merely as boyish fantasy but as *stupid* boyish fantasy. Standing on the Plainfield High School ball field, the sweat of a game running down his forehead, Black pretended that he'd been joking. "Oh, sure," he said to the scout. "Just forget it."

That night he took his scrapbook from a drawer and studied it. Every face, Gehrig, Ott, Waner, Derringer, the others, *all* were white. Without tears Joe began to shred the book in his big hands. But before he did, he carefully clipped a picture of Hank Greenberg, crashing out a long home run. He could not bear both, to have the dream dead and to have nothing, nothing at all to show from the scrapbook of his boyhood.

The best scholarship offer came from Morgan State, a black liberal arts college in Baltimore. If he played baseball and football at Morgan, he'd be granted room, board and tuition for $10 a month. Joe's oldest sister became a stock girl in Bamberger's Department Store in Newark and at the end of the summer she and Joe's mother pooled funds. Using the Bamberger's employee discount, they bought Joe a new pair of pants, two shirts, five pair of underwear and a raincoat. Despite the discount, there was not enough for an overcoat or a suit. "You're not going to college to get pretty, Joe," the mother said. "You're going to get an education."

The first thing for Joe to learn was that he was black. At Morgan State he was assigned a room in Banneker Hall, the dormitory named for Benjamin Banneker, a freeborn Maryland Negro who taught himself astronomy and published an almanac in 1790. Black had never heard of Benjamin Banneker. During a student assembly, someone asked that everybody join in the Negro National Anthem. Joe was preparing to begin, "Oh, say can you see," and was surprised when the others sang something else. "Hey, man," he said to the student at his right, "what's this you're singing?"

"You must be kiddin'."

"I'm asking."

The song, popular among Negroes at the time, was called "Lift Every Voice." " 'The Star-Spangled Banner,' " the other Negro said, "is the *white* people's anthem."

The denouement approached comedy. During a time-out at a varsity football game, Joe, ball carrier and linebacker, pulled off his helmet and rubbed the back of one hand upward against his brow. It was a habit he had acquired playing with whites at Plainfield.

"Hey," said a Morgan State lineman, "what's that you're doing?"

"Brushing the hair out of my eyes."

"What hair? Colored people's hair doesn't grow that way."

"I mean I'm wiping sweat," Joe said.

"You don't know what you mean."

All at once, when he was eighteen, Black confronted his color, and as he did he confronted bigotry. He remembers hating whites for several months before deciding that hate held neither profit nor the keys to any kingdom. As long as he was a Negro, he reasoned, he ought to find out what a Negro was and what a Negro could become and then make the most of himself. He would not let white prejudice warp him. He wanted to live by a motto he had heard somewhere once: "Grab onto life when you're young. You aren't going to pass this way again."

He served the U.S. Army more as athlete than as soldier. "Sixteen months after I was drafted before I touched a rifle. I pitched a lot." After World War II he signed with the Baltimore Elite Giants of the Negro National League and resumed studying at Morgan. Pitching earned enough to pay full tuition. With a degree, he could coach and teach. His own lot would be better than his father's. If not content, he was amiably resigned.

Then in 1946 Rickey signed Robinson. Black ball players rooted. "Come on, Jack. Come on, big black man. Show those white guys. After you, comes us." The new hope receded cruelly. Black was the fastest pitcher on the Baltimore Elites, but year after year no white cared. White scouts picked the very best of a rich plantation harvest—Robinson, Newcombe, Campanella, Monte Irvin, Satchel Paige—to fill the narrow quotas. Baseball was not segregated one day and integrated the next. First came one black, then two, then four, then ten. The Yankees carried none as late as 1954. Branch Rickey made a mistake with black pitchers. The first one he signed, Dan Bankhead of Empire, Alabama, lacked major league ability. Bankhead was failing before Brooklyn scouts signed Joe Black to a minor league contract in 1950.

Black felt pleased, but not exhilarated. He was a twenty-six-year-old college graduate who had erased white baseball from his plans. All right. He'd go. There was nothing to lose. He'd have to accept abuse, but he might as well give the white minor leagues a try. He signed to play where Robinson had, far from the American South in Montreal.

He can still imitate a sound from opposing benches, ringing in two notes, a mix of bird call and obscenity. "Black," begins a voice, stretching the vowel sound so that the name sounds "Bla-a-a-ack." Then, a few tones higher, "nigger." The second word is tightly clipped. The sound went "Bla-a-a-ack nigger, bla-a-a-ack nigger. Nigger!" He ignored it and took his pitching pay.

No other career on the team was both so brilliant and so brief. I can still see Black trudging from the bullpen, in foul territory beside the right-field corner of Ebbets Field. He wore Number 49 and he approached with all deliberate speed, holding a jacket in one hand, reaching the mound, exchanging a sentence with Dressen, who was half his size, taking a ritual pat on the flank from the pitcher he replaced and, with evident confidence and a certain impatience, going to work.

Black coming in against the Giants, whose bean balls disquieted Hodges and Campanella, threw at heads. In 1952 the Giants were afraid of Black. They could not beat him when they had to. Black stopped Stan Musial in St. Louis and Del Ennis in Philadelphia and Ted Kluszewski in Cincinnati. He stopped all the best hitters by throwing to spots and keeping them loose, and his relief pitching won the pennant. But the next season Dressen's tinkering and Black's own concerns shunted him back to the second line. A year later he was in the minors. Then back again; then Cincinnati and a final weary effort for Washington. He was not a star, but a nova, appearing, flaring and disappearing, each phase following the other so rapidly that before there was time to contemplate one phenomenon it had been succeeded by another.

As we sat in the rectangular house on Yates Street, almost everything in Black's life, and everything that we discussed, hinged about the single year 1952, and actually less than that, the brevity of a season. Out of the forty-six years, everything built toward and sloped from a starburst.

"Does it seem real?"

Black laughed, sound gurgling up from his big chest. "You trying psychological stuff on me?" The laugh exploded. "What's that over there to my left?" The bronze glove. "You want to see my trophies? They're in the basement. I show 'em to Chico when he visits. Yes, it seems real. I remember it very clearly. You trying to psych a psych major?"

"What happened, Joe?" I said.

"The last time I pitched in the Stadium, I could hear Stengel yelling at the hitters, 'Don't let him fool ya. Watch out for the fast ball. He can throw harder than that.' But I couldn't. My arm had started to hurt a few years before. I had them take X-rays. The humerus was cracked. Throwing. I don't know when I'd cracked the bone. The Stadium was the finish. I packed up and came back to Plainfield and took courses for my master's, and went to work teaching. And I figured, what the hell, there's a lot worse ways to end up."

A young teacher, where twenty-five years before he had worn frayed shirts to school, he had seen black America and white America and come to believe in the unity of both, a moderate position to which he brought immoderate intensity. About 60 percent of the students at Plainfield Junior High were black. Most of the white 40 percent were Jewish. One Friday, late in the autumn of 1959, Black learned that some of the Negroes were extorting money from some of the Jews. On the next Monday, he stood up, moved to the front of his desk and began to address his home-room class. "People should live," Black said. "I've been some places and I've seen some things and pitched in the World Series, and I can tell you that is basic. We've got this one life, and it isn't very long, and we all want to live. I'm going to talk to you about living.

"Some of you are black and some of you are white and I know it's hard to get along. It was harder when I grew up. I honestly think things are easier now. There's more bread. But things aren't the same. They're different. You with me?"

A noncommittal murmur.

"All right, you black kids. I was a black kid here. I know the disadvantages. But I know some of you are punching the white guys and don't try to deny it. And I know why. Because every day you can get fifty cents not to hit him. Well, that's against the law. If I brought a policeman in here and made you admit what you were doing, which I am strong enough to do, you'd get locked up.

"Now you white guys, you got a little money. You've got the fifty cents. I want to ask you right here and now, why don't you fight back?"

A Jewish boy said, "They can beat us up."

"Okay. That's a good reason not to fight. You don't want to get killed. But we've got the gym on Wednesday and I'm going to teach combatives. Boxing. We're gonna have headgear, that's like helmets, and mouthpieces, and big sixteen-ounce gloves. Nobody's gonna get hurt bad."

In the gymnasium on Wednesday, the boys were loud with excitement. The black children arrayed themselves at one side of the ring. "Get in there, man, and dig, dig, dig, dig."

The middle-class Jewish children stood at another side. Black walked toward them towering.

"Don't worry. You box in your own way. They're gonna bang on you in the beginning. Let them bang on you. I'm the referee. Nothing terrible will happen."

In each of a half dozen bouts, the black banged on the white. But heavy gloves softened the punches, and after the first blows, the blacks became less violent. Throwing punches with heavy gloves is exhausting. A boy swings hard for thirty seconds. Then he loses the desire to swing and wants very much to lower his arms.

When the boxing was done, Black again stood among the Jewish children. "So they banged on you," he said. "Bomp, bomp, bomp. And you didn't die, did you?"

The boys began to smirk.

"All right," Black said. "Your turn is coming."

A day later he asked one of the whites, a wiry boy of one hundred pounds, to meet him in the gymnasium. "I want to show you judo," Black said. "You're gonna throw me."

"I don't want to, Mr. Black. You're too big."

"It's not size, it's weight distribution and leverage."

They worked together, and in an hour the hundred-pound boy was able to throw the compliant 250-pound teacher. The boy would grab an arm, press hard and move into Black, who yielded to the pressure and rolled over the boy's shoulder. Black then slammed against the mat on his back. There is no way a hundred-pounder can throw a powerful 250-pound man who does not want to be thrown. Effect was what Black sought. Effect would be enough.

"All right," Black announced the next Wednesday, "today we wrestle."

The Negro children chattered, "Say, Mr. Black. We're gonna do our thing."

"Hold it," Black said. "There's a difference between wrestling and *rasslin'*. You guys are thinking about rasslin'. In *wrestling* there are rules."

"What rules?"

"Well, there's a lot to learn, and the first thing is how to fall." Black contemplated. "I've got to get somebody to fall. Let's see." He looked about. His eyes found the white hundred-pounder. "You," Black said. "Come on out."

"Hey, wait, Mr. Black," one of the Negroes said. "He's too small. You shouldn't throw him."

Black said easily, "He's gonna throw me."

Black students laughed. "That kid's gonna throw you, teach? Ain't gonna. Hey, kid, don't get hurt throwin' Mr. Black."

Gigantic Joe Black and the small white child met at the center of the mat. In seconds the boy threw his teacher. As Black landed, he struck the mat with open palms for volume and added a resounding "Ooof!" Then he rose and proceeded to teach serious wrestling.

He laughed to himself as he remembered. "You know what happened in a few weeks? The Jewish kids, who were pretty sheltered, got over their fear and whipped the black guys good. They paid attention to my talks, and when they got into the ring, they knew how to maneuver. The black guys kept trying to get a gargantua hold. Instead, they ended up pinned. All right. What happened?

"The Jewish kids found out that because a guy is black doesn't

283

mean he's tough. The black kids found out that because a guy is Jewish doesn't mean he's chicken. The extortion stopped all by itself. By the end of that year they were getting along."

"Since then?"

"Since then there's been trouble in Plainfield. They brought in a player from somewhere else and a black television announcer. Celebrities. What do celebrities mean to these kids? You have to get somebody to sting conscience. It isn't just that I could relate to tough black kids. I'd gone to school with their mothers and fathers. I'd *lived* where they did, in the shanties by the track. Sting a boy's conscience and reward him with a little honest hope. The day is done when it was niggers across the tracks, white trash down the dirty end of the river and the rich living upstream. You got to get those words to the kids."

"Does it bother you to have left the ghetto?" I said.

"I didn't leave it," Black said. "I got pushed. Society told me, 'Joe, get out.' I've got alimony, and child support for Chico. I thought I was doing good work in the ghetto. But society didn't rate it very high. To teach and coach with a master's degree, my salary was forty-two hundred a year."

"That was before everybody got frightened," I said. "Now you could get Ford Foundation grants. Real money."

"Maybe. But what you learn is that then and now don't mix. If I'd gone into organized ball at eighteen, the way I could throw . . . But I couldn't go into organized ball until Jackie made it and the quotas let me, and if we want to get sad, we can think that I pitched my greatest games in miserable ball parks, in the colored league, with nobody watching.

"But I'm not a sad guy. Things are bad in Plainfield. My sister stays in school all day with her kid. Parents patrol the halls. But look here, I'm a black executive in a big corporation. That's now, and now is my chance to show that this big colored guy, me, is no dummy."

Martha Jo had finished her bottle and fallen asleep on her

father's shoulder. We adjourned, to resume the next day at the headquarters of the Greyhound Corporation, 10 South Riverside Plaza in downtown Chicago, close to ghettos, to be sure, but 850 miles away from the railroad tracks in Plainfield, New Jersey.

The Greyhound Corporation, Gerald H. Trautman, president, is not, as Black is always telling somebody, a bus company. It is that mixed bag of industry and finance, legerdemain and hustle, the conglomerate. The bus company is a subsidiary. So is a moving company, a computer company, a finance company, a range of a dozen businesses all joined under Greyhound, Inc. Joe Black is vice president for special markets. He works among Negroes and among whites. He stood among whites, speaking at a dinner of advertising men in Tulsa, Oklahoma, on the day Martin Luther King was shot. He sensed a stirring and someone handed him a note saying, "Dr. King shot. Not serious." The white chairman did not want to unsettle the black guest. The chairman waited until the speech was over and then, privately, recounted what had happened. Black flew to Atlanta and served as an usher at the funeral. Although King was an idol, he remained composed and after the services found himself clearing a path for Sammy Davis, Jr., among poor Atlanta blacks.

"My people, my people," Davis cried. He threw out both hands in deep emotion.

"Some," Black said, "are your people. Some will steal the rings off your fingers. Stay close and keep your hands in your pockets, Sam."

Black's office at Greyhound was a large square, with cold fluorescent lighting and a picture window over the Chicago River. Black pointed out several awards. I asked why he lived far south on Yates when, as a corporate vice president, he could afford a fashionable neighborhood.

285

"It's a nice house," he said, "and a nice mixed block. It's comfortable. I want to be comfortable where I live, same way that I want to be comfortable with myself."

"Meaning?"

"There are plenty of places where, if a black man wants to live there, he has to fight a war. The war affects his family. I speak English, right? My wife is not ugly, right? I have a college education, a good job. I'm a vice president. I'm in five figures, right?

"One afternoon Mae Nell and I visited white friends in Lombard, a suburb on the North Side. We saw signs advertising a development, nice houses with a garage for thirty-two thousand dollars. This was one of those places with a community pool and tennis court and a big social room where everybody meets socially.

"We applied. The manager had a list of names. Next to it were the people's salaries and how much each person had to make as a down payment. Nobody on the list was making what I am. I could tell because I can read upside down."

"How much down?" he had asked the manager.

"We'll get to that. Where do you work?"

"The Greyhound Company."

"What are you? A driver?"

Black handed him a card. "A vice president," the manager said. "That's very good. What do you make?"

"Put down in excess of thirty-five thousand a year."

"In excess of thirty-five. Not bad. Say, do you travel?"

"Quite a bit," Black said. "Making speeches. Things like that."

"Well," the manager said, "you certainly earn enough, but if you travel, I can't encourage you to buy. We don't let anyone use the recreation room until they're eighteen, and some of these seventeen-year-olds, pretty husky fellers by the way, are kicking up a fuss. Rebelling. Throwing stones. Acting up. Now,

286

Mr. Black, it certainly would be a terrible thing if these white seventeen-year-olds threw rocks through the window of your thirty-two-thousand-dollar house, possibly injuring your wife while you were traveling and not here to protect her."

Later Black's friends in Lombard offered to buy one of the development houses. "Then, instead of us, you and Mae Nell move in."

"Like hell," Black said. "Something like that happens to you every day in your life if you're black."

He has adjusted to bigotry, without accepting it. His talks argue against nihilism and riot.

"Dropout," he tells black youths, "is another word for quitter. Quitting is a cinch. You walk away. For the time being you're the boss. Free as a bird. And because you're young, people excuse a lot of things. But when you get older, people stop feeling sorry, and that gets you sore, but what are you good for? A quitter is trained for nothing but being angry.

"This reawakening of racial pride," he tells black adults, "is a fine thing. African styles in clothing, jewelry and hairdos are important. But what's more important is what we do to solve community problems. The future is the young; it's in the schools. A new hairdo solves no problems, but wearing the new hairdo to PTA meetings is something else. That's feeling racial identity *and* trying to make the ghetto school a better place. But if you had to pick one to skip, skip the hairdo. Make the PTA."

During a recent Honors Day Program at Virginia Union, a black university in Richmond, Black spoke about the responsibilities as well as the rewards of black power: "Our efforts have to be more positive than shouting, 'Sock it to him, Soul Brother,' or, 'We are victims of a racist society,' or, 'Honkey!' I'm in favor of black history because it makes whites realize that American blacks have done more than make cotton king. But I'm opposed to all-black dorms, and to violence. If the black *student* wants to use a loaded gun to make a point, what can we expect of *uneducated* blacks? By now some of you may be saying I'm a Tom, a window-dressing Negro. But I learned two things early. A minority cannot defeat a majority in physical combat and you've got to let some things roll off your back. Because my name is Joe Black, whites called me 'Old Black Joe.' After a few years of scuffling, I still hadn't silenced all of them and throwing all those punches had made me a weary young man. Call me 'Old Black Joe' today and you agitate nobody except yourself."

He makes one point to everyone. It is bigotry to exalt the so-called special language of the blacks. "What is our language?" he asked. " 'Foteen' for 'fourteen.' 'Pohleeze' for 'police.' 'Raht back' for 'right back.' 'We is going.' To me any man, white or black, who says whites must learn our language is insulting. What he's saying is that every other ethnic group can migrate to America and master English, but we, who were born here and whose families have all lived here for more than a century, don't have the ability to speak proper English. Wear a dashiki or an African hairdo, but in the name of common sense, learn the English language. It is your own."

At lunch, he handed me a sheet of paper. "This is a part of my philosophy," he said. "And by the way, notice the use of English vocabulary."

I read:

> blackball,
> black book,
> black eye,
> black friday,
> black hand,
> black heart,
> blackjack,
> black magic,
> blackmail,

          black market,
          black maria,
          black mark,
little black sambo.

          white lies.
          Black is Beautiful.

"If that's what you make it, Joe," I said.
"Well," he said. "You got the point."

THE ROAD TO VIOLA

Because it was remote, of rugged territory and off the main track of the Western surge, Arkansas was slow to develop.

MOTTO: *Regnat populus* (The people rule)
NICKNAME: Land of Opportunity
PER CAPITA INCOME: $1,655

Mobil Travel Guide

During the summer of 1955, Elwin Charles Roe, a guileful man from the Ozark hills, where cottonwood and yellow pine grow thick, cut across the American grain. For a fee of $2,000, Roe confessed in *Sports Illustrated* magazine that he had put more than his left hand on what he threw. The title read: "The Outlawed Spitball Was My Money Pitch."

Although the article won a prize for Dick Young, who wrote it, certain baseball people and laymen expressed distaste and disbelief. It was not, I suspect, that Preacher's spitters shocked anyone. A man does what he has to in order to make a living. Rather, the act of public confession bruised a tender area in the national ethos. It was if a Frenchman had sold *Réalités* an essay on his coy mistress, and used not only her name but his own.

"Spitter, bah," Larry Goetz, a large, gruff umpire, was quoted as telling a reporter from the *Sporting News.* "I worked a lot of games behind the plate when Roe was pitching. I never once saw him throw a spitter and I've seen some thrown by real experts like Burleigh Grimes."

"I doubt that he got away with as much as he says," announced Ford Frick, the Commissioner of Baseball. "I believe he has done a little bragging. We have a rule in baseball, 8.02, which says that if a pitcher throws a spitter, he shall be removed from the game and suspended for ten days. If Roe were still in baseball, we would do something, but he has retired now and is beyond our reach."

Away from official stuffiness, one could scent traces of amusement. "He never threw one against me in batting practice," said Pee Wee Reese, "so I take it he never threw one in the game." Writing in the New York *World Telegram & Sun*, Bill Roeder concluded that Roe would have to wait until he was sixty-seven before returning. Multiplying the ten-day suspension by a thousand spitballs, Roeder wrote, "he owes 10,000 days or more than 27 years."

That season the Dodgers defeated the Yankees in the World Series for the first time and John Podres became a Brooklyn hero. Talk about the spitter faded while trees still wore green, darkening after Roe's confessional summer. The Preacher himself disappeared into the Ozarks. A gifted raconteur, he shunned requests to speak at Rotary luncheons in St. Louis and at supermarket openings in Pittsburgh. Later his teammates gathered for old-timers' games at Walter O'Malley's handsome new ball park in Los Angeles and at Shea Stadium, a cylinder set on the old marshlands of Flushing, New York. Reticent Billy Cox showed up for one. Jackie Robinson flew to Los Angeles to play second base at fifty. There were no reunions for the Preacher. His sins confessed, Elwin Roe remained in a corner of Missouri, twenty-five miles from his old Arkansas home, selling groceries and leaving the world alone.

To reach the village of West Plains, you sweep down Illinois flatlands into Missouri and move southwest beyond St. Louis on Route 44, until you reach Rolla, a town supposedly named by a homesick settler from North Carolina, who spelled "Raleigh" as he pronounced it. At Rolla you leave the mainline and bend south through villages called Yancy Mills and Willow Springs and Cabool. Amid a subtle beauty of fields, rounded hills and scattered copses, the soil is touched with red. Ozark land is just promising enough to make a man want to farm it and just poor enough to starve him when he tries.

At the end of the 1953 World Series, after Mickey Mantle beat him, 4 to 2, with an eighth-inning home run, Preacher asked if I would give him the lapel button that newspapermen wear as an admission token to the food, drink and gossip of press headquarters. "What I like to do," he said in a drawl, preserved with as much care as his pitching arm, "is to get trinkets from all my World Series and put 'em on this bracelet of my wife's. It sure does mean a lot to Mozee." He was thirty-eight years old, and there was not much baseball left in his skinny body. If he were asking for Mozee Roe, his wife, he was also asking for himself.

"Sure, Preach," I said, "but we oughta trade. I'll give you the button. Then, in a couple of months, you give me a story."

"What kinda story? I'm no writer."

"Just a letter from the Ozarks," I said, and handed him the button.

With December, Roe made good the bargain. Several cobra being shipped to the zoo at Springfield, Missouri, had squirmed loose from crates in a heated railroad car and, presumably, frozen to death. Roe used the snakes as a departure point:

I like to hunt deer and rabbit [the letter began], but Old Preach ain't in no hurry to find no cobra. I have kept my eyes open but I have had

292

no luck; or maybe I should say I had good luck. I did not see one.

We had Sniders for 3 days and we done a little horseback riding. Snider is no fisherman, so we did no fishing. However we were boating one day and we looked at my trot line and lo and behold if we didn't get a 20-pound catfish. That was quite a bit of luck as that is considered a large one of its kind and on top of that I had the Duke with me.

He couldn't pitch much the next season. He was an elegant competitor; twice at Brooklyn he led the league in winning percentage. But in 1954 he lost four and won three. He understood, and when the Dodgers sold his contract to Baltimore, Roe retired.

Now two letters went unanswered. Finally, I telephoned— there is only one Elwin Charles Roe in the West Plains book— and simply said I'd arrive in a day or two.

"Well, we're busy at the store," Roe said. "I get up at six every morning for inventory. Jes' what do you wanna see me about?"

"For some visiting. Look around where you grew up. I've never been to Arkansas."

"We live in Missouri now. Moved 'crost the line because the schools were better and we had two growin' boys. But, sure, you could come down here. Things are changing. Maybe the people should know about it. We got a Holiday Inn. How's Pee Wee and Erskine and Jack? You seen them? How they look?"

Physically he had changed more than any other Dodger. Roe, the pitcher, was all bones and angles, even to a pointed nose and a sharp chin. Greeting me in the lobby of the Holiday Inn stood a portly man of fifty-five, who wore eyeglasses and had grown jowls. "Welp," Preacher said, brusquely. "Ready? I'll show you what there is to be showed."

We drove a mile south on Highway 63. On the side of a tidy, one-story brick rectangle, a sign read "PREACHER ROE'S SUPERMARKET." "Not what you'd call a supermarket back east," Roe said. "More like a grocery store, ain't it? We deliver. We give

293

personal service. Now the big shopping centers are comin' in, with the giant supermarkets. I don't mind tellin' ya, it's got me worried."

"What kind of car we driving, Preacher?"

He laughed. "I do believe," he said, "they call this a Cadillac." He turned off Route 68 and up a gentle rise toward a big two-story white frame house. "My home," he said. "Seventeen acres. Good huntin' dogs. I got it cheap. But with the land and all it's worth somethin' now. Come out and take a look around."

Beyond a back lawn, land rose and fell to the west. Overhead clouds rushed across a wide, bright sky. "Windy," I said.

"That wind's all right, long as it's blowing straight. It's when it starts a-circling that you have to watch it." He winked. "This here's tornader alley. Look, this isn't where I growed and that's what I'm gonna show you. Heck, we can talk about any of it, then, now, the spitter, but I'll bet you one thing. After you see how it was where I started out, you won't believe the feller riding you went from there to being a major league pitcher. Come on, I'll run you down to Viola, Arkansas. The population is a hundred eighty."

His father, Dr. Charles Edward Roe, had wanted above all things to be a ball player. He was bigger than Preacher and stronger, but he never got far. A look at Memphis in 1917. A season with Pine Bluff of the Cotton States League in 1918, when Preacher was three years old. And that was all. Afterward Dr. Roe concentrated on medicine and studied his six sons in search of the major leaguer he had wanted to be. Preacher was the fifth-born boy, and Vince Scully remembers a day in St. Louis when Preacher shut out the Cardinals and a tall, bony country man walked up to strangers near the ball park and said to one after another, "Did you see what my boy did? That was my boy who pitched that game today." The old doctor's eyes were wet.

"My dad," Preacher said, pointing the Cadillac south, "was a

fast righthander, the rubber-arm type. In the Cotton States
League he pitched both games of a double-header three times.
He couldn't understand why I wasn't rubber-armed, but I
wasn't, so that's the way it was.

"There was a lot of land. Hell, all there was was land, and a
few dirt roads. My dad used to make his calls on horseback. He
wasn't no doctor in a Cadillac. People paid him with chickens
and sacks o' grain.

"Up till I was in high school we had outdoor plumbing. A little
shack with one hole in the door and another hole inside. There
was the six boys and a girl and we all threw and they tell me,
the funniest thing, when I was little, my dad always said, I was
the one. I'd be the major league pitcher."

"You ever think of medicine?"

"Not so's I can remember. None of us went into medicine.
Fact is, my brother Roy and I—he's a school superintendent—
are about the only ones who went into something more than
labor. I guess it was we seen how hard a country doctor works
and fer how little. I hung around Dad's office and made calls
with him. I saw him sew people after knife fights, and I heard
him getting up at all hours when people banged on the door.

"That was work. Baseball was the other way. Fun. Every
Saturday afternoon and every Sunday afternoon there was a
ball game and we Roes was always in it. We played for the Viola
team.

"We'd go to a ball field and all the people from two towns
would be there and we'd have two baseballs which cost a dollar
each, lot of money in Arkansas then. Course it was wide-open
spaces and all the people who came to the game knew that if
those baseballs got lost, the game was over. So when a ball got
hit, no matter how far out into the bushes, play stopped until
you found it. If both was in the bushes, you'd have the whole
population of two towns, Viola and Calico Rock, a-trampin'
around looking. Afterwards you passed the hat and if you was

lucky you took in two dollars, for new baseballs.

"The umpire was some interested person in the community who worked for nothing, and he'd stand behind the pitcher's mound, call it all. Balls and strikes. The bases. Only thing he couldn't call was the foul balls. So there the catcher was on his honor. He'd always do real good till the last inning. Then he was liable to get hooked.

"Biggest games come around July 4. We'd have a three-day picnic and there was three kinds of events. The ball game. A bunch of fights. I ain't gonna mention the third. That's no different here than anywhere else.

"The picnics had some side shows and we got speeches and we was supposed to be dry. Notice I say, 'supposed to be.' A sheriff would catch some old guy making bootleg and get him in the pen a year. Soon's he'd come out, he'd start making it again. Wasn't the world's biggest secret what was in them Fourth of July jugs.

"One time I said to a farmer, 'Hey, Ben, how's your corn crop comin' in?'

" 'Fine, Preach,' he hollered back. 'Looks like thirty gallons to the acre.' "

Roe pulled off the blacktop road and stopped. "That was Moody, Missouri, you just went through, only you didn't look real quick, so you missed it. This here's Moody Park, where I got a great deal of training. There's the same boards in that backstop that was there forty years ago. It's eight miles from here to where I was raised. A lot of guys had horses or a bicycle. Us Roes had two horses and the older ones grabbed them. So on many a Saturday I'd walk eight miles to play the ball game and then walk eight miles home, and couldn't wait for Sunday so's I could do the same thing again."

We had stopped on a rolling hilltop. Moody Park rolled eastward, on upland meadow, reaching toward ridges. A small white-stone building rose behind the backstop. "Ozark hillbilly land is what you're seein'," Preacher said. "Good for sage and hardwood and, Lordie, how the grass grows. People are doing good grazing livestock." A cattle fence bounded right field. "I never will forget the day another boy hit one over that farmer's fence there. I thought it was a mile. You want to pace it off. Maybe 250 feet. A mile here was a pop fly in the major leagues."

"Where are the grandstands?" I said.

"The dirt is the grandstands," Preacher said. "That's where people sat. You're a ways outa New York City. Even St. Louis is near two hundred miles."

He started the Cadillac south again. "My dad had very strong ideas about pitching. He worked on my curve-ball form, but he wouldn't let me pitch in the games until I was sixteen. He wanted the arm to develop slow, natural and strong.

"Up until sixteen I played the outfield. The year I was sixteen, there was a kid could throw so hard nobody could handle his stuff, so I started catchin'. When I went into pro ball, the kid that was pitching to me, Charles Carroll, had become a catcher and I'd become a pitcher, which, of course, was always intended anyways. Charles Carroll had good ability but he jes' quit. My younger brother Roy, the school superintendent, had good ability, but he was too hardheaded. He had to roll separate. A lot of things come together in making a ball player.

"Now you're gonna ask about hitting. I was a *good* hitter in town games. Even in the minor leagues I hit fairly well. But, boy, I'll tell you that major league curve ball isn't as good to hit as them other things. What did I hit as a Bum—.032?"

"The book says your lifetime average is .110."

"Ya looked the dang thing up, did ya? Well, you remember, then, about 1953. Big game in Pittsburgh and some young feller out there for the Pirates ain't jes' throwin'. He's shootin'. He got a gun fer an arm. Here comes that ball, a-smoking and about ta burst into flame, and Old Preach swings, you remember?" In July 1953, Roe hit a 336-foot fly to left that fell a few inches beyond the fence. Led by Billy Cox, the Dodgers spread sweat towels from the dugout toward home plate so that Roe, the home run hitter, could tread a carpet. "That young feller found out right then, you didn't just blow one by Old Preach."

"The book also says you came to bat 620 times and that was your only home run."

"Yep. You got a secret weapon like that, you don't want to go showing it around."

A small black and white sign announced the border of Arkansas. "My first time in this state," I said.

"That right?" Preacher said. "Well, nice to have you."

A blue Oldsmobile whipped up the winding road, passing unsteadily in a seventy-mile-an-hour rush of air. "Lotsa people git hurt driving that way," Roe said. "My dad got hurt bad in an auto wreck back around 1950. He lived up till '52, but he weren't the same man afterwards.

"My dad seen to it that I got myself educated and went to a good college, Harding College, in Searcy, Arkansas. It was a church school and the president was a baseball nut and I had good stuff and got publicity. Like that kid in Pittsburgh ya caught me being comical about, I had smoke. Only I'm serious. And a good curve ball. I'd strike out twelve and walk seventeen. Pitched that way till Branch Rickey said, 'Son, if you walk five more than you strike out, you're five behind.' At Harding, I averaged eighteen strikeouts a game.

"Here come the scouts and offers from, I believe, five teams. It was the Yankees and the Cardinals made the best, but this part of the United States isn't Yankee country, if'n you get me. The Yankees was thought of as the best club in baseball, which no doubt they was, but down here we *talked* about the Cardinals.

"Branch Rickey sent his brother Frank to see me and my dad in my junior year. He said they'd pay a bonus of five thousand dollars, worlds of money. My dad and I drove from Viola to West

Plains, and went to the First National Bank. My dad took out the contract and showed it to the bank president. He read it slow and then said, 'Dr. Roe, this seems like a good contract for the boy.' I signed and the bank president got no fee for his advice, 'cepting for a pretty good deposit.

"Counting that trip to the bank, I'd been in Missouri twice. Never seen a city. Never worn a necktie in the daytime. The Cardinals bought me a suit and put me on a train to New York and said when I reached there to go to the Hotel Lincoln. They was expecting me.

"I got off the train and found me a taxicab. With my hillbilly ways, ya coulda seen me comin' five miles. 'Hotel Lincoln,' I said in a deep voice, to show the driver I been around. Okay. We get there. This is '38, the Depression. Nine bucks is what the meter says. My bonus is now $4,991.

"We play a couple games in New York and some fellers take me in hand. Pepper Martin, he was from Oklahoma and they called him 'The Wild Hoss of the Osage.' And Lonnie Warneke, he's from my own state, and they called him 'The Arkansas Hummingbird.' Pepper and Lon and me stayed at the hotel a couple days. Then we were due to leave town and I said, 'Train time's 'bout an hour. Let's get a cab.'

"Warneke said, 'What's this?'

"I said, 'Get in the cab.'

"Warneke said, 'That's the station twelve blocks down Eighth Avenue. Keep your legs strong if you wanta pitch. We'll walk.'

"That first cabbie took me to Brooklyn, the Bronx, Astoria. Man, I saw it all. The country boy's nine-buck city tour.

"So I'm grateful to Warneke, but my gratitude had limits. He was through 'round '45 and commenced to become an umpire. Now by the time I got to Brooklyn and I was working the wet one, I didn't have that real hard fast ball any more. I needed the corners. I pitched to four-inch spots. Figuring both ways, that means I needed an ump could see two inches. And one day in a tough game I was passing Lonnie Warneke and he said, 'Preach, I may have my superiors on the bases, but when it comes to balls and strikes, I'm second to no man.'

"And I commenced thinking careful and when I was done I told him, 'Horseshit, Lon.'

"See that gas station up there? Well, that's Viola. You done brung me home."

The gas station, old pumps and graveled driveway, stood at an intersection. Small clapboard houses, mostly white, were scattered beyond it. You could see in one glance school, church, houses and the little sign that read: "VIOLA. POP.: 196."

"Growed," Roe said. "Another sixteen. I told you things was picking up."

At the crossroad he turned right and drove six hundred yards up a narrow country road and parked in front of a sprawling white house, with a sheet-iron roof. "The clinic my dad run burned down, but this is my home, just about the way it was. Over here, I want to show you something. Let's get out." We walked to a retaining wall, between lawn and blacktop road. Someone had written in the wet cement:

> Roe Construction Company
> July 15, 1934
> Wayman B. Roe, Superintendent
> Elwin C. Roe, Foreman

"We were kids," he said, "but we built the thing ourselves."

The house stood against the sky on a grassy crest. "We played some ball right here," Roe said. "I want to show you the school over yonder. That big brick building's the Wayman B. Roe building. He was my older brother. Died in an auto crash." There was no sadness, but a kind of resignation, that country people acquire to survive.

Roe walked with long strides, his head bobbing on the long neck. "Now here's something else." A stone gatepost bore an

inscription: "GIFT OF CLASS OF 1934–35. ELWIN C. ROE, PRESI-
DENT. VEDA E. UPTON SECRETARY." "I finished third. The secretary finished second. Her boy friend finished first. We're all
pretty old and scattered now. That little house across the way,
not fancy, is where my wife was raised. She and me used to sit
on fences here and spark.

"Over there you seen the Methodist church, where I was
raised in all my life. That's all there is of Viola. I've hunted and
fished every hill and stream in this country. I grew up in the
woods here and the fields. Let's commence back country a
ways, unless you're tired."

We drove and turned onto a dirt road for two miles. He
stopped between two houses and a clearing in oak woods. "This
was my real home field," Preacher said. "Old backstop's gone
now. There's some stones come up. Native flint rock. And as you
see, it's all overgrown."

"What's that, rye grass?"

"Sage. Let a field be and the sage takes it." We got out of the
car and sat on a bank at the side of the road.

"Here's where it really begun," Preacher said. "One of my
brothers and I lived in those two houses once. We had a regular
Roe community, but when I was a boy, there weren't any
houses at all. Just woods and this field, trimmed neat. Gray
Field, owned by Mr. Gray, and open spaces. Can you imagine
startin' here and getting to pitch for the championship of the
World Series in New York City?" Roe shook his head in wonder.

"Can you imagine it?" I said. "Can you make it come alive?"

"All of it," Preacher said. "One thing makes a feller sad is
knowin' that's behind, and what's wrong with him is nothing
that giving back twenty years wouldn't cure. 'Cept they don't
do that, do they? Say, we had some pretty good days."

Country quiet held us briefly.

"That Mr. Rickey," Preacher said. "First time he talked to me

301

he told me two things. He said, 'Son. Always be kind to your fans. You get back what you give and when you're through, you're just one more old ball player, getting back from life what he gave.' I heeded that and I wisht someone would give advice to Joe Namath. I don't know the man personally, but I get the impression he ought to walk more humble.

"Second, Mr. Rickey said, 'Remember, it isn't the color of a man's skin that matters. It's what's inside the individual.' And he said some of the people with the whitest skins would be the sorriest I'd meet and some of the darkest ones would be the best. That was 1938. I know now that Rickey had in mind breaking the color barrier almost ten years before he did. I respect him for that, and I went through my career with that respect always in mind.

"I first seen colored at Searcy, 'cepting colored passing through on trucks and once a year a colored team'd come down from Missouri for an exhibition game in Viola and draw a crowd.

"Now I'm playing with Jack. I'm gonna tell you frankly I don't believe in mixed marriages."

"Neither does Robinson," I said.

"Well some do, and I won't argue with 'em. But as far as associatin' with colored people and conversing with them and playing ball with them, there's not a thing in the world wrong with it. That's my way of looking at the thing.

"Lots of people here reckoned like me. And some did not. A few times people come up to me in the winter and said, 'Say, Roe. If you're gonna go up there and play with those colored boys, to hell with ya.' But very few. I always said, 'Well, if that's how you feel, I considered the fellers I play with, I considered your remark, and to hell with *you!*' "

The sun was lowering toward a line of oaks. Before us stretched a wide, bright sky, big sweeping woods, a field of sage. "When I was starting," Roe said, "the Cardinals would look at me in the spring and send me back and take another look in the fall. For five years I pitched at Rochester and Columbus. Then Frankie Frisch, who'd managed the Cardinals when I first come up, moved on to Pittsburgh and wanted me there. I pitched opening day, 1944, the first year he had me. Threw a two-hitter and got beat, 2 to 0.

"In Pittsburgh I commenced to change my style. In '45 my control was a lot better and I led the National League in strikeouts.

"I came back to coach basketball and teach a little high school math that winter. At one game I didn't like a referee's call and I shouted something.

"He shouted, 'Shut up.'

"I thought he shouted, 'Stand up.'

"He decked me. My head hit the gym floor. I got a skull fracture and a lacerated brain. The fracture ran eight inches long.

"I wasn't much good the next couple of years; but I was changing my style and messing with the wet one. I won less than ten games in the next two years, but I was learning.

"Then Rickey got me and Billy Cox for Dixie Walker and Vic Lombardi, a little lefthander, and Hal Gregg. Years later, they said, Rickey put a gun to the Pirates, but hell, he wasn't dealin' with dummies. Billy had been shook by the war. Close as I been to that man, he never talked about it. So what was Rickey getting? An infielder who had been shook real bad and a skinny pitcher with a busted head.

"Now we come to where I quit flyin' in airplanes. For 1948 the Dodgers trained in the Dominican Republic, so Jack and the other colored guys wouldn't have the pressure of bein' in Florida. I went to Miami by train and got on this airplane to the Dominican Republic. Then I flew from there to Puerto Rico and back and then on to the States, and that began and ended my career flying.

"On one of them flights, the plane ahead of us took off into

303

a cross wind and almost wrecked against a hangar. After our pilot assured us he won't do that, we all had to get off. Overloaded. He took off a little gasoline. I knew we was running heavy, and forty minutes out Duke called to the hostess, 'Why isn't this thing flyin' right?'

"She said, 'Look out your window.'

"One of the inboard motors was stopped. We turned back and a little later there's more bucking and Duke said, 'What's doing that now?'

"The girl said, 'Look out the other window.'

"Another inboard motor was stopped. Here we are loaded to capacity, two engines out, and we come over a mountain so low, if I coulda pulled down the window, I'da grabbed me a handful of leaves. We get over the coast and the right outboard motor starts smoking. You counting? Three stopped. We're down to one. Pilot comes on and tells us to buckle in; he might set down in the water. No sharks, he says, just barracuda, so stay on top o' something that floats. We made the airport, and landed among a mess of fire-fighting stuff.

"Couple of days later, we fly back to Florida and we're to take the Dodger DC-3 from Miami to Montgomery, Alabama. Pilot run into a storm. There was twenty-one on the plane, and twenty of 'em was sick. Only Jocko Conlan, the umpire, was okay. Sickest crew you ever saw. We finally had to set down in Tallahassee and we come staggerin' off, and somebody says, 'Lunch is being served.' That was it. I had to see me a doctor. Then someone with the ball club says, 'Preach, go home for three days and pick us up in Asheville, North Carolina.' I caught up with them ten days later in Washington, D.C., by train. I've never been on an airplane from that day to this.

"In '48 we started with three lefthanders, Joe Hatten, a boy named Dwain Sloat and me. Durocher's managing. He calls in me and Sloat and says, 'Hatten's made the club, and I'm only gonna keep two lefthanders. I'm gonna start you both in Cincinnati and the one that looks best gets to stay.' We all shook hands. Then we flipped a coin and I got to pitch first. I had a good game, a three-hit shutout. Next day when Sloat worked, he gave up about as many hits as I did, but Pee Wee kicked one. It beat him his game.

"Now we have another meeting. Durocher says, 'Preach, you won, but you have to admit Sloat looked as good as you did. Remember, I didn't say who won. Just who looked better. You looked the same. So we're gonna do it all over again in Chicago.' And we three shake hands again.

"Welp, if you look into the records, you'll see that in Chicago in '48 I pitched my second straight shutout. Next day the Cubs got to Sloat for five. He goes. I stay. That began my Brooklyn success. Those were the only two shutouts I got all year."

According to the story in *Sports Illustrated*, Roe decided over the winter of 1947—before coming to Brooklyn—that he would try to use the spitter. "But," he said, "I believe I admitted in the article to throwing exactly four specific wet ones. It was a helluva pitch, but it was just one of my pitches; and just one part of my pitching. I ain't gonna tell you now I only threw four at Brooklyn, but, cripes, don't make it come out like the spitter was my only pitch. Some seem to think I threw a hundred spitters every game."

Sitting on the woody roadside, beside a settled, fiftyish man, I could almost see the skinny lefthander who at thirty-three learned above all things to win. His Brooklyn winning records were phenomenal. He had the league's best winning percentage in 1949 and in 1951. During the three years from '51 through 1953 he won forty-four games and lost only eight. He kept ahead. He yielded more homers than most pitchers, but almost never let a home run cost a ball game. He stood on the mound fidgeting, walking in little circles, muttering, scheming. It could take him three hours to win, 3 to 1. He was always chewing gum, touching his cap, tugging his belt or chattering to the air.

"Everybody on the staff threw curves off their fast ball," he said. "They used the fast one to set up the hitter. That helped me. I used one curve to set up another. I had some tricks."

Roe chewed Beech-Nut gum, which he says gave him a slicker saliva than any other brand. To throw a spitter, you use a fast-ball motion, but squeeze as you release the ball. The effect you want, Roe says, is like letting a watermelon seed shoot out from between your fingers. The fingertips have to be both damp and clean. Before throwing the spitball, Roe cleaned his fingers by rubbing them on the visor of his cap. Between innings he dusted the visor with a towel. To "load one," Roe wiped his large left hand across his brow and surreptitiously spat on the meaty part of the thumb. The broad base of the hand was his shield. Then, pretending to hitch his belt, he transferred moisture to his index and middle fingers. Finally, he gripped the ball on a smooth spot—away from seams—and threw. The spitter consistently broke down.

The other Dodgers knew about the spitter. Carl Furillo says that he could tell all the way from right field. "When Preach went to his cap with two pitching fingers together, that was our signal," Furillo says. "That meant it was coming. If he went to his cap with fingers spread, then he was faking."

Within the year 1948 word spread that the skinny Pittsburgh lefthander had learned a great new drop in Brooklyn. Hitters talk to one another. They knew what Preacher was throwing. But no one caught him. While he fidgeted, Roe studied the umpires, as a prisoner might study turnkeys, always on his guard. His closest call came when he had wet the ball, and suddenly Larry Goetz charged from his blind side. Goetz had been umpiring at second. "The ball, the ball, Preacher," Goetz roared.

Roe turned and flipped the baseball over Goetz's head, perhaps six inches out of reach. Reese scooped the ball, rubbed it and threw to Robinson. Jack rubbed the ball again and flipped to Hodges, who threw across the infield to Billy Cox. Cox examined the baseball. It had been rubbed dry. Then he said to Goetz, "Here, Larry. Here's the fucking ball." Roe's control was never better than when he was under pressure.

An extra pitch developed when several hitters read a connection between Roe's touching his cap and his new drop. Did he have vaseline on the visor? A sponge worked into the fabric? No one knew. Everyone theorized. The dry cap on which Roe cleaned his fingers was regarded as the source of moisture.

"Soon as I figure *that* one out," Roe said on the Viola roadside, "I got *another* pitch, my *fake* spitter. I go to my visor more and more. Jim Russell with the Braves one day was looking when I went to the cap and he stepped out. He comes back in. I touch the visor again. He moves out. This went on three or four times. Finally, Jim said, 'All right. Throw that son of a bitch. I'll hit it anyway.' He's waiting for that good hard drop. I touch the visor and throw a big slow curve. He was so wound up he couldn't swing. But he spit at the ball as it went by.

"So you see what I got. A wet one and three fake wet ones. Curve. Slider. Hummer. I'd show hitters the hummer and tell reporters that if it hit an old lady in the spectacles, it wouldn't bend the frame. But I could always, by going back to my old form, rear back and throw hard. Not often. Maybe ten times a game. Right now I could still throw pretty good, if you had a glove and the sage was down and we walked over there into Gray Field. But for just about ten minutes, that's all. And I wouldn't be able to comb my hair tomorrow.

"Well, now, pitchin', you know, is a shell game. You move the ball. You make the hitter guess. There's more than two pitches you can throw at any one time, so the more often he's guessing, the better off you are. The odds are he'll guess wrong. That was mostly how I won so many dang games. Thinkin' ahead of 'em.

Foolin' 'em. Slider away. Curve away. Fast one on the hands. Curve on the hands. Curve away. There's a strikeout in there without one spitter, but maybe I faked it three times."

"Why would you do that article?" I said. "What was the point in confessing?"

"Bad reckoning, I got to say. It wasn't money. Frankly, we were trying to legalize the pitch. The objection to the spitter is that it was supposed to be hard to control. Not everybody can control it and not everybody can throw it, but I controlled mine and Murry Dickson controlled his, which broke upward, and so did Harry Brecheen. I was famous as a control pitcher and here I was gonna knock the argument to pieces. I was led to believe that if one man could prove that it wasn't a dangerous pitch, the spitter would be legalized. That's what I set out to do. But the article made it appear, or the folks who read it seemed to think, that the spitter was all I had. Made me look bad, an', of course, nothin's been legalized. The game is all for the hitters. The other year hitters had a bad season, so they got hysterical. They lowered the mound. Hitters come back strong. Now are they gonna come back and do something for the pitchers? Hell, no.

"The batter's sitting in the circle with a pine tar cloth. Puts tar on his hands, up to his elbows, if he wants, and rubs that bat and gets up there and squeezes and it sounds like a dad-gum car comin' by you, screechin' its wheels.

"But if it's a poor old pitcher, he better not put his hand in his pocket, or touch his hat ever, 'cause they're gonna come runnin' to shake him down. I don't get it."

The sun was flickering behind a stand of oaks.

"Here," Roe said, "to prove my argument, do you think that, as smart as umpires were then and as smart as they are today, a man could have stood out and throwed the spitter time after time without one of them snapping onto you? When people say *all* I had was a spitter, I tell 'em they're insulting the intelligence of umpires."

"But when umpires asked you for the ball, you rolled it to them."

"That's right. They had no business asking. If a man is runnin' around on his wife, there's only two ways he can be caught. That's for him to be seen or for him to admit it.

"If they want to say I'm breaking the rules with the spitter, to hell with 'em. I sure wasn't goin' to admit it when I was pitching."

"Was there a sign, Preacher?" I said.

"In the very beginning, but not fer long. Campanelly would sit back an' shake his head. I'd stand on the mound and shake mine. We'd go on a bit and all the time he'd never give a sign. Heck, he told me one day, 'Preach, I don't need a sign for the spitter. I caught 'em for years in the colored leagues.' "

Roe laughed. His laugh is warm and youthful. Laughter is the youngest part of Preacher Roe.

"How come that field's overgrown?" I said. "Where do Ozark kids play baseball now?"

"Don't," Preacher said. "We got Little League and school ball, 'course, but the old town teams is gone. We got all these new roads. And tourist business. People are eating better. But the young fellers, 'steda workin' on pitching, drive over to Memphis, in three hours, and spend time listening to rock music. They *tell* me it's good for the region, but look at that field." The pale-green sage shivered in the wind. "Funny, isn't it?" Roe said. "Same thing in these woods as where Ebbets Field was in Brooklyn. There'll never be a ball game here again."

A SHORTSTOP IN KENTUCKY

So came the Captain . . .
And when the judgment thunders split the house,
Wrenching the rafters from their ancient rest,
He held the ridgepole up. . . .

EDWIN MARKHAM

Pee Wee Reese was riding a ship back from Guam and World War II when he heard the wrenching news that Branch Rickey had hired a black. Reese had lost three seasons, half of an average major league career, to the United States Navy and he was impatient to get on with what was left when a petty officer said, "It's on shortwave. His name's Jackie Robinson. A colored guy to play on your team."

"Is that a fact?" Reese said, deadpan.

"Pee Wee," the petty officer said, in a needling, singsong way. "He's a shortstop."

"Oh, shit," Pee Wee Reese said.

Across a brace of nights, Reese lay in a bunk, measuring his circumstances and himself. He'd won the job at short, in the double caldron of two pennant races. Now the old man had gone and hired a black replacement. The old man didn't have

310

to do that. But wait a minute (Reese thought). What the hell did black have to do with it? They'd signed a ball player. They'd signed others during the war. White or black, this guy was gonna learn, like Cowboy Bill Hart and Fiddler Ed Basinski, that the war was over now, and the *real* Dodger shortstop was still named Pee Wee Reese.

"Except—except suppose he beats me out. Suppose he does. I go back to Louisville. The people say, 'Reese, you weren't man enough to protect your job from a nigger.' " In the bunk, only one response seemed right: "Fuck 'em." "I don't know this Robinson," Reese told himself, "but I can imagine how he feels. I mean if they said to me, 'Reese, you got to go over and play in the colored guys' league,' how would I feel? Scared. The only white. Lonely. But I'm a good shortstop and that's what I'd want 'em to see. Not my color. Just that I can play the game. And that's how I've *got* ·to look at Robinson. If he's man enough to take my job, I'm not gonna like it, but damnit, black or white, he deserves it." Reese did not speculate on the reactions of other white ball players, but before the Navy transport docked in San Francisco he had made an abiding peace with his conscience.

Three themes sound through the years of Harold Henry Reese, son of a Southern railroad detective and catalyst of baseball integration. The first was his drive to win, no less fierce because it was cloaked in civility. A second theme was that civility itself. Reese sought endlessly to understand other points of view, as with Robinson or with Leo Durocher or with a news photographer bawling after a double-header, "Would ya hold it, Pee Wee, for a couple more?" The final theme echoed wonder. He played shortstop for three generations of Brooklyn teams, and came to sport droll cockiness. Yet near the end, sitting on a friend's front porch and watching a brown telephone truck scuttle by, he said with total seriousness, "I still can't figure why the guy driving that thing isn't me."

Reese played Dodger shortstop the year I entered high school. He played Dodger shortstop when I covered the team. The year I left the newspaper business, he batted .309. He was still able to play twenty-two games at short when he was forty and the Dodgers had moved to Los Angeles, in 1958. "He came from Kentucky a boy," Red Barber liked to say, his voice warmed by sparks of Southern chauvinism. "And he-ah, right he-ah in Brooklyn, we saw him grow into a man, and more than that, a captain among men."

By the time I met Reese he had been team captain for five years and had devised an unpretentious twinkly style of leadership.

"Good God A'mighty," he'd cry in the batting cage after cuffing a line drive to right. "*Another* base hit." The big hitters relaxed and laughed and winked.

"How ya doin', Roscoe?" he greeted McGowen once after a long night game in Philadelphia.

"Not so good, Pee Wee," the gray-haired *Times* man said. He began a monologue on the bad hands he had lately drawn at cards.

Reese listened sympathetically. Then he said, "Roscoe. Did it ever occur to you that maybe it isn't the cards, that you just might be a horseshit poker player?" Even McGowen smiled.

It all seemed so casual that Reese stepped with apparent ease from pleasant trivia to more serious things. He was Jackie Robinson's friend. They played hit-and-run together and cards and horses. Anyone who resented Robinson for his color or— more common—for the combination of color and aggressiveness found himself contending not only with Jack, but with the captain. Aware, but unself-conscious, Reese and Robinson came to personify integration. If a man didn't like what they personified, why, he had better not play for the Dodgers.

Duplicity annoyed Reese. A young Dodger pitcher sat drinking with a girl once when two newspapermen drifted into a hotel bar. "Christ," the ball player said. "Gotta get outa here, 'fore them guys see me and put it in the paper."

Splitting beers with Snider nearby, Reese called, "Hey. You have it wrong. The writers don't want to be treated like stool pigeons. You got caught with a dolly. Run and you make yourself look worse. Buy them a drink. Hell, writers get caught with dollies, too."

In the clubhouse Reese's drawl rarely showed an edge, but between games of one important double-header Billy Cox angered him. "I can't play no more today," Cox said. "Bushed. I gotta save something." Gil Hodges gazed into a locker. Carl Furillo shrugged. But no one spoke. Finally Reese called, "What are you saving something for, Billy? An exhibition game in Altoona?" Cox played the second game.

Reese could have managed the Dodgers. After the overthrow of Dressen, he towered, the obvious successor. "It was not specifically offered," he says, "but they gave me the impression that if I wanted to run for the office, ask real strong, I could have it. Thing was, I didn't want to run." Later he spent one season as a coach. From that point he might have succeeded Walter Alston and he certainly could have managed somewhere. But he quit after a single season. He was rejecting the eternal pressure, the abrasive life, the suffocating responsibility and, I suppose, the eventual firing that is part of a manager's condition of employment. His reason cut deeper than the outward calm. Before Pee Wee Reese retired as shortstop, he had developed a case of stomach ulcers.

He took a job telecasting ball games once a week for NBC. "How do you like that?" he said, with cultivated mildness. "They're paying me to talk into a microphone and I still pronounce the damn word 'th'owed.' " But he was proud of this success, as he was proud of the others, and losing the NBC job to Mickey Mantle wounded him. When I telephoned Reese in Louisville, I said that I was sorry.

"That's show biz," Reese said. "Don't get lost coming here. Make it for brunch. The house is out in Bealesbranch Road."

He was comfortable, I knew. He owned a storm window business and a bowling alley and part of a bank in Brandenburg, Kentucky, and the Cincinnati Reds had hired him to broadcast for a season. "I liked the old NBC job," he said, "but face it. I was never a name like Mantle. I was hanging in and my time ran out. Now it's running out in Cincy, too."

The contentious present has whirled his name into controversy. According to newspaper accounts, a black group in Louisville accused Reese of renting bowling lanes only to whites. Driving out of Roe's Ozarks, through forests, into the Mississippi flats across west Kentucky hills, I wondered intermittently what could have happened. The man had worked ten years for integration, sharing a measure of Robinson's triumph, and ten years after that he stood accused as a segregationist.

"Come in," Reese said, at the door of a rambling, unpretentious house. Bealesbranch is a street of comfortable homes, with tidy lawns and landscaped plots, bespeaking means, if not wealth. Reese guided me through a large carpeted living room, to a veranda under a viny lattice. "Beulah will get coffee," he said. He wore slacks and a knitted shirt. His body looked trim. He eased onto a pale chaise longue. His hair was sandy. You could still read Puck in his face. A choir of birds saluted the morning.

"Nice here," I said.

"We like it."

"What's this racial stuff about you?"

Reese sat up. "What racial stuff about me?"

"The papers said your bowling alley was lily-white."

He winced.

"Could Robinson bowl at your alley?"

"Look," Reese said. "What happened was that a black team wanted to use it on a night when all the alleys were taken by a league. Now maybe that *league* was all-white. I don't check on all the customers. In this climate, charges get wild. But hell"—disgust sounded—"I wouldn't run a segregated *anything*. A little while later, just by accident, I bumped into Robinson at an airport. He'd been speaking somewhere. He came over and asked if I was trying to make him look bad. I began to tell him what I told you, and he just started laughing."

Reese shook his head. "That Robinson. You remember the time he first got into the Chase Hotel in St. Louis. We're all on the bus and the black guys got in cabs to go to their hotel in the colored section. And Jackie gets on the bus.

" 'Hey,' Campy shouts. 'Come with us, Jack.'

"Jack says, 'No, I'm going to the Chase.'

"Campy says, 'Oh, man. Come *on*. We'll all get in the Chase eventually.'

"Jack says, 'I know. But I'm getting there *today*.' "

The housekeeper appeared with coffee. "I'm gonna make this man work," Reese told her. "He intends to write about me because he's forgotten how hard I am to write about. What I mean," Reese said, "is that Robinson or Durocher, stories about them write themselves, don't they?"

"Red Smith says he's waiting for a story that writes itself. He says he always has to push the keys himself."

"But there's nothing *colorful* about me."

"Well, why don't we start by talking about other people, say someone who's doing what you didn't want, managing—Gil Hodges."

"Okay, but I don't have a real good memory."

Reese raised his feet and sipped coffee. "When Gil first came up, a catcher, there were two other catchers around. Bruce Edwards, who was fine, until he put on weight. And Campy. We could play three catchers at once. Edwards at third, Hodges at first. And Campy where he belonged. Gil could play anywhere, but I didn't think he would *ever* manage. It's like me being a telecaster. If someone had told me I'd be doing national TV, I'd have said, '*No way.*' I wasn't that clever. I wasn't that much an extrovert. Rooming with Gil, and we roomed together on one of the trips the team made to Japan, I didn't think he'd be able to take over a club. He wasn't tough enough. Once Dressen put money in Gil's hand and said, 'If there's a play at first and you think the guy is out and they call him safe and you get th'own out of a ball game, I'll give you fifty.' Gil wouldn't do it. People like Maglie always knocked him down. I said, 'Gil. When one of those guys th'ows at you, why don't you drop that bat, or after the game just go up and grab him'—strong as Gil was—'and say, "If you ever come close to me again, I'll *kill* you." ' Gil laughed. Nothing riled him. I didn't think he'd be tough enough. But he's become real tough, I hear. And I can't believe that's Gil."

"To your right," I said, "Billy Cox."

"Best glove I ever saw. He could be compared only to Brooks Robinson, but he had a better arm than Brooks and more speed. A lot of times he'd field the ball absolutely wrong." Reese sprang up and crouched to field a ball hit to his right. "Instead of backhanding, Cox would go for them like this." Reese reached right, but holding up his palm. "That's so awkward you know it's wrong. 'Cept Billy did it. They talk today about the six-finger glove. Billy wore a four-finger glove. So he picks up this terrific smash wrong, with a terrible glove, making it look easy, and then he'd hold the ball. I'd holler, 'Billy. Th'ow the damn ball.' Ol' Cox, he'd just set there, then he'd get the man by half a step."

"Campy was a man you enjoyed."

"Oh, I sure did," Reese said. His voice had been even and cheerful. Now sadness touched him. The voice changed from major to minor. "Damn terrible thing," Reese said. Then, picturing Campanella well again, "Campy was the best I ever saw at keeping the ball in front of him. Watching Johnny Bench, who will be one of the great catchers of all time, that's one thing he has to learn. On the breaking ball that bounces, don't try to catch it. Just keep it in front of you.

"Playing short, I was aware of signs. We might use the first sign after 'two.' A catcher goes 'one-three-two-one,' that's fast ball. The 'one' after the 'two.' But you have to change once in a while." Reese learned sign stealing on the 1940 Dodgers under Durocher and carried the lesson into the fifties. Whenever he reached second base, he tried to read the opposing catcher. If he detected a sign, he had ways of tipping the batter. Leading away in a crouch, hands on knees, might mean he had seen a curve sign. Leading away with hands on hips or standing straight might mean fast ball. "Robinson never wanted signs. Hodges always did."

"Of course," I said. "Hodges needed all the help he could get against good righthanders."

"Didn't we all?" Reese said. "But you see why I was so aware of signs. Once in a while Campy would just go down and pump 'two' for a curve, and I'd think, 'Hell, they're gonna pick that one off.' But, what the hell, maybe I was giving the other teams too much credit."

Beulah brought more coffee. Reese was relaxing and moving easily from man to man. "Carl Furillo," he said, "had this great arm, but he threw a tough ball to handle. He was so close, especially in Ebbets Field. He played that wall better than anyone. If it hit the screen, the ball came straight down. If it hit somewhere else, it came straight back. If it hit another place, it went sort of up in the air. The guy, Furillo, would never miss. And here was a runner coming into second base and Furillo threw so damn hard the ball shot off the grass. You could get to dread that play. But you had to make it.

"Late in my career, I found out Carl was bitter against what he called a clique. Snider, Erskine, some of us out in Bay Ridge, our wives were close together, and we played bridge. Carl lived over in Queens. You didn't just drop by. I talked to Carl about it. I said, 'We have no clique. We have nothing against you. It's one of those things.' I don't remember what he did. I think he nodded. He feels he wasn't close to me, but, hell, I could never get close to Carl."

The telephone rang. Reese answered it and said softly that the figures seemed good. They seemed fine. But he wanted to think them over. He'd call back.

"Selling some shares in the bank," he said. "Where were we? To the Duke? I think he was an only child. They didn't call this guy 'Duke' for nothing. A big man in high school. Good basketball player. Could th'ow a football seventy yards. And he was hitting forty home runs. He could be tough to handle.

"Duke was the greatest going against the wall and catching the ball, but ground balls gave this guy a fit. With a man on first and a ball hit to center on the ground, Duke would not charge. The runners didn't even hesitate at second; they'd just go into third and all the time I'd say, 'Duke, goddamnit. Charge the ball. Sure you're going to make some errors, but you'll make the runners stop at second.' Duke would say, 'Pee Wee, I used to be an infielder. The reason I moved out here is that I hate those damn ground balls.'

" 'All right,' I'd holler in a game. 'Move in.'

"He'd yell back, 'Ah, the hell with it.'

" 'Goddamnit, Duke. Come in a couple steps.'

" 'What kinda steps, Pee Wee? Giant steps or little steps?' In the middle of a damn major league game."

Reese laughed. "There was a day I heard him telling newspapermen, 'The fans right here in Ebbets Field are the worst fans in the world.' They'd been on him or attendance was off or something.

"Well, you know you can't win *that* one, and I said to one

318

writer, Jack Lang, 'He's just hot. Don't use this.' Lang said he
had to use it to protect himself. The way Duke shouted, ten
writers heard and some of *them* were going to use it. So I
hollered, 'Hey, Duke. You don't mean any of this.' He hollers
right back, 'The hell I don't. The Brooklyn fans are the worst
in the world and I want everyone to print it.'

"I said, 'Duke, you're gonna crucify yourself.'

"The Duke said, 'Fuck 'em.'

"The papers came out rough. Next game, we're playing Cincinnati and of all things a lefthander named Don Gross goes
against us. Duke didn't care for lefthanders and he knew he was
in for it from the fans. He didn't feel so mighty then. He
wouldn't go out to warm up. Hell, they had signs: 'Snider, Go
Back to California.' Finally I went out with him and started a
catch. Man, they're booing like hell. Duke got mad and bore
down hard and for as long as that lefthander was in there, he
got base hits. And then they cheered him.

"I hated to be booed. I never read the papers when we lost
or when I had a bad day. The guys may write tough things.
You're better off not reading them. That helped with the writers, but you can't do anything about being booed. I didn't mind
so much on the road or the Polo Grounds, but being booed in
Brooklyn used to *kill* me. Maybe I'd booted a ground ball the
night before. Then I'd tell my wife, 'Dottie, stay home from the
next one. I *have* to do this, but I don't want you there if I'm
being booed.'

"Once she said, 'Look, honey, they never boo *you*.'

"I said, 'You must not listen sometimes then.'

"When I read a ball player saying he doesn't hear the boos,
I think one thing: '*The hell you don't!*'"

"Preacher said after the first pitch he heard nothing."

"Pitchers are different," Reese said. "But did Preach try to
tell you he didn't worry? In '49 we lost the first game of the
World Series, 1 to 0, when Tommy Henrich hit one off Don

Newcombe in the ninth. The next day we're ahead by 1 to 0, and it's a late inning and here comes Henrich and Preacher calls me in. You know how he used to take his cap off and play with his hair and mumble. It took him three hours to pitch a low-run game. I wanted to keep moving. I asked what the hell he wanted.

" 'Man,' Preacher said. 'I see this Henrich up here and it sort of bothers me. I want you to talk to me awhile.'

"I said, 'What the hell we gonna talk about, Preach?'

"He says, 'Fishin' and huntin' are the only things I know enough to talk about.'

"I say, 'All right, Preach. How many hunting dogs you have?'

"I stood there talking for a bit. Then he says, 'Okay, I'm all right.' I go back to shortstop. He gets Henrich. We win, 1 to 0."

Reese remembered Erskine's reluctance to throw at batters, Labine's breaking stuff, Black's big year and how that season, 1952, he himself had lost his poise on a ball field. "I started slow," Reese said, "and one night Dressen sent George Shuba to hit for me. When Dressen whistled and here came Shuba, I couldn't believe it. They didn't hit for me much, not that I was such a great hitter. They just didn't. I saw George and I took my bat and heaved it against that little rack next to the dugout. Those damn bats in there ricocheted for five minutes. The people booed like hell. They were booing Dressen. To make things worse, George struck out.

"The next day in the clubhouse meeting, Dressen walked up and down kind of slow. In my own mind, I'm apologizing like crazy. Dressen said, 'I'm managing this club and if I feel I want someone out of the line-up, that's my decision and don't try to show me up. When you don't get a base hit, I don't raise hell with you. So I don't want you showing me up, but that's what you did to me last night, Reese. You showed me up.' And I said, 'Yeah, yeah. I did show you up and I showed George up and I'm sorry for it and I'll never do it again.' "

The remembrance troubled him. He sipped his coffee and thought and said, "It's funny. When you start talking about the team, I realize how great a ball club this was but how after we left the ball park we were not over all real close. Once you got in the clubhouse, you played bridge. Then boom. The game is over with and, as Furillo says, 'We all went off in our little cliques.'

"And now the guys and I—what is it, ten years, fifteen?—we almost never see each other any more."

He was born July 23, 1918, during the last summer of World War I, on a farm, between the Kentucky villages of Ekron and Brandenburg, forty miles downriver from Louisville. People were leaving farms, and three years later Carl Reese moved his family into the city and went to work for the Louisville and Nashville. As Pee Wee remembers him, his father had racial attitudes characteristic of his time and station. A railroad detective cleared bums out of the yards. Black bums were niggers.

Pee Wee grew, a slight, well-coordinated boy who won marbles tournaments but seemed a questionable baseball prospect. In his senior year at Du Pont Manual High School, he weighed slightly over 110. "I was strong," he says, "for a 110-pounder." He played second base for Manual that season and graduated and found a job with the Kentucky Telephone Company, splicing cables. The pay was $18 a week.

Baseball was for Saturday and Sunday. He had wanted to be a ball player, but his size kept him from taking his own prospects seriously. He spent two years with the phone company as cable splicer, and weekend shortstop, and ballooned to 140. Then, to his surprise, the Louisville Colonels signed him out of a Presbyterian Church League. He had a good year for the Colonels, batting .277. He moved well. His hands were fast. He ran bases brilliantly. Then the Boston Red Sox bought the Louisville franchise for $195,000, and someone suggested that "five thousand was for the franchise. The rest went for the kid at short."

The next year, 1939, Reese blossomed. He led the American Association in triples and he led with thirty-five stolen bases. He stole the thirty-five in thirty-six attempts. But, in a move of minor, enduring mystery, the Red Sox sold him to the Dodgers for $150,000. Tom Yawkey, the president of the Red Sox, ran the franchise as a hobby. He hungered to have his team defeat the Yankees and spent millions in search of a winner. Why, then, would he countenance the sale of Reese?

At the time Larry MacPhail bought Reese's contract, Joe Cronin, the manager of the Sox, was also the shortstop. Cronin was thirty-four. A suspicion persists that Cronin looked south and saw a rival of such talent as to drive him from the field. Cronin says no. Whatever, it is a matter of record that while Reese reigned in Brooklyn, seven men moved into and out of the shortstop's job at Fenway Park, Boston.

Leo Durocher became Reese's champion. He invited Reese to share his Brooklyn apartment and blanketed the rookie with advice and gifts. "Leo was a sharp dresser," Reese says. "I was a kid in polo shirts. If I liked one of his sweaters, he'd give it to me. Year or so ago, he's managing the Cubs and I saw him in Cincinnati. He wore a nice orange sweater and I said I liked it. Damn if the same thing didn't happen. I'm getting to be fifty years old and he's still giving me sweaters and I can't tell him no without hurting him."

Over two seasons, Reese acquired a toughness, somewhat like Durocher's, without developing the older man's abrasiveness. Reese's first year went badly. He broke a bone sliding and later a pitcher named Jake Mooty beaned him. The next season, 1941, his batting average sank to .229, and he made forty-seven errors, more than any other shortstop in the league. Durocher believes that Reese was asking out. "One day in August," Durocher says, "he kicked one in a spot and we got beat. I jumped him hard. He was down, and hoping that I'd take him out and play myself. But errors don't mean that much by themselves. The kid had everything, and the errors were just mistakes. I mean I couldn't field with him by then. So I said, 'Pee Wee. If you think I'm going in there to bail you out, you're nuts. You're playing even if you make twelve errors a day.' " Durocher pauses, milking the moment. "You know what happened then? Pee Wee didn't just play a good game. He played the game of the century. That's right. The kid played the fucking game of the century. And we won the pennant." The next season his batting recovered and he picked up more ground balls than any infielder in baseball. He married a sleek, black-haired Louisville girl named Dorothy Walton in 1942. He was maturing, everyone said, when he went off to war.

In the end his first concern about Jackie Robinson proved groundless. Robinson spent his prime at second base, complementing rather than challenging Reese at shortstop. Indeed, Reese found then that he had to fight for Robinson's job, rather than his own.

In 1947, Rickey delayed promoting Robinson from the International League. The Dodgers and Montreal trained together in the Dominican Republic, and Rickey hoped that the Dodger veterans, seeing Robinson's skill, hungering for a pennant, would demand that Jackie join the team. Never was anyone more deaf to the tenor of his team.

On an exhibition series in Panama, Robinson batted .515. A half dozen Dodgers responded with a petition demanding that he not be allowed to play for Brooklyn. If Robinson was promoted, the petition read, the undersigned would refuse to play.

Reese, not captain then, was respected as a sensible young man. Dixie Walker of Villa Rica, Georgia, presented the petition and Reese shook his head. "I can't sign this thing. I don't know about you guys, but this is my living. I got a wife and a child. I *have* to play ball." Others, like Ralph Branca, a sensitive man from Mount Vernon, New York, and New York University, also declined to sign. But it was Reese's decision that shocked the petitioners. He was a Southerner and confidant of many. The petition was not presented to him again. It failed, and later Walker was traded and Robinson stayed.

After snacks, under the latticework, Reese began to talk about his old friend. His tones had warmth when he mentioned other teammates, but only Robinson moved him to intensity.

"Listen," he said. "This fella was a helluvan athlete. Tennis. Golf. Ping-Pong. You name it. And making that double play, they didn't move him. He'd get over that damn bag. He didn't care how big you were, how hard you slid. He challenged you and he had those big legs and, playing alongside him seven, eight years, I don't remember seeing this guy knocked down. He didn't fear *anything*.

"Al Gionfriddo had a hearts game going in 1947 and Jackie was in it and they asked and I said, 'Yeah. I'll play.' Somebody said to me, 'Damn. How can you sit and play cards with *that* guy?' I said, 'What the hell's wrong with playing with a guy on your own team?'

"I don't know how he took it, to be frank. Mr. Rickey made me captain, maybe for the team but maybe to make me come out a little more, to come on stronger. I remember guys from other teams kidding Jackie. 'Hey, you have your watermelon today?' Or somebody trying to stick the baseball in his ear. Or yelling, 'You black bastard.' And the fans as we came north. Terrible. He didn't let on, but he musta heard.

"One time in Fort Worth, Texas, this guy was really on Jack. I said, 'Hey, Jackie. Don't pay any attention to that son of a bitch. I'll take care of it.' I gave the guy a pretty good blast. He completely forgot Jackie and took off after me. 'You ol' bastard, Reese. You shouldn't even be playin'. You're too damn old!' I laughed at him. He left Jackie alone.

324

"Jackie showed me letters he got. In Atlanta the Klan said they would shoot him if he played. During warm-up I said, 'Jack. Don't stand so close to me today. Move away, will ya?' It made him smile.

"There were times when I went over to talk to him on the field thinking that people would see this and figure we were friends and this might help Jack. And there were times when he was on his own. In Tampa, Florida, Ben Chapman had been cutting Jack strong. I wasn't aware how bad it was. Maybe Jack heard things I didn't; naturally I wasn't listening for them like he would be. Chapman was coaching third for the Reds in this exhibition game and we throw the ball around the infield and my throw goes to Jack pretty hard and he looks at me and makes a little motion shaking his hand. Ben Chapman hollered, 'Hey, Pee Wee. Don't throw it too hard to little Jackie now. You're liable to hurt his little hand.' Jack came across from second base, walked right in front of me, almost to third and said, 'Look, Chapman, you son of a bitch. You got on me for two years and I couldn't say a word. Now you open your mouth to me one more time during this game, I'm gonna catch you and I'm gonna kick the shit out of you.' Jack just turned around and walked back to second and Chapman did not say another word. Chapman was rugged, but you better believe Robinson would have been something in a fight. A guy that agile—and I've seen him kidding around with his fists. Well, you could see from the way he moved that he'd be something."

"The bean balls," I said. "Did Jack get the worst you saw?"

"I guess so," Reese said, slowly. "Yes, sure, I would guess so. You know eventually they have had to have black people in baseball, but just thinking about the things that happened, I don't know *any* other ball player who could have done what he did.

"To be able to hit with everybody yelling at him. He had to block all that out, block out everything but this ball that is

325

coming in at a hundred miles an hour and he's got a split second to make up his mind if it's in or out or up or down or coming at his head, a split second to swing. To do what he did has got to be the most tremendous thing I've ever seen in sports."

He rose and broke out a bottle of Scotch. "Okay?" he said. "Or am I still bad copy?"

"Excellent for a man with a poor memory."

He seemed settled now. The ulcers were healed. He looked contented. Mark Reese came home from school. Mark was twelve, very serious, very polite. "Could you and the gentleman throw some forward passes to me?" he asked.

"Soon as we finish the drink, Mark."

"Yes, sir. I'll meet you out front."

"How's your arm?" Reese said.

"Chicken."

"Don't worry about that," he said solemnly.

We walked to the front lawn. Mark began running what he called a post pattern, starting straight and curling toward a sycamore tree that symbolized a goal post.

Pee Wee threw flat hard passes to Mark's fingertips at the base of the sycamore. To throw the same distance, I had to loft the ball. The first throw brought down a few leaves. So did the second. After my third pass through the sycamore to Mark, Pee Wee looked at me and made a little grin.

"Hey," he said, "you got something against my tree?" I kept the next throws lower. Settled at fifty, the captain is the captain yet.

THE HARD HAT
WHO SUED BASEBALL

Disability directly resulting from injury . . . shall not impair the right
of the Player to receive his full salary for the period of such disability or for the season in which the injury was sustained.

Clause in the Official Player's Contract,
cited in the original *Baseball Encyclopedia*

The wine has soured. There are not going to be any more
hurrahs for Carl Furillo, and those that he remembers, if he
truly remembers any, are walled from him by harsher, newer
memories. His career ended in anger, lawsuits, frustration. He
speaks of one prominent baseball official as "that prick." Another is "a lying bastard." One of his lawyers "ended up buddies
with the guy I paid him five thousand bucks to sue."

When I found Carl Furillo, he was a laborer, installing Otis
Elevator doors in one tower of the World Trade Center, rising
bright, massive, inhuman, at the foot of Manhattan Island. We
sat in a basement shack, beneath incalculable tons of metal and
cement, and talked across ham sandwiches at lunch. Furillo
seemed to enjoy being interviewed. He wanted to hear about
some of his teammates, Carl Erskine and Preacher Roe. But
mostly he wanted to spit rage. He believes that he has been
cheated. The Dodgers released him while he was injured. He

fought back with litigation. "You can't beat them bastards," he says. "I won. I got my money. Then all of a sudden I was black-listed. Nobody wanted me to coach, to pinch-hit, not even in the minors. You seen me. Could I play ball?"

Carl Anthony Furillo was pure ball player. In his prime he stood six feet tall and weighed 190 pounds and there was a fluidity to his frame you seldom see, among such sinews. His black hair was thick, and tightly curled. His face was strong and smooth. He had the look of a young indomitable centurion. I can imagine Reese running a Chevrolet dealership and Andy Pafko coaching high school football and Duke Snider operating a dude ranch in Nevada. But I cannot imagine Carl Furillo in his prime as anything other than a ball player. Right field in Brooklyn was his destiny.

He was a solitary, private man, but not unhappy. He had stopped school at the eighth grade, and on a team of facile, verbal athletes, he felt self-conscious. He thought that he and his wife, a Pennsylvania Dutch girl named Fern, were treated as outsiders. His locker stood diagonally across from the tumult of Reese, Robinson and Snider. "Where I dress," he said, "is where I am. They don't want me in the middle of things."

"Does that bother you?"

"Nah. I ain't got the mouth for that crap"—he said, nodding at the others—"if you know what I mean."

He played with dedication and he played in pain and he was awesome in his strength and singleness. People came early just to watch Furillo unlimber his arm. The throws whined home-ward, hurtled off a bounce and exploded against Roy Campanella's glove—pom, pom, pom, pom—knee-high fast balls thrown from three hundred feet. Throws climaxed his most remarkable plays. With a man on first, someone stroked a hard, climbing line drive. It was going to hit the wall, then carom at one of five angles. Furillo glanced up and ran to a spot. The drive cracked into cement and bounced into his hands. He whirled and loosed a throw. The base runner had to stop at third. The batter had to settle for a single. The crowd gasped at the throw, and then Dodger fans, appreciating how Furillo had read the right-field wall, began to clap, not wildly but rather with respect. Throughout the grandstands men said to one another, "He's a master."

Off the field, Furillo sized up people slowly, then made intuitive, unshakable decisions. He hated Leo Durocher. He disliked Jackie Robinson. He respected Campanella. He admired Dick Young. For reasons I never knew, he accepted me. He spoke with honesty rather than discretion and trusted you to keep him out of trouble. Once in a while, when something he said fired controversy, he stood by his remark. "Maybe I shouldn'ta said it, but I did." He was a man of uncomplicated virtues.

He was proud of the way he had learned to hit good right-handed pitching and of the way he played the wall, but his deepest pride was in his arm. After Willie Mays followed a remarkable catch by whirling and throwing out Billy Cox at home, Furillo said, "I'd like to see him do that again."

"Well," I said, "he did it once."

"I'd like to see him do it again, know what I mean?" Furillo said.

"He can't throw with you," I said, and Furillo nodded.

He seemed enduring as granite in Ebbets Field. It shocked me to see him playing in Los Angeles. Without the old wall, he had lost his native backdrop. He ranged an Antony without the Capitoline, a gladiator in a cardboard coliseum.

I had not kept close track of Furillo when *Newsweek* magazine dispatched me in 1959 to Los Angeles, where the Dodgers and White Sox thrashed through a World Series. In a crowded press row, I found myself beside the Hollywood columnist for the *Herald Tribune*, who had been ordered to cover the Dodger clubhouse and complained periodically, "I don't know what I'm doing here. I haven't seen any baseball since I was thirteen, and I never liked it."

329

Furillo was no longer starting, but that day he pinch-hit a single with the bases loaded. The ball scooted up the middle, hopping narrowly over the shortstop's glove. It was not an old-time Furillo hit, but it won the game. (And the Dodgers went on and won the Series.) Some ninety thousand people cheered, and I told the columnist, "If you think that's something, you should have seen the homer Furillo hit off Allie Reynolds."

The columnist frowned. Near dusk I saw him alone in the press row, crumpled yellow paper scattered about his typewriter. He seemed near tears. "I can't write *anything*," he said. "I don't know these people, so I thought I'd write down quotes and look at their backs and get the numbers and check the program later and see who it was who'd said what. But"—terror touched his face—"they take off their *clothes* in the dressing room. They weren't wearing shirts. Who is the black-haired, handsome guy who talks in short sentences?"

That is how I came to write three sports stories for an infirm *Herald Tribune* under the by-line of a gossip columnist. It was fun trying my hand again and the columnist provided obbligatos of Hollywood chatter, plus door-to-door transportation in the Mercedes-Benz he said had been given to him by Lauren Bacall. But among the shine of walnut dashboards, the glitter of pool parties, I thought, what a hard way for stolid Carl to finish: pinch-hitting in a strange town and being interviewed by people who were surprised to discover that a baseball was stitched with red yarn.

That next spring the Dodgers fired Furillo. Newspapers told a fragmented story of lawsuits, and Furillo faded. Episodic publicity greeted his reappearance as part owner of a delicatessen in Queens, but then he sold his interest and no one seemed to know where he had moved. Several ball clubs offered me addresses, but Furillo no longer lived at any. The telephone company had no record of him in New York City. Someone said he had gone south. Someone said he was living out west. Someone

330

else was certain he had remained in Queens, under another name. I looked for months and mailed half a dozen letters, but I had all but given up when the telephone rang at 9:30 of a Friday morning and a large voice boomed my name.

"Who's this?"

"Carl Furillo."

"Where in the world are you?"

"Downtown. The family's back where I come from, but I'm working in the city during the week."

"Nobody knows that."

"You want to be bothered a hundred times a week? But I got your letters and I been thinking and it's okay. But look, when you come down, do me one favor. Put it down right. I ain't greedy. I ain't nuts. I only wanted what I had coming. I read my fucking contract so many times I got that part memorized by heart." Then he recited the lines that precede this chapter.

By the time Furillo called, winter had come. One tower of the World Trade Center had been topped and sheathed. It stood 1,350 feet, the tallest building on earth, an aluminum hulk against the sky. The other tower still showed girders. Wind was slamming across the Hudson, blowing bits of debris from unfinished floors. Four thousand men had been working for two years, and the sprawling site had acquired the scarred desolation that comes with construction or with aerial bombardment. The sun gleamed chilly silver. It was 11 degrees and getting colder.

A broad stairway led below grade to a cement floor that was wet and patched with ice. Enough daylight entered the vast basement so that wall signs were clear. "TO HELL WITH GOODELL." "VOTE BUCKLEY." "VOTE CONSERVATIVE." This was hard-hat country.

"Otis is over there," someone said, pointing toward a

331

clutch of unpainted wood cabins. "Furillo? The ball player? He dresses in that one."

Inside, a workman standing under a bare bulb said Furillo would be down in a minute. "See that paper bag on that bench? You *know* he's gonna be here. That's his lunch."

The workman's name was Chester; Chester Yanoodi. "Carl stays with me out on the island," Chester said. "He's moved his family back to Pennsylvania. He's in good shape. Real good." Chester was a compact man, with leathery skin and eyeglasses. "I've played some ball myself. On the Grumman Aircraft softball team. I could hit a few."

Furillo entered. "Ho," he called for "hello." Then, "Cold mother out there, huh?" He wore baggy brown pants and layers of clothing. His hair was still black, but he looked heavier. He peeled off a windbreaker and walked in front of an electric heater, beating his arms and blowing on his hands. "Ho," he said again. Then, "Hey, what do you think of the building? It's something, huh? I'm still learning about elevator doors, but I'm not bad. Do I look fatter? I go around 220. Preacher called me one time, and when I told him, he said he was ready to wrestle. Him, that skinny guy, Preacher weighs 223. How do you like that?"

According to a spokesman for the Port of New York Authority, each tower of the World Trade Center requires a thousand elevator doors. "What do you do, Carl," I said, "when all the doors are in and the job is through?"

"Then I'm through."

"Meaning?"

"Back to Pennsylvania. Hunt. Fish. You remember my boy, Butch? He's gonna be a trooper. We'll be all right where we came from. I like to hunt and fish."

"And clam," Chester Yanoodi said. "He's a helluva clam-digger."

"I'm bitter about baseball," Furillo said.

"He could break some necks," Yanoodi said.

332

"Lousy bastards," Furillo said.

He sat on a bench and opened a sandwich and offered me half. Chester handed me a Thermos cup full of coffee. Three other workmen ate silently along the opposite wall, under another naked bulb. Furillo was one of them in the work clothes, but an interview reminded them that he was set apart, too. They knew it. They sat respectful. Furillo began to tell what had happened.

He never won the batting championship again after 1953, but he had six more good years. In 1955 he hit 26 homers and batted .314. In 1958, when the Dodgers sank to seventh at Los Angeles, he was still the solid man, with a .290 average and 18 homers. By then he was fighting pain. Under the beating of fifteen thousand innings and five thousand sprints to first base, his legs began to cramp. He had to miss days and later weeks. Professionalism and toughness drove him, but in 1959, the year of the World Series ground single, he played in the outfield only twenty-five times.

During the first week of the following season, Furillo was running out a ground ball, hurrying across first base, when his left foot found a soft spot on the floor of the Los Angeles Coliseum. Something tore in the calf. Pain crippled him.

Buzzy Bavasi wanted change. The Dodgers of 1959 were ribbed by Brooklyn veterans. Nineteen-sixty was a time to turn over personnel. A team must change constantly if it is to win. The calf injury convinced Bavasi that Furillo's glories were history. He summoned Furillo to his office at the Statler Hilton Hotel and asked, "What do you think of Frank Howard, Carl?"

"I don't think he hits the curve good."

"But he has promise."

"You don't hit the curve, you don't belong here."

"How's your leg?"

"Coming along, but slow."

"That Howard's gonna be something," Bavasi said.

Bavasi was bearing a message down Byzantine ways. He was suggesting that Frank Howard had arrived, and that Furillo, like Carl Erskine, should make way gracefully to the judgment of years. Retire. Then, perhaps, the Dodgers would find him a job.

Fighting for his career and the last days of his youth, Furillo beat off that conclusion. Three days later, as the Dodgers prepared to fly to San Francisco, an official telephoned and said, "Carl, don't bother to pack." Furillo decided that Bavasi was giving him more time to rest his leg. But after the series Bavasi himself called and said, "I'm sorry to have to inform you that you've been given an unconditional release."

Furillo cursed and hung up. Then he studied his contract. He drove through thirty-two arid paragraphs until he found the clause he wanted. He was hurt, unable to play, and the Dodgers had released him. It didn't matter how slick Bavasi was or how much money O'Malley had. They *couldn't* release him when he was hurt. He took out a pencil and began to calculate.

His salary for 1960 was to be $33,000. He had drawn $12,000. That meant the Dodgers were welshing on $21,000. "You know, Fern," he said, "I think I'm gonna do something. I got an idea."

Within an hour reporters came unannounced to the house he rented in Long Beach. A Dodger official had tipped them to the story. "What do you think about being released?" one sportswriter said.

"I don't like it."

"Are you hurt bad?"

"I can't play, and that means they can't release me." Furillo explained the official contract succinctly.

"What are you going to do?"

"You asked me so I got to tell you. I'm gonna talk to two guys I know."

"What two guys?"

"You asked me so I got to tell you. Two guys who're lawyers."

Furillo had not intended to reveal his scheme, but he felt that principle forced him to speak. When a man is released, he has to face reporters, and when he faces reporters, he has to answer what he is asked. He was surprised the next day to see his name and projected lawsuit in headlines.

Bavasi's secretary called and asked him to stop in again. "Soon as I take care of something," Furillo said.

He found Bavasi enraged. "Of all the dumb dago things to do. I was going to find a spot for you. Now I can't. You've made trouble for you and me and everybody. What a rock."

"Hey, Buzz," Furillo said. "I got a message for you. It's from the clubhouse man."

"What's that?"

"In my pocket here." Furillo reached into his jacket and withdrew a subpoena.

Bavasi maintains that he "would really have looked after the guy, but not at $33,000." He speaks of sending Furillo to Spokane and developing him into a coach. O'Malley shakes his head and says a man has to learn to accept things as they are. Both feel Furillo broke a code. In the extralegal world of baseball, a dissatisfied player may protest to the Commissioner, who is supposed to look upon club owners and their chattels without partiality, but is hired and fired by the owners. Turning to the courts is considered nihilistic. No one in baseball, or in the law, knows just when a judge will decide that the official player's contract is itself invalid. The people who run baseball regard anyone exposing them to such risk as indecent. "I'm not sure what would have happened with Furillo," Bavasi said, "but there were options." Hiring lawyers foreclosed every option but one. There would be battle.

While the legal proceeding dragged, one of Walter O'Malley's representatives asked if Carl would settle for a job as counselor in the Dodgertown Camp for Boys at Vero Beach. Furillo moved toward court and the following spring wrote letters to eighteen major league teams. He would pinch-hit or play; he had plenty left. Nobody hired him. "It's gotta be because I'm hurt," he said. "That damn injury is still messing me up." He wanted to sue for two years, instead of one.

In May of 1961, a year after the injury, Furillo met with Ford Frick, the Commissioner, and Paul Porter, Frick's attorney. According to Furillo, he collected the $21,000 due for 1960, and collected nothing for 1961.

If one thinks of blacklist in terms of the old McCarthyism when the three television networks in concert refused to employ writers or actors with a so-called radical past, then Carl Furillo was not blacklisted. As far as anyone can learn, the owners of the eighteen major league clubs operating in 1961 did *not* collectively refuse to hire him. What they did was react in a patterned way. Here was one more old star who wanted to pinch-hit and coach. He could have qualified marginally, but once he sued, people in baseball's conformist ambiance decided he was a "Bolshevik." Hiring him at thirty-nine was not worth the potential trouble. Walter O'Malley was no Borgia, plotting to bar Furillo from the game. Only Furillo's decision to hire lawyers was at play. The existential result was identical.

Furillo returned to Reading, investigated several businesses and liked none. In 1963 he resettled in Queens. Then he bought a half interest in a small delicatessen and restaurant on Thirty-second Avenue under the shadow of a Consolidated Edison gas tank. At Furillo and Totto's cheeses hung from the ceiling. Neighborhood people bought prosciutto and Italian sausage. Children loitered and in the afternoon you could hear Furillo's voice booming. "Hey, kid. The candy's for buying not for touching." Late at night, in the restaurant, you could order hero sandwiches prepared by Furillo himself.

The trouble, said Fern, was the hours. Carl had to get up early and he had to work late. "You hardly see the family any more," Fern said.

"I got to make a living."

After seven years, Furillo sold his share in the store and moved his family back to Stony Creek Mills, on the north side of Reading, where he was born. Then he took his job with Otis. He wanted to think several years ahead. He would work hard until he was fifty, spending only weekends with the family. But then, with the money he made in construction and with his pension, he would be set. There would be nothing but time for hunting and fishing, for Fern and the boys. That was how, he explained, he had come to be wearing a yellow hard hat and these rough clothes in this barren workingman's shack.

"You've missed some damn nice years," I said.

"They really screwed him," pronounced Chester Yanoodi.

"Aah," Furillo said. "It ain't been bad."

He reached back in memory beyond the bitter time. He could always play ball, he said. He could throw, and his brother Nick encouraged him to play and, hell, he said, when he got through with grade school what were the jobs? Picking in an apple orchard for $5 a week. Helping in a woolen mill for $15. But the family kept him close, and it wasn't till he was eighteen and his mother died that he could go off to be a professional. He spent a year at Pocomoke City on the Eastern Shore of Maryland and hit .319. A season after, he played at Reading under Fresco Thompson, who watched him throw, gasped and encouraged him to pitch. "The experiment," Fresco said, "ended within three games. He could certainly throw, but who knew where? He broke four ribs and two wrists before we decided as an act of public safety to make him spend all his time in the outfield."

He came to Brooklyn in 1946, the vanguard of Branch Rickey's youth movement, and moved into center field between Dixie Walker and Pete Reiser. Once he spoke to Reiser about a radio program he enjoyed. "Hey," Reiser shouted. "This guy thinks 'The Dorothy and Dick Show' is 'The Dorothy Dix Show.' What a rock. Hiya, Rock." With Furillo's hard body and deliber-

337

ate ways, ball players thought the cruel nickname fit. Furillo felt like an outsider because in many ways he was made to feel that way.

"I started having trouble with Durocher the year after that," he said in the Otis shack. "A guy's no good, he's no good. He didn't want to play me against righthanders, and Mike Gaven asked how I liked being platooned. He asked. I had to tell. I didn't like it. He wrote the story. Durocher said, 'Hey, kid. You trying to run my team?' Why didn't he get on Gaven?"

"It's a good thing for Durocher Carl can't get his hands on him today," Chester said.

"Forget it," Furillo said.

In 1949 Durocher was managing the Giants, but before one game in Brooklyn he poked his head into the Dodger clubhouse. Furillo was sitting on a black equipment trunk. "Hey," Durocher shouted. "We had you skipping rope with the left-hander last night. Tonight we got the righthander. You'll be ducking."

"Go fuck yourself," Furillo said.

A minute later Herman Franks looked in. "In your ear," he cried. "Tonight we get you, dago."

Chester broke into the story. *"Dago?* They called *you* 'dago' to your face?"

"All the time," Furillo said. Then, kindly to the old Grumman softball player, "Things are different in the big leagues."

That night the righthander, Sheldon Jones, hit Furillo with a pitch. The next afternoon, Jones visited the hospital where Furillo was recovering from a concussion. "I'm sorry, Carl," Jones said. "It was a curve."

"First fucking curve that never bent," Furillo said.

"I just threw what Durocher told me to," Jones said.

"I know," Furillo said. "I ain't blaming you." He promised himself to get even. It was that 1949 promise that flared at the Polo Grounds when Furillo charged to tackle Durocher and the entire Giant ball club in 1953.

"Six times I got hit in the head," Furillo said. "Maybe I ducked slow, but they was always gunning for me. So I had a right to gun for the guy that started it. Right?"

"You gunned 'em yourself," I said. "How many did you throw out from right field?"

"They all the time write eight. They count seven I caught rounding the bag. I threw behind them. There's only one guy I really threw out. A pitcher. Mel Queen. He hit a liner at me. I grabbed it on a hop and my throw beat him. Write the truth. I threw out *one* guy."

"About the right-field wall," I said.

"I knew you'd ask that." His dark face lit.

"Well, how did you get to play it like that?"

"I worked, that's fucking how. I'd be out early and study it. Preacher and Billy Cox hit fungoes for me. Now as the ball goes out you sight it, like you were sighting down a gun barrel. Except you got to imagine where it's going. Is it gonna hit above the cement? Then you run like hell toward the wall, because it's gonna drop dead. Is it gonna hit the cement? Then run like hell to the infield. It's gonna come shooting out. Now you're gonna ask me about where the scoreboard came out and the angles were crazy. I worked. I worked every angle in the fucking wall. I'd take that sight line and know just where it would go. I wasn't afraid to work."

"Do you still play ball?" I said.

"He don't even play catch," said Chester.

"Arm still hurt?"

"It ain't that. The Mets were after me when I had the store. Play in old-timers' games. I figured, why? I got the store and I got to work at it, but once the Yankees was having one and Fern said, 'Go ahead. See the guys you played with.' I went. I put on spikes. I'd been off 'em ten years. I rocked. I thought I was gonna fall over. I couldn't walk on spikes. I made it to the outfield. Someone hit a little fly. I ain't caught a fly in ten years. Son of a bitch, the ball looked as though it was six miles up. I said to myself, 'See the old guys if you want to, but for Christ's sakes, don't do this no more. Don't ever put on spikes again.' "

The three young workers across the shack sat wide-eyed. "You got to watch out for yourself," Furillo told them. "There was this guy on the team, Carl Erskine, and he was such a nice guy that when they ordered him to throw at a hitter, he'd throw ten feet over the man's head. And he had arm trouble and he quit young and they put out stories that they were really looking after him. He was through in 1959, the year before I got hurt. I said to him, 'Hey, is that right? The ball club treated you fair?' He didn't want no trouble, but I'll never forget what he told me. He said, 'Carl. Take care of Carl.' "

Furillo puffed air and offered me more coffee. "If I really wanted to hit 'em," he said, "I'd have another suit. Two back operations. The bad leg had me walking funny and I had to have two operations for a ruptured disc. That come on account of the injury, but I figure, fuck it, I got to take care of myself and I can do it." The young hard hats nodded vigorously.

"Hey," Furillo said, "what is it with the colored today? They got to get welfare? It's tough, but was it easy for the Italians? Five dollars a week in the apple orchard, was that easy? Why should the colored have it easier than anybody?"

More nods.

"It isn't the same," I said. "You were playing ball and Robinson couldn't."

"He wasn't the only guy got thrown at."

"Ah, you're talking like a hard hat."

"That's what I fucking am. But when this building gets through, it's in the barrel. I put the lid on this city, New York, where I had some good times, and Los Angeles, where I should never have gone, and back with Fern up around Reading and hunt and fish and take my pension. I'll be fifty. Hey, I like a lot of colored. Campy and Joe Black, he was a nice guy. I don't think they ought to have it easy, that's all."

He does talk like a hard hat and he was a baseball Bolshevik. He fits no label. He is too human, too large, too variable, too much the independent. In one voice he talks against welfare, like a Buckley, and in another voice, which is the same, he talks about ball players' rights and defies a system, like Bartolomeo Vanzetti.

"Hey," he shouted. "Who got a hammer? I need a hammer. Having trouble with a door." He turned. "I got plenty tricks to learn," he said. Someone found him the hammer and he began zipping into his winter clothes, gruff, cheerful and defiant of pity.

"Come 'round in spring," Furillo said, slamming a yellow hard hat on his head. "In spring we'll sit outside and you and me can take a little sun."

ONE STAYED IN BROOKLYN

The New York Mets were the worst team in the league during the days of Casey Stengel; their players were bitterly, hopelessly humiliated. When some of the youngsters showed signs of becoming first-rate professionals, Gil Hodges was named manager and the Mets became serious.

CURT FLOOD (WITH RICHARD CARTER), *The Way It Is*

Late spring is the time to see Gil Hodges work. Not summer. Then heat sits on the cylinder of Shea Stadium and a baseball season, like New York summer, grinds down strong men. Not September. The weather cools, but then the final pressures of a pennant race clamp Hodges into a vise. He manages the New York Mets, contenders like the Dodgers, but a generation younger than he, people playing the same game in a different time, and by September his face shows leather strain lines and his soft voice becomes ever more tightly controlled. But in late spring Hodges watches his ball club settle in. He almost relaxes. There are no baseball irrevocabilities in the month of May.

During August of 1968, Hodges suffered the forewarnings of a heart attack. The Mets were moving from ninth place to eighth amid dizzying waves of adulation. Hodges, the still point,

342

smoked heavily and tried to bury tension within his large frame. On about September 19, 1968, he felt what he calls "pain like a drill boring into my chest." It was not excruciating, but neither did it go away. For five days he ignored the boring, the way his old roommate Carl Furillo might have done, although the pain disrupted sleep and shattered concentration. "Did I know what it was?" Gil Hodges says. "I suppose so. Yes. Did I *want* to know what it was? No." He continued managing for a week. Then, during the second inning of a night game at Atlanta on September 24, he excused himself from the dugout, walked into the dressing room and lay down on a training table. His skin was ashen and he felt chilly. "I got to rest," he told Gus Mauch, chief trainer of the Mets, who had followed him inside.

A local physician put a stethoscope to Hodges' chest, and said he thought Gil could go home and check into a hospital the next morning. Mauch, who is not an M.D., was more cautious. He had suffered a heart attack himself. He urged Hodges to ride a taxi with him to Crawford W. Long Hospital, which is named for the man who first mastered the use of ether. By midnight Hodges lay under intensive care. He had suffered a myocardial infarct, a heart attack of so-called "mild" proportions. He had walked about for a week, hit fungoes, pitched batting practice, with a developing coronary. The strongest of the Dodgers was fortunate still to be alive at forty-four.

As far as researchers can tell, six specific factors contribute to the heart attack that strikes a man in his mid-forties: poor diet, insufficient exercise, overweight, heredity, smoking and— catchall for most ills of modern man—stress. Only the last two considerations apply directly to Hodges. Still two out of six were enough. He built an outer barrier of calm, but he churned beneath the way the sea churns below a pale, rippled surface. "And the smoking got out of hand," he says. "I knew I was smoking too much. Don't write I've stopped. I sneak one every so often. But I'm fine. I do sit-ups, push-ups, run. I do everything

I ever did except pitch batting practice. I'm perfect, if you can overlook a few mental hang-ups."

"Such as?"

"You have one of those things, you don't forget it."

Gil Hodges the ball player cast a sense of strength. He stood six feet two, and with no extra fat he weighed more than two hundred pounds. After playing cards once, he returned to his compartment on a train and found Dick Williams reading in the lower berth. "How did you do?" Williams asked.

Hodges smiled faintly. Then he slipped both arms under Williams, 190 pounds himself, and lifted him into the upper bunk.

He had the largest hands in baseball. "Gil wears a glove at first because it's fashionable," Pee Wee Reese said. "With those hands he doesn't really need one." People were always kidding about his physical powers.

Hodges has to be the strongest human in baseball.

What about Ted Kluszewski?

If he's stronger than Hodges, he ain't human.

Did you hear what went on after Hodges hit the beach at Okinawa?

The Japs surrendered.

Not only that. Half our Marines did, too.

You know what happens when big Gil squeezes that bat?

No. What?

Instant sawdust.

Beyond the jokes stood a large, quiet, intense man, somewhat surprised at his own success and damned to cringe before tough, righthanded pitching. Remembering Hodges against Sal Maglie or Allie Reynolds, I see a man hating to come to bat against such intimidating stuff and hating more the fact of his own fear.

One's response to a curve ball and its illusion of impending concussion is almost reflex. One wants to duck. Some, like Billy Cox, conquer the reflex with comparative ease. Most do not.

Athletes as heroic as Jim Thorpe never learned to control the reflex well enough to hit a good curve. Without precisely knowing—good hitting remains as mysterious as any other art—I suspect a mild phobia is at play. Mild, because batting is genuinely a high-risk occupation. It is normal for a hittter to be aware of the danger.

Few of us are anxious to paint bridges; real risk exists and our sense of self-preservation asserts itself in distaste for high winds that keen through suspension cables. Conversely, the fearless bridge painter may himself be discomfited by tunnels or by ocean breakers. No one is a coward because he shuns suspension towers, or because he draws back from a baseball hurtling toward his head. Rather it is a measure of courage that Hodges fought his cringe reflex year after year. To taste fear as he did and to choke it down and make a fine career is a continuing act of bravery.

Hodges hit 370 home runs, four in a single game. Swinging hard, he batted .273 across eighteen seasons. But his conflict, the reflex to duck contending with the desire to hit, almost snipped his career before he was thirty.

On September 23, 1952, the day on which the Dodgers clinched a pennant, Hodges singled off Karl Drews, a Yankee reject who had joined the Phillies and threw hard sinkers. Hodges did not hit safely again that week. Humiliation came with the World Series. Hodges went to bat twenty-six times, and during these tense games, when men about him rose to the drama of the days, he suffered in a public impotence. He walked five times, but he made no hits in any of the seven Series games.

The spring brought no relief. Hodges outran a ground ball for a single on opening day, but by the middle of May he was batting .187 and Charlie Dressen sent him to the bench. The fans of Brooklyn had warmed to the first baseman as he suffered his slump. A movement to save him rose from cement sidewalks and the roots of trampled Flatbush grass. More than thirty people a day wrote to Hodges. Packages arrived with rosary beads, rabbits' feet, mezuzahs, scapulars. One man wrote that pure carrot juice would restore the batting eye. "Vitamin A," he explained.

Charlie Dressen knew what was wrong. He ground his teeth and swung his arms. "The trouble," he said, "is they won't let ya teach 'em till they is real down." Without telling Hodges, Dressen asked Barney Stein, the team photographer, to shoot hundreds of feet of movies. A few days after the benching, Dressen thought Hodges was ready to be taught and called him into his office, beside the clubhouse.

In the most telling strip of Stein's film, Hodges was hitting and Andy Seminick was catching for Cincinnati. As the ball approached, Hodges drew back his bat, and stepped toward the third-base dugout. His stride carried him away from home plate. He followed the pitch into Seminick's glove, certain that it was outside. It was a strike. Had Hodges swung, his weight would have gone toward the safety of a dugout, while his arms and bat moved toward the ball. He was off balance. His timing suffered. He got neither weight nor accuracy into the swing. "See it, see it," Dressen cried.

"Mmmm," Hodges said, for "yes."

"Now ya been stepping that way for a long time and maybe ya ain't gonna stop," Dressen said, "but I can fix it so a step like that don't hurt ya, if you're willing to listen."

"I'm listening right now, Charlie."

"Keep your front foot where it is, but move the back foot farther from the plate. See what I mean. Now when ya pull back, the way ya do, you'll just be stepping into line. It won't hurt ya so much, stepping outa the way like ya do, cuz ya won't be really stepping out of the way, you'll really be stepping into it. I wancha to overcompensate, or some word like that."

That season, 1953, Hodges batted .302. In the World Series of 1953 he led all the Dodger hitters with .364. His weakness persisted, but his career was saved.

346

"I remember that slump very well," Hodges said softly, as we left his house on Bedford Avenue near Avenue M. It is a large, unpretentious, comfortable home—the Hodges have four children—in a quiet neighborhood that has shown little outward change since the 1940s. We were going to drive from the house to Shea Stadium, where that night the Mets would play the Chicago Cubs. "Having had to fight slumps, does that help you manage?" I said, as we climbed into my car.

"Not by itself," Hodges said, "although I understand you can't help a man until he's willing to be helped. I probably would have understood that anyhow. Charlie's way isn't the same as mine. Take the man in the other dugout tonight, Leo Durocher; not in any way criticizing, he makes noise. I'm not built that way. I communicate through my coaches. I have rules that I want obeyed, but I keep the coach between myself and the player, which establishes a distance that I like and prevents arguments. You don't want to be arguing with them yourself when you're manager."

"How is it working with people of a different generation?"

Hodges mused. "Go left up here," he said. "We want to hit the Shore Parkway. Then into Van Wyck. That'll take us in."

Silence. Hodges uses silences. He seems to enjoy them.

"Is it tough working with kids?" I said.

"Oh," Hodges said. "That's right. You had a question in there, didn't you? No. I haven't found it all that tough."

"Your background is different from theirs. You came out of the mines."

"No. I was never down in the mines. My father never would let me go down in the mines."

"Mining country."

"That's true."

"Well, you came out of hard times, and when you broke in, the game was all-white. Now you're managing men who've gotten good money to sign, and they're black and white."

Hodges looked over oncoming traffic as we pulled onto the

Shore Parkway. "I can honestly say that color was never a problem to me," he said. "It wasn't to Pee Wee or the others either. And it isn't now." He puffed his lips in a faint sigh and began to talk easily about his background.

Princeton, his hometown, lies below the White River in the southwestern corner of Indiana. You can make a triangle from Anderson to Princeton to Louisville—Erskine, Hodges and Reese—and plot the Dodgers from the Middle Border. Princeton was coal country, and (as Gil remembers) his father rode down to deep veins in order to support his family and died slowly, one part of his body at a time. An accident cost an eye. Another cost some toes. At fifty-four he injured a knee and as Big Charlie Hodges lay in a hospital recovering from surgery, an embolism stopped his heart in 1952.

"Did *you* want to go down into the mines?" I said, as we drove beside the foul blue waters of Jamaica Bay.

"I didn't want to go down," Hodges said. "I didn't want to ever work down there."

Charlie Hodges had two sons, Gil, called "Bud," and Bob. Both were big and well coordinated and Charlie taught them what he knew about playing ball. If he could not escape the mines himself, at least he'd show the boys a better way. After high school they went to St. Joseph's College near Indianapolis. Bob, fourteen months older than Gil, entered the Army in 1942. Gil, who ran track, and played football, basketball and baseball, caught the attention of Stanley Feezle, the scout and sporting goods man who signed Carl Erskine. Feezle sent Hodges to a tryout camp at Olean, New York. From there Hodges went to Brooklyn, for personal examination by Branch Rickey. He was, as someone has said, "the kind of prospect who secures a scout's job for life."

Over three morning workouts, Rickey moved Hodges through eight positions, every one but pitcher. "You ever think of catching, young man?"

348

"No, sir."

"You have a little hitch in your throw at shortstop. Catching would be a marvelous opportunity."

Hodges signed for a $500 bonus and joined the 1943 Dodgers, a team of Durocher, Luis Olmo, Mickey Owen, Billy Herman and a waning Dolph Camilli. Hodges played one game—at third. He walked once, stole a base and struck out twice. Then he was drafted into the Marines, where he spent the next twenty-nine months. Whatever heroics he may have worked, he keeps to himself. He says only that he started smoking "to have something to do sitting in those holes in Okinawa."

Bob Hodges' baseball career ended with a bad arm in the low minors. Then he went to work for the U.S. Rubber Company. When Gil returned to baseball, Rickey gave him another $500, and sent him to Newport News to master catching. A year later Hodges leaped to Brooklyn and became catcher number three.

The next season, 1948, the outlines of the team began to show. Billy Cox took over third. Jackie Robinson moved to second base. Snider and Shuba appeared in the outfield. Roy Campanella caught and Hodges, handed Robinson's discarded mitt, was assigned to first.

He had to struggle. That season he batted .249. But he hit twenty-three home runs for the pennant winners of 1949 and led the league in fielding. In 1951 he hit forty homers, the second highest total in baseball. He seemed to have arrived. Then the slump seized him.

"With me," he said, as we parked close to the players' entrance at Shea Stadium, "it was a battle. I *always* had trouble with the outside pitch. Some don't. I did." He shrugged.

We walked through the Mets' dressing room, carpeted and empty, into Hodges' office, a large underground room without windows. "Did you plan on managing?" I said.

"How can you plan on getting a job that may not be offered? I suppose I hoped, but when George Selkirk asked me to take

349

over Washington, I didn't jump. I called some people. Talked to my wife, Joan."

"Do you find it hard?"

"Sending out an older player, telling him he's released, is hard."

"How about strategy?"

"Most is simple logic. I don't think it calls for any great thinking."

"Hello, Dad," called Gil Hodges II, a cheerful, chunky boy of nineteen. "I thought me and my friend Jack here could work out."

Hodges looked at his oldest son. "Since you got a haircut, okay." Someone appeared and began to talk to Hodges about the jewelry he could get wholesale and Hodges nodded and said he had to go out for a minute and look for Rube Walker, his pitching coach.

The two boys dressed quickly. "Hey," the younger Hodges said to Jack, "what kind of spikes you wearing?"

"What do you mean what kind?"

"They got white tops."

"That's right. The uppers are white."

"Well, you can't use them here. My father's a kind of conservative man."

"He don't seem bad."

"He isn't. He's just kind of conservative."

Hodges returned. "Your hair should be even shorter," he said. Young Gil grinned and shook his head. The father dressed silently. "I'm not a Durocher type," he repeated at the batting cage. "I can't get that worked up all the time."

"Or even talk that much," I said.

"You got it," Hodges said.

I turned and suddenly he was gone. I found him back in his office, speaking with Harold Weissman, the Mets' publicity director.

350

"Tommie Agee," Weissman said, "is having chest pains."

"How old is Agee?"

"Twenty-seven."

Hodges looked pale and concerned. "Don't tell the papers just yet."

"A city edition will be closing," Weissman said. "We can't withhold something like that."

"Don't tell them," Hodges said.

"You're losing points with me, Hodges."

"If it was a matter of needing your points, I wouldn't be behind this desk. You're losing points with *me*."

"Give a man an office," Weissman said, "and he goes wild."

"We should wait," Hodges said. "Wait for the cardiogram. Then if it's nothing, you can announce it as chest pains that *weren't* a coronary."

"Got you," Weissman said.

"The word scares people," Hodges said.

"We'll wait," Weissman said.

"Rube out there?" Hodges asked.

"Ru-u-ube!" someone called.

Rube Walker, the catcher who backed up Roy Campanella, has grown bald and portly.

"How's Koosman?" Hodges said.

"No complaints," Walker said.

"Good," Hodges said. The phone rang on his desk. Someone from the front office was calling. "Yes," he said. "Yes. I've taken care of that. Long distance? Sure. Put it on the other line."

Gil Hodges' salient quality, strength, works a strained contrast against the tension of his silences. A slim fierce infielder named Don Hoak appeared with the Dodgers during Walter Alston's first year and established himself as a neurotic. Hoak liked to be called "Tiger," and he raged several times a day, as others might take meals, or yawn. Hoak had fought professionally in Pennsylvania and when he became angry—at a train schedule, at an umpire or at the color of the sky—he cocked his fists. Visiting the clubhouse once, I saw him chattering at Hodges, then suddenly throw two punches to the upper arm. Hodges is fair-skinned. The blows left small red marks. Expression flowed from Hodges' face. He stared at Hoak, his pale eyes the more menacing because they showed no emotion. Hodges himself did not so much as make a fist, but before the gaze Tiger Hoak retreated.

A sense of strength stays with a man. When Hodges managed the Washington Senators, he learned once that four players were violating a midnight curfew. Hodges believes in curfews and he convened his ball club and announced: "I know who you were. You're each fined one hundred dollars. But a lot of us are married and I don't want to embarrass anyone. There's a cigar box on my desk. At the end of the day, I'm going to look into that box and I want to see four hundred dollars in it. Then the matter will be closed." Hodges gazed. At the end of the day, he looked into the cigar box. He found $700.

Against this sense of power and command beat the serious silences of Gil Hodges. Always (it seemed to me) the silences were tense. Yes, he could lift Dick Williams, flatten Don Hoak, physically awe an entire team. But he knew how weak physical strength really was. He had learned that watching his father die one part at a time. And he learned it again, when smaller, weaker men mixed fast balls at his head with curves. It was fine for Reese to talk about flattening a pitcher, as if flattening one man would work. But the game was played by rules and one rule commanded him to stand in and take it and he believed in rules. He practiced a devout, quiet Catholicism and he sought humility, but he drove himself to move ahead and drove himself to fight down fear, and what can give a strong athletic man a frightful heart attack at forty-four is the war he wages within himself, even if he is soft-voiced, like Hodges, and blankets the conflict under casual remarks, a hard blank look, bantering ways and the faint, almost casual smile.

Tommie Agee had not suffered a coronary. By nine o'clock he was back in Shea Stadium. "Chest pains," Harold Weissman announced in the press box, "which were probably caused by indigestion. We had a precautionary cardiogram and it proved negative." A crowd of 50,586 appeared, but it was not an easy night. The Cubs scored three in the first inning when Jim Hickman, an original Met, who was traded in 1967, hit a home run. After one of Koosman's pitches in the second inning, Jerry Grote, the catcher, called time. Hodges walked toward the field and Grote said, "He had nothing on it. Something must be hurting." At the mound Koosman admitted that his arm ached and came out of the game. Later a downpour stopped play for fifty-five minutes. The Cubs stayed ahead and won, 6 to 4.

Hodges had promised to talk on a Chicago television program after the game. Still in uniform, sweating from the sultry heat, concerned about Koosman, reminded of heart pains by Agee, he made his way up runways to the corner of the press box that would serve as the studio.

"Yes," he told the announcer, an ebullient man named Jack Brickhouse, "I'm disappointed in the loss, but the Cubs played well. Agee is fine. He'll play tomorrow. Koosman? We'll have to wait a day. We're hoping it's nothing." Then, "Thank you, Jack. Thanks for having me. I've enjoyed talking."

The television lights blinked off. We started down the runway, myself and the manager of the Mets, a forty-five-year-old postcoronary. In the half light his face seemed dry and gray.

"Tough night?"

"They're *all* tough. I mean it. I'm being serious. In this

353

job the days don't get easier. I thought maybe we could sit up a while, but with the rain and all the problems, when I go home, I better go to sleep. The one thing after a heart attack is you don't want to overtire yourself."

I said, "Sure. You need a lift back?"

"I'll go with Gilly. You can go home. I guess you're tired, too."

I said yes, but I wasn't. We parted, and in the large empty ball park I tried to imagine how this job and night and life felt to a man with mine deaths in his past and a heart condition in his present and I missed a sense of joy. He has been close to the peaks of baseball for a quarter century and, though he has gained things he wanted, Hodges has paid. He had seemed more tranquil as a player struggling to hit Maglie than as a pennant-winning manager. In the empty ball park, where my footfalls on cement made the only sound, I wondered whether Gil Hodges truly was better off with the satisfactions and fierce strains of his success or whether sometimes he envied his older brother Bob, who always talked a better game, but disappeared into the chasm of corporate life during the 1940s when all his talk and scheming ended with a dead arm on a Class D ball club playing in West Central Georgia. And here it was, only May.

MANCHILD AT FIFTY

Sometimes the answer to fear does not lie in trying to explain away
the causes. Sometimes the answer lies in courage.

J. ROBERT OPPENHEIMER

For half of Roy Campanella's ten seasons behind the plate the
Dodgers won a pennant, and when each World Series came and
the dreary ball-park railings flowered with bunting of red,
white and blue, and politicians strutted in the pocked cement
runways and four hundred newspapermen gathered to watch
batting practice, Campanella's round face glowed and he broke
into patter. "Yessir, it gets me real excited to be in a Series and
see these writers here and all them flags. It makes me feel like
I was at a circus. There's nothing a boy likes better than a circus,
and to play this game good, a lot of you's got to be a little boy."

That pleased the sportswriters. It gave them something for
their first edition, to set against ponderous prebattle statements
and wordy medical reports. Campanella was indeed excited as
he spoke and his voice rose to a tenor pipe. "Ol' Roy," the
writers said, "is lotsa fun."

After the game began far below the press box, Campy, Number 39, came striding to the plate, swinging a bat, serious, intent

355

but also portly. There was none of Snider's limber grace, no long-muscled fluidity, to his walk. He pumped his bat toward Allie Reynolds, then swung at a fast ball, dropping his right knee so that it almost touched the earth. The mighty uppercut produced a foul tip and Campy shook his head, indignant at the wasted exertion. "Old colored gentleman," Red Smith repeated, quite softly.

In the sunburst of his prime, Roy Campanella, pale-skinned, round, doggedly jovial, played at 190 pounds. When he gained weight, it showed first at the belly and Charlie Dressen talked about "putting him in a rubber suit and runnin' him." Usually Campanella was roundness without flab. He stood a big-boned five feet nine, with massive arms and torso, a sumo wrestler pared to catcher's size.

Given a relaxing day and an audience, he broke into stories as naturally as someone else would whistle. "Did I ever tell you how it was in the colored league when I was playing down in Venezuela? You talk about catching double-headers. Oncet I caught three double-headers in a day, from ten o'clock in the morning till past midnight, and all they paid me was sixty dollars a month, plus fifty cents a day for meals. That was the onliest money we had, but I was catching so much I didn't have *time* to eat. Yessir."

Whenever Campanella hit a foul into the rows behind a dugout, he stooped to retrieve the other catcher's mask. He chattered with opposing hitters all game long, as though he were running for office. Except for a questionable outburst against bean balls and another against characteristic Southern segregation practiced in Bradenton, Florida, he chose to ignore the facts of American bigotry. He moved smooth, pale and placid against Jackie Robinson's dark fire.

The contrasting styles fed an ironic rivalry. Both men broke pathways, but by different methods, and in the competition of seasons forgot that their divergent roads led toward one goal.

Sometimes when Robinson denounced reporters and umpires, his clear voice rising into long, shrill paragraphs, Campy shook his head as if despairing to find a black man so fierce, so wanting tolerance. Sometimes after Campy had retrieved a mask, or ignored someone's taunt of "nigger," Robinson told intimates, "There's a little Uncle Tom in Roy."

Covering the team intensely, you were driven toward one or the other. I drew closer to Jackie Robinson, perhaps because his bellicosity fit my preconception of what black attitudes should be, perhaps because I believed that his road was the more difficult, perhaps because I knew he had few allies in press boxes. Dick Young had already embraced Campanella. Magnificent in 1951, Campanella won the first of three Most Valuable Player awards, and after that chose Young as his collaborator on an autobiography. He then insisted that Young keep the entire $1,000 advance against royalties. "You gotta do the work, buddy," he said. Subsequently Young brought ardor to his Campanella rooting. "Mighty Roy," he said, after the movie about a genial gorilla known as *Mighty Joe Young.* "Come on, Mighty Roy," he cried. "Hit one. Sell a book."

Despite moments of bickering, I enjoyed Campanella. Delight brightened his eyes when he talked about electric trains, tropical fish, baseball or his children. There was that habit, annoying, actually dangerous to reporters, of making one statement on Tuesday and then, when controversy rose, denying on Wednesday that he had said any such thing. The Dodgers did not lack for lay analysts, and looking at Roy, with the toy trains, the fish, the petulance, analysts said, "He really is, in a sense, a boy." But at the same time he was Red Smith's dark, old gentleman. I felt I understood Roy Campanella less than any of the Dodgers, although it is possible that in those days there was really nothing much to understand.

357

The catching trade makes messy, painful work. In midsummer heat a man straps on mask, chest protector, shin guards and stuffs sponges into a fat round mitt. His laboring posture is a squat. Years of catching turn the thighs to lead.

Crouched, offering the glove as a target, he has to catch a ball moving one hundred miles an hour, or break forward for a bunt or spin backward for a foul pop. Almost every time the pitcher throws, the catcher throws, too, returning the ball to the mound. In addition, a catcher, if he is a good one, can fire a baseball 130 feet to second base without rising. Roy Campanella was a very good catcher, and some seasons he became a great one. He was elected to the Baseball Hall of Fame in 1969, and if one part of the vote was sentimental, some surely stands in cold tribute to his record.

But Hall of Fame catchers even as schoolboys sweat into their masks, strain their arms, and suffer knotted legs, foul tips cracking into fingers and the frightful pounding of fast balls into the left hand. Campanella's three best years, 1951, '53 and '55, were interrupted by seasons in which he could neither hit .300 nor catch every day. Bruises and fractured metacarpals stopped him. At his best, in 1953, he clouted 41 homers and won game after game with clutch hits. He drove in 142 runs, which, Allan Roth pointed out, "would be a record, most runs batted in for a catcher, except they don't figure batting records by fielding position." Roy loved those great years. Then his stories sparkled and his eyes shone with the dark devil's wine of success. The bad years frustrated him; pouting, he would say, "Maybe I ain't hittin', but it ain't as easy as it looks. Like to see one of you fellers in the press box come down and try to hit Robin Roberts with sore hands."

"I couldn't do it with good hands, Roy."

"Sheet. You couldn't even come close."

"I'm not arguing, Roy."

"Sheet."

358

He had no good seasons after 1955, and by 1957, the Dodgers' last year in Brooklyn, he caught only one hundred games. He was thirty-six that November, his body worn, and a new black catcher, John Roseboro, was pressing. Still the catching job was Roy's and he rose to challenges. Carl Erskine was not the only man who believed that the short left field in the Los Angeles Coliseum would inspire a revival.

In mid-January 1958 one of Ruthe Campanella's brothers was involved in a minor automobile accident, which disabled Roy's station wagon. The family also owned a Cadillac hardtop. Ruthe usually drove the Cadillac and Roy used the wagon to commute from Long Island to his successful new business in central Harlem. With help from Walter O'Malley, a man of increasing political power, Campanella had obtained a liquor license and opened Roy Campanella Choice Wines and Liquors on the corner of Seventh Avenue and 134th Street. After the accident, Campanella drove to work in a rented Chevrolet.

At suppertime on January 26, a clear, bitter cold evening, Campanella was hurrying to Salt Spray, his waterfront home on Morgan's Landing, an expensive section on the north shore of Long Island, between the Scott Fitzgerald country of Sands Point and Oyster Bay, where the Republican Roosevelts reigned. Salt Spray had cost almost $75,000, and newspapers ran occasional features describing the playthings with which it was filled. The collection of tropical fish was "impressive"; the electric trains, running intricate courses down hundreds of feet of track, were "any child's Christmas dream come true."

Five miles south of Salt Spray, on a two-lane blacktop road, Campanella rolled onto a slab of ice, at a sharp bend to the left. The rented Chevrolet skidded, slammed almost head on into a telephone pole and turned upside down. Seat belts were uncommon at the time. Campanella's body crashed heavily into the steering wheel. Then his head whipped backward. A rescuer found him conscious and badly frightened. "Would you please turn the key in the ignition," Campanella said. "Turn off the engine. Please. I don't want to burn to death." He had fractured the fifth cervical vertebra—broken his neck—and injured his spinal cord.

An ambulance bore him to Glen Cove Community Hospital, where a surgeon tried to repair the damage. It was three months before Campanella was strong enough to be moved to the Institute of Rehabilitation Medicine at New York University. There he came slowly to recognize the full measure of his injury. He was a quadriplegic. He could not walk or use his arms or hands. For the rest of his life his lungs would be threatened by every cold and his kidney and bowel functions would have to remain under almost continuous medical monitoring. In one physician's description, "Even though he survived, such sweeping paralysis loosens his grip on life itself."

The return to Salt Spray brought a burst of joy that changed at once into more pain. The paralysis had not left Campanella impotent but had robbed him of motion, the push-pull, so to speak, of sex. Dr. Valery Lanyi, a physician who has worked at the NYU Institute, explains; "In such cases the man is still capable of intercourse, although his pleasurable sensations are diminished. Women coming to such a man with tenderness and love can lead fulfilling sex lives. We have many cases of this. In practice a little training is necessary for each partner, with which we can help, but the woman must be willing to be gentle." Ruthe Campanella would not be gentle, and a story most uncongenial to small boys or old colored gentlemen soon exposed the private life of the Campanellas in the courts.

On August 2, 1960, Roy instituted a suit against Ruthe for legal separation. Through his attorney, Harold Stackel, he charged that Ruthe had said "she doesn't love me, I'm a helpless cripple, I serve no purpose in her life and she intends to come and go as she pleases." Campanella cited occasions when he was cuckolded "in Atlantic City," in "another man's apartment," and "once at 2 A.M. outside our home she got into a car with a man and they embraced passionately and made love with abandon." When he complained the next morning that the children had heard her cries, Ruthe "raised a fork to me and said, 'I'll give my body to anybody I desire. You can't do anything about it.' "

Ruthe underwent surgical sterilization because "I want to enjoy life." She drank heavily, Campanella said, and sometimes struck him during arguments, although he was unable to raise his arms and defend himself, much less strike back. After the charges produced headlines in New York's tabloid press, Campanella temporarily withdrew his suit.

But by spring, 1962, Roy had moved into an apartment in Lenox Terrace, a complex of high-rise apartment buildings inhabited by middle-class blacks that rises near his liquor store. Ruthe remained in Salt Spray, which Roy sought to sell. The house was too costly now that the marriage was spent. Between 1960 and 1963 the Campanellas shuttled in and out of court at least three times. Ruthe complained he had taken away her charge accounts. Roy said she was irresponsible, but paid her more than $800 a month for child support. Meanwhile Ruthe's romance with a musician fed the gossip which babbles through the bars and living rooms of Harlem.

On November 27, 1962, Salt Spray was sold at auction. Thirty-one people bid. The house had been appraised at $60,-000. But trouble—others' knowledge of family trouble—undercuts the price of a house. The best bid was $47,000, which did not leave much cash after fees were paid to the auctioneer and lawyers and after a bank equity of $29,000 was satisfied. One scene remained to crown the tragedy. On January 26, 1963, Roy and Ruthe were talking by telephone. He heard a gasping sound and a crash. Ruthe had suffered a fatal heart attack.

When she died, she was forty years old.

Surely, he had been the manchild with toy trains and pet fish in the promised land of baseball, but time had torn at him and now he could no longer hit or run or walk. In June 1964 the tabloids reported that he had married his Lenox Terrace neighbor, Mrs. Roxie Doles. May 5 was the wedding date; the newspapers had missed it at the time. "She lives right next door," a tabloid columnist wrote in June, "so all wunnerful Roy has to do to have family life again is to break down the walls."

"How has he weathered these tragedies?" I'd asked Joe Black in Chicago.

"For a time bad, now good," Black said. "He's got a nice house up near White Plains and this wife is very good for him. Used to be, when Camp was in trouble, and you had a chair for a hundred and fifty dollars, he'd have to buy one for two-fifty. The department stores loved that. But this wife has settled him down. Don't worry about a visit being depressing. You'll probably enjoy the day."

When I telephoned the liquor store months later, Campanella said, "I know what you been doing. I heard about it." The old piping voice was lower, more breathy. Paralysis cuts a man's wind. "I'm real busy at the store, but Saturdays is good. I try to take Saturdays off. The house is close to Tarrytown Road. I'm gonna look forward to talking about the old times."

"You don't sound like an old-timer."

"Buddy," Campanella said, "I was born in 1921. I'm fifty years old right now."

The large, brick house sits on a knoll, close to others in a comfortable suburban cluster. Roxie, a pretty, soft-voiced woman who looks to be in her thirties, met me at the garage. A Cadillac bore the license plate "ROY—39." "That's Roy's elevator over there," she said, pointing. "We have some ramps inside. He gets around just fine."

She led me upstairs into a rectangular living room, walled in wood, with a raised fireplace facing a picture window. "Roy said why didn't you talk in the den. It's brighter and some of his baseball things are hanging there."

The den, an airy corner room, was bright with early afternoon sunlight. The walls flashed the jewels of a great career. The three Most Valuable Player plaques, 1951, 1953, 1955, hung close together. Nearby in a framed cartoon, Campanella stepped into a pitch, the right knee trailing low, power bursting from the vital frame. A mix of bronze and silver awards celebrated later work with disabled children. A twenty-five-year-old photograph of Jackie Robinson, lean-faced and intense, smiled from a table. A pair of spikes cast in dull bronze made the most elaborate display, above a caption that read: "The last pair of shoes worn by Roy Campanella as a player; Brooklyn Dodgers vs. Philadelphia Phils, September 29, 1957." The spiked shoes that would not be worn again hung above everything else, dominating.

A whir announced his coming. Campanella rides a battery-powered wheelchair and he has just enough control over the heel of his hand to move a control stick back and forth. His hair was black. He had grown a mustache. His legs were withered. He greeted me with an odd little wave and it was an instant before I realized that he can move his arms from the shoulder, as in the beating of a wing, but the hands and forearms are dead.

"Good to see ya," he said. "Real fine. Roxie, this is one of my real favorite writers."

"Helluva ball player," I said, but I was shocked by the beating wing, and surprised that he had said I was a real favorite.

"The writers was fine," Campanella said. "I've had a lotta time to think and you know I got a lot of people wanting me for this thing and that thing but when I heard it was one of the old Dodger writers, well—this day, I just set aside." He beamed out of the wheelchair and I felt a rush of warmth and I remembered Carl Erskine talking about his own tears and I said quickly, "Roy, you look fine."

"Oh," he said, "I am. I am. I got something I want to get across if it's all right." His torso looked sturdy but not stout.

"These awards all around here didn't mean so much to me, but today, what is it, thirteen years later, they mean so much I can't find the words, just like Ebbets Field does, in my memory. I didn't realize at first when I did get the opportunity but, gee, how it dawned on me later. To talk to my sons—I have three boys—and some of their friends from high school and college. Being one of the first blacks to play in the major leagues with this, as they say, revolution taking place today, these teen-agers refer back to Ebbets Field. And I tell them the press, the white press, really helped me, and the fans across all the years, I never had a single racial slur happen to me from the fans, nothing out of the way, and maybe they been listening to people talking about hate and I want to tell them it isn't all hate, hate don't do good and I have no hate but"—he paused and looked about—"no hate but friends. Would you put that better and write it for me?"

"You put it fine."

"I wasn't never that good with the words."

"What do you tell these kids when they ask you how it was?"

He paused, frowned in thought and said, "You was there. I was one of the first. And when I was startin', I was a black man giving signals to pitchers, telling them what to throw. Now there was some fellers on the Brooklyn Dodgers which didn't care for a colored feller telling them anything. Hugh Casey. When I was catching Hugh Casey, who come from Georgia, if I called for a curve, he'd want to throw a fast ball. And if I called for a fast ball, he'd want to throw a curve. He'd shake me off, no matter what I called. I always tried to study and I thought I was a pretty good analyzer of the other fellows. Like one time with Robin Roberts. I never will forget, it was an All-Star Game at Detroit. When I hit against Roberts, he threw this fast pitch that would always slide away from me. At the All-Star Game I'm his catcher and I said on a certain pitch, 'I'll give you a sign for a slider.' He said he didn't have one. I told Robin, 'Hey. Wait a minute. Don't get cute with me. I *hit* against you, buddy, and you *throw* it to me.' He said, 'Roy, that's my fast ball.' I said, 'Robin, they're all fast, but you throw one straight and another breaks. If you expect me to catch it, I better be expecting it.' Well, turned out he didn't realize hisself that with some fast balls he'd twist the wrist a little. He said, 'Roy. You know you're teaching me something.' So I knew something about what they was throwing. Hugh Casey didn't have to be shakin' me off. But he did. Later the poor guy killed hisself, Lord forgive him."

"You used to say they threw at you because you were black. Do you tell kids that?"

"If they ask. I had this run-in with Lew Burdette." A chuckle rumbled in his chest. *"Little* run-in, is what I tell them. It was in Milwaukee and he threw at me twice in one turn at bat. After the second one I hollered, 'Now damnit, throw the ball over the plate.' Burdette said, 'Nigger, get up and hit.' I got so damned mad I missed the next pitch. He called me 'nigger,' then he struck me out. And I was goin' out there. But you know after I was paralyzed and retired from baseball Burdette seen fit to come to my office at the store and ask how I was feeling. I didn't want to be called 'nigger' by no one. I was gonna fight him. But now I can't swing a bat, or nothin', he comes by. I tell ya, hate don't get you nowhere. Don't keep hate stirring down inside. The onliest thing I want to remember about Lew Burdette is that whatever he called me, and he shouldn't have, later on he come all the way to Harlem to say hello."

Sometimes a man who has endured great pain acquires a curious gentleness. I saw that in the eyes of a football player named Ernie Davis who was dying of leukemia at twenty-two. People were haggling over the terms of a contract for his life story; Davis listened, tolerant, disinterested, beyond contentiousness. He had left such things behind and he was living out his span utterly alone, but tranquil, at peace with life and at peace with death. Campanella radiated a similar transfiguration. He is mobile in the wheelchair, beating the dead arms, twisting his trunk, growling, smiling, shrugging as he tells a story. No harshness lingers in his voice or in his words.

"Nicetown," he said, under the bronzed spikes. "That's where I come from in Philadelphia. That's what they called the section. It was integrated when we moved there, my father had a grocery store. There were few other colored in the neighborhood, but a lot of Polish people.

"I never had any idea I was gonna be a ball player. I loved to play. I mean any sport. Gee, I played baseball, basketball, football. But I was gonna *be* an architect. I would have loved that, drawing plans."

"Can you hold a pencil now?"

"No, but I can feed myself. I've learned to do that. Most of the time for autographs,–Mrs. Campanella signs. She writes the name as good as me. But I control my wrist pretty good and if I have to, they strap something to my arm with a pen in it and I can write." He made a little shrug. "You get so you're glad for anything you can do.

"I used to like to run. I was on the track team at Simon Gratz High School. It wasn't more than 10 percent black. But the first baseball uniform I got came from a colored paper. The Philadelphia *Independent*. The owner lived in our neighborhood and all us paper boys asked this man to buy us uniforms because we wanted to have a team. And he did. It said 'NCAC' on the shirt. 'Nicetown Colored Athletic Club.'

"I played outfield and infield and sometimes I catched, but I thought I couldn't see through a mask. I was a catcher without a mask until one day a foul ball popped me right in the center of my forehead. I run home to Mama. Oh, my goodness. I had a big knot on my head. And Mama said, 'Oh, what happened?' I said, 'I been hurt the worst ever.' That taught me to catch *with* a mask. I found out the next time I could see through a mask just fine."

He chuckled at his own story and asked if I wanted a Scotch. Mrs. Campanella mixed drinks and served canapés. "I'm not supposed to drink," he said, "but now and then I take a small one. See, with so much of me paralyzed, I'm not supposed to strain the kidneys any way. But you go ahead, if Chivas Regal is all right."

"It's all right."

"I was not thinking about college, but my family was. I had a big sister who run off to Tuskegee Institute down in Alabama. But while I was still in high school a team, the Bacharach Giants, asked my mother if I could play with them for a weekend and go to New York. I'd get out of school Friday and they'd see I was back Sunday night. Mama said okay. The first game we played was in Beach Haven, New Jersey, on Friday night. Then we went to New York City to stay over. Saturday we played a double-header at Torrington, Connecticut, and Sunday we played a double-header at Hartford and we drove back to Philadelphia and I went to school on Monday. I caught five games and they gave my mother twenty-five dollars. Holy gee, but that was good.

"Now while we had stopped at this hotel in New York, the Woodside, the Baltimore Elite Giants of the Negro National League was there. One of the fellers with our club told Biz Mackey, who was the catcher and manager for the Baltimore Elites, 'We got a fifteen-year-old kid with us, and you should see *him* catch and throw.'

"Biz Mackey got up early Saturday morning and said did I want to go with them. They was asking a fifteen-year-old boy into the colored big leagues. But I was a kid and my mother had only give me permission to play with the Bacharachs. So I told Biz Mackey, no, no, no.

"He took my name and address and got in touch with my

367

parents, Ida and John Campanella. Mama didn't want to hear nothing about that. She was thinking of college.

"I used to go and sit up on a roof back of Shibe Park in Philadelphia. You paid a quarter to a superintendent and you could watch the old Athletics. I saw some great ones. Jimmie Foxx, Doc Cramer, Max Bishop, Mickey Cochrane, and the visiting players, Babe Ruth. I saw Lou Gehrig. That old right-field fence was no higher than this ceiling, and when Connie Mack found out how many people were seeing his games from the roof, he built that high right-field fence to block the view."

"You hit some against that fence," I said.

Campanella nodded vigorously. "And over," he said. "They talk about hitting in Ebbets Field. The ball carried even better in Philadelphia."

"Did you know that the game was all white, that there wasn't any place for you?"

He thought, and pushed a flat lever with the heel of his right hand. The motor whirred and the wheelchair moved back, then forward. "Yes," he said, "by the time I was in my teens. But it didn't faze me. I was young. I even went to the Phillies for a tryout. Hans Lobert was managing; they were a bad team and needed help. Lobert didn't know how to tell me no, so he referred me to the owner, which was Gerry Nugent, and he didn't know what to tell me neither. He said there weren't going to be tryouts that day. After I got to the Dodgers, they hired Lobert as a scout. One day I saw him sitting in our dugout and I said, 'See what the Phillies missed. A *pretty* good catcher.'" Campanella smiled and shook with soft laughter.

"I played twelve years in the colored league. I started out with the Elites at sixty dollars a month and I went up slowly. I used to tell stories, but in later years I was really getting six hundred a month, plus expenses, for six months. Then I'd play all winter in South America and get pretty near the same. I never had to pay room and board and I wound up getting about seventy-five hundred for playing every day around the calendar.

"The Elites was good, but so was the team Josh Gibson caught for, the Homestead Grays, and so was the Newark Eagles. They had Monte Irvin and Newcombe and Larry Doby. Satchel was with Kansas City. That was out in the Negro American League. The National League was in the East. Western teams played in the American League. Jackie played with Kansas City for a year, and I got to know him."

"Was he angry then?" I said.

Roy shook his head. "No." He paused. "Let me see." Another pause. "I want to put this right. You see, playing in the colored league, he wouldn't have all those things to be angry *about.*"

The picture of Jackie stared at us from a wall. He wore a baseball cap and an undeterminable uniform. He was young, fine-featured, black-haired. The smile curled mysteriously from the corners of his mouth.

"A lot of people try to take different sides with me or Jack. I didn't push hard enough. He pushed too hard. Well, Jack had his moods and I had my moods, but deep down I believe we were always friendly. On a day off, Jack liked to go to the racetrack. I wasn't a racetrack man. You'd never see Jack or me together. You might see Newk and me at a movie. On a day off at Chicago, I'd be in Shedd Aquarium. I'm just crazy about tropical fish. That's not Jack's speed; him and Pee Wee and Duke would go to the track or play golf. I never did that either. My legs had enough work getting up and down catching every day. So people figured that because me and Jackie didn't pal around together that we were always having words. It wasn't true, whatever people said. Jackie comes over here now when the weather is good for cookouts. You know I admire him. I know how it was. And I think Jack knows I admire him, too." He looked at me evenly. "It wasn't easy for any of us," he said.

"How did you hear about Jackie's signing?"

"We was in a hotel together in New York. We were both on a black all-star team that was going out to play twenty-five games in Venezuela. I'd just played for the all-star team against major leaguers in Ebbets Field. It was right after the season of 1946. Ralph Branca was the major leaguers' pitcher. Charlie Dressen was their manager. Charlie said did I know my way to the Brooklyn Dodger offices on Montague Street. I said no. He said could I be in their office at ten the next morning. I told him, 'Mr. Dressen, I may have some trouble finding it. I don't know my way round the subways of New York well enough to get to Brooklyn, but if the *Brooklyn Dodgers* want to see me, I'll find the way.'

"When I got there, holy gee, Mr. Rickey had a scouting report on me a whole loose-leaf book thick. They'd had Clyde Sukeforth following me and they knew how I catched and hit and threw and Mr. Rickey told me everything from school to my mother and father to what I did off the field. And he signed me and then he signed Newk.

"But we wasn't definitely assigned to any club. That was 1946 and something happened in Florida, where Jack was training with Montreal. A sheriff came and threw him off a field. There was talk they was gonna run Jack out of town. Now Mr. Rickey said, 'If they want to run out Jack, you better stay North.' I'd played all winter in Venezuela. I thought, 'Okay, I'm in good shape.' Later I met Rickey in his office in Brooklyn. I sat there and he called every general manager in the system, fifteen, twenty men. 'Would you accept Roy Campanella?' None of 'em would touch me. He called Buzzy Bavasi. Buzzy was the onliest one to say, 'Yeah. I will accept him.' Mr. Rickey said, 'Roy. You will go to Nashua and play.' I said what did he mean; where was Nashua? I thought he was telling me Nashville.

"Newk and I went to Nashua, New Hampshire, and if you don't believe I could run, I stole sixteen bases that year. There were no colored people in the town 'cept for Newk and me.

Rickey wanted us to work together. Walter Alston was the manager. One night in Lynn, Massachusetts, I hit a couple of home runs and Newk pitched good and after the game Buzzy went in to get his money and the manager of Lynn said, 'If it wasn't for them niggers, you wouldn't have beat us.' Buzzy jumped him. And they were swinging and all the players came running in. Buzzy was fighting him for what he said. It was always some sly thing. I never did let it peeve me.

"The next spring, I was training with Montreal and we flew to Panama for games with the Dodgers. Jackie was with Montreal. We had a pretty good club. Hugh Casey was pitching, listen to this, and Jack faked a bunt toward third. Casey broke that way and Jack bunted the ball slow up toward Eddie Stanky, who was playing second. Stanky didn't have a play so he picked that ball up and threw it over the top of the grandstand in Panama. Stanky can't deny that neither. It was the worst thing I ever seen on a ball field."

Campanella was not appearing to tire. "I'm in good shape," he said. "Most everybody paralyzed like me has to take regular exercises. I don't seem to have to. I thank baseball for that. I believe it put my body in this good condition where being paralyzed wasn't as bad for me as it would be for some."

"But it *is* bad for you," I said.

Roy shrugged; a look of hurt invaded his eyes.

"I mean you were really a physical man. You'd lived a physical life. That was everything to you and this thing happened and you can't be physical any more."

"That's true."

"Well, where did you get the courage to go on?"

"Uh-huh," Campanella said, as though he had been waiting. Now he spoke very slowly and softly, and before he was done his eyes would film with tears.

"After the accident," he said, "and laying in the bed and realizing that I was paralyzed. No. At first I didn't realize. It happened January the twenty-sixth and I was laying there in Glen Cove Community Hospital and I thought in a few weeks I would be well and go to spring training. They had my arms strapped out and my legs and I couldn't move them. Suddenly I couldn't move my arms and my legs. When you get like that and lie in that position, you start trying.

"I tried to move my right leg. My right arm. No reaction.

"I tried to move my left leg. My left arm. No reaction.

"I tried a little every day. The doctors weren't disclosing a whole lot. You don't think, 'I'm *paralyzed*,' right away. You think, 'Hey, I can't move my arm.'

"After a lot of days, I started wondering to myself. Gee, I can't move this, I can't move that, I can't move *anything*. I was a good one for prayers and I prayed to the good Lord to let me accept whatever was happening.

"One day it started getting tough to breathe. The shortness of breath was getting worse and worse. They put me in an oxygen tent. I realized then that it was pretty bad. They never told me that the way it was going I was about to lose my life.

"A doctor said they wanted to perform a tracheotomy, make a hole in my throat, let me breathe through that, and hope. And the best I could do, paralyzed in that oxygen tent, was nod my head. It was my life and all I could do was nod. Now I knew it was real bad.

"I got through it. The next day I felt a little better and I started to ask questions. It was tough to talk. They had my trach plugged with a cork and when the cork was in there I could say something. If the nurse wanted to quiet me, she pulled the cork.

"They told me I had broke my neck and what vertebrae and how they had operated on my spinal cord. They said they were still waiting for reactions. I might be in shock.

"But I still wasn't moving or anything. I gave up the idea of going to spring training. Then Walter O'Malley sent Dr. Howard Rusk from NYU to look me over, and he checked me and said, 'Roy. You can't run water through a broken pipe. It's just that simple. Your spinal cord has been messed up. You may get to walk again and you may not. If you don't, you have to learn how to live with it.' "

Very softly, Campanella said, "I think I've learned how."

"You sure have," I said, and that was when I saw the film of tears.

"I've accepted the chair," he said. "My family has accepted it. My wife has made a wonderful home. I'm not wanting many things. Sure, I'd love to walk. Sure, I would. But I'm not gonna worry myself to death because I can't. I've accepted the chair, and I've accepted my life.

"My oldest son, Roy Junior, is twenty-two years old and teaching at Harvard. I never went to college. Tony is a sophomore at Elmhurst right outside Chicago. John is a senior at Windsor Mountain, a prep school in Lenox, Massachusetts. And Princess, my baby, seventeen years old, is waiting for me in the kitchen. Why don't you go downstairs with Mrs. Campanella and look at the playroom we got? I'll be talking to Princess."

He pushed the lever and the wheelchair started off bearing the broken body and leaving me, and perhaps Roxie Campanella as well, to marvel at the vaulting human spirit, imprisoned yet free, in the noble wreckage of the athlete, in the dazzling palace of the man.

13

THE DUKE OF FALLBROOK

When I'm watching the Pacific ten years from now, I know I'll miss
my baseball friends. Maybe I'll even get a twinge when I hear about
some other center fielder helping another Dodger club to a pennant. But the first time one of my neighbors tells me how soft I had
things, I'm gonna get that neighbor into a chair. Then we can have
a little talk.

DUKE SNIDER, C. 1955

During my last trip with the team, I finished the story of an
easy victory in Milwaukee, stowed my typewriter in a bare
room at the Hotel Schroeder and, rather than consider prints
of strawberries, I walked across Wisconsin Avenue to a bar
called Holiday House. Inside, Duke Snider gestured for me to
join him.

Across drinks, Snider was serious, soft-voiced, opinionated
and quietly insistent that each opinion was correct. The more
intense he became, the more softly he spoke. "Did ya write a
good story?" he asked in a low tone. "What'll you drink?"

"Medium. It was a medium game. Scotch, thanks."

"I'm buying," Snider said. "Bring him a double Scotch and
soda."

"Something bothering you, Duke?"

"Something? Everything."

"You're hitting .335."

"I know." The long face fell into a pout. "But it's this whole damn life. You know what I'm gonna do? Get some good acreage. I know a place south of Los Angeles. I'm gonna move there and raise avocados."

"You're kidding."

"I'm not kidding. I dreamed of being a big leaguer once, but that's not it for me any more. Last fall in the World Series, I'm out there. Big bat. Seventy thousand watching. Great catch. You know what I'm dreaming then? About being a farmer."

"There's the money."

"That's right, and if it wasn't for the money I'd be just as happy if I never played a game of ball again." He was twenty-six years old.

"Duke, if you mean what you're saying and you're willing to put your name to it, we can both make a little money just by printing it."

"I mean it," Snider said. "You go write it, just so's it comes out I'm explaining, not complaining."

I put off the story for years. Then Gordon Manning, the penultimate managing editor of *Collier's*, called me for lunch and asked if I had any article ideas. "We'll give you enough for the Jaguar you always wanted, or the down payment anyway," he said.

When I mentioned the old conversation with Snider, the editor glowed faintly and made a fair offer for each of us. A week later he handed me a round-trip ticket to Los Angeles and an expense check of $500.

"I'll only be a day or two," I said.

"Spend it all. Keep the Duke happy."

The Sniders owned a small white house on a quiet street in Compton, which lies just south of the Los Angeles city line.

Duke was grossing $50,000 a year, but his house could have belonged to someone earning a fifth as much. The rooms were compact. The children slept in bunks. "We aren't getting anything fancier until we're sure it's for keeps," said Beverly Snider, a trim, forceful woman. "Baseball isn't all that secure." Duke was large, long-striding, somewhat jowly. Beverly was petite, unlined, determined. As I set up a recorder and Duke groped for the sources of his disenchantment, Beverly wandered in and out of the small living room monitoring.

A few fans threw marbles at him when he chased fly balls, Duke said. The endless travel bothered him. The press could be cruel. "It isn't any one thing, but when they all come at the same time, when you get off a train after a couple of hours' sleep and a manager snipes at you before the game, and the fans throw stuff during the game, and the writers second-guess you after, you begin to wonder about baseball as a trade."

"Could you think of one particular bad day?"

"No," Duke said, "but lots of bad times. Like once when Charlie was managing a bunch of us went to see *The Caine Mutiny* in Philly. Well, in the movie Captain Queeg blew up over a quart of strawberries. The next damn day Charlie blew up over an order of creamed cauliflower. The Warwick Hotel was expensive and someone had a good meal and added creamed cauliflower à la carte for an extra seventy-five cents. That night it was drizzling and we got stuck in the clubhouse and Charlie opened up. 'You damn wise guys. You got nothing better to do than order creamed cauliflower, seventy-five cents extra?' He kept repeating it and it wasn't raining that much and around the fifth time I said, 'Hey, Charlie. What say we go out on the field?'

" 'What you trying to do?' he hollers. 'Run this ball club?'

" 'Hell, no. I just want to loosen up.'

" 'You'll loosen up when I tell you to loosen up. Now about this creamed cauliflower, you listening, Snider?'

" 'Look,' I yelled. 'I didn't even eat at the hotel on the club. I ate in a restaurant with my own money. Why don't you deduct the seventy-five cents for the cauliflower from the six-bucks meal money I didn't use?' "

Remembering, Duke made a little laugh. "And then he reamed me."

We walked out of the white house in Compton to a clothing store where Duke said he would sell sports jackets during Christmas week. We stopped in a bar and he drank Seven Crown and Seven-Up. When he tried to take the bill, I explained about the $500 expense check.

"Keep the money," he said. "Bev and me don't need entertaining."

"Well, I have it. Why don't we go to a club tonight on Sunset Strip?"

"It's Saturday," Snider said. "We couldn't get in anywhere good."

"Can I use your name for the reservation?"

"Sure but that won't help. They don't know me here. I'm not a coast league ball player."

We reached Ciro's at 8:30. "Mr. Snidair," cried a maître d', in great excitement, "we didn't think it was really *you*. People call all the time and use famous names. What a pleasure." Bus boys began chattering and pointing. The maître d' led us toward the stage and placed us at a table, second row center.

"I don't know," I said, "if I should have tipped, or if movie guys have all the first rows tied up."

"I'm just surprised they know me," Duke said.

Beverly considered a menu and cried, "Look at these prices."

"I don't see any creamed cauliflower," Duke said.

Eartha Kitt's act at Ciro's built to a climactic number in

which she stripped to black brassiere and underpants, while singing variations of a lyric:

> I'm getting nothing for Christmas,
> That's why little Eartha is sad.
> I'm getting nothing for Christmas
> 'Cause I didn't want to be bad.

At the final chorus she leaped into the arms of a Latin, who suddenly appeared at one wing and carried her off, presumably to ecstasy and other Christmas gifts.

"Well," said Beverly Snider, as the lights came up. "Well!" Duke gazed toward a wall. "Certainly not the sort of thing," Beverly said, "one could recommend to one's friends."

"Depends on the friends," I said. *Collier's* paid our check. We departed in silence.

In the spring of 1956 *Collier's* published the article, Snider and myself sharing the by-line. The piece stands as accurate, reasonably balanced and mild compared to the commercial sports iconoclasm of the 1970s. Snider described some of his disillusion, said he hoped to play through 1962 and then looked forward to retirement. He imagined a California Elysium, with avocados bursting from every tree. For all its bluster, the story was genial, no more mature than either author, harmless.

But the sporting press hurried to flagellate us for unorthodoxy. At least fifty newspaper articles described Snider as an ingrate. Red Smith composed an arch column in which Snider was said to have grabbed my lapel and wept. Stanley Woodward, rescued from Miami, was working for the Newark *Evening News*. He wrote that I had sat in a little room, invented the article and gone forth to find a ball player, any ball player, to lend a name and share the profits.

"Son of a bitch," I told him afterward. "You were wrong."

"Not wrong," Woodward said. "Entertaining and short of libel. And that's my definition of a good column."

Only John Lardner, who was writing for *Newsweek*, took us seriously. He was a tall, bespectacled, profound man, infinitely gentle to his friends, and typically he found depth in the article beyond what Snider and I had conceived.

"You see," Lardner said at the long bar of the Artist and Writers Restaurant, "Duke thought if his dream came true he would be a different person. He's not unhappy about the dream. He's unhappy that he is still the same man. Happens to a lot of us. We get somewhere we wanted and find we're still ourselves." Lardner had revealed more than he intended. He said quickly, "Needles has the staying power to win the Belmont."

"I don't like to bet horses," I said. "You really think the dream is killing Snider?" Lardner gazed at me with kind, despairing eyes.

I telephoned Gordon Manning and said that we ought to do something for Duke. "You could write an editorial, for example. He's getting murdered."

"He should have thought about reaction before he did the piece," Manning said.

"I didn't think about it. He certainly couldn't have."

"But you each have the down payment on a Jaguar," Manning said. He was closing another issue, he said. If I had any other story ideas, would I let him know?

Snider played for more seasons than anyone else—curiously, none of the team had an exceptionally extended career—but in the 1959 World Series he strained a knee. After that he had to cramp his swing. In 1963 the Dodgers shipped him to the Mets, where he was a sentimental favorite and batted .243, a hundred points below his best standard. A year later the Giants signed him to pinch-hit. He batted .210, and a few months after his thirty-eighth birthday he retired. He had hit 407 home runs, more than any Dodger, more than all but about a dozen men in baseball history. And he had found forty rolling acres outside

379

the village of Fallbrook, California, and bought his farm.

To reach Fallbrook, you drive south from Los Angeles down Highway 1, out of yellow haze into an open country of tan beaches and golden fields. You pass San Juan Capistrano, the Marine base at Camp Pendleton, and then you turn into a smaller road toward handsome uplands and a crossroad village called Bonsail. There you follow a two-lane blacktop winding among citrus trees. Two miles before Fallbrook, a narrow road cuts toward Green Canyon, and a few minutes down Green Canyon Road, in a pleasant ranch house looking toward Mount Palomar, one finds the Duke of Fallbrook. The setting is attractive but not overwhelming. Eight years out of baseball, Duke Snider has had to sell the large home, the avocado trees, the farm.

He seemed cheerful, almost unchanged. He had put on weight at the jowls, but he always did tend to go puffy. His hair, gray in 1953, was black. He had performed on television for a hair darkener and the contract required him to keep using dye. Beverly, still trim, made soup for lunch, and Duke asked if I wanted to see the town and the countryside. He walked his two acres lovingly, showing me a small pool and dwarf lemon trees. A few avocados stood on a slope where he had installed sprinklers. "Bev and I like to grow things," he said. We got into a car and drove slowly over rolling dun ridges, green where irrigation touched them. "See that," Snider said pointing to a rambling Spanish-style manor on the shoulder of a hill. "That was our house. And that all over there—those rows of avocados—was the farm."

"I'm sorry it didn't work out."

"Aaah," Snider said. "I made a bad guess. Look at those things. I owned them all." Avocados grow short, stumpy and gnarled. Against a memory of Eastern maples, they are not handsome, but Duke considered the stumpy rows tenderly. "They were bearing fine," he said. "Then we decided to do a

little more, invest in a bowling alley near Camp Pendleton. The
Marine families would be permanent customers. Vietnam happened. The families were broken up. The recruits want more
action than a night of bowling. So I had to get out of the business.

"By the time I did, I'd lost a lot. There went the farm. But
Buzzy's taken care of me. I broadcast for his San Diego club and
do some coaching."

"Back on the damn road."

"It's not that bad," Snider said, "but you know what bothers
me. This house there"—he pointed at his lost manor—"is set so
high we could get TV stations from L.A. and San Diego both.
Now where we are, down Green Canyon, we only get San
Diego." A breeze stirred through the avocado fields. "Come
on," Duke said. "Let's get a brew."

We drove into Fallbrook, a low, sprawling town, and as we
walked into the bar, men called greetings. Snider introduced
me and one of the men said, "Keep your money in your pocket.
You come all the way from New York, we won't let you buy."

"Thanks."

"But if you come all the way from New York, how can you
speak English? I didn't know they spoke English in New York."
Others nodded. "How do you like it out here?" the man asked.

"It's great," I said, quoting Fred Allen, 1938, "if you're an
orange."

"Hey," said the man, "that's all right." He was wearing work
pants and a khaki jacket. "You know we let Duke in our softball
game once."

Snider nodded. "They told me it was fast pitch, but everything I hit went foul. Fast pitch to these guys, but I pulled
everything inside first base."

They took softball seriously, said the man in khaki, as someone bought a second round. They played through the summer
in informal leagues, building to "a kind of world series." A year

before, the Fallbrook team had reached the series against a team from an Indian reservation. The Indians went ahead, three games to nothing. The Fallbrook team sent for the Duke.

"Right," Snider said, "and I said I'd help if I could use a hardball bat."

"I don't remember what he used, but we put him at shortstop, and from losing three games to nothing, we won the series four games to three."

"He still hits good," someone said.

"Different league," the Duke said. "My round." And he bought the beers with a flourish.

As we drove home, he reminisced. "My dad, Ward, come out west from Ohio. He used to see Cincinnati play. He kept putting the bat on my left shoulder when I was little because he knew the right-field fences were closer. Pete Rozelle and I were forwards on the same basketball team in Compton and he wrote for the newspaper, the *Tartar Shield*. My wife was with him the day he went ice skating and fell and lost his two front teeth. I could throw a football seventy yards. Pete says I coulda been a T quarterback. But I liked baseball. The Dodgers give me seven hundred and fifty dollars to sign and I took a train acrost the country to Bear Mountain, where they were training. I was seventeen and I never owned a topcoat."

"Did you buy one?"

"No. I stayed indoors a lot." Snider smiled at his own joke. "That was '44 and I got in an exhibition game at West Point and Glenn Davis was in the outfield for Army. I was the professional, but I got a thrill being on the same field with the amateur.

"I made it to Brooklyn in '47. In the first game Jackie Robinson played, I pinched hit for Dixie Walker. Base hit to right. I sent the clippings to my mother and I wrote that it wasn't only a colored person's first game in the big league, it was also her son's.

"I really made it after 1951. You know I struck out eight times in five games during the 1949 Series. I don't remember it bothering me much in '50, but in the last month of 1951 I kept thinking I was gonna face those Yankee pitchers again. I went in a terrible slump. I'm no psychologist, but I know that was in the back of my mind. I didn't hit and then we lost the play-off. The next year, you were there, I got straightened away and *that* Series I hit four home runs.

"I could always go back good in the outfield, and when I went to my left, Furillo and I had this trick. If we thought we might collide, I'd take a step in and try to catch the ball high and Furillo would take a step back and try to backhand it low. Not much got through us all those years and we never did run into each other."

When we reached his house, I said maybe we ought to go out for dinner again. "If we can find where Eartha Kitt's playing."

"You remember," Beverly said. "Well, there isn't any of that kind of thing in Fallbrook, but there is a fine restaurant called Valley Forge."

"An old Marine sergeant is behind the bar," Duke said, "and if you wear a tie, he clips it. I'll call ahead and fix it so he won't cut yours."

The sergeant, a massive man with a great waxed mustache, waved as we entered, winked to indicate that my tie was safe and made drinks. "Did you see *The Graduate?*" Beverly said.

I nodded.

"You work hard for your money. Why give it to a dirty movie like that?"

"It wasn't much good, but I wouldn't call it dirty."

"Well, I sing in the Methodist choir," Beverly said, "and a lot of us don't see any reason for putting sex on a movie screen."

"Sex exists, Bev."

"I know it does, and it's very beautiful and *very* private."

Duke seemed to be considering the oak floor. "I've always meant to tell you two that I was sorry about the reaction to the *Collier's* story," I said.

"Fergit it," Duke said. "Like Rickey put it, don't worry what they say about you, as long as they say something. Boy, I sure got my ink.

"And most of that story still goes. Except after I got done playing, I come to realize that baseball was what I knew, *all* I knew. When we had losses, and I *had* to get back, it wasn't like before. I'm older. I don't mind things so damn much."

"He misses the old team," Beverly said. "Everyone was so close."

"Heck, once in Pittsburgh," Duke said, "after a day game we went to watch the Kentucky Derby at the men's bar of the Schenley Hotel. There was nineteen of the twenty-five ball players in that bar. Lots of time after a game, there might be fifteen of us go to the same place. I credit Rickey, from the way he was working to bring us together. Hey, who you seen?"

I told him and mentioned Pafko's remark that Duke was so fine a ball player he deserved a steak. Snider nodded. That seemed fair. We went to eat. Brooklyn or Fallbrook, his swagger endured. Over the sirloins I told Beverly Pee Wee Reese's favorite Snider story. Four players rode a car pool from Bay Ridge to the Polo Grounds in 1951, and on Reese's night to drive a motorcycle patrolman stopped them. Approaching, the policeman burst out, "Pee Wee. It's you. Why you driving so fast?"

"Big series with the Giants, officer. Kind of nervous."

"Don't listen to that, officer," Snider said. "He deserves a ticket."

"Hiya, Duke," the cop said. "Gee, fellers. What a thrill for me. Good luck, and take it easy, will ya, Pee Wee?"

Snider drove the next night and within a mile of the same spot another policeman sounded a short siren burst from *Die*

Walküre. Then he took Snider's license and started writing.

"Say, officer. That Edwin Donald Snider is *Duke* Snider. I'm the Dodger center fielder."

Without looking up the policeman said, "I hate baseball." He handed Snider a ticket for speeding.

Beverly smiled faintly. Duke nodded. "That's about right, and I woulda had to pay it, too, if John Cashmore, the Borough President of Brooklyn, hadn't fixed it for me." And buoyant and boyish though fifty was approaching and the farm was gone, Duke resumed his attack on the steak.

THE LION AT DUSK

A free man counts tomorrow and yesterday and both of them are his; hunger and there's no master to feed you, but walk with long steps and no master says go slowly.

HOWARD FAST, *Freedom Road*

Of all the Dodgers, none seemed as able as Jackie Robinson to trample down the thorns of life. Indeed, the thornbush became his natural environment. But here, on the night of March 6, 1968, not a dozen years after his last World Series, Robinson stood among television reporters, a bent, gray man, answering questions in a whisper, and drawing shallow breaths, because a longer breath might feed a sob.

Jackie Robinson, Jr., no more the large-eyed imp, had been arrested in a one-night-cheap hotel. The police of Stamford, Connecticut, charged him with possessing a tobacco pouch filled with marijuana, a .22 caliber revolver and several packets of heroin which he may have wished to sell. Outside a suburban courthouse, television reporters, who had never seen the father play baseball, called hard questions with extravagant courtesy.

"Sir, are you going to stick by your son?"

"We will, but we'll have to take the consequences."

"Were you aware that he had certain problems, Mr. Robinson?"

"He quit high school. He joined the Army. He fought in Vietnam and he was wounded. We lost him somewhere. I've had more effect on other people's kids than on my own."

"How do you feel about *that*, sir?"

The gray-haired black man, Jackie Robinson, shook his head. "I couldn't have had an *important* effect on anybody's child if this happened to my own."

I turned away and Jack answered another question at length, as if in relief, as if in penance. He had not faded from public sight like most of the others. Even Robinson's declining baseball years crackled with controversy. During Walter Alston's first spring as manager, he said in Vero Beach, "Every man on this ball club will have to fight for his job." Some veterans laughed. Duke Snider did not expect to spend the season of 1954 on the bench. Pee Wee Reese was offended. Jackie Robinson spoke out. "I don't know what the hell that man is trying to do. Upset us all?" That year a strong, mismanaged, discontented Dodger team finished second.

In succeeding seasons the Dodgers won two pennants, but for Robinson the old spirit was vanished. He felt out of things, he said. This manager was hostile. This front office did not provide support. Then, after the 1956 season, Walter O'Malley traded him to the Giants. "We hate to lose Jackie," O'Malley said, "but it is necessary for the good of the team."

To find similar cynicism, you had to go clear back to 1935 when the Yankees dumped Babe Ruth on the old Boston Braves. But then the star was being sent to another league. Robinson, the embodiment of the loud, brave, contentious Dodgers, was being assigned to his team's great adversary. Sports pages flapped with excitement. Robinson deserved it. O'Malley was outrageous. The Polo Grounds was no Valhalla.

Ed Fitzgerald, the editor of *Sport* magazine, commissioned

an artist to paint a cover portrait in which Sal Maglie, who had come to Brooklyn early in 1956, stood at the mound, glowering at Giant base runner Jackie Robinson. "Maglie of the Dodgers against Robinson of the Giants," Fitzgerald said. "*Un*-believable. But would you first find out if Jackie's gonna play?"

Robinson was vague when I telephoned. The money was good, he said. The Giants were offering $40,000 for one year; then they'd pay him $20,000 for each of the next two seasons as a part-time scout.

"So you're going to accept?"

"You know me."

"Well, do you expect to play?"

"Whatever I do, I'll give it all I got."

What Robinson was trying to say (and has never known how to say) was "No comment." A month later on a chilly Sunday afternoon in January, *Look* magazine called "a press conference of major importance involving Dodger great Jackie Robinson."

At four o'clock in a wood-paneled conference room off Madison Avenue, *Look*'s promotion men distributed press releases and tearsheets of an article "copyright 1957, Cowles Magazines, Inc." Above Robinson's by-line, the story was headed: "Why I'm Quitting Baseball." Robinson explained that he was thirty-eight and had a family to support. He had been offered a job as vice president for personnel at Chock Full O'Nuts, a chain of lunch counters staffed almost entirely by Negroes. He was "to keep turnover at a minimum." "So," he wrote, "I'm through with baseball. From now on I'll be just another fan—a Brooklyn fan."

Reporters sat in overstuffed black-leather chairs and sipped Scotch. Their first questions were gentle. Help? Yes, Robinson conceded, he'd had help with the article. Had the Giant trade made him quit? No, he'd already begun working on the story when Buzzy Bavasi called him.

"Didn't you lie to your friends?" someone said suddenly.

"I did not lie."

"Mislead?"

Dan Mich, a large, square-faced man, stepped forward. "I run *Look,*" Mich said, in a presidential tone. "Any statement Jack made that may have been misleading was out of respect for us. I've never met anyone more honest." The conference descended to chatter and morning newspapermen left to make their deadlines.

Back home in Stamford that night, Robinson faced doubts that would not down. He had said that he was quitting and he had meant that he was quitting, but a Giant executive called to propose a still better contract. If the offer improved further, Jack simply would have to change his mind. *Look*, Robinson reasoned, would be getting $50,000 worth of publicity. He was square there, he felt. Now it might be fun making Walter O'Malley look like a clown of a trader. Then two days later Buzzy Bavasi told reporters, "Robinson will play. I know the guy and he likes money. Now that *Look*'s paid him, he'll play so he can collect from the Giants, too."

Reading these sentences, Robinson knew: the retirement would have to be permanent. Already Red Smith was attacking him "for peddling a news story, the rights to his retirement." If he did play again, critics would denounce him as a phony. His baseball years, begun with heroic pioneering, could end amid cries of fraud. "Goddamn, I can't play," Robinson told himself, cheerlessly, but the doubts endured until the first day of the 1957 season. That morning his right knee, crippled by a thousand slides, was so swollen he could not get out of bed.

"I'll miss the excitement of baseball," Robinson wrote in *Look,*

but now I'll be able to spend more time with my family. My kids and I will get to know each other better. Jackie, Sharon and David will have a real father they can play with and talk to in the evening and every weekend. They won't have to look for him on TV.

Maybe my sons will want to play ball, as I have, when they grow up. I'd love it if they do. But I'll see to it they get a college education first, and meet the kind of people who can help them later.

Just now Jackie still feels badly about my quitting. It's tough for a ten-year-old to have his dad suddenly turn from a ball player into a commuter. I guess it will be quite a change for me, too. But someday Jackie will realize that the old man quit baseball just in time.

He telephoned two seasons after his retirement and asked if I'd talk to him about a biography he was preparing, helped by Carl Rowan, the black journalist. We lunched in Janssen's, a restaurant on Lexington Avenue, and Robinson immediately told me how difficult it was to be a writer. "First I picked the wrong collaborators," he said, and mentioned two white newspapermen. "I tell one of them something for the book. He tapes me and two days later uses it for a column. Now I'm squared away on that, but I've got other problems. Campy. I told you there was a little Tom in him. Suppose I go into that. I'm hitting a cripple."

"Write the damn thing the way you feel it," I said.

"And then there's a point about women. When I was at UCLA, more white women wanted to go to bed with me than I wanted to go to bed with white women."

"Congratulations."

"Everybody thinks it's all the other way. All the black guys are panting to get into bed with white women. Well, a lot of white guys are just dying to get hold of black women. I'm not kidding. I've seen it. And, for me, with white girls, like I said, I didn't have to make much of a move."

"You've *got* to write that. A chapter. Write it goddamn tough."

"I don't know," Robinson said.

"Pliss," said a short, elderly man, bending so that his bald head dropped between us. "Be a good boy and give your autograph."

"What?" Robinson's tenor clanged through the restaurant. The man started. "I said, could I have your autograph?"

"That isn't what you said." Robinson's voice drew eyes toward our table. The man was frightened. "Who's this for?" Robinson shouted.

"My grandson."

"All right. I'll give you the autograph to your grandson, but not because I'm a boy." Robinson scribbled on the menu. The man took it and hurried away.

"You're a fierce bastard," I said.

"He won't call a black man 'boy' again," said Robinson.

The biography, called *Wait Till Next Year*, told several plain, hard stories. Robinson was born near Cairo, in southwestern Georgia, during the Spanish flu epidemic of 1919, the fifth and last child of Mallie McGriff Robinson. The father, Jerry, deserted Mallie six months later and she bundled her children onto a train for California. There she found work as a domestic. Mallie Robinson taught her children to look after one another. She tried to fill them with a sense of pride. At eight, Jack was sweeping the sidewalk in front of the house, a small frame building in Pasadena, when a white Southern girl shouted from across the street, "Nigger, nigger, nigger."

"You're nothing but a cracker," Robinson answered.

The girl had played this scene before. She chanted:

> Soda cracker's good to eat.
> Nigger's only good to beat.

At fourteen, Robinson went wading in the Pasadena City Reservoir. The municipal pool was closed to blacks. Someone saw him splashing, and a few minutes later a sheriff arrived and drew his gun. "Looka here," he roared, behind the .38. "Niggers in my drinking water."

Robinson grew up tough, running with street gangs, but the 1930s were not revolutionary years. Street boys believed aspects of the American Dream, and Robinson rode his athletic skill to junior college and then to UCLA. Although in *Wait Till Next Year* he cannot say it, Robinson was a superathlete, probably the best in the United States. He was a star forward in basketball, an extraordinary running back in football, a record-breaking broad jumper. And he played baseball.

As a college man, he was commissioned an infantry lieutenant during World War II and assigned to Camp Hood, Texas. After a general order forbade segregation within military installations, a driver ordered Robinson to move to the rear of an Army bus. Robinson stood his ground. The driver called the military police, and a captain named Gerald Bear wanted to know if Robinson "was trying to start a race riot or something." Robinson spoke heatedly about civil rights. Captain Bear's secretary said Robinson had "some nerve being sassy."

In the ensuing court-martial, Robinson stood accused of disturbing the peace, of disobeying an order, of acting with disrespect toward a civilian woman and of "contemptuously bowing, giving sloppy salutes to Captain Bear and repeating several times, 'Okay, sir. Okay, sir.' " Robinson's lawyer suggested that this was not a case in which the articles of war had been violated; rather a few people "were working vengeance against an uppity black man." The court-martial concurred and dismissed all charges.

This was the man Branch Rickey hired, proud, as his mother had wanted him to be, fierce in his own nature, scarred because white America wounds its fierce proud blacks. I once asked Rickey if he was surprised by the full measure of Robinson's success and I heard him laugh deep in his chest. "Adventure. Adventure. The man is all adventure. I only wish I could have signed him five years sooner."

As surely as Robinson's genius at the game transcends his autobiography, it also transcends record books. In two seasons, 1962 and 1965, Maury Wills stole more bases than Robinson did in all of a ten-year career. Ted Williams' lifetime batting average, .344, is two points higher than Robinson's best for any season. Robinson never hit twenty home runs in a year, never batted in 125 runs. Stan Musial consistently scored more often. Having said those things, one has not said much because troops of people who were there believe that in his prime Jackie Robinson was a better ball player than any of the others. "Ya want a guy that comes to play," suggests Leo Durocher, whose personal relationship with Robinson was spiky. "This guy didn't just come to play. He come to beat ya. He come to stuff the goddamn bat right up your ass."

He moved onto the field with a pigeon-toed shuffle, Number 42 on his back. Reese wore 1. Billy Cox wore 3. Duke Snider wore 4. Carl Furillo wore 6. Dressen wore 7. Shuba wore 8. Robinson wore 42. The black man had to begin in double figures. So he remained.

After 1948 he had too much belly, and toward the end fat rolled up behind his neck. But how this lion sprang. Like a few, very few athletes, Babe Ruth, Jim Brown, Robinson did not merely play at center stage. He *was* center stage; and wherever he walked, center stage moved with him.

When the Dodgers needed a run and had men at first and second, it was Robinson who came to bat. Would he slap a line drive to right? Would he slug the ball to left? Or would he roll a bunt? From the stands at Ebbets Field, close to home plate, the questions rose into a din. The pitcher saw Robinson. He heard the stands. He bit his lip.

At times when the team lagged, Robinson found his way to first. Balancing evenly on the balls of both feet, he took an enormous lead. The pitcher glared. Robinson stared back. There was no action, only two men throwing hard looks. But time suspended. The cry in the grandstands rose. And Robinson hopped a half yard farther from first. The pitcher stepped off the mound, calling time-out, and when the game resumed, he walked the hitter.

Breaking, Robinson reached full speed in three strides. The pigeon-toed walk yielded to a run of graceful power. He could steal home, or advance two bases on someone else's bunt, and at the time of decision, when he slid, the big dark body became a bird in flight. Then, safe, he rose slowly, often limping, and made his pigeon-toed way to the dugout.

Once Russ Meyer, a short-tempered righthander, pitched a fine game against the Dodgers. The score going into the eighth inning was 2 to 2, and it was an achievement to check the Brooklyn hitters in Ebbets Field. Then, somehow, Robinson reached third base. He took a long lead, threatening to steal home, and the Phillies, using a set play, caught him fifteen feet off base. A rundown developed. This is the major league version of a game children call getting into a pickle. The runner is surrounded by fielders who throw the ball back and forth, gradually closing the gap. Since a ball travels four times faster than a man's best running speed, it is only a question of time before the gap closes and the runner is tagged. Except for Robinson. The rundown was his greatest play. Robinson could start so fast and stop so short that he could elude anyone in baseball, and he could feint a start and feint a stop as well.

All the Phillies rushed to the third-base line, a shortstop named Granny Hamner and a second baseman called Mike Goliat and the first baseman, Eddie Waitkus. The third baseman, Puddin' Head Jones, and the catcher, Andy Seminick, were already there. Meyer himself joined. Among the gray uniforms Robinson in white lunged, and sprinted and leaped and stopped. The Phils threw the ball back and forth, but Robinson anticipated their throws, and after forty seconds, and six throws, the gap had not closed. Then, a throw toward third went wild and Robinson made his final victorious run at home plate. Meyer dropped to his knees and threw both arms around

Robinson's stout legs. Robinson bounced a hip against Meyer's head and came home running backward, saying "What the hell are you trying to do?"

"Under the stands, Robinson," Meyer said.

"Right now," Robinson roared.

Police beat them to the proposed ring. Robinson not only won games; he won and infuriated the losers.

In Ebbets Field one spring day in 1955 Sal Maglie was humiliating the Brooklyn hitters. Not Cox or Robinson, but most of the others were clearly alarmed by Maglie's highest skill. He threw at hitters, as he said, "whenever they didn't expect it. That way I had them looking to duck all the time." The fast pitch at the chin or temple is frightening but not truly dangerous as long as the batter sees the ball. He has only to move his head a few inches to safety.

On this particular afternoon, Maglie threw a fast pitch behind Robinson's shoulders, and that *is* truly dangerous, a killer pitch. As a batter strides, and one strides automatically, he loses height. A normal defensive reflex is to fall backward. When a pitch is shoulder-high behind a man, he ducks directly into the baseball.

I can see Maglie, saturnine in the brightness of May, winding up and throwing. Robinson started to duck and then, with those extraordinary reflexes, hunched his shoulders and froze. The ball sailed wild behind him. He must have felt the wind. He held the hunched posture and gazed at Maglie, who began fidgeting on the mound.

A few innings later, as Maglie continued to overwhelm the Brooklyn hitters, Pee Wee Reese said, "Jack, you got to do something."

"Yeah," Robinson said.

The bat boy overheard the whispered conversation, and just before Jack stepped in to hit, he said in a voice of anxiety, "Don't you do it. Let one of the others do it. You do enough."

Robinson took his stance, bat high. He felt a certain relief. Let somebody else do it, for a change.

"Come on, Jack." Reese's voice carried from the dugout. "We're counting on you."

Robinson took a deep breath. Somebody else? What somebody else? Hodges? Snider? Damn, there *wasn't* anybody else.

The bunt carried accurately toward first baseman Whitey Lockman, who scooped the ball and looked to throw. That is the play. Bunt and make the pitcher cover first. Then run him down. But Maglie lingered in the safety of the mound. He would not move, and a second baseman named Davey Williams took his place. Lockman's throw reached Williams at first base. Then Robinson struck. A knee crashed into Williams' lower spine and Williams spun into the air, twisting grotesquely, and when he fell he lay in an awkward sprawl, as people do when they are seriously injured.

He was carried from the field. Two innings after that, Alvin Dark, the Giant captain, lined a two-base hit to left field. Dark did not stop at second. Instead, he continued full speed toward third base and Jackie Robinson. The throw had him beaten. Robinson put the ball into his bare right hand and decided to tag Dark between the eyes.

As Dark began to slide, Robinson faked to his right. Dark followed his fake. Robinson stepped aside and slammed the ball at Dark's brow. To his amazement, it bounced free. He had not gotten a secure grip. Dark, avenging Davey Williams, substituting for Sal Maglie, was safe at third.

Both men dusted their uniforms. Lockman was batting. Staring toward home, Robinson said through rigid lips, "This isn't the end. There'll be another day." But when the game was over, Dark asked a reporter to carry a message into the Brooklyn clubhouse. "Tell him we're even," the Giant captain said. "Tell him I don't want another day."

The next afternoon I stood in the Giant clubhouse, watching a trainer rub Dark's shoulders. Alvin had straight black hair and deep-set eyes that seemed to squint, the kind of face, Leonard Koppett said, that belonged on a Confederate cavalry captain.

"What do ya thinka Robinson?" Dark said softly, as the trainer bent over him.

"A lot. I think a lot of Robinson."

"I don't know how you can say that," Dark said. "Do you know what he is?" He sought a metaphor to stir me. "Don't you understand?" Dark cried. "He's a *Hitler*." ("And Maglie is Mussolini," I thought.) "Anybody can do something like that to Davey is a Hitler," Dark said.

He paused in thought. "Ah know ahm right," Dark said. "A little higher, Doc." Watching the deep-set angry eyes, I could not forget that when combat reached close quarters, it was the Southerner not the black who had backed off.

After baseball, the executive saddle was something Robinson bore to earn a living. He moved from Chock Full O'Nuts to an insurance company to a food franchising business. Politics was his passion. He supported Nixon for President in 1960, when Kennedy won, and he endorsed Rockefeller for the Republican candidacy in 1964, when Barry Goldwater stormed the San Francisco convention. We met from time to time and chatted.

"I wanted to be fair about things," he said, "so I went to see both Kennedy and Nixon. Now, Nixon seemed to understand a little bit of what had to be done. John Kennedy said, 'Mr. Robinson, I don't know much about the problems of colored people since I come from New England.' I figured, the hell with that. Any man in Congress for fifteen years ought to make it his business to know colored people."

"Credibility is the question."

"Well, I trust Nixon on this point."

"All right," I said. "Even if your analysis is right as far as it goes, civil rights isn't the only question. There are a dozen other issues."

"Sure," Robinson said, "and there are pressure groups working on all of them. I'm a pressure group for civil rights."

Goldwater's capture of the candidacy shook him. He recognized the nature of the campaign, Goldwater playing to conservative whites, Lyndon Johnson courting liberals and blacks, and said that we could well have a white man's party and a black man's party in America. "It would make everything I worked for meaningless," he said, "if baseball is integrated but the political parties are segregated." In Nelson Rockefeller he saw a great dark hope. He might have been appointed to the cabinet if Rockefeller had been elected President, but Robinson's political career, unlike his baseball life, trails off into disappointments and conditional sentences.

He came walking pigeon-toed through the doors of the Sea Host, a food franchising company, at 12:30, suddenly and astonishingly handsome. Under a broad brow, the fine features were set in a well-proportioned face. What was most remarkable was the skin. It shone, unsullied ebony. I should expect that Shaka, the chieftain who built the Zulu warrior nation, had that coloring, imperial black. Robinson's hair had gone pure white, and the contrast of skin and hair make a dramatic balance.

"You look better than when you played," I said.

"Lost weight," Robinson said. We walked to Morgen's East, a restaurant off Madison Avenue, which Robinson finds convenient. A few heads turned when we entered, but no one bothered him. "I lost weight on doctor's orders," he said. "I have diabetes, high blood pressure, and I've had a heart attack." He grinned. "That's because I never drink and I don't smoke."

"Bad heart attack?"

"Bad enough. I was at a dinner. It started out like indigestion, only worse. I had three weeks on my back." He looked at the menu and ordered a salad and said, "Low cholesterol."

"I don't know how to ask you about your boy."

"You just did."

"And the arrest."

"Two arrests, one in March and one in August. The second time the court ruled that he was a narcotics-dependent person. I can talk about Jackie. Rachel and I have been able to piece things together. He's a bright boy and a good athlete. If he'd worked, I think he could have become a major leaguer."

"Would you have liked that?"

"Yes," Robinson said, "I would have liked that. But he's an independent kid, and look where he was. You know Rachel has a master's degree. She teaches at Yale. So there was the culture stuff. He felt blocked there. And he was Jackie Robinson Junior so he felt that he was blocked in sports. He wanted to be something; he wanted to be great at *something*. So he decided, when he was pretty young, that he was going to be a great crook. There are some Mafia people around Stamford. It began with smoking pot. And after a while, it turned out, he knew about Mafia contracts, about murdering people. Then he went off to the war. He was wounded. He learned how to kill. When he came back, he couldn't handle anything himself. Heroin. When he was picked up, with some other kids who possessed marijuana, he started fighting the police.

"It could have been jail, but the sentence was suspended with the understanding that he'd go into treatment to cure himself of addiction. There's a place called Daytop, in Seymour, Connecticut, where rehabilitation is done by former addicts. That's where he decided to go.

"When he went in, a psychiatrist talked to Rachel and me for a long time. They wanted to explain what was going to happen so we could deal with it. The psychiatrist said that in the cure Jackie would have to confront himself and that one of the pat-

terns is that the addict runs home to his parents. It seems to
happen.

"Now, he told us, the important thing was that when Jack
came home, we shouldn't let him in. He had to confront himself
and this thing on his own. If we let him in, then all the Daytop
work could be undone. Jackie might see it as something he
could quit when the going got tough. So there we are, Rachel
and me, and there is the psychiatrist saying when your own son
comes to the door begging for help, you must not under any
circumstances let him in.

"And I nodded and I didn't look at Rachel, because I knew
if I looked at her and she looked at me, she'd start to cry."

"How could your son have been involved with dope and
crime without you or Rachel suspecting?"

"I told you that he wanted to be a great criminal. I didn't tell
you what he really was."

"What was he?"

"A great liar," Robinson said.

We sat silent. Robinson continued to eat slowly. "You see any
of the old writers?" I said. "Dick Young?"

"I respected Dick as a good writer. We disagreed, but I give
him that. A lot of writers were as uninformed as fans. What did
they know how it was? What did they know how it felt to win,
to lose? And they expected me to be grateful for what they
wrote. Once a writer came up and said I better start saying
thank you if I wanted to be Most Valuable Player. I said if I have
to thank *you* to win MVP, I don't want the fucking thing. And
I didn't thank him, and I won it.

"I was a great thing for those guys. They could sell magazine
stories about me. That was the difference between hamburger
and steak." He picked at his salad.

"How do you do with the young militants?"

"A while ago in Harlem these kids started threatening me.
The Governor asked me to speak for the new state office thing
and it got rough."

Nelson Rockefeller had sponsored a high-rise state building at Seventh Avenue and 125th Street, the core of Harlem. The plan would encourage integration, Rockefeller said. But ever baronial, he neglected to bring local black leaders to planning conferences. The initial leveling was messy. People had to be dispossessed. To certain blacks, the whole scheme reeked of colonialism. One night, thirty militants advanced with pup tents and occupied the site. Without neighborhood support for his benign intention, Rockefeller turned to Robinson.

"When I went there to talk," Robinson said, "the kids were angry. A detective with me said I better watch it, but I've been in that scene before, with angry kids. They see me in a suit and tie and they look at my white hair and they're too young to remember what I did, or they don't care. I began to talk and some shouted 'Oreo.' You know. The cookie that's black outside and white underneath.

"When I get with militant kids, I can handle myself. I curse." Robinson smiled to himself. "All of a sudden this gray-haired man in a suit and tie is calling them mothers. Well, you know."

He repeated some of the speech he had made. " 'Maybe this isn't the best thing in the world, but it's something. It's a chance. And if you block it, then that's it. You've lost, not Governor Rockefeller. Nobody's gonna try and build here again. And it'll be over. Nobody'll invest and nobody'll want to come here and nothing will happen except the neighborhood'll get worse. You bastards are wrong to turn against this thing.'

"There was this white man, sixty years old, maybe five feet five, walking down the street and a couple of the young militants went up behind him and knocked him flat. I went over and helped him up. That's when they really started with the 'Oreo.'

"The gang was tough. The police didn't want to get involved. That old man could have been murdered. They said he was an accountant at Blumstein's and they don't like Blumstein's." It is the principal department store on 125th Street, free with credit, persistent with demands for payment, the very cliché of the usurious, exploitive, Jewish white.

"The militants," Robinson said, "just want to burn. And maybe white society will have to burn, but they are hitting the wrong targets all the time, like an old man."

"Or you?"

"Or me."

He does not want society to burn. Burn America and you burn the achievements of Jackie Robinson. After ruinous, anarchic blaze, who will remember the brave, fatherless boyhood, the fight for an inch of Army justice, the courage in baseball, the leadership and the triumph, of a free man who walked with swift and certain strides?

It was a cold day. After lunch the wind, biting up Fifty-third Street, bothered him. He walked deliberately, and it shocked me in the street to realize that I was slowing my own pace so as not to walk too quickly for Jackie Robinson.

The noontime of the American Dream glows briefly. One is continuously being persuaded to purchase washing machines and dryers, spare television sets and youth furniture, to add a room or to move into a larger home, and then when the hardest payments have been met, and the large family is suitably housed, the children begin making their way into dormitories and shared single rooms, the world beyond the hearth.

The children were all gone from the big stone house in Stamford, which the Robinsons built in mid-1954. Jack Junior was fighting for stability, and doing well. He had stopped using heroin and joined the staff of Daytop; he talked of wanting to run a community center in a ghetto. Sharon, born in 1950, married young, was living in Washington, D.C. After a good career at Mount Hermon Prep, David has gone clear across the country to Stanford. "But we're busy, you can be sure," Mrs. Robinson said on an afternoon when Jack asked my wife and me to visit. "We're both quite occupied."

402

In at least one sense, the years had treated Rachel Isum Robinson kindly. She remained a handsome woman, with soft, unlined skin. Escorting guests into the living room, she bore herself elegantly, and there was a warmth to her manner, and the two, elegance and warmth, blended into graciousness.

"Won't you sit down? Can I fix drinks?" An ebony piano stood at one side of the spacious room, which was carpeted and high-ceilinged. A window wall overlooked a bright lawn, sloping toward water, the Stamford reservoir. Opposite, gray stone arched above the fireplace. One had to look closely to notice a pride of the mason's craft; no visible mortar interrupted the flow of stone. "The builder," Rachel said, "was marvelous. He meant this place to be a monument; of course, we have never been sure whether for us or for him."

She climbed two carpeted stairs into a dining alcove and returned with drinks in mugs of heavy glass. She sipped at a martini. "One thing about my background in California was that I was brought up to be as ladylike as possible. I was taught not to be aggressive. And then, marrying Jack I was in the middle of a struggle where—well, without aggressive behavior it would have failed. There was an aggressiveness to Jack's whole career in baseball. It was a kind of objection to the white society."

"A very mild objection." Treading softly, on the balls of his feet, Robinson entered his living room. He found an easy chair and reclined into a graceful slouch. He wore dark slacks and a blue knit shirt with sleeves that ended in mid-bicep. "Go on, go on," he said in a soft voice.

"How did you find spring training in the South?"

"Humiliating," Rachel said. Jack half-closed his eyes. "One of the many mistakes we made with Jackie," Rachel said, "was trying to shield him from the way the South was. When we just had little Jack, we lived in the barracks at Vero Beach, like some other families, but we were limited to camp, which made us different. The white wives were always going on shopping trips

403

to Vero Beach. Black people weren't welcome to shop there. The hairdresser said he couldn't work with black women's hair. Well, one day I found a black hairdresser, and telephoned Vero Beach for a taxi. I was standing with little Jack when the driver pulled up. I started in, but he said wait, he wouldn't take us. I'd have to call the colored cab.

"The colored *cab!* It was a big, ugly bus. I got in with Jackie, and the driver had to swing around near the swimming pool where all the white wives sat with their children. I shrank in my seat. I didn't want anybody to see me. But just as we were turning little Jack stuck his head out of a window and called, 'Good-bye, good-bye.' All the white wives looked up and saw me in this awful bus, the colored taxi, we had to ride in.

"After I was done at the hairdresser I decided instead of the bus I'd walk back the five miles. It was slow going with little Jackie. He couldn't make it all the way. And then that colored taxi came by again, only this time it was full. It was bringing the help to serve the evening meal. The driver stopped and Jackie and I got on again. I hated to, but that was the only way we could get back to camp.

"Another time the Dodgers were playing in West Palm Beach and I took Jackie and when we got there they wouldn't let us through the turnstile. No colored, the man said. Go around to the outfield. The colored *entrance*, they called it, was where they'd taken some boards out of the outfield fence. You had to climb over boards. Skirts were long then. I remember holding little Jack's hand and helping him through.

"I never discussed any of these humiliations. I tried to pretend they weren't there. And young Jack never discussed them with me. But he must have noticed. He had to notice, don't you think?"

"He noticed," Robinson said.

"My husband underplays things," Rachel said. "That's his style. Don't let him fool you. What he came up against, and what we all came up against, was very, very rough."

Robinson's eyes remained half closed.

"He was explosive on the field," Rachel said, "and reporters used to ask if he was explosive at home. Of course he wasn't. No matter what he'd been called, or how sarcastic or bigoted others had been to him, he never took it out on any of us.

"After we moved up here," Rachel said, "there was one clue to when he was upset, when things had gone particularly badly. He'd go out on the lawn with a bucket of golf balls and take his driver and one after another hit those golf balls into the water."

Robinson sat up. His eyes grew merry. "The golf balls were white," he said.

"We wanted this house," Rachel said. "We lived in St. Albans, a mixed neighborhood in Queens, but we wanted something more and we began to look, and there were more humiliations, although, by this time, it was almost the mid-fifties. We answered ads for some places around Greenwich. When the brokers saw us, the houses turned out to be just sold or no longer on the market, phrases like that. The brokers said they themselves didn't object. It was always other people. The Bridgeport *Herald* got wind of the trouble and wrote it up and then a committee was formed in Stamford with ministers and Andrea Simon, the wife of Dick Simon of Simon and Schuster. They asked what we wanted. We said view, privacy, water. They lined up a broker with six places. The first five houses were all bad for different reasons. Then we saw this site. It had"—Rachel smiled—"view, privacy, water.

"But we weren't done with it. We had to find a builder, and some banks up here were dead set against us."

Robinson had reclined again. "We lower real estate values," he said.

"The banks had power over the builders," Rachel said. "They could stop credit. But finally we found one builder, Ben Gunner, a bank operated by two Jewish brothers, and they'd take

405

the chance. Ben Gunner and I used to sit out and watch the water and talk and one day I told him I'd always wanted a fireplace for the bedroom. To surprise me, he built one. Then Ben thought children should have a secret staircase. He put one in, and a firemen's pole for Jackie to slide down and so many extra things, for which he didn't charge, he may have gone broke building this house for us. Nothing shakes it."

"And in this neighborhood," Robinson said, "real estate values go up every year."

"I'll get strawberries and cream," Rachel said. "Would everybody like strawberries and cream?"

The unshakable house was a pivot to their lives. Rachel enrolled at NYU and in 1957 took a master's degree in psychiatric nursing. From Stamford she commutes to New Haven, where she is assistant professor of psychiatric nursing at Yale's graduate nursing school. Jack commutes the other way.

Over strawberries, he said, "The baseball years seem very long ago. When I quit, I went into the NAACP, and the conservatives found me hard to take. They were men of eighty. Their attitude was: don't rock the boat. Today militants find me hard to take. Their attitude is: burn everything. But I haven't changed much. The times have changed around me. Now we're coming to the black-black confrontation, extreme against moderate. After that the rough one, black and white. Blacks aren't scared any more. If the Klan walked into a black neighborhood now, the people would rip the sheets right off them.

"Only the President of the United States can cool things, if anything or anybody can, and we have a President who surrounds himself with Mitchell and Agnew. Why the hell didn't he make Mitchell Secretary of State?"

"World War III."

Robinson grinned slightly. "Well, anyway, you see, the baseball years and the baseball experience not only seem long ago, they were long ago."

"But you're more proud of it than anything."

"Sure. No pitcher ever made me back up. *No one.* And they all tried. Near the end Sam Jones—you remember him with that big sidearm stuff—brushed me and I got up and hit the hell out of his curve."

"I'm not proud just that he performed with excellence on the field," Rachel said. "I'm proud that as a man he had integrity and strength." She paused. "Remember, don't let him fool you. When I hear him talk about it to others, it always seems less devastating than it was."

It grew late. The time was dusk. Near the door he showed me a box of candy. "I used to buy chocolates for Rachel when we were courting," he said.

"It's been nice talking again, hasn't it?" Rachel said.

"I'll try not to hit nerves writing about Jack Junior."

"Oh," Rachel said. "Don't concern yourself. Every nerve has been hit already." Then, "How are the other wives you've seen?"

"Well, Betty Erskine has her hands full with their boy. Dottie Reese seems to be bowling a lot."

"See," Rachel said to Jack. "What would you rather have me doing, bowling or working? A working wife isn't the worst thing."

He grinned a private grin and they exchanged soft looks as men and women do when there is love and respect and vintage between them.

We visited again, late in a cool wet May, this time by day and with our children. He had more questions now than before. How was Carl Erskine? He had enjoyed playing on the same team with him. Labine? Had Preacher really put on weight?

Rachel was away, and "Jackie got himself in a scrape last night in New Haven," Robinson said. "He's in bad neighborhoods working with addicts and it caught up with him. Someone hit him with a board and split his forehead. They woke me, New

Haven Hospital, at 6 A.M. I've got to drive there and pick him up a little later." Then Robinson was talking to my children, who warmed to this large gentle man.

When Robinson found the older boy wanted to become an architect, he showed him something of how the house was built. My younger son wanted to fish. Robinson found him a pole and baited the hook and pointed out a rock. "That's the best place to fish from." He was playing peekaboo with my three-year-old daughter when the time came for him to leave. "You and the children stay," he pleaded. "I wish Rachel could see them playing. That's what this house was built for, children."

We meant to drive off before father and injured son returned, but the children delayed us and we had just reached the station wagon when they drove up to the house. Jack Junior stepped out of his father's car slowly and turned so that his back was toward us. "Say hello," Jackie said. "It's all right." The young man had a strong straight body. He turned. He wore a beard. Bandages covered the forehead.

He started unsteadily toward the house, resting on his father's arm. I called, "My wife can drive our kids home, Jack. Let me give you a hand."

Robinson put an arm around Jack Junior, and said softly, tender as Stephen Kumalo, the umfundisi, "No. Thank you. It's all right. I can take care of my son."

The death facts may be stated simply. On June 17, 1971, at about 2:30 A.M., Jackie Robinson, Jr., twenty-four, was found dead in the wreck of a yellow MG. He had driven off the Merritt Parkway at such high speed that the car, which belonged to his brother David, demolished four wooden guard posts. One door came to rest 117 feet distant from the chassis, which looked like a toy car, bent double by the hammer of a petulant child. Police theorized that death was instantaneous. The coroner fixed the cause as a broken neck. David Robinson identified the car and his brother's body. Jackie broke the news to Rachel.

People at Daytop believe that young Jackie fell asleep behind the wheel. He had been organizing a benefit jazz festival, which was indeed held, but as a memorial. "Jackie was putting in very long hours," says Jimmy DeJohn of Daytop. "He just must have got exhausted."

The body lay in an open coffin, among floral wreaths. The family had chosen Antioch Baptist church in Brooklyn for the funeral, and June 21, the day of the services, broke with oppressive heat. Mourners crowded the church and sat beating fans.

"In Memoriam," said the program, *"Jack Roosevelt Robinson, Jr., 1946–1971."* I looked up. An open coffin downs hard and when we heard my wife gasp, Al Silverman, the editor of *Sport,* and I made heavy funeral gossip. There was Hugh Morrow from Nelson Rockefeller's office. There was Don Newcombe. There was Monte Irvin, the glorious old Giant outfielder. But the coffin was open. No chattering could obscure that for long and I looked at the leonine head of the young man newly dead. His beard was trimmed. For an instant I allowed myself to think of what lay locked within the skull, Gibran and Herbie Mann and the old colored taxi at Vero Beach and night patrols near Pleiku and the narcosis of heroin and the shock of withdrawal and a father's tender voice. And then I would not let myself think like that any more.

The family was escorted to their pew at 1:15. Rachel was clinging to another of her children. Two men had to help Jack walk. He was crying very softly for his son, his head down, so that the tears coursed only a little way before falling to the floor.

A small chorus from Daytop sang "Bridge over Troubled Water" and "Swing Low, Sweet Chariot." A solo flutist played "We Shall Overcome." One is prepared for music at funerals, but then something happened that surprised everyone: Monte Irvin, Hugh Morrow, the people of the parish, who had known the Robinsons twenty-five years ago as neighbors. David Robinson, who was nineteen, walked to the pulpit and read a eulogy. David had written it in a single afternoon and while riding to church that morning had asked his father if he could speak it.

"If you want to," Jackie Robinson said.

"He climbed high on the cliffs above the sea," David called in a resonant tenor, "and stripped bare his shoulders and raised his arms to the water, crying, 'I am a man. Give me my freedom so that I might dance naked in the moonlight and laugh with the stars and roll in the grass and drink the warmth of the sun. Give me my freedom so I might fly.' But the armies of the sea continued to war with the wind and the wind raced through the giants of stones and mocked his cries, and the man fell to his knees and wept."

David wore a dashiki. He had finished his freshman year at Stanford. Soon he would travel through Africa. Jackie Junior had intended to buy the yellow MG and help David to a stake.

"He rose," David's voice called from the pulpit, "and journeyed down the mountain to the valley and came upon a village. When the people saw him, they scorned him for his naked shoulders and wild eyes and again he cried, 'I am a man. I seek the means of freedom.'

"The people laughed, saying, 'We see no chains on your arms. Go. You are free.' And they called him mad and drove him from their village. . . ." The man walked on, "eyes red as a gladiator's sword," until he came to a stream where he saw an image, face sunken in hunger, "skin drawn tight around the body.

"He stood fixed on the water's edge and began to weep, not from sorrow but from joy, for he saw beauty in the water. He removed his clothing and stood naked before the world and rose to his full height and smiled and moved to meet the figure in the water and the stream made love to his body and the majesty of his voice was heard above the roar of the sea and the howl of the wind, *and he was free.*"

David hurried from the pulpit. His mother rose to embrace

him. Sobs rang through the old church; it was five minutes before formal worship resumed. But even as our small group drove back to New York, wondering how to make memorial, we had seen Jackie Robinson after the services, white-haired, dry-eyed and sure, as when he doubled home two runs, walking among street people outside the church, talking perhaps of the hell of heroin, touching or being touched by children, and we thought how proud his first-born son would have been, not of the ball player but of the man, had he lived, if only the insanity of the present had given him a chance.

BILLY ALONE

He wasn't with us after the last part o' May, but I roomed with him long enough to get the insomny. I was the only guy in the club game enough to stand for him. And do you know where he is now? I got a letter today and I'll read it to you. No—I guess I better tell you somethin' about him first.

RING LARDNER, *My Roomy*

The Juniata River runs down Black Log Mountain, and through the Tuscarawas its gorge curves like a bow. All the factories are shut at Cuba Mills and Mifflintown, and downstream, when the Juniata sweeps along past Newport, the hurrying waters are clean enough to fish.

On the interstate highways that band Pennsylvania no signs announce mileage to the petrified village of Newport, where Billy Cox, the great third baseman, tends bar. Like Clem Labine's Woonsocket, Newport lies close to arterial roads, but bypassed. You drive west from New York into Pennsylvania Dutch country, and at Harrisburg the main routes press farther west and south. To reach Newport, you turn north along the Susquehanna until it forks just past Duncannon. The left fork is the Juniata River.

I had found everyone now but Cox, that odd, incongruous figure, hints of intelligence set in curious camouflage. The others remembered him as solitary, strange, gifted, troubled. Some reminded me that Preacher Roe had done a lot for Billy, by rooming with him and buoying his spirits. Pee Wee Reese called Cox the greatest glove and least likely-looking major league infielder he'd ever known. I can still see him going toward the line, the barehand side, and reaching across the wiry body, slapping that Whelan glove, capturing a two-base hit, and turning it into a ground out. "Five to three if you're scoring," Connie Desmond, the sportscaster, liked to say.

Even in the major leagues third base begins with the hard, wordless truths my father and I explored thirty years ago. You have to see the ball. You have to look the ball into your glove. But as you do, your face is bare to any sudden hop, and as you lower the glove, the way you must, you leave torso and groin unguarded.

It is the same in the majors. The fields are better, making truer bounces, but then the batters hit harder. The balance holds, and sometimes you want to cringe for a third baseman, but not for Billy Cox. With Billy crouched, motionless, staring down a hitter's craw, the ball, not he, would be the victim.

Hoss Cox had a long face, thin hair and a sorrowful, inward expression. Along with the index-finger wag, for "Fuckit," he put off serious talk. "Ah," he would say, "don't start that shit." At times, when something odd, comical or ghastly happened, the long sad face transformed. He cocked his head and pursed his lips and seemed about to grin. "Look at this," Hoss Cox's expression said. "Look what the sonsabitches are up to now."

When I telephoned, he explained carefully that he had left the job tending bar at the American Legion. His Cousin Gumby worked there now. He himself was at the Owls Club.

413

"Elks?"

"Nah. Not Elks. *Owls.* You cross the bridge to the Gulf Station and you turn left."

We made a date to meet at four o'clock on Thursday afternoon. I knew Billy liked the night. I packed a few things and the glove, the Wilson A-2000. Each Dodger had signed it. Fingers read Joe Black, Jackie Robinson, Preacher Roe. Only Cox was left to close the circle of nostalgia.

Newport sits among ridges and cuts in cold, handsome country, a town of perhaps fifteen hundred on the south bank of the Juniata. I crossed an old bridge and made the left at the Gulf Station. Near the end of a narrow street stood a two-story building, faced with dull, glossy slabs of mica. A sign etched in light gray read, "SOCIAL ORDER OF OWLS (PRIVATE)."

Cox has not yet reported for work. "Wait for him over at the Newporter," suggested the day bartender. "It's half a block away." The Newporter, a frame building three floors high, is the town hotel. The main entrance leads to a foyer feeding a wooden stairway. A registration desk and newsstand lie off to the right, in a bare square room that serves as lobby. Beyond, the bar was dark. Four men sat drinking quietly. A chubby blonde, with a farm girl's face but pressing thirty, was sipping beer and giggling. An older woman watched her, with intent amusement.

I ordered Rolling Rock, a beer that calls itself the pride of Pennsylvania. Suddenly an old man, beyond the two women, called hoarsely, "Big Bill." Cox had entered. He wore an open-collared plaid shirt and work pants. "Yeh," he said to me. "Yeh. How ya doing? Need a room? Jack here, he'll get you one. I come here to eat. Then I gotta work. Then we can talk. Maybe I'll take ya up the hill like the other time, or maybe we'll go to the Vets. Hey, Jack, a meat loaf. And another drink for him. He's a writer from New York."

"I grew up with Bill," said the bartender, a short, stumpy man in eyeglasses. "My name's Jack Heisey. I knew him as a boy."

"Don't believe any shit he tells you now," Cox said.

He has grown a belly and he was bigger than I remembered. He is no taller, of course, perhaps five feet nine, but above the new paunch powerful high shoulders hunched. Among Hodges, Snider and Robinson, you overlooked the power in Cox's build.

"Hey," he said. "Lookit this, will ya?" Cox extended his right hand. The middle finger ended between knuckles. The skin was smooth. It looked like a normal finger end, a dwarf finger, without the nail.

"What happened?"

Cox jerked his head back, and pursed his lips. "Dumbness," he said, "dumbness. I thought the power mower was off. I put my hand in to find out. It got the longest finger. Started spurting blood. Didn't hurt. I'm standing there with part of my finger on the grass looking at the blood, saying, 'Dumbness, dumbness.'"

"When was this?"

"Last summer."

"Can you throw? You ought to have a sinker now."

"Yer right, but I don't know. I ain't tried to throw a ball since it happened."

The blonde girl's cry filled the bar: "Billy Cox."

He started and drew back his head.

"Are you really Billy Cox? The third baseman? Who played for the Dodgers? Really? I use to watch you."

"You was six months old."

"Oh, Billy." The girl sprawled away from the bar stool. She was wearing tight blue slacks and a white blouse. "Would you give me your autograph?"

Cox turned to his beer. "Can't write."

"I never met a major leaguer before."

"I got to work a while," Cox said to me, pointedly ignoring the blonde. "We can talk after. Jack here'll take care of ya. Get ya a room. Private bath, if you want it."

415

The girl pressed pencil and paper between us. Cox shook his head and signed his name.

"Here's the meat loaf, Bill," Jack said.

"Big Bill," said the old man in the corner. He offered me a hand. "I'm Kenneth S. Smith."

"Above your name," the blonde said to Cox, "you have to write 'love and kisses.'"

"No," Cox said.

"Suppose I go out and buy a baseball and a pen."

"Can't get a baseball in this town no more."

"Sure I can."

"Hey," Cox said, jerking his head. "You find a baseball left in this town, I'll sign anything."

The women walked out into Main Street, the blonde rolling in the slacks. Cox shook his head and said to no one, "Whoosh. She's trying to get me in trouble."

"She's a secretary over to Harrisburg," said Kenneth S. Smith. "The older one runs a bar."

"I don't want no trouble," Cox said to me. "This here's a small town. Everybody knows what ya do."

In a few minutes the girl came squealing back. "I found it, I found it." She carried a dollar baseball in a box and a yellow pen.

"Son of a bitch," Cox muttered.

"It's not much of a ball, miss," I said.

"But it's a baseball," Cox said. "She found a baseball in Newport."

"Now you got to sign 'love and kisses,'" the girl said.

Cox pursed his lips and signed. The chubby girl put her arms around him and kissed his cheek. His eyes glinted with amusement.

"This happen every day, Willie?" I said.

"This is the first real ball player I ever met," the secretary said.

"Over ta York," Cox said, "Kenny Raffensberger lives there."

The girl paced. Cox finished his meat loaf and put sixty cents on the counter. "When I get done, we get together," he said. Jack Heisey called, "See ya," as Cox left. The blonde stopped pacing. She clutched the baseball at a hip. "Hey," she said to her friend, "let's go on over to Enola or Duncannon and see what's doing there."

Jack Heisey said room Number 8, one flight up, came with a private bath. "Cost ya more, though. Five dollars." I took the key and followed the wide staircase to a landing and an inked sign marked, "This way to public bathroom." In Number 8 a double bed, covered with a tea-rose spread, stretched diagonally. The private bath was an unenclosed toilet in one corner of the room.

Downstairs a man in the lobby sat studying a television set that showed a basketball game among commercials. He had a long face and a thick chin. "Yes, sir," he said to the announcer of commercials. "You're right, sir. I *will* get some Kellogg's bran cereal. I know, sir. It *is* good for my system. I should have it more." He looked toward me. "You eat bran cereals?" he said.

I crossed into the bar where Jack Heisey and Kenneth S. Smith waited. Billy had told them I would be coming back, and they both began to speak, almost in turn.

"We had some good ball players round here," said Kenneth Smith. "I oughta know. I managed the town team starting in '27. Charley Zeidders, he was fast. Les Bell. A pitcher named Red. They were the good ones."

"Billy," Jack Heisey said, "used ta stand down by the Pennsy tracks. If there was nobody to play with, he'd pick up stones and hit 'em with a stick."

"The day he come out for the team he was so skinny, his shadow looked thinner than a bat."

"His mother died. The Cox kids didn't have no mother."

"The other fellers on the town team didn't want him there. He was so small."

"When he was ten, he fielded like a man."

"I said, 'He stays. The rest o' you can go.' "

"But he got lonely. He was always getting lonely."

"Over ta Marshall Field, that's Agway now, Charlie Zeidders hit one out to left."

"He didn't never want to leave this town."

"Billy said, 'Gimme a bat. Come on. I'll show ya who's skinny!' "

"He was always quitting to come back."

"Billy hit one clear outa sight to center."

"We never seen a ball player like him in Newport or Port Royal."

"Or Mifflintown."

"We won't see one like Billy Cox again."

"The tannery; you heard about the tannery? When I first come here, people said, 'Ken Smith, the tannery is where you oughta work. Secure. We got a mountain town, you know, and times get hard.' Hell, I was a salesman. I traveled some. Bucks County. Seen New York. I was selling when the tannery got closed. Depression come and went. The tannery was dead. There was no call. You don't tan leather goods with tanbark these days. Chemicals, that's what it is."

"Bill's father worked the tannery. Fred Cox. When it closed down, he went to WPA. They never had no decent meals, them kids."

"Billy kept playing baseball."

"We had a common near the ironworks."

"He'd pick up anything, off grass or rocks."

"They closed that, too. Play an' watch baseball was all we had to cheer us."

"The Pirates signed him ta play over ta Harrisburg."

"And he was proud."

"He didn't have no clothes. I ran the town collection. We gave him clothing and a send-off."

"A month later he come home."

"He got too goddamn lonely."

"The next year I sent Red, the pitcher, too. He'd never make it, but he'd sit with Billy."

"The Pittsburgh Pirates. Billy was their shortstop."

"Shoulda played third. He played third for my team."

"Fast company in Pittsburgh. He did fine."

" 'Cept they was drinkers on that club."

"He got to like it there in Brooklyn."

"Poor guy come out of the war and had to play with boozers."

"The Brooklyns let him go. The best third baseman anybody saw."

"He shouldn't be *here* now. Should be on top of the world."

"The Brooklyns sent him to the other league. Then he come home. Showed me his legs. All swole and purple. Thirty-six and they was gonna teach him how to slide. 'Fuckit,' he said."

"Jack," said Kenneth Smith, "would you pipe down so's I can tell this here man how Billy Cox played ball?"

The reasons for which Newport was built died along with the tannery and ironworks. A river bend no longer makes a town and jobs are so short at the Penn Central that only men with twenty years' seniority survive recurrent layoffs. But Newport is not dying; the petrified village may even grow. It is a refuge for certain whites, raising young families, who talk about "the niggers stealing America." No black man lives in Newport, Pennsylvania. None wants to come and none is asked. A few blacks who work for Bethlehem Steel have built a cabin near Lost Creek Gap, but the Newport elders say these aren't bad ones. Hunting and fishing is what those fellers like, the elders announce in the barrooms. No boozing or womanizing. (But the blacks and the white secretaries have not yet found each other.)

419

As much as excellence and pride, the team was black and white together. Preacher Roe felt it and Joe Black, and this untinted friendship was the richest element in Carl Erskine's career. But here was Billy Cox, who was not very good at talking or dealing with other people, not brilliant at anything truly but picking up ground balls, alone now in a prison of intolerance.

"The Vets," he said. "Come in my car." Kenneth S. Smith, past seventy, declared that he would have to go to sleep, but Jack Heisey announced that he would stay. Halfway up a midnight hill, windows of the VFW shone bright. Inside, twelve high stools rimmed the bar. A pool table filled the other space.

"Goddamn catcher's mitt," Cox said, picking up the Wilson A-2000.

"When we played near the tracks" Jack Heisey said, "the gloves wasn't bigger than yer hand." Cox slipped fingers into the glove. "Not bad," he said. "Ain't heavy like a catcher's mitt." He flexed his hand. "Good leather." He swept the glove across his chest, one way, then the other. In the movement, eighteen inches, you could see, if you had ever seen baseball close, that the old hand in the new glove was phenomenal.

"All right," Cox said. "Ya shouldn't miss too much."

He sipped beer. His look softened. "Do you think about Brooklyn much?" I said.

"Oh," Cox said. "Oh." The long face jerked and he nodded.

"You remember?"

"Hey," Cox said, "there was this day Preach was pitching. I put on a catcher's mask and shin guards and a chest protector and I said, 'Okay, I'm ready.' Preach said, 'Wear anything you want, long as you're there.' It wasn't trouble to make the joke. Campy's locker was right near mine."

Someone else prattled about niggers. "You was lucky, Cox. It wasn't like today. You didn't play with no niggers. Campanella was a gentleman. Robinson been to college. You didn't play with no niggers." A film fell over the eyes of Billy Cox. He walked to the pool table and began practicing shots. "Ah," he said at a billiard ball. "Get the fuck down." He was throwing himself into pointless practice.

"New York's fulla niggers," the man said.

Before he spoke again, a shapeless woman marched up and shouted, "I know about the redhead." The woman wore a teal kerchief and brown-rimmed eyeglasses. She started swinging. The man hunched shoulders and held his drink. "You been with that redhead," the woman screamed. "I know, ya lousy bastard." But her blows were not equal to her fury. While she pummeled and shrieked, the man sat, feeling embarrassment more than pain, and tried to focus on his glass of Rolling Rock beer.

I stepped off the bar stool. The sign, "WILLIAM GAYLOR POST, V.F.W., #34," was blue and white.

Cox looked at me, the film lifting from his eyes, and he jerked his head. "Now look at this, willya. Look what the sonsabitches are up to now."

He bent and stroked the cue ball. It caromed far across the table and gently tapped an eight-ball toward a pocket. The woman swung. She cried, "You rotten fucker."

No one present, I thought, except myself, witnessing this 2 A.M. talk of niggers, the ugly woman clouting the sodden man, could have realized that this broad-shouldered, horse-faced fellow tapping billiard balls, missing half a finger on one hand, sad-eyed, among people who would never be more than strangers, was the most glorious glove on the most glorious team that ever played baseball in the sunlight of Brooklyn.

INTERLUDE II

I can never be sure whether it is arrogance, hostility or a streak of good sense that prevents me from taking millionaires as seriously as they would like to be taken. In the course of an education by journalism one frequently sees millionaires naked of press agents, but such intimacy breeds an unpredictable variety of attitudes.

Jack Tibby of *Sports Illustrated* once quoted Henry R. Luce on what he wanted of the magazine. "He put it all into a word," Tibby said. He paused and made a small, smug smile and said, "Excitement."

"They want that on the *Tribune*, Jack. Everywhere."

"Excitement," Tibby repeated, as though oracular, trying to freight a rich-man's offhand banality with wisdom.

Having audited many scenes played by millionaire and vassal, and lacking Tibby's native reverence, my own situations with the rich tend to crumble. George Bernard Shaw said after meeting a film producer, "All he wanted to talk about was art and all I wanted to talk about was money." That is continually happening in more complicated ways, but Walter Francis O'Malley, of Dodger Stadium, Los Angeles, is a rare millionaire in that he senses the limits of his expertise. I have never heard O'Malley discuss a second baseman's hands, the speed of someone's swing or the rotation of a curve. O'Malley considers people, whom he manipulates, and money, which he appears to coin in incalculable quantities, while saying from time to time, "I'm just a fan."

Although he pretends to be pure Brooklyn Celt, O'Malley is the offspring of a German-Irish marriage, who grew up at Culver Military Academy, the University of Pennsylvania and Fordham Law School in the Bronx. In the first trough of the Depression, he scratched out a living servicing bankrupts.

Our lives touched after O'Malley had re-entered the middle class and moved into a private home five blocks from the family apartment at 907 St. Marks Place. I had been enrolled in a small grade school called (for the creator of the first kindergarten) Froebel Academy, and housed at the corner of Brooklyn and Prospect avenues in a building once occupied by Charles Evans Hughes. Names such as Kahn and O'Malley appeared rarely in this Protestant bastion where, during the 1936 Roosevelt landslide, my class supported Alf Landon, by nine to one. But rejecting the clichés of a Roman Catholic upbringing, O'Malley sent his daughter, Terry, to Froebel. Presently, with each man pursuing an area of interest, my father was coaching Froebel sports and Walter O'Malley had become a Froebel trustee.

After my first *Herald Tribune* stories in 1952, O'Malley said what pleased him was that they were the work of a Froebel boy. I mouthed thanks, a mute, inglorious Robinson, wishing people would stop calling me "boy." O'Malley's style was regal, but he was accessible and responsive to questions. Later I composed an enthusiastic feature about him for the *Tribune Sunday Magazine*.

Disenchantment struck after my story about the Gilliam affair. The phrase I had heard, "How would you like a nigger to take your job?" was, O'Malley insisted, the same as "another Jewish judge," cacophony piped by unchosen lawyers in courthouse smoke rooms. "It's rude, but doesn't mean much," O'Malley said, "and I'm surprised that you were taken in."

My defense—"I'd write 'another Jewish judge,' too"—drew a wintry response. "A Froebel boy should know how to evaluate things realistically," O'Malley said, and "Froebel boy" had never sounded so pejorative.

Patches of geniality survived a hardening relationship. O'Malley believed that the first function of the press was to praise, and as his fortune grew, pettiness invaded his style. At one corner of the Ebbets Field press box, a phone was tied into the switchboard. Sportswriters could make local calls without charge, a courtesy that O'Malley ended in 1953, by substituting a pay phone. Subsequently, he complained about "freeloading writers," and ball players who were "money-hungry."

But he understood the New York press better than Rickey had. He knew whom to flatter, whom to cajole, whom to browbeat. He discussed stocks with one writer, baseball broadcasting with another and politics with a third. He possessed the high skill of talking into another man's interest and making that interest appear to be his own. Many baseball writers took him for a warm friend, without recognizing that, as with an underboiled potato, O'Malley's warmth was mostly external.

The shock was all the stronger when he led the Dodgers out of Brooklyn and left some journalists to cover golf matches contested by wiry women. Hypocrisy rose from cry to clamor. "For ten years he told us he was a fan. Then he pulls out for money."

It amazes me to this day that once I stood in the ranks of journalists who, in the most furious words they could summon, indicted a capitalist for being motivated by a passion for greater profits.

The Dodgers prospered in Southern California. After 1958 in which the bones of the team—Hodges hustling in the same infield with Dick Gray, Snider playing outfield beside Gino

Cimoli—finished seventh, the Los Angeles Dodgers rebounded to a pennant and world championship. It had taken Brooklyn seventy-five years to win a World Series; Los Angeles won it in Year Two.

World Series attendance exceeded ninety thousand each afternoon in the Los Angeles Coliseum, but O'Malley's odd frugality persisted. He insisted on closing the so-called press room, a hotel banquet hall where journalists and baseball men eat and drink without charge, at 10 P.M. (Bill Veeck, whose White Sox played docile opposition to the Dodgers, responded by keeping the Chicago press room open twenty-four hours a day. "You can have Scotch for breakfast," Veeck cried, and many did.)

Buzzy Bavasi built the Western Dodgers. The old sluggers yielded to a club of pitchers, Koufax and Drysdale and fast feathery batsmen like Maury Wills. Including 1959, they won three World Series in a decade. The Hollywood community embraced them, and playing at handsome new Dodger Stadium, they drew 2,755,184 customers in 1962, by far the largest total in the history of baseball to that time.

Newspaper accounts described Walter O'Malley entertaining governors, dominating baseball meetings, trudging through East African safaris, a happy man. Then, when the National League expanded to twelve teams in 1969, Bavasi assumed the presidency of the San Diego Padres. Now at length the men who directed the team were co-equals, and after my voyages with Robinson and Cox, Labine and Roe were done, I boarded a plane to California to meet both again. He would book me into the Statler Hilton in downtown Los Angeles, O'Malley said. It was a good functional hotel. "Why not sleep at my place?" said Bavasi. He lived on a mountaintop in La Jolla. "Come over and we can watch the whales migrating in the Pacific."

Beneath the head of a sable antelope who looked wounded, Walter O'Malley smiled and said that only half the lies the Irish tell are true. At almost seventy, he appeared as he had at sixty and fifty: round face, round spectacles, bouncy jowls and a voice sounding a pure Tammany basso. Beyond a window wall, Dodger Stadium spread in what Red Smith has called the green and brown and white geometry of the diamond. "I'm proud of this park," O'Malley announced. "If someone tried to give it to the government, I'd fight. I like things the way they are, private enterprise. I don't like rebelling students. I'm a Tory. An O'Malley a Tory? Why they'd string me up in County Mayo. But Tory is what I am."

Despite the girth, no sense of jolliness flows from the man. The chuckles seem a camouflage for growls. Sidney Greenstreet conveyed such things in the movies of the 1940s.

"Have you heard," O'Malley said, "that anyone mentioning Rickey after he left our office was fined a dollar? I respected Rickey but knew him for what he was. Not quite the idealist some would have him.

"Rickey's Brooklyn contract called for salary plus a percentage of the take, and during World War II the take fell off. It was then Rickey mentioned signing a Negro. He had a *fiscal* interest.

"Rickey suggested an infielder Leo Durocher said could make any major league club. We anticipated opposition within baseball and they asked if I would fly to Havana. The player's name was Silvio Garcia. Third base. I flew in a little DC-3 over the Havana waterfront covered with tar, from American tankers that German submarines had sunk. Garcia had personal problems. Besides, he was in the Cuban Army, a conscript. I advised the directors that the Brooklyn club would not do well to hire someone out of the Cuban Army to replace an American boy who had gone to war.

"This episode opened the door. It gave Rickey complete authority to find his own Negro and he found Robinson.

"Rickey played professionally, but I came into baseball in an

426

unusual way," O'Malley said. "I never practiced law in Brooklyn. I worked in the Lincoln Building, on Forty-second Street in Manhattan. But I lived in Brooklyn and I needed clients and one season during the 1930s I bought a box to take prospective clients to Ebbets Field. Everyone said I was crazy. Yankee Stadium was the place. But I could get a good location in Brooklyn. That began it.

"Now I was doing legal work for the Brooklyn Trust Company, a bank owed a lot of money by the club. It was possible the Brooklyn franchise might go under, but George McLaughlin, the president of the bank, was a tremendous fan. He kept the club afloat. He was under pressure from the superintendent of banks because he had carried the Dodgers' loan too long.

"Things got better with Larry MacPhail, but there was still this loan. Wendell Willkie became club lawyer in 1941, and when Willkie resigned, McLaughlin assigned me as club lawyer.

"Do you know when Brooklyn baseball reached its height? Just before the television era. We had a talented broadcaster, Red Barber, good lights, then Robinson, and we drew 1.8 million fans into a bandbox ten years after the club darn near went bankrupt.

"Three of us were the quickest to recognize the wisdom of acquiring stock: Branch Rickey, John Smith, from the Pfizer chemical company, and myself. By the late 1940s we agreed not to sell stock to an outsider without first offering it to ourselves. Then Smith was taken terminally ill. Lung cancer.

"One day I learned Rickey had been talking to Joseph Kennedy, the Ambassador.

"I said to Rickey, 'What's going on?'

" 'Well, with John Smith dead, I feel it's time to sell. I told Mr. Kennedy you might disagree, but if he acquired my stock and Mrs. Smith's, he'd have control. He's got this son,

John, who is brilliant in politics but has physical problems. Mr. Kennedy thinks running the Dodgers could be the greatest outlet in the world for John.'

"It might have been Jack Kennedy, president of the Dodgers, but Joe rejected the deal when he found he'd face an unhappy minority stockholder in myself. He didn't buy, but if he had, Jack Kennedy could be in this chair and alive today.

"Next Rickey negotiated with William Zeckendorf. I invoked the old agreement, and whatever Rickey and Zeckendorf were planning, I got the stock. The price seemed high. The total was two million dollars.

"In my first year as president, Bobby Thomson hit his home run. I attended a banquet at the St. George Hotel, and in the elevator this night was Thomson. He got out on one floor and someone said, 'Hey, you know what that guy cost me? Twenty-five bucks.' The elevator boy pointed to me. 'You know what it cost him? A quarter million.'

"Well, then we started winning, but we had to keep on winning and that was expensive. After the Braves moved to Milwaukee I saw some developments you may remember."

Mentioning Milwaukee loosed currents of recollection. The 1953 Braves, an ordinary team with Andy Pafko playing left, sold out night after night. O'Malley flew into Billy Mitchell Field whenever the Dodgers played at County Stadium. He likes German food and staged parties at restaurants called Mader's and Karl Ratsch's. "There's a problem," he said one night across platters of Milwaukee bratwurst. "They're going to draw a million customers more here than we will back in Brooklyn."

"Temporary thing."

"But we can't afford even a few years of this. The Braves will be able to pay bigger bonuses, run more farm teams and hire the best scouting talent. The history of the Brooklyn club is that fiscally you're either first or bankrupt. There is no second place."

He had spoken of a roofed stadium, and for years a model stood in the foyer of the Dodger offices, called "O'Malley's Pleasure Dome" and drawing laughter. Then in 1955 a bill passed the New York Legislature establishing a Brooklyn Sports Center Authority. O'Malley expected the Authority to condemn a sufficient number of buildings to create a site for the new super ball park.

Currents met at the crossing of Atlantic and Flatbush avenues downtown. Two subway lines join there, alongside the Long Island Railroad Depot, the tallest building in Brooklyn and the Academy of Music. But along Atlantic Avenue wholesale meat markets led toward slums. Condemnation proceedings begun by the Sports Authority could clear land there. O'Malley peddled Ebbets Field for $3 million, sold two minor league parks at $1 million and announced that he was prepared to put the $5 million into a stadium in downtown Brooklyn. Robert Moses, politician, urban planner, said the stadium would create "a China wall of traffic." Until he measured Moses' power and found it greater than his, O'Malley says he did not intend to move the Dodgers.

In 1956 he purchased the Los Angeles minor league franchise to "get an anchor windward," and when the Mayor of Los Angeles appeared in Vero Beach, O'Malley demanded that the city improve Chavez Ravine, the ball-park site; build access roads; offer a ninety-nine-year lease; and grant him half the rights to minerals, a euphemism for oil, under three hundred acres. He won most points and the Dodgers, profitable in Brooklyn, fled to the West and Coronado.

"They called me carpetbagger," O'Malley said. "One man wrote I left because I believed the colored, Puerto Ricans and Jews were taking over Brooklyn. Lies. Pejorative lies. My son, Peter, came home from Penn and said, 'Dad, what are we going to do? The things in the papers are terrible.'

" 'They are, Peter, but they will pass and the great ball park

I'm going to build in California will stand. That will be remembered' "—he looked through a window wall and beamed—" 'a monument to the O'Malleys.' "

"Walter," I said, "putting this aside, what are you worth?"

He blinked, unoffended, and said, "I can't tell you exactly. There are still some litigations."

"Well," I said, remembering the old Froebel Academy Trustee with $15,000 or so in a bank, "suggest a sensible figure I can quote."

O'Malley brushed his jowls. "A fair figure," he said, "would be twenty-four million dollars." He turned and gazed at his California stadium with delight.

Buzzy Bavasi's window wall commands the sea. Rounder, balder, with sadder eyes than I had known, Bavasi gazed toward the Pacific in winter where young people swam. "The water stays warm and we don't have much pollution yet," he said. "This is the highest hill in La Jolla, and the only person with a higher house is Dr. Seuss, who writes the children's stories. He lives above us and we have to watch it. If a child walks onto his land, Dr. Seuss beats him."

Bavasi smiled at his own joke. "A nice guy," he said. "Let's have some Chivas."

In the bar off the living room a foot-high Frankenstein monster stood beside a pleasantry of bottles. I pushed a red button on a black base and the monster made a strident sound. His face turned green. Then the sound stopped and the monster's trousers fell. His undershorts were polka-dotted. Green faded from the face, the monster blushed a brilliant pink.

"I want to ask about a sentence," Bavasi said. He walked to a high bookcase in the paneled room and took down *The French Lieutenant's Woman*. "Look at this," Bavasi said, showing me the beginning of the book:

An easterly is the most disagreeable wind in Lyme Bay—Lyme Bay being that largest bite from the underside of England's outstretched southwestern leg—and a person of curiosity could at once have deduced several strong probabilities about the pair who began to walk down the quay at Lyme Regis, the small but ancient eponym of the inbite, one incisively sharp and blustery morning in the late March of 1867.

"Is that a good first sentence?"

"Well, it's out of Hardy, and the author says so, and you more or less have to see what comes after."

"But that isn't the way you wrote or Dick Young." Bavasi strode about the hard-bought room. "Great team you got to cover. Best team I ever saw. The game, it worries me. Arnold Smith, the man whose money started it down here—I got a cut —they hit him hard. And now we're trying to sell tickets with the ocean to the west, the desert to the east, Mexico south and two established teams north, including the Dodgers. The game isn't changing as fast as it should, not getting young people. They should have hired Senator McCarthy as Commissioner. Young people follow him.

"You know all those years in Brooklyn I never got paid. Less than twenty thousand dollars for a couple of seasons and never an offer of a piece of Walter's action. Even after I put together the L.A. team, Walter didn't pay me enough.

"After I became an owner we were sitting at a league meeting and Walter said, 'Well, Buzzy, now that you've seen *all* the books, I guess you think I was cheating you.' I could have told him something, but I said, 'No, Walter, I've got the World Series rings.' I was thinking about the old team, Erskine and Campy. I had associations that were priceless. Was I gonna bitch now because he stiffed me?"

Bavasi walked to a telescope. The air curling about the hills was warm and clear. "Look through this," Bavasi said. At the other end of the telescope, a half dozen miles away, a Little

League field stood flat on a hilltop. "I can watch my youngest boy play ball there," Bavasi said. "That's something, isn't it? Drive him to the game. Come home. Have a Scotch. And watch him hit six miles away."

He talked for a while about the great players with calm professionalism, how Reese endured and Furillo cruised in right center and how he wished he had come really to be Jackie Robinson's friend. His lips set when he asked about O'Malley. "What did that man tell you he was worth?" Bavasi said.

"About twenty-four million."

Bavasi looked at me and shook his head and mused, and when he spoke, his voice was charged but soft. "That's true," he said. "That's honest. All Walter left out were three hundred acres of downtown Los Angeles."

AFTERWORDS
ON THE LIFE OF KINGS

In the days after the Dodgers had found their way west and the Brooklyn team withered into retirement, John Lardner introduced me to a wheezing journalist who stood at the long bar of the Artist and Writers Restaurant and tried to talk baseball with us, and drank. He had been blacklisted for his politics, and this cruel deed bowed the man's spirit and made him afraid. Only the cold fire of Leo Corcoran's martinis revived a touch of the dashing fellow who had been. Sober, the man spoke banalities. "Say, you guys really like sports, don't you?" Drunk, he recited a poem he had composed on the creation of the atom bomb. Each stanza drew imagery from a different Shakespearean play. I don't remember if the poem was good or bad, but the recitation sounded overwhelming.

Throughout the shattering seasons in which he could not work, the journalist studied Shakespeare, and one evening announced that he had grasped the basic universal theme. "What's going on," he said, "is war between generations. It's waged everywhere, if you know how to look. *Romeo and Juliet,* of course, but why can't Lady Macbeth kill the king? He looks too much like her father. How does Cassius rouse Brutus? 'Rome, thou has lost the breed of noble bloods. . . . There was a Brutus once,' and so on . . . King Hamlet's ghost tortures the

433

young prince. *Othello* begins with the senator raging at Desdemona's marriage. And *Lear*, the greatest play, is the final battle. Generations war in Armageddon and all must die."

Lardner gave a brief smile of commendation, and said it was tricky to slip in the premise that *Lear* was a greater work than *Hamlet*.

"Anyway, your theory dies at *The Tempest*," I said.

The writer wheezed. Excitement and English gin had brought color to his skin. "Not at all," he said. "By the time of *The Tempest*, Shakespeare knew that even he, Prospero, the Magician, had lost the generation war. The rage is spent. The *Tempest* is *King Lear*, seen again, from the other side of the curtain. No rage at all. The author pleads for prayer."

Lardner is ten years dead and I have not seen the bowed journalist for still longer, but wandering among old Dodgers I again heard the echoing Shakespearean theme. There is only so much space on the planet. Fathers perish to make room for sons. At the end, some go with grace, but the middle years—and these Dodgers are striding through middle years—shake with contention. Jack and Jackie Robinson; Clem and Jay Labine, father and son circling one another in a spiky maze of love.

It is too easy to lay griefs on the end of summer. Once I wrote the poet Robert Graves, asking, among other questions, how it felt to be seventy years old. He could not tell me, Graves responded, because in his own mind he still was twenty-one.

When what Walter O'Malley called the Dodgers' Official Family tore apart, it was not a sliding man's knee or a hitter's dimming eyes that mattered. Rather, another episode in the transcendent generation war came crashing among unathletic men.

After the Dodgers' fifth California pennant, Buzzy Bavasi says that he became conscious of a challenge to his position. Walter O'Malley's son, Peter, was maturing, and had inherited the father's strain of uninhibited ambition. By 1968 Bavasi faced an ultimatum. He was to find another position that autumn or be dismissed.

During June Bavasi became president of the new San Diego franchise, beating O'Malley's deadline by four months. In the way of things, O'Malley appears to have been angered. He had specified autumn and he was used to being obeyed. Fresco Thompson replaced Bavasi and his first assignment was to make a flight to Albuquerque, where Bavasi's oldest son, also called Peter, was directing a Dodger farm team. Thompson, who had wheeled Peter Bavasi in a carriage, was enjoined to fire a godson. The loyal Fresco was torn asunder, like a wild Irish harp.

When he reached Albuquerque, he prepared for duty by consuming a quart of Scotch, and soon after firing Peter Bavasi he needed help to climb into bed. Thompson did not feel well the next morning, or ever again. The final bout with whisky unmasked cancer symptoms, and after a long and painful time, this man of wit and irony found a ghastly death on November 20, 1968. He was sixty-six years old.

Now the Dodgers' family was rent. The Bavasis had been beaten southward to a patchwork team in San Diego. Peter O'Malley, at thirty-three, became president of the ball club. Walter O'Malley, retaining his large desk under the slain African antelope, declared himself chairman of the board.

Wanting, needing, but being unnerved at a trip back to the Brooklyn of the Dodgers, I rode a subway train. Rightness is often an accident, and on the morning I chose for the revisit, my wife commandeered the car.

Down all the season when I longed to flee college, mornings began with a cry from my father, "Okay, Cheezix." Cold hands pressed to my belly, and after this gruff tenderness the world began. Each day's trip toward New York University, from a station called Eastern Parkway–Brooklyn Museum to another called 181st Street, the Bronx, consumed an hour and twenty minutes. Classmates joined me at Nevins Street and we practiced holding textbooks buttock-high and standing against pretty girls. The back of the hand is an imperfect vehicle of sexual delight. My subway memories are noise, odor and a vaguely faint feeling behind the knees that tells one he lacks sufficient sleep.

Now impelled toward old, unfamiliar places, I paid a subway fare six times what it had been. People complain, but the cars looked neither better nor worse than I remembered. Men jostled as they had jostled in the days when I had covered the City Hall–to–Coney Island walking race. Newspapers blew on dirty floors. Littering is an ancillary function of the free press.

As I rode back, stations showed unforgotten names. Chambers Street. Fulton. A round man was rattling a *New York Times* and a black teen-ager drummed fingers on his own knees. Wall. Did anyone remember what Harold Ickes said in 1940? "Wendell Willkie is a simple, barefoot Wall Street lawyer."

The train veered left, iron wheels keening. The entry to Brooklyn began with eardrums slightly stopped. Air pressure builds underneath the East River. Then with a faint relief from unfelt pain, I heard the train screech into Clark Street. Brooklyn began.

Memories came flooding into consciousness. Above the Clark Street station rises the St. George Hotel. Advertisements once pleaded, "Swim in our *salt water pool.*" For fifty cents everyone was given a knitted bathing suit, and you could watch the girls in clinging wool: flat globes for breasts, a mound of belly and, as they climbed out of the green water on scaly metal ladders, a clear outline of the magic triangle.

After the swelling days, I had come back to the St. George, when Walter O'Malley chose it as press headquarters one World Series. Baseball men crowded one another, standing on cigarette butts before the bar.

Henry Ughetta, justice of the New York State Supreme Court, director of the Dodgers, found two steps in the ballroom and pitched headlong. Frank Graham, the late columnist, remarked in his soft way, "Sober as a judge."

The eight cars of the New Lots Local-Express drew into Borough Hall. It is disquieting to ride within a tiled, unchanging tube and to know what stood above and what is gone and what has come. The old Dodger offices, 215 Montague Street, have been destroyed. The old Brooklyn *Daily Eagle* is dead as *The Tattler*. Above Borough Hall station now blank Federal architecture rings an artless plaza. Above, too, in a pleasant narrow apartment Olga Kahn survives, brave as Brünnehilde in viduity. The age of seventy is her unwelcome beckoner. Still, she has found a place to teach and from time to time she asks, "Would you stop by and tell my people at the New School how Robert Frost said to write, although there are newer poets you should pay attention to?"

The train entered the Nevins Street station. Close to the old kiosks a boy and girl could find the Brooklyn Paramount or the Fabian Fox. We saw Susan Hayward there and Barbara Stanwyck, and Lana Turner in *The Postman Always Rings Twice*. Trying—why was it always so *easy* for John Garfield?—I slipped a hand around a back and under an arm. Arm and body tensed, pinning my hand against a rib; another milkless breast of Israel went unsullied.

"Atlantic Avenue," called the conductor, ordering me into the present. "Change here for the BMT."

Where O'Malley planned his Xanadu, blight had descended. "GEM JEWELERS," read a sign where O'Malley would have parked a hundred cars. "LOANS." "CASA DE EMPEÑO. SUITS $4.95 UP." Five streets angled into the unplanned crossing and black strips of trolley track showed through asphalt on Flatbush Avenue. O'Brien's Bar was open, but the Blarney Stone, under the Hellenic American Democratic Club, had closed. A breeze whipped around the Williamsburg Bank Building. Storefronts gaped empty. Traffic was light.

It took twenty minutes to walk where I had to go. At Bedford Avenue and Sullivan Place a billboard announced, "The happiest families live in New Ebbets Field Apartments." The sign was ten years old and faded. Behind it rose a tall stand of faceless, red-brick buildings.

Mr. Caulfield, a tall, brown-haired English teacher in eyeglasses, was supervising dismissal at IS 130 on McKeever Place, which had paralleled the left-field line. The children left quietly and Mr. Caulfield said that by and large they were a good bunch. "About 70 percent black, to 30 percent white," he said, "but everyone gets along. Some of them know there was a ball park here; not all of them care. But say, I was a fan. I remember Billy Cox and Pee Wee Reese, even if most of the kids never heard of them."

"Jackie Robinson?" I said.

"Oh, yes," said Mr. Caulfield, with a glint of pride. "We've made Jackie Robinson part of our social studies curriculum."

"I'm not supposed to say anything to writers," said Patrolman Greene. "The rule is everything got to be cleared downtown. But I remember maybe better than him. Erskine. Furillo. I'd make sure no one banged their cars."

White teacher and black policeman nodded and moved separately from the place where Ebbets Field had stood. On a handball wall children had scrawled their names: "Shass." "Rossnean." "Spain."

If the Dodgers ever had a decent team, my father told me. They had a decent team. Billy and Pee Wee and Campy and Jack. Loner, captain, colored gentleman, crusader. But what is that to Shass, Rossnean and Spain?

Sweet Moses, white or black, who will remember?

Is that the mind's last, soundless, dying cry? *Who will remember?* There was no rustling of old crowds as my long, wrenching, joyous voyage ended, only the question, "Who will remember?" and a small sign in the renting office at New Ebbets Field Apartments saying, as if about the past, "NO VACANCY. Files closed."

And then it was time to start uphill toward another morning and another home.

December 15, 1968–May 21, 1971
New Marlborough, Massachusetts,
and New York City

AN ACKNOWLEDGMENT

Readers may be amused to learn that even as details of this book were being completed, it had become the stuff of competition among the old Dodgers themselves. "Hey, Carl," Joe Black shouted to Erskine before the old-timers' game at Los Angeles in 1971, "you must have told some stories. I hear you come out *good* in your chapter." Put an old ball player back into uniform and the first thing that returns is the habit of bench jockeying. *The Boys of Summer* could not have been written without the help of the old Dodgers. They were generous with their time and with their memories. I want to thank particularly Carl Erskine, for his sensitivity to the work and his encouragement; and Mr. and Mrs. Jackie Robinson, who were kind and forthright, in the face of difficult questions and trying personal circumstances. A special quality of the old Brooklyn team was a concern for others less famous and less fortunate. The Dodgers' compassion, it seems to me, began with their captain and shortstop, Pee Wee Reese, now justly celebrated in the Baseball Hall of Fame.

After he closed down the *Herald Tribune* in 1966, Jock Whitney offered its morgue—that is, the files, library and copies of the paper and its antecedents reaching back more than a century—to the Columbia University School of Journalism. The gift was declined on the grounds of a space shortage. Whitney repeated his offer to New York University, which accepted, and where the morgue may be found today, cheerfully cared for by Mrs. Mae Nyquist Bowler. Both the files and Mrs. Bowler's assistance were most valuable.

A number of people have helped along the way. Clearly, I was blessed to have worked beside Red Smith. Covering a team against Dick Young had its difficult moments, like translating Cicero, but when you were done, as Latinists say, you were the better for it. When Ed Fitzgerald edited *Sport* magazine, he consistently guided me toward stories that were more complex than my newspaper pieces. To describe Smith, Young and Fitzgerald as teachers may embarrass them, but so they were.

Dick Passmore copyedited the book with intelligence, tenderness and care, policing commas, images and metaphors splendidly.

Gerald Astor points out that the lines from *King Kong,* quoted on page 128, were actually spoken by the actor, Robert Armstrong, not Bruce Cabot. We are left then with a correctly quoted misattribution. Many persons offered stories and recollections; I am particularly thankful to Frank Graham, Jr., Harold Rosenthal, Allan Roth, Irving Rudd and Vince Scully. Mr. Rudd still owns a button urging, "KEEP THE DODGERS IN BROOKLYN!" He has, however, moved to the Borough of Queens.

I knew little about cameras. Martin Blumenthal, staff photographer for *Pageant* and *Sport* magazines, introduced me to the world of f/stops and the single-lens reflex. Barney Stein, once the official Dodger photographer, made his complete file available. So did *Sport* magazine, through its editor, Al Silverman. All photographs not otherwise credited are mine.

My son Gordon has contributed one photograph to this book; my younger son, Roger, brought back other times by rooting for today's beleaguered Yankees, with what appears to be the same intensity I offered the comic-opera Dodgers of the 1930s. My daughter Alissa, who is four, contributed giggles. Despite unpredictable pressures, my wife Alice showed consistent grace, as is her wont.

Finally, my literary agent Don Gold of the William Morris office introduced me to M. S. Wyeth, Jr., the executive editor of Harper & Row. Buz Wyeth's patience and belief were such that my gratitude to him is greater than I can suitably say.

Roger Kahn at bat. *Photograph by Wendy Kahn.*